T0147043

Mary of all Virgins
Our Lady of the
Holy Trinity of God

Mary of all Virgins Our Lady of the Holy Trinity of God

María de todas las Vírgenes Nuestra Señora de la Santísima Trinidad de Dios

JUAN DE LA CRUZ

Número de Control de la Biblioteca del Congreso de EE. UU.:   2020906929
ISBN: Tapa Blanda   978-1-5065-3225-7
             Libro Electrónico   978-1-5065-3224-0

Información de la imprenta disponible en la última página.

Fecha de revisión: 22/04/2020

Para realizar pedidos de este libro, contacte con:
Palibrio
1663 Liberty Drive
Suite 200
Bloomington, IN 47403
Gratis desde EE. UU. al 877.407.5847
Gratis desde México al 01.800.288.2243
Gratis desde España al 900.866.949
Desde otro país al +1.812.671.9757
Fax: 01.812.355.1576
ventas@palibrio.com
619531

CONTENTS

Mary of all Virgins

Our Lady of the Holy Trinity of God

"Queen Conceived without Original Sin"

Hail Mary, Full of Grace,
The Lord is with thee.
Blessed art thou among women, and
Blessed is the fruit of thy womb, Jesus.

Holy Mary, Mother of God,
pray for us sinners
now, and at the hour of death.

Holy Mother of God, glorified with the Son, in the Holy Spirit.
Amen.

1.0.- Introduction

During the course of human history, great controversies have arisen on the subject of God. Most of the ancient peoples believed in the existence of multiple gods, but the Hebrew people very early managed to establish the belief in the existence of one and only one true God. After the life, work, death and resurrection of Our Lord Jesus Christ, this belief was strengthened by the Christian church, but adding the confession about the existence of the Holy Trinity of the Holy Spirit; in a consubstantial composition of God the Father, God the Son and God the Holy Spirit, in a single Being as we know it until today.

The great Christian erudites have deeply debated their different thoughts and ideas about the trinity of God, but, whether by mistake or omission, none have had the privilege of revealing the true composition of the Holy Trinity as we do now, in this book.

With a direct and simple language, supported by the Faith, we will guide the readers on the path of revelations of the true composition of the Holy Trinity of the Holy Spirit. We will see how the Holy Spirit is revealed in the Bible, as well as the different interpretations that have been made of the Holy Spirit, the gifts and characteristics of the Holy Spirit, following the true composition of the Holy Trinity of the Holy Spirit and the different people or human figurations assumed by the Holy Spirit during the course of human history.

In our analysis we begin with The Holy Spirit as "The Father", then with the Holy Spirit as "The Son", Jesus Christ, to conclude with the revelation of the Virgin Mary proceeding and assumed in the Holy Spirit; her incarnation, her mission on earth before and after her Assumption, and her Works and Miracles through her different advocacies, which shows that she possesses Divine Power as the Holy Spirit, Father and Son, and that the three At the same time, they are the same and only Being called the Holy Spirit who is the true God, the eternal and almighty Creator God.

To guide the reader in the search for this truth, we will make extensive use of Biblical references, of different gospels and of some books by different analysts who have treated the subject in one way or another, to reinforce our arguments and make this book a document valuable for the study of the true composition of the Holy Trinity of the Holy Spirit, placing the Virgin Mary in her rightful place as Mother and Spouse of the Holy Spirit, her Own Being.

We have titled this book "Mary of all Virgins; Our Lady of the Holy Trinity of God," to lay the foundations for the development of an important debate about the true composition of the Holy Trinity of the Holy Spirit of God; his person, his composition and his work. Since by becoming aware of the true composition of the Holy Spirit, we can learn more about the ways and means through which he acts on each individual people in the Universe.

The first part of the book's title; "Mary of all Virgins" makes it clear that, although there are many advocations with different names and different physical faces and images, there is only one Virgin Mary, Mother of God. The second part of the title; "Our Lady of the Holy Trinity of God" establishes that the Virgin Mary forms an integral and undivided part in the Holy Spirit, with "the Father" and "the Son"; the three are one in the Holy Spirit who is the God of creation.

The christian erudites state that "The Holy Spirit is the third person in the undivided trinity of God; that eternally proceeds from the Father and the Son; true God with them, of majesty and glory equal; like them eternal, omnipotent, omnipresent, omniscient, just, merciful; that together with the Father and the Son is the Holy One, the Lord of hosts. As such he can do the work that he, according to God's counsel, must do - the sanctification of sinful humanity, bringing sinners to faith in their Savior, preserving and strengthening them in this faith, empowering them to demonstrate their faith with good works, and finally gathering them in the heavenly barns." (Abiding Word, Barbara Reid and Cardinal Francis George, Vol. I, p. 57).

As you can see in the previous quote during the course of the history of Christianity, the great analysts have considered the Holy Spirit as the third person of the divinity of God, however, this time We are going to demonstrate to the readers and to the world that all the theories exposed until now are incorrect or incomplete, since the Holy Spirit is actually the Spirit of God, that is, the Holy Spirit is the divine essence of "That All" called God, and personified in the Father "God," in Jesus Christ "the Son of God" and the Virgin Mary "the Mother and Wife of

God." So, the Holy Spirit is the Father, the Holy Spirit is the Son and the Holy Spirit is the Mother and the Wife of God at the same time, and the three are a unique and undivided Being called the Holy Spirit who is God eternal.

> *"The earth was total chaos, the darkness covered the abyss, and against a cold, dark, lifeless background, the Spirit of God moved on the face of the waters." (Genesis 1:2)*

In this book We will demonstrate that the Virgin Mary is not a simple human being, she is not a simple servant, more than that, She is the Living Expression that originated the "Divine Entity of Creation," She is consubstantial with the Father and the Son in the Holy Spirit that is God, therefore, She is, in herself, the Infinite who, that because it has no beginning, will also have no end.

The only true God, the Holy Spirit, who is eternal, omnipotent, omnipresent, omniscient, immeasurable, just, merciful; As such in order to carry out his works with humanity, he has revealed himself chronologically in different temporal personal figurations; as the Creator Father to the Ancient Patriarchs, as the Redeeming Son through Jesus, and in modern times as the Spirit of the Virgin Mary in her appearances in the different towns around the world. The Holy Spirit is the element and the whole of the universe, it is the true essence that unites all creation, it is the Father who generated himself in himself as the Son, in the eternity of the Divine Womb of his Own Being.

But before going into the details that demonstrate our approach, let us first analyze, in our Theological Framework, the different approaches of Christian erudites and the different theories and interpretations that have been given about the Holy Spirit during the course of the history of humanity.

2.0.- Theological Framework

It is necessary for all generation to be concerned and interested in the study of the Work of the Holy Spirit. During his ministry Our Lord Jesus Christ spoke abundantly about the full and varied ministry of the Holy Spirit. In Acts we find specific details of the blessed results of the ministry of the Holy Spirit in the lives of individuals and congregations. Also the Epistles of Paul of Tarsus contain abundant references on the Work of the Holy Spirit, "when people became aware of the Divine Spirit, when they lived and walked in the Divine Spirit, the church was strengthened and extended."

The Holy Spirit has the full characteristics of a person - Isaiah 11: 1-2 - He has wisdom, above all human imagination; Romans 8:27 – He has an ultra or super human mind; 1 Corinthians 12:11 – He possess a will; He acts and reacts like a person - Genesis 6: 3 - He loses patience with increasing wickedness; John 15:26 – He serves as an instructor; Ephesians 4:30 – He saddened by ungodly life; Acts 5: 3-10 – He can be lied to with fatal consequences; He has pronouns that indicate it is a person - John 16: 13–14.

"There is no matter more important in religion than that of the Holy Spirit. Unless properly understood, a large portion of the Bible, and especially the New Testament, will remain indecipherable. On the other hand, a fair review of the subject will help more than an illustration of any other particular topic to give harmony, clarity and consistency of what could be learned from all the other matters presented in the Word of God." (The Office Of The Holy Spirit, Richardson.)

But despite its importance in understanding the Scriptures as a whole, there is much confusion and superstition in the minds of many people regarding the Holy Spirit and His Holy Trinity.

First, the Holy Scriptures establish that Christ is eternal (John. 1: 1–3, 15:30; 8:58; Matthew. 23:37; 12:41; 17: 5–24; Isaiah 44: 6; 48: 12–16; Col. 1: 15–17; Revelation 1: 8–17) That is, he never had a beginning and he will never have an end, being eternally God (John.

1: 1; Heb. 1: 8; Col 2: 9), sharing the essence of deity with the Father and the Holy Spirit (John. 10: 30–33; 1 Cor. 3:16; Romans. 8: 9; John. 14: 16–23), equal in value and in substance.

Micah 5: 2, But you, Bethlehem Ephrata, although you are small among the families of Judah, from you will come the one who is to be ruler in Israel. And its origins are from ancient times, from the days of eternity.

John 1: 1, In the beginning was the Word, and the Word was with God, and the Word was God.

Colossians 1:17, And He is before all things, and in Him all things abide.

Hebrews 13: 8, Jesus Christ is the same yesterday and today and forever.

Jesus Himself affirms and confirms that He is eternal:

In John 8: 57-58, the Temple priests said to him, "You are not yet fifty years old, and have you seen Abraham? Jesus said to them, Truly, truly, I say to you, before Abraham was born, I am."

In John 17: 5, when he says "And now, glorify me, Father, next to you, with the glory that I had with you before the world existed."

In John 17:24, exclaiming "Father, I want those you have given me to be with me where I am also, so that they may see my glory, the glory that you have given me; because you have loved me since before the foundation of the world."

In Revelation 2:8, he commands John: "Write this letter to the angel of the church in Smyrna. This is the message from the one who is the Alpha and the Omega, the beginning and the End, who was dead but came to life, says this …"

Isaiah 44: 6-8, Thus says the Lord, the King of Israel, and his Redeemer, the Lord of hosts: "I am the first, and I am the last, and there is no God besides me..."

We have already seen how the Holy Scriptures reveal the Holy Spirit with attributes that only a person can possess. For example, He speaks clearly; in 1 Timothy 4:1, Acts 8:29, Acts 10: 19-20, Acts 13: 1-4. He taught all things to the apostles, according to John 14:26. He was going to testify about Jesus as you can read in John 15: 26-27. Jesus always referred to Him as a person, using the personal article "he", according to John 14: 16-17. He would carry on and complete the work begun by Jesus, as read in John 16: 12-13. He warned Paul and his companions to go to certain areas of Asia; this he did by "forbidding" them, and not "allowing" them despite their initial efforts, according to Acts 16: 6-7.

The Holy Spirit himself intercedes for us, as Paul tells us in Roman 8:26, just as Christ "intercedes for us," according to Roman 8:34. And Roman 8:27 tells us that He has a mind, so He has thoughts of His own. He "knows the things of God", 1 Corinthians 2:11. In Roman 15:30, Paul speaks of "the love of the Spirit." Corinthians 12:11 tells us: "But all these things are done by one and the same Spirit, distributing each one in particular as he wants." It was the Holy Spirit who decided which person received such gifts. He suffers rebuffs and insults "do not grieve the Holy Spirit", Ephesians 4:30. He can be saddened through our voluntary negligence. Attributing their actions to the work of Satan is "unforgivable sin", Matthew 12: 31-32. Someone who has "trampled on the Son of God" has also "insulted the Spirit of grace," Acts 10:29. Those who lie to the Holy Spirit, like Ananias and his wife Safira were blamed for doing so "... why did Satan fill your heart to lie to the Holy Spirit ...?" Acts 5:3.

Tertullian was the first to use the term Trinity (trinitas), in the year 215 A.D., although previously, Theophilus of Antioch had already used the Greek word τριάς (triad) in his work A Autolic (180 A.D) to refer to God, his Word (Logos) and his Wisdom (Sophia). Tertullian would say in Adversus Praxeam II that "the three are one, because the three come from one, per unit of substance."

The formula took shape over the years and was not definitively established until the fourth century: The definition of the Council of Nicaea, sustained since then with minimal changes by the main Christian denominations, was to affirm that the Son was consubstantial with the Father (ὁμοούσιον, homousion, literally of the same substance as the Father). This formula was questioned and the Church went through a generation of debates and conflicts, until the "faith of Nicaea" was reaffirmed in Constantinople in 381 A.D.

At the Council of Nicaea (325 A.D.) all attention was focused on the relationship between the Father and the Son, including through the rejection of some typical Arian phrases through some anathemas attached to the creed; and no similar statement was made about the Holy Spirit completely concealing the feminine part of God.

At the Council of Constantinople (381 A.D) it was stated that the Holy Spirit is worshiped and glorified together with the Father and the

Son (συμπροσκυνούμενον καὶ συνδοξαζόμενον), suggesting that he was also masculine and consubstantial to Them. This doctrine was later ratified by the Council of Chalcedon (451 A.D), without altering the substance of the doctrine approved at Nicaea.

Christian doctrine is based on monotheism; the existence of one God. Therefore, at the Council of Nicea it was necessary to make the necessary adjustments to what Scripture said regarding the Father, the Son and the Holy Spirit. The Christian theologians who structured the books that were included in the Bible produced confusing explanations that generated various currents of thought and intense controversy. This controversy was accentuated with the Roman emperor Constantine I having to take action on the matter to reach a consensus and it is from this situation that the leaders of the Church began to count on imperial support and it is the emperor who specified what the unifying doctrine shared by the various Christian communities, thus giving birth to the Roman Catholic Church. Thus, in the face of this position, some theologians suggested that, if these three people shared different qualities and divine characteristics exclusive to God: lordship, eternity, omnipotence, omniscience, omnipresence, holiness, etc., the mathematical formula 1x1x1 = 1 would have to be used instead of 1 + 1 + 1 = 3, since it breaks the monotheism of God and becomes polytheism or henotheism. The Roman emperor Constantine I was the one who decided that the three divine people would be Father, Son and Holy Spirit, thus sealing the exclusion of the feminine part of God and instead placing the figure of the Holy Spirit, when in reality the Holy Spirit is the everything that is personified in multiple human figurations, according to his will. That is, they are all one and one is all.

2.1.- The Trinity of the Holy Espirit; Biblical perspectives

In the Bible there are allusions to the Father, the Son, and the Holy Spirit that have been presented as implicit mentions of the Trinitarian nature of God.

- Quotations from the Tanach (Jewish Old Testament) in which references to God appear in the plural:

- o "God (the Holy Spirit) said:" Let us make man in our image, after our likeness ..." (Genesis 1:26)
- o "Man has become like one of us in the knowledge of good and evil." (Genesis 3:22)
- o "And Yahweh said:" I see that they all form one people and have the same language. If this goes ahead, nothing will prevent them from now achieving everything they set out to do. Well, let's go down and confuse their language right there, so that they don't understand each other." (Genesis 11:6-7)
- o "I heard the voice of the Lord saying: 'Whom shall I send, and who will go for us?' I replied: "Here I am: send me!""" (Isaiah 6:8).
- o The use of the word Elohim, which is plural, to refer to God is also presented as an argument (Genesis 20:13 and 2 Sam 7:23).

- • New Testament quotes in which Jesus is identified as God:
  - o The beginning of the Gospel of John: "In the beginning there is the Word and the Word was with God, and the Word was God." (John 1:1)
  - o The recognition of Thomas towards Jesus with the expression: "My Lord and my God." (John 20:28)
  - o The recognition of the omniscience of Jesus, attribute of God (John 21:17; John 16:30)
  - o "Who has seen me has seen the Father" (John 14:9)
  - o "I am in the Father and the Father is in me" (John 14:11)
  - o "All that the Father has is mine" (John 16:15)
  - o The accusation of the Jews of making themselves Jesus equal to God (John 5:18)
  - o Jesus' ability to forgive sins (Mark 2:5-10).

- • New Testament quotes in which the three entities are mentioned:
  - o Baptism in the name of the Father and of the Son and of the Holy Spirit (Matthew 28:19);
  - o The Pauline greeting: "The grace of the Lord Jesus Christ, the love of God and the communion of the Holy Spirit be with you all." (2 Corinthians 13:13).

o Outside of the books considered canonical, the Trinitarian formula is present in the Didaché, a Christian document dated from the 1st century by most contemporary scholars: "You will be baptized in the name of the Father and of the Son and of the Holy Spirit in living water. But if you don't have running water, then get baptized in another water [...]. But if you have neither, then pour water on your head three times in the name of the Father and of the Son and of the Holy Spirit." (Did 7:1-3).

o In addition to the controversy over the nature of Jesus —if he was human, divine, or both at the same time—, of his origin —if everlasting or temporary— and similar questions related to the Holy Spirit, the central problem of the trinitarian dogma is to justify the division between single "substance" and triple "personality." Most Protestant churches, as well as Orthodox and the Catholic Church, maintain that this is an inaccessible mystery to human intelligence.

2.2.- Perspectives of the Christian Churches on the Trinity of the Holy Spirit.

According to the Catholic Encyclopedia, the Holy Trinity of God is both a dogma and a mystery, for which reason it states that: Such a mysterious dogma presupposes divine revelation.

For the Roman Catholic Apostolic Church "The Trinity of God is the term by which the central doctrine of the Christian religion is designated ... Thus, in the words of the Quicumque Symbol: "the Father is God, the Son is God and the Holy Spirit is God, and yet there are not three Gods, but one God." In this Trinity [...] the Persons are co-eternal and co-equal: all, equally, are uncreated and omnipotent. [...]" (The Catholic Encyclopedia).

For the Greek Orthodox Church the Trinity is the following: "God is triune and one. The Father is totally God. The Son is totally God. The Holy Spirit is totally God." (Our Orthodox Christian Faith)

The Evangelical Christian Churches propose that within the unity of a One God there are three different persons; the Father, the Son and the Holy Spirit. All three share the same attributes and the same nature, therefore these three constitute the one God.

According to all these doctrines:

- The father. He is uncreated and not begotten.
- The son. He is not created but begotten eternally by the Father.
- The Holy Spirit. He is not created, nor begotten, but proceeds eternally from the Father and the Son (according to the Evangelical Churches and the Roman Catholic Church) or only from the Father (according to the Orthodox Catholic Church).

According to the Catholic Dogma defined in the First Council of Constantinople (381 A.D), the three persons of the Holy Trinity are really different, but they are one true God. This is something possible to formulate but inaccessible to human reason, for which it is considered a Mystery of Faith. To explain this mystery, Christian theologians have sometimes resorted to similes. Thus, Augustine of Hippo compared the Trinity with the mind, the thought that arises from it and the love that unites them. On the other hand, the classical Christian theologian Guillermo de Occam affirms the impossibility of an intellectual understanding of the divine nature and postulates its simple acceptance through faith.

The Gospel of Philip says: "Some say that Mary has conceived by the work of the Holy Spirit: they are wrong, they do not know what they say. When has a woman never conceived of another woman? Mary is the virgin whom no Power has tainted. She is a great anathema to the Jews, who are the apostles and the apostles. This virgin that no Power has violated, (... while) the Powers were contaminated."

If we analyze this paragraph by part we will see that Philip here is referring to that Mary is in herself the Holy Spirit "... a woman has never conceived of a woman," this means that Philip had full knowledge that the Holy Spirit is female Even more clearly, Philip in his limited knowledge knew that the Holy Spirit had a female personification, but he did not understand that in reality the Holy Spirit had both personifications, female and male. From here we can gather that the Holy Spirit "is a unique substance" that presents himself to humanity in multiple and infinite "personalities" being the three main Yahweh, Jesus Christ, and the Virgin Mary in her different advocations.

Jesus is God and eternal, this leaves a conclusive affirmation that Mary is also God and eternal. In such a way, Mary is the feminine personification of the Holy Spirit made woman to be Mother. The Holy Spirit masculine part engendered in Mary, her feminine part, her own being, in a divine process and incomprehensible to current human knowledge. The Holy Spirit is male and female at the same time and his Divine Being can be together as one or reproduced, in both sexes, in as many times as the human mind cannot imagine.

"The Holy Spirit encloses everything in himself - be "man", be "woman", be "angel", be "animal", be "tree", be "rock", ... or be "mystery" - even Father, Mother and Son at the same time, and They at the same time enclose Him, since they all form one Being, the Holy Spirit."

"The Holy Spirit is the true God, the God of Abraham, and they are indeed found everywhere: above, below, in the secret and in the manifest. The Holy Spirit is in the revealed, below, in the secret, and above. The Holy Spirit is the Father of Jesus: "Jesus was conceived by the work and grace of the Holy Spirit in Mary." Jesus is the Holy Spirit incarnate as a man to be the son of God, Mary is the Holy Spirit incarnate as a woman to be the mother of God. The Holy Spirit said to the Prophets of old "... I will send a woman who will crush the offspring of the serpent of evil", ¡And here is Mary!

"The evil Powers are at the service of the saints, after having been reduced to blindness by the Holy Spirit so that they believe that they are serving a man, and thus they are operating on behalf of the saints. So, (when) one day a disciple asked the Lord for something from the world, He said to him: "Ask your mother and she will share with you the things of others." Philip's Gospel.

"The apostles said to the disciples: "May all our offering seek salt for itself. "They called (the Sophia) "salt", (for) without it no acceptable offering (es)." "Sofia is sterile, (without) child (ren); that is why it is called (also) "salt". The place where they (...) in their own way (is) the Holy Spirit; (for this) his children are numerous." Philip's Gospel.

"... The Holy Spirit feeds everyone and exercises his dominion over (all) the Powers, the same over the docile as over the (unruly) and lonely, since he (...) secludes them so that (...) when want." Philip's Gospel.

"If someone — after going down to the waters — comes out of them without having received anything and says 'I am a Christian', this name has been received (only) on loan. Even more if he receives the

Holy Spirit, he remains in possession of (said) name by way of donation. Whoever has received a gift will not take it away, but whoever is given a loan will be asked for it." Philip's Gospel.

Here we see how the apostle Philip states that it is more important to receive the Holy Spirit than to say that you are a Christian simply by having received the baptismal water.

"We are - it is true - begotten by the Holy Spirit, but re-begotten by Christ. In both (cases) we are likewise anointed by the (holy) spirit, and — by being begotten — we have also been united." Philip's Gospel.

"Let us say - if it is allowed - a secret: the Father of All joined with the virgin who had descended and a fire illuminated him that day. He unveiled the great bridal chamber, and so his body — which originated that day — came out of the bridal chamber as one that has been begotten by husband and wife. And likewise, thanks to these, Jesus straightened the All in her, requiring each and every one of his disciples to enter their resting place." Philip's Gospel.

In the previous paragraph, the apostle Philip clearly establishes that the Virgin Mary was not begotten, but descended that day with the illumination of the Holy Spirit, His Own Being. And at the same time he makes it clear that the Father, the Mother and the Son are one same person, and that the three entities had a body that same day; all three coming from the same substance called the Holy Spirit.

The Holy Spirit is the Divine Entity of Creation, He was the one who appeared to the Patriarchs of the Old Testament on each occasion, He was the one who gave the Commandments to Moses, He was the one who was incarnated in the figure of Mary, He was the one who gave birth to his Son, Jesus, in the womb of his own Being in a process through which he gave his life for us. He is the true and only God. He is the one who personifies the divinity of the Father, the Mother and the Son in Himself.

2.3.- The Ministry of Jesus is based on its essence in the Holy Spirit of God.

Let's look at some biblical statements about the Holy Spirit that corroborate with this reasoning: "He is the **Original Spirit**". "(...) There is (...) only He, the only one (...). He has existed from all eternity, and His existence will have no end. He has no one like him either in Heaven or on Earth…" "…The secrets of nature are in the hands of God. Because the world, before it appeared, already existed in the depth of Divine thought; it was made material and visible by the will of the Holy Spirit." "When you turn to Him, turn again like children, for you know neither the past nor the present nor the future, while God is the Master of all time" "(He) is a Monocracy with nothing above Him. (…) He is God and Father of everything, the invisible Spirit Who is above everything, (…) Who is in pure light, who no eye can see. (The Life of Saint Issa, 11:12-15).

> "He is the Holy Spirit. It is not correct to think of Him as gods or something similar. (…) Everything exists in Him. (…) He is unlimited, because there is nothing prior to Him that limits him. (…) He is immeasurable, because there was no one before Him who measured Him. (…) He is eternal (…). He exists eternally (…). There is no way to say His quantity (…). He is not contained in time (…)." (The Apocrypha of John, 4:35; 5:10-15)

> "The Great Creator has not shared His Power with any living being, (…) He is the only One who possesses omnipotence." (The Life of Saint Issa, 5: 16-17)

> "The Eternal Legislator is one; there is no God other than Him. He has not divided the world with anyone, nor has He informed anyone of His intentions. " (The Life of Saint Issa, 6:10)

The Lord our God is all-powerful, omniscient and omnipresent. It is He who has all the wisdom and all the light. It is He, to whom they must turn to be comforted in their pain, helped in their works and cured in their diseases. Whoever turns to His Holy Trinity their request will not be denied.

> "(…) He is the Life That gives life. He is the Blessed One Who gives the blessing. He is the Wisdom Who gives wisdom. He is the Love Who gives salvation and love. He

is immovable; He resides in tranquility and silence. (...) He directs His desires within His flow of Light. He is the Source of this flow of Light (the Holy Spirit)" (The Apocrypha of John, 2:25-4: 25).

"This is the message we have heard from Jesus, and we manifest it to you: God is Light, and in Him there is no darkness at all." (1 John 1: 5).

"(...) The blessed and only Sovereign (...) Who exclusively has Immortality and dwells in the Light (...)" (1 Timothy 6: 15-16).

"Now to the eternal, immortal, invisible King, the only wise God, be honor and glory forever and ever. Amen" (1 Timothy 1:17).

Most of these words of Jesus were not included in the New Testament by fourth-century church leaders, when the compendium of the Bible was prepared by order of Emperor Constantine I. Most Christians have forgotten God the Father, although He and the Way to Him were the essence of Jesus' preaching. But even more, the essence of these words was distorted in which it is clearly deduced that Jesus calls the Holy Spirit "Father". The terms "God is Light"; "God is spirit"; "God is invisible"; "God has Immortality and dwells in the Light"; "God directs His desires within His flow of Light"; "God is the Source of this flow of Light"; "God is the Spirit ... Everything exists in Him"; "Against a cold, dark, lifeless background, the Spirit of God moved on the face of the waters." And many others that we will continue treating in this book demonstrate not only that the Holy Spirit, but, that God is in Himself the Holy Spirit.

In such a way, Jesus is in the Father and in Mary; The Father is in Jesus and in Mary; Mary is in the Father and in Jesus. The Father is the Holy Spirit; Jesus is the Holy Spirit; Mary is the Holy Spirit. The Holy Spirit is presented in one of the three divine personalities separately, but on some occasions He has been presented to some people as the Holy Trinity of the Holy Spirit, in an entity of Light with movement from which three different voices have come out: the of the Father, that of the

Virgin Mary and that of Jesus Christ, each voice with its peculiar timbre and tone that allows people to identify who is speaking at each time.

The Holy Trinity of the Holy Spirit is the only Divine Entity, the Supreme Being, God, therefore, there is only one and only Divine Being called "Holy Spirit," God, which is composed of the three divine persons, who are: the Father, Mother and Son. The Holy Spirit (Father) called himself YHVH (which in the ancient language of the Jews means – "He who exists" - and is pronounced Yahweh and in English the pronunciation was adapted to Jehovah and Yahweh, the Mother is called Virgin Mary or Our Lady Mary, and the Son is called Jesus Christ. In such a way, we have three people in the same and unique Being, who by their divinity, omnipotence, omniscience and omnipresence can present together and / or separately and at the same time each of them can assume different figurations regardless of time or space.

3.0.- The Holy Spirit; sex, origin and provenance

The word "spirit" comes from the Greek "πνευμα" (pneuma) and the Hebrew "ruach or ruaj". It is an incomplete translation since "ruaj" and "pneuma" are also translated as "air" (hence the word "tire"). Air and spirit are different things for us today, but they appeared related to each other, in the ancient Greek and Hebrew. What is currently a double meaning was in those languages an identity of concepts.

On the origin of the Holy Spirit, there is a certain unanimity between the different Christian confessions. With the exception of the tritheistic interpretation, which assumes the Holy Spirit as an uncreated being and independent of God, the other interpretations consider that it comes from God, although they differ in form. For example; in modalism he proceeds as a force, in Arianism as a creature and in trinitarianism as a person. Trinitarianism also addresses an additional question proper to its theological framework, distinguishing between the origin of the Father and the origin of the Son, an issue known as the filioque clause.

The only true God, the Holy Spirit, has revealed himself chronologically in three different temporal Personalities; as Creator Father in the Old Testament, as Redeeming Son during the life of Jesus, and finally through the different advocations of the Virgin Mary in the different towns of the world.

Until now, no theory had dealt with the feminine part of the Holy Spirit, that is, with "The Virgin Mary" as an inherent part in the Holy Trinity of God.

The Virgin Mary must be glorified as an integral part of the Holy Spirit, together with the Father and the Son (συμπροσκυνούμενον καὶ συνδοξαζόμενον), modifying the doctrine ratified by the Council of Chalcedon (451 AD). Fulfill this mandate before it is too late.

3.1.- Nature of the Holy Spirit.

In Christian theology, the Holy Spirit (or its equivalents, Spirit of God, Spirit of truth or Paraclete: action or presence of God, from the Greek παράκλητον parakleton: Who is invoked, and Which comes from the Latin Spiritus Sanctus) is an expression Biblical that refers to a complex theological notion through which a supreme spiritual reality is described, which has had multiple interpretations in the different Christian confessions and theological schools.

This spiritual reality is spoken of in many passages of the Bible, with the expressions quoted, without giving a single definition. This was the reason for a series of controversies that took place mainly over three historical periods: the 4th century as the quintessential Trinitarian century, the East and West schismatic crises that occurred between the 9th and 11th centuries, then the different doctrinal reviews born of the Protestant reform, and, finally, the actually one, that expressed in this book.

Regarding the nature of the Holy Spirit, the Christian erudites basically maintain four interpretations that We indicate here in broad strokes, to later elaborate on each one of them, and then conclude with the real and true composition of the Holy Trinity of the Holy Spirit:

- For modalists, the Holy Spirit is a divine force or quality such as wisdom, beauty, love, or goodness. The theory of Unitarianism, although it has basic theological differences with that of modalism, shares this vision of an impersonal Holy Spirit who acts being the Power or Active Force of God. In any case, both currents share the vision that the Holy Spirit is not "someone" but "something."

- According to Arian interpretations of character, the Holy Spirit is a spiritual entity or angelic nature of exalted character, very close to divinity, but different from it due to its condition as a creature.

- According to the interpretations of a tritheistic character, the Holy Spirit is another God, perhaps inferior in character to the main God, but who shares with him the quality of being uncreated.

- Trinitarian interpretations consider the Holy Spirit as a divine person, a notion with which the divinity of the Holy Spirit is assumed, maintaining, however, the uniqueness of the divine principle. This is the doctrine of Catholic Christianity, Orthodox Christianity, and some Protestant denominations.
- The Holy Spirit is the only God, a divine person, a notion with which the divinity of the Holy Spirit is assumed, maintaining, however, the uniqueness of the divine principle. This is the doctrine of Catholic Christianity, Orthodox Christianity, and some Protestant denominations.

As we have been able to see from the first centuries of the Christian church, theologians have had great confusions about the Holy Trinity of the Holy Spirit. East and West have had different points of view; On the one hand, the distinction of the Father, Son and Holy Spirit has been strongly proclaimed, on the other hand the proclamation that God is one was maintained. Both East and West were struggling to avoid what for them is the error of Tritheism, or the false doctrine that there are three gods.

Towards the end of the second century, as a result of these struggles to find the truth, a doctrine known as monarchianism began in the East and spread to the West. It was an attempt to proclaim the unity of God, who unfortunately destroyed the Trinity. One form of this doctrine sought to preserve the unity of God, the deity of Christ, and the deity of the Holy Spirit, teaching that the Son and the Holy Spirit were only modes or manifestations of God the Father. It was called modalist monarchianism, (modal, which appears in different papers, monarch, a main being). Another name was Patripasionism, because it insisted that the Father suffered in his role as Son.

Another distinct monarchian doctrine, dynamism monarchianism, also attempted to preserve the unity of God, but did so by denying the deity of Christ and of the Holy Spirit. He speculated that God, the sole ruler, raised Jesus to an almost divine level, filling him with powers, called "the logos" and "the spirit."

Furthermore, a third destructive conclusion about the Trinity speculated that the only true God is the Father and that the other two divine persons are only temporary, somewhat inferior manifestations, which flow from the Father. This doctrine became known as subordinationism.

"At the time of these controversies there were many different opinions about the Holy Spirit who was identified by some theologians as an energy, a creature, or an angel. However, we can be sure based on the simple statements of the Apostolic Creed that the ancient church believed in the personality and deity of the Holy Spirit. "But it was not until the fourth century that the personality and divinity of the Holy Spirit became prominent." (E. H. Klotsche, The History of Christian Doctrine, Grand Rapids, MI: Baker Book House, 1979, p. 69; Neve, A History of Christian Thought, The United Lutheran Publication House, 1943, vol. 1, p. 119;)

About 150 A.D. Certain people in the Greek part of the church who wanted to avoid what they considered to be the heresy of Tritheism declared that Jesus Christ is not God, but He is almost God. They said that the Logos, who became flesh in Jesus Christ, was on a lower level than the Father.

Origins of Alexandria in Egypt polished some of the rough edges of this thought known as subordinationism (from Latin, having an inferior nature). Fighting against the monarchists, he insisted that the Father, the Son and the Spirit were three eternally different people, but he did not think they were the same. His concept of the Trinity was three concentric circles that formed an inverted triangle, and it extends from God to man. Origen reasoned that "since all things have come into being through the Logos, it follows that the Holy Spirit is the first of the spirits begotten of the Father through the Son." He taught that all three people have the same essence, but not the same existence. Jesus and the Holy Spirit were part of a bridge that descended between heaven and earth. The role of the Holy Spirit was to proceed from the Father through the Son to sanctify men. (Neve, op. Cit. Vol. 1, p. 87)

Thus, according to Origen, the Son and the Holy Spirit were subordinate to the Father and the Holy Spirit was also subordinate to the Son. This distortion, which became widely distributed, was not clearly corrected until the Council of Nicaea in 325 A.D.

Theodotus of Byzantium tried to preserve the unity of God in another way. He stated that Christ and the Holy Spirit are not equal to God the Father, holding that the man Jesus was raised to a level similar to God when he received dynamis, a power that came from God. Near the end of the 2nd century Theodotus moved to Rome, taking with him his theory, which became known as dynamism monarchianism or adoptionism. According to this doctrine, "as a result of the abode of the Logos and the Holy Spirit, Jesus was" adopted "as the Son of God, received the power to perform miracles, and finally achieved permanent unity with God." (Pieper, Francis D.D., Christian Dogmatics, St. Louis, MO: Concordia Publishing House, 1951, Vol. 1, p. 383.)

The Lutheran confessions in the Main Articles of Faith, Article 1, of God, condemn the teaching of the Samosates for denying the personality and deity of the Logos and of the Holy Spirit. They also reject that of the samosatenses, ancient and modern, who maintain that there is only one person and sophistically assert that the other two, the Word and the Holy Spirit, are not necessarily different people, but that the Word means the eternal word or the voice, and that the Holy Spirit is an energy generated in created beings."

Athanasius, bishop of Alexandria, declared, at the general council of the eastern bishops of Nicaea in 325. A.D., that the Father and the Son are a God, that they have the same substance or nature, which he summarized using the word homoousios. He also defended the homoousios of the Holy Spirit at the synod of Alexandria in 362 A.D., teaching that the Holy Spirit is God, because only a divine Spirit could make people "partakers of the divine nature." Athanasius was convinced that the formula for Baptism reveals the divine nature of the Holy Spirit. If the Spirit were only a creature, it would not be included under the same name with the Father and the Son. (Eerdman's Handbook to the History of Christianity, Grand Rapids, MI: Wm. B. Eerdmans Publishing Co., 1977, p. 164)

Until then not much had been said about the third person of the Trinity, but in the following years much more attention was given to the identity of the Holy Spirit. The Macedonian Bishop of Constantinople opposed Athanasius's position and insisted that the Holy Spirit is a creature subordinate to the Son.

But the 362 A.D. synod of Alexandria, prompted by Basil of Caesarea's treatise on the Holy Spirit, condemned both Arianism and the similar teaching of the pneumatomachians (from the Greek, those who fight the Holy Spirit), who were also called Macedonians. Basil was the first to formalize the accepted terminology for the Trinity: one substance (ousia) and three people (hopostaseis).

Basil's friend, Gregorio Nacianzeno, noted the biblical distinction between the three persons of the Trinity, that is, that the Father is unbegotten, the Son is begotten, and the Holy Spirit proceeds from the Father by the Son. This useful distinction was accepted by the church at a synod held in Rome in 380 A.D. A year later, in Constantinople, the church followed a step further by affirming the full deity of the Holy Spirit, declaring that He was the Lord and giver who came from the Father, adored and glorified with the Father and the Son. In 451 A.D., in Chalcedon, the eastern and western parts of the church formally adopted this expression in the Nicene Creed. (J. L. Gonzalez, A History of Christian Thought, Nashville, TN: Abingdon Press, 1970, vol. 1, p. 323)

Tertullian fought against modalist theory, correctly teaching that the Father, the Son, and the Holy Spirit are three distinct, eternal, coexisting persons, who together make up the one triune God. To express his thought he used the word trinitas (Trinity). Tertullian, however, was not without errors. He sustained a subordination of the Son and the Spirit to the Father. To illustrate this he drew analogies from nature. The Father, the Son, and the Holy Spirit are related to each other like a spring, a riverbank, and a river. The Father is all substance, while the Son and the Spirit descend from the Father. (Neve, op. Cit., Tome 1, p. 107; Klotsche, op. Cit., P. 54)

Augustine added a new emphasis to the relationship of the three persons of the Trinity 200 years later, when he formed the habit of saying that the Spirit comes from both the Father "and the Son" (Latin, filioque). When he spoke of the procession of the Spirit, he spoke of the eternal procession of the Spirit of the Father and the Son, not just the sending of the Holy Spirit at Pentecost. Augustine reasoned that if the Holy Spirit comes from the Father, it must also come from the Son, because they have the same divine nature.

But Augustine also contributed to the confusion of modern theology when he tried to explain the inexplicable. To make a distinction between the "generation" of the Son of the Father, and the "procession" of the Holy Spirit of the Father and of the Son, he expressed the theory that the Holy Spirit is a mysterious, eternal substance, common to both the Father and the Son, which can also be called a "friendship" or "bond of love." In his great work The Trinity wrote: "Therefore the Holy Spirit, whatever it may be, is something common to both the Father and the Son, but that communion itself is inherent and coeternal, and if it can be properly called friendship, then it is called, but more aptly it is called love. And that is also a substance, since God is a substance, and God is love, as it is written." (González, op. Cit., Pp 340-341)

In 589 A.D., in the third council of Toledo in Spain, is the first evidence that the filioque has been found in a western version of the Nicene Creed. This was done to refute the Arians. The Spanish church was disturbed by a group of Arians, who denied the full deity of the Son, but those Arians were willing to say that the Holy Spirit was God. That made his opponents answer that Jesus also has to be God, because the Spirit comes from the Father and the Son, filioque, and God can only come from God. This does not mean that the term filioque was widely accepted at that time. In fact, filioque was resisted in both the west and east for generations. Western theologians knew that the eastern church had not accepted the concept. Pope Leo III, for example, refused to allow the phrase to be added during his lifetime. In fact, he ordered to inscribe the Creed in Latin and Greek without filioque on two silver plates to adorn the walls of St. Peter's Basilica in Rome. He did so despite the fact that he agreed with the filioque regarding doctrine.

Eastern theologians, who feared that the filioque taught Sabellianism, insisted that there could only be one God who is the Father, and that the Father must be the source of both; of the Son and of the Holy Spirit.

When Pope Benedict VIII officially declared that the filioque statement would be part of the Creed that was confessed at the Latin Mass in 1014 A.D., deeply offended the leaders of the eastern church. Forty years later, in 1054 A.D., after several centuries of controversy about doctrine and practice in relation to this and other matters, a rupture occurred between the Roman church of the west and the orthodox church of the east that lasts until today.

In the modern era, theologian Robert W. Jensen considers that he has a mission to amend the doctrine received so far. According to him, Spirit was a term that biblical theology supplied to describe what precedes an encounter between God and the believer. The "Spirit" is "the knowledge of God by faith." He held that: "Truly, the Trinity is simply the Father and the man Jesus and his Spirit as the Spirit of the believing community." He calls the "Spirit" a "dynamism" that the church caught when he expected the future return of Jesus. Because he believes that the Holy Spirit is not a person of the Trinity, but a power that comes from God, Jensen is a modern example of dynamic monarchianism. Pieper, in turn, writes that "the majority of English,

North American, and German Unitarians are dynamic monarchists." (Braaten and Jensen, editors, Christian Dogmatics, Philadelphia, PA: Fortress Press, 1984, tome 1, p. 93, 108, 155, 156, 400; Pieper, op. Cit., P. 383)

Modern theology, with its rejection of the authority of Scripture, presents human speculation about the Trinity. Liberal scholars openly deny the deity of the Son and the Holy Spirit. They use the words Father, Son and Holy Spirit, but they explain them as three divine operations of a divine person, which denotes a modalist monarchianism. (Braaten and Jensen, editors, Christian Dogmatics, Philadelphia, PA: Fortress Press, 1984, tome 1, p. 400)

The Prussian Reformer theologian, Schleiermacher, recommended that the name Father be used for the true God, and that the names Son and Holy Spirit be used to represent the temporal ways in which the Father revealed himself. "The Holy Spirit was only the spirit of the believing community that proceeds from Christ, an active spiritual force" that according to him tended to agree with Imanuel Kant who thought that God cannot be known. He suggested that giving the Spirit at Pentecost only meant that the risen Christ had caused the beginning of an organized entity known as the church. (Neve, op. Cit., Tome 2, p. 113; Justo González, A History of Christian Thought, New York, NY: Abingdon Press, tome 3, p. 329)

Later, in the 9th century, Alberto Ritschl, an agnostic, repeated and slightly modified Schleiermacher's doctrine by saying that the Holy Spirit was an impersonal power emanating from God and dwelling in the church. (Neve, op. Cit., Tome 2, p. 151)

Modern modalism tries to make the doctrine of the Trinity reasonable by saying: "God is love. The Father is the love that has been given in the past, the Son is the love manifested in the present and the Spirit is the love that extends to the future."

There are also modern subordinationists, including some Arminians, who argue that the Son is younger than the Father, and that the Holy Spirit is younger than both because he comes from them. In contrast, the Athanasian Creed says: "And in this Trinity none is first or last; none major or minor; but all three people are co-eternal together and co-equal."

In this book we maintain that the Creator, the Supreme Being, the only God who exists and gives life is the Holy Spirit, and He has revealed Himself to human beings in different human figurations or expressions. The most connoted expressions or personal figurations that the Holy Spirit has assumed during the course of human history are: that of the Virgin Mary, as Woman and Mother, and that of Jesus, as Man and Son. When Jesus spoke of His Father, He was speaking of the Holy Spirit.

God in essence is Spirit, immeasurable energy, as Sacred Scripture says: "... Jesus was begotten by the Work and Grace of the Holy Spirit in the womb of Mary." In an unprecedented fact and beyond all logic of current human knowledge: Mary is Mother and companion at the same time and both entered the threshold of human incarnation at the same time as Philip establishes in his Gospel: "Let us say —if it is allowed— a secret: the Father of All was united with the virgin who had descended and a fire illuminated him that day. He unveiled the great bridal chamber, and so his body — which originated that day — came out of the bridal chamber as one that has been begotten by husband and wife. And likewise, thanks to these, Jesus straightened the All in her, requiring each and every one of his disciples to enter their resting place." Philip's Gospel.

The Holy Spirit of God in his omnipotence and omnipresence became woman and man at the same time. What for the human being seemed to happen in distant times, actually happened in the same instant of life. From before creation and for all eternity; The Virgin Mary is the Holy Spirit, Jesus is the Holy Spirit and the Father is the Holy Spirit in a unique and absolute consubstantial and coeternal essence called the Holy Trinity of the Holy Spirit.

3.2.- The Holy Spirit; Qualities, Names, Gifts and Fruits.

Concerning the qualities of the Holy Spirit, Christian theologians assume that he is the bearer of very diverse supernatural gifts that can be transmitted to man through his mediation. Although the enumeration of the gifts may vary from one author to another and between different confessions, there is a broad consensus regarding their excellence and magnanimity.

Most of the Christian churches, and among them the main ones, declare themselves Trinitarians. There are also non-trinitarian churches that confess some of the other interpretative modalities. (Christian Interpretations on the Holy Spirit, Wiki asked, 2012)

The Jewish-Christian texts contain a set of expressions that allude to a "divine reality" in which Judaism and Christianity believe, the main ones are: Holy Spirit, Spirit of God, Spirit of Truth, Spirit of Holiness, Straight Spirit, Generous Spirit, Spirit of Adoption, Mind of Christ, Spirit of the Lord, Lord Himself, Spirit of Liberty, Finger of God, Paraclete and Holy Spirit of God. Of all these, "Holy Spirit" is the main expression, the best known and the most used in Christianity.

In Judaism and Christianity it is believed that the Holy Spirit can approach the soul and transmit certain dispositions that perfect it. These habits are known as the "Gifts of the Holy Spirit." The gift ratio varies between different Christian denominations. In the Bible there is a quote from the prophet Isaiah where the "Gifts of the Holy Spirit" are listed, these are:

> Spirit of wisdom, intelligence, advice, strength, science, godliness and fear of God. (Isaiah 11: 2)

These gifts are complemented by the "7 fruits of the Spirit" that appear in the Epistle to the Galatians:

"But the fruit of the Spirit is: charity, joy, peace, tolerance, kindness, goodness, faith, meekness, temperance; against such things there is no law." (Galatians 5: 22-23)

All these names, gifts or fruits are implicit in the expression "Holy Spirit of God" and enrich all theological notions. However, despite this diversity of names, in Christian theology it is said that there is only one and only Spirit: The Holy Spirit of God, which is expressed through different divine personalities: Yahweh, the Virgin Mary and Jesus Christ.

3.3.- Personality of the Holy Spirit.

The way the scriptural truth that God the Father subsists or exists in three Persons - the Father, the Son and the Holy Spirit - was defined, was erroneously recognized by the vast majority of Christian congregations. Basing their definition on their interpretation of Scripture they state that the Holy Spirit is a Person as much as God the Father and God the Son, and that as seen in the study of the doctrine of the Trinity, the three Persons form a God and not three. The error of this interpretation is that the Holy Spirit is considered as one person and the Father as another person, but no mention is made of the feminine personality of the Holy Spirit. However, when we analyze the Gospel of Philip we realize that the Trinitarian reality is that the Holy Spirit incarnated at the same time as a woman in Mary to be the Mother of God and in Jesus to be the Son of God. In such a way, the Holy Spirit is "the whole" that contains the parts that make up the three realities known to Christianity: the Father, who is the Holy Spirit, the Mother (the Virgin Mary), who is the Holy Spirit, and the Son (Jesus Christ) who is the Holy Spirit, and the three are in themselves a single Being called the Holy Spirit.

In interpreting the fundamental truths concerning the Holy Spirit we must make special emphasis on the fact of his personality. Since the Holy Spirit does not speak of himself; According to John 16:13 and Acts 13:2, He speaks what He hears, and John 16:14 says that He has come into the world to glorify Christ, thereby also glorifying the Father and the Virgin Mary. Instead, Scripture only represents the Father and the Son, speaking of themselves with final authority and in eminent conversion, one with the other. But the truth is that none of this tends to make the personality of the Holy Spirit less real. The fact that He does not speak of Himself is that He preferred to speak to His Work through the Virgin Mary and Jesus who are both Himself, and through the true bearers of the faith who are inspired to write in his Glorious Name.

3.4.- The Holy Spirit; founder and main head of Christianity.

The Holy Spirit created Christianity thousands of years before his human incarnation as Jesus, when he inspired the prophets and patriarchs of old to propagate and write about the coming of the Christ, the Messiah, the Son of God, the Son. from his own womb, the one who would give his life to save humanity. That is to say that before Jesus came to the human world he already had followers, people who followed all the signs given about the way and place in which he would reach the world, among these were the kings or magicians of the East and the Essenes.

This is what the prophet Joel said: "And in the last days, says God, I will pour out my Holy Spirit on all flesh, and your sons and your daughters will prophesy; Your young men will see visions, and your old men will dream dreams; And verily on my servants and on my handmaids in those days I will pour out my Spirit, and they will prophesy. And I will show wonders in the heavens above, and signs on the earth below, ... before the day comes that I demonstrate to the unbelievers That I exist, great and manifest; and everyone who invokes my Name will be saved".

All who prophesy are among those servants who are enlightened, thanks to the Holy Spirit. Using Scripture as his tool, the Holy Spirit leads us to proclaim the "mystery that has been hidden from everlasting time," that Jesus Christ, the Lamb of God, is the Savior of mankind. He is the Savior that everyone needs to know and whom they need to trust to get rid of the coming judgment of the Holy Spirit. The Holy Spirit is the Spirit of God, the Spirit of YHVH "who exists," the Spirit of the Father, the Spirit of Jesus, the Spirit of Mary and the Spirit of faith in "the only God who exists."

It is the Holy Spirit who gives life, who creates our faith in the divine, who baptizes us, who turns bread and wine into the body and blood of Christ, who consecrates all the sacraments, is who guides our lives in faith as believers and who empowers us for our activity to proclaim Jesus as our Savior, Yahweh as our heavenly Father and the Virgin Mary as Our Lady of the Holy Trinity of God, all the miracles done on the face of the earth are made by the Work and Grace of the Holy Spirit.

The apostle Peter made an important announcement that is written in the book of Acts, in describing the miracle taking place in Jerusalem at Pentecost, he declared the beginning of the special coming of the Holy Spirit. This had been promised to the Old Testament prophets as a sign of the last days before Christ's glorious final advent. But this story was manipulated by men from the beginning of the Christian era, to hide the true origin of the Virgin Mary. Actually, on the day of Pentecost, when all the Apostles were gathered together in fear and incredulity about the power of Jesus, the Virgin Mary appeared to them and revealed to them that She is the Holy Spirit incarnated in the figure of a simple woman and that Jesus is the Holy Spirit incarnated in the figure of an apparently mortal man, that the three are one Being, and that although Mary and Jesus looked like flesh and bones, in reality their bodies did not possess elements of corruption like those of the human body.

On the day of Pentecost, the Virgen Mary, clothed with the Holy Spirit, is the one who gives the gifts that inspire and give sufficient strength to the Apostles to go out to preach the gospel after the ascension of Jesus, and She is who has continued to inspire millions of men and women to maintain and promote the faith of the Christian Church throughout the world, through her different advocations such as the Virgin of La Altagracia, the Virgin of Guadalupe, the Virgin of the Mercedes, the Virgen de la Caridad del Cobre, the Virgen del Rosario, the Virgen de Fátima, the Virgen de Pellevoisin, the Virgen de Regla, the Virgen de Lourdes, the Virgen del Carmen, the Virgen del Pilar, the Virgen de La Salette, the Virgin of Rome, the Virgin of Paris, the Virgin of Syracuse, the Virgin of Knock, the Virgin of Pontmain, the Virgin of Beauring, the Virgin of Banneux, the Virgin of Hollywood, the Virgin of the Miraculous, the Virgin of Kibeho, the Virgin of Caacupé, the Virgin of Chapi, the Virgin of Czestochowa, the Virgin of China, the Virgin of Akita, the Virgin of Vang, the Virgin of Sufanieh, the Virgin of Velankanni, among many other advocations, which do not are more than the different ways of naming the female personification of Holy Spirit in the Virgin Mary.

The Bible testifies in 2 Peter 1:21 about our Savior Jesus Christ only because the writers of it were "prompted" to do so by the Holy Spirit, like ships powered by the wind. It was the Holy Spirit who taught the prophets and the apostles what to say and what to write. The Holy Spirit is the true author of the real Sacred Books, which is also revealed in these books, although these were manipulated by man over time, which has resulted in different versions of the Bible that we have today, that have many alterations of the Word of the Holy Spirit.

"God is not the author of confusion." (1 Corinthians 14:33) The manipulation wicked men have done in the scriptures for their own profit has created confusion. When Jesus was referring to the Father he was speaking of the Holy Spirit. The Bible itself says: "Mary (the Mother of God) conceived her Son Jesus (the Son of God) by the Work and Grace of the Holy Spirit (God)." Here it is clear that "God the Father" is the Holy Spirit himself.

The first sentences of Genesis provide a dynamic introduction to the Holy Spirit, when he says: "Against a cold, dark, lifeless background, the Spirit of God moved on the face of the waters." (Genesis 1:2; Romans 16:25). Genesis does not refer here to Yahweh, or the Father, but here it is clearly stated that the Holy Spirit is the Entity of Creation and exists forever.

Again and again, seven more times, the Pentateuch reveals the power of the Holy Spirit, saying that He gave exceptional ability and knowledge to certain chosen people (once again we must emphasize that the Holy Spirit is being spoken of). Sometimes He gifted them physically, but more often He blessed them spiritually in matters of faith. Among them are Joshua, Gideon, Samson, and Saul who became outstanding leaders of Israel under the influence of the Holy Spirit. David, the king who wrote the Psalms, explained his lyrical gift saying: "The Spirit of God has spoken for me, and his word has been on my tongue." The Spirit is also credited with putting David's plans for the future temple in David's mind. The Old Testament repeatedly says that the Spirit of God, or the Spirit of the Lord, came upon the prophets, guiding their thoughts, words, and actions. The Holy Spirit of God receives praise and blessing throughout the entire Old Testament. (Genesis 41:38; Exodus 31: 3, 35:31; Numbers 11:17, 11: 25,26; 27:18 and 34:9 the seventy elders; Judges 3:10; 6:34; 13:25;14: 6,19 and 15:14;1 Samuel 10:6,10; 11:6 and 19:23; 2 Samuel 23:2).

"Just as in the beginning, before there was life in the world, the Holy Spirit was already moving on the waters," so also when the fulfillment of time arrived, the omnipotent, omnipresent and omniscient incarnated in the Virgin Mary to be Mother of God and in Jesus Christ to be the Son of God, as the essence of his own essence, the substance of his own substance. Long before the beginning of that great event, the Holy Spirit made person after person testify about Jesus, his own incarnate himself. He began with the Prophets and Patriarchs of the Old Testament and then with Elizabeth, Zechariah, and the Magi, and followed with the Shepherds, Simeon, and Anna. Then the Holy Spirit anointed Jesus himself, his Incarnate himself, to preach the good news to men of good will. After the ascension of the Messiah the Holy Spirit poured out his gifts on his disciples, through the divine person of the Virgin Mary, so that they understood the Scriptures and preached it throughout the world, and gave them power to forgive the sins in his name. The Holy

Spirit removed language barriers, dissolved fears, and prepared believers to bear witness to Jesus as our Savior. What he began to do at Pentecost, the Holy Spirit has continued to do for all eternity through the Virgin Mary. "The Holy Spirit will come upon you, and the power of the Most High will cover you with his shadow. The Spirit of the Lord is upon me, because he has anointed me to bring good news to the humble; This is what the Spirit said that those who believed in him were to receive; for the Holy Spirit had not yet come, because Jesus and the Virgin Mary had not yet been glorified; But when the Spirit of truth comes, He will guide you into all truth. He blew and said to them, receive the Holy Spirit to those who remit sins, they are remitted; and those who withhold them are withheld." (Luke 1:35; 4:18; John 7:39; 16:13; 20: 22,23; Acts 2:1; 1 Corinthians 12:11)

3.5.- The Holy Spirit has names and attribute divines

The Scriptures reveal that the Holy Spirit is God crediting him with divine names, works, and attributes. We have already seen that the word spirit literally means air, "breath" or "wind" and that it comes from the Hebrew (ruach or ruaj) and the Greek (pneuma). The word "spirit" in itself does not imply divinity, just as the words Father and Son do not in themselves imply divinity. But the fact that this Spirit is often called the Holy Spirit clearly indicates that he is God. Bible translations generally recognize this, capitalizing the word Spirit when the context reveals that it is speaking of the Holy Spirit. (Psalm 99: 9 "Exalt Jehovah our God, and prostrate yourselves before his holy mountain, for Jehovah our God is holy." Isaiah 6: 3 "Holy, holy, holy, Jehovah of hosts; the whole earth is full of his glory.")

The apostle Paul gave the names "Lord" and "God" to the Holy Spirit when he wrote of spiritual gifts: "There are diverse gifts, but the Spirit is the same. And there is a diversity of ministries, but the Lord is the same. And there are diverse operations, but God, who does all things in everyone, is the same ... But all these things are done by one and the same Spirit (the Holy Spirit of God)." (1 Corinthians 12: 4; 6:11). Saint Paul also said in 1 Corinthians 6:19, "Your body is the temple of the Holy Spirit, which is in you," meaning that the Christian's body is a temple of God since the Spirit dwells in it.

The Nicene Creed praises the Holy Spirit as "the giver of life." It is an appropriate description of the divine activity of the Holy Spirit during the creation of the world. It also deserves this praise because the gift of life can be transmitted from one generation to another. As Job said, "The spirit of God made me, And the breath of the Almighty gave me life." But even more important than the gift of physical life is the new birth, the spiritual life that the Holy Spirit works through the Gospel in the Sacrament of Holy Baptism and through the Gospel itself. God "saved us ... by the washing of regeneration and by renewal in the Holy Spirit." "God has chosen you from the beginning for salvation, through sanctification by the Spirit and faith in the truth, to which he called you through our gospel, to achieve the glory of our Lord Jesus Christ." (Genesis 1: 1,2; Job 33: 4; Titus 3: 4,5; 2 Thessalonians 2: 13,14).

Furthermore, the Holy Spirit also preserves the lives of his people by praying for them: "And in the same way the Spirit helps us in our weakness; for what are we to ask as is fitting, we do not know, but the Spirit himself intercedes for us..." (Romans 8:26). These activities of creation and preservation affirm that the Holy Spirit is God. Like God, the Holy Spirit also convicts us of sin, testifies of Christ, leads us to faith in our Savior, and preserves our faith.

It should be noted that the three people who make up the Holy Spirit; the Father, the Mother of God and the Son of God, They do all these divine works in common. All three persons have the same divine nature and together they are active in all the divine works that are done outward from the Holy Spirit, for creation, preservation and evolution of creation. The world is full of miracles performed by the three divine persons, who is just one, the Holy Spirit.

When baptism was instituted, the three people who make up the Holy Spirit were named, but the maleness of the time eliminated the feminine part of the Supreme Being and to achieve this they doubled the mentions of the Holy Spirit as such and as Father. In Matthew 28:19 it is read; "Baptizing them in the name of the Father, and of the Son, and of the Holy Spirit." According to theologians, the fact that the Holy Spirit was named last does not indicate that he has an inferior position, or that he originated in another time, nor does the fact that each of the three persons are named separately mean that each has their own divine nature. The divine nature of the Holy Spirit is not separate from the divine nature of the Father, the Mother and the Son. Scripture teaches that there is a God, with a divine nature. The appropriate words are: "I baptize you in the name of the Holy Spirit, who is Father, Mother and Son." Since there are not three gods with three divine natures, there is only one Holy Spirit who has possessed three different figurations to carry out different actions. Each of the three persons assumed by the Holy Spirit has a unique and indivisible divine essence in its entirety. Because in truth there is only one God who receives the name of Holy Spirit and that this one has been made present among humans in three persons or divine figurations; the Father, the Virgin Mary and Jesus, and that each culture has called them by different names. In fact, the Hebrews, before the coming of Mary and Jesus, called the feminine part of God with the name of Asherah to which they paid tribute as the wife of God, but all of this was edited from the Christian bible.

"Sometimes we read a plural reference to the Holy Spirit in the Bible. That may have reference to the sevenfold characteristics of the Holy Spirit that were given to Christ as the prophet Isaiah predicted: "And the Spirit of Yahweh will rest upon him; spirit of wisdom and intelligence, spirit of counsel and power, spirit of knowledge and fear of Jehovah." (Revelation 1: 4; 3: 1; 4: 5; 5: 6; Isaiah 11: 2; Luke 4:18)

The Holy Spirit was given to Jesus human nature "without limit" for this reason and also because Jesus and the Holy Spirit, there is only one, with the same divine nature, Jesus can be called, "the Lord who is the Holy Spirit." The perfect divine cooperation and unity of these two personalities of the Divine Being does not change the fact that the two persons are distinct and separate in space and time. The Son is in the Holy Spirit and the Holy Spirit is in the Son, the same thing happens with the Virgin Mary. The Three divine people; Father, Mother and Son are in the Holy Spirit as much as the Holy Spirit is in each one of them. The Holy Spirit is like an equilateral triangle formed by the Father, the Virgin Mary and Jesus where they are the whole and the parts at the same time.

"For the Lord is the Spirit; and where the Spirit of the Lord is, there is freedom. Therefore, all of us, looking at the naked face as in a mirror the glory of the Lord, we are transformed from glory to glory in the same image, as by the Spirit of the Lord." In this passage the words "the Lord," "the glory of the Lord," and "the same image" have reference to Jesus Christ. "The Spirit" has reference to the Holy Spirit. Similarly, the

Son is the Father, and the Father is the Son, since Jesus said, "Me and the Father are one," and "Who has seen me has seen the Father." (John 3:34; 10:30 and 14: 8-11; 2 Corinthians 3: 17.18). When Jesus speaks of the Father, He is referring to Himself as the Holy Spirit.

"For the one whom God sent, the words of God speak; for God gives us the Spirit by measure."

Scripture warns against offending the Holy Spirit. When King Saul turned away from God, "the Spirit of God" turned away from him. When King David recognized that his sin and unrepentance had grieved the Holy Spirit, he repented with all his heart. God warned unrepentant Israel that they were "rebellious, and angered his holy spirit" and that was why "he made them an enemy, and he himself fought against them." A terrible judgment fell on Ananias and his wife Safira when they refused to repent or even admit that they had lied to the Holy Spirit.

In the same way the Hebrews were warned: "For if we will sin voluntarily after having received the knowledge of the truth, there is no longer any sacrifice for sins, but a horrendous expectation of judgment, and of boiling fire that will devour the adversaries. He who violates the law of Moses, by the testimony of two or three witnesses, irretrievably dies."

How much more punishment do you think he will deserve who tramples under foot the Son of God, and considers the blood of the covenant in which he was sanctified as unclean, and offends the Spirit of grace? For we know the one who said: Vengeance is mine, I will give the payment, says the Lord. And again: The Lord will judge his people. It is a horrible thing to fall into the hands of the living God! (1 Samuel 16:14; Psalm 51: 1-11; Isaiah 63:10; Hebrews 10: 26-31).

The Holy Spirit deserves the adoration and respect of the people of God. Sin saddens him, sanctified life honors him. "And do not grieve the Holy Spirit, with whom you were sealed for the day of redemption. Take from you all bitterness, anger, rage, shouting and slander, and all malice." Ephesians 4:30-31

Or do you not know that your body is the temple of the Holy Spirit, which is in you, which you have from God, and that you are not yours? Because you have been bought with a price; Therefore glorify God in your body and in your spirit, which are from God. 1 Corinthians 6:19-20

Since the Holy Spirit provides the power for sanctified life only through the gospel in word and sacrament, we honor it by keeping in touch with these means of grace, so that we do not quench the fire of the Spirit by being negligent of the gospel.

3.6.- The true dynamic of the Holy Spirit.

In the ancient Christian church, a group of Jewish Christians known as the Ebionites held the belief that the Holy Spirit was the female person in the Divine Trinity. A modern theologian whose writings have recently appeared on the internet also speculates about the feminine gender of the Holy Spirit. She then proceeds to develop her own theological system, suggesting that a female Holy Spirit explains the female characterization of "wisdom" in Proverbs 8:12:31. Also some modern feminist theologians prefer to worship God like Sophia, a goddess, they have the same heterodox opinion. (Neve, op. Cit., Tome 1, p. 51; www.theology.edu/pneumato.htm)

These beliefs add to all of the above which have been based on many misconceptions about the identity of the Holy Spirit. Among their great confusion some see the Holy Spirit as a mystical force. Others understand the Holy Spirit as the impersonal power that God makes available to followers of Christ.

We have seen that the Bible says clearly and precisely that the Holy Spirit is God. It also tells us that the Holy Spirit is a Person, a Being with a mind, emotions, and a will. The fact that the Holy Spirit is God is clearly seen in many parts of Scripture, including Acts 5: 3-4. In this verse, Peter confronts Ananias for having lied to the Holy Spirit, and tells him that he had not lied to men but to God. It is a clear statement that lying to the Holy Spirit is lying to God, that is to say that both are the same essence. We can also know that the Holy Spirit is God, because He possesses the attributes or characteristics of God. For example, as we could see earlier, the fact that the Holy Spirit is omnipresent, in Psalms 139: 7-8 "¿Where will I go from your Spirit? And ¿Where will I flee from your presence? If I go up to heaven, you are there; and if I make my platform in Sheol, behold, there you are". Then in 1 Corinthians

2:10 we see the characteristic of the omniscience of the Holy Spirit, but God revealed them to us by the Spirit; because the Spirit searches everything, even the depths of God, ¿For who of men knows the things of man but the spirit of man that is in him? So also no one knew the things of God, but the Spirit of God.

We can know that the Holy Spirit is truly more than a Person, "Who Exists", who ordered and gave the Commandments to Moses, because He has a mind, emotions and a will. "The Holy Spirit thinks and knows" (1 Corinthians 2:10). "The Holy Spirit can be afflicted" (Ephesians 4:30) "The Holy Spirit intercedes for us" (Romans 8: 26-27). "The Holy Spirit makes decisions according to His will" (1 Corinthians 12: 7-11). "The Holy Spirit is God. As God, the Holy Spirit can truly function as a Counselor and Comforter, just as He promised through Jesus." (John 14:16, 26; 15:26).

With all that we have seen so far about the Divine Persons that make up the Most Holy Trinity of the Holy Spirit of God, we must conclude that in reality Yahweh and the Father, are exactly names by which the masculine expression of the Holy Spirit of God; When Jesus is speaking of His Father, He is referring precisely to the Holy Spirit of God. The Holy Spirit of God has never incarnated as "The Father"; He incarnated as a Woman to be a Mother, in Mary, so that through His feminine incarnation, He incarnated at the same time as Man and Son in Jesus Christ, Our Lord. If the scriptures that confirm and speak of the nature of God are studied carefully and objectively, there would be no possibility of confusion. In such a way that it has not been by confusion that the ecclesiastical hierarchs have kept humanity misinformed about this matter, rather they have done it blinded by the macho selfishness that has clothed the different churches throughout the course of the history of the humanity. "And Jesus, after he was baptized, immediately went up out of the water, and at that moment the heavens were opened to him, and he saw the Spirit of God descending like a dove and alighting on him. And at that moment a voice was heard saying: This is my beloved Son, in whom I am well pleased." (Matthew 3: 16-17).

If you carefully analyze the passages in the Bible where God has made contact with a human, it will be verified that he has never presented himself with a figure of man or Father, he always did it in the form of a burning bush, fire, light source and wind. The only parts where God the

Father is spoken of is when Jesus is referring to his Father, the Creator Father, my Father's Temple, my Father's house, etc., if we link this with the part of the Bible that He speaks of his way of coming to the human world, which says: "He was begotten by the Work and Grace of the Holy Spirit," then it is clear that the Father of Jesus is the Holy Spirit, while Jesus is also the Holy Spirit. Later in another passage in the Bible it says: Before he returned to heaven after his ministry on earth, Jesus spoke of the coming of the Holy Spirit:

"But when the Comforter comes, whom I will send to you from the Father, the Spirit of truth, who proceeds from the Father, he will bear witness about me" (John 15:26). If we consider that Jesus said: "Me and the Father are only one." And he added "Who has seen me has seen the Father." In such a way that Jesus here is promising to return Himself, sent by Himself, although he is emphasizing that his return will be in a different way, in a different expression of his own Divine Being, which is precisely the form and essence of the Holy Spirit who at the same time is his Father is himself.

"And I will ask the Father and he will give you another Comforter, to be with you forever: the Spirit of truth, whom the world cannot receive, because it neither sees it nor knows it; but you know him, because he lives with you and will be in you" (John 14: 16-17). Who more than the Holy Spirit in the Virgin Mary to comfort Believers. "But when the Comforter comes, to whom I will send you from the Father, the Spirit of truth, who proceeds from the Father, he will bear witness about me." (John 15:26).

"Manifest are the works of the flesh, which are: adultery, fornication, filth, lust, idolatry, witchcraft, enmities, lawsuits, jealousy, anger, strife, divisions, heresy, envy, selfishness, homicide, drunkenness, orgies, and things equally to these. Regarding this, I warn you, as I have already told you before, that practical stories things will not inherit the kingdom of God. But the fruit of the Spirit is love, joy, peace, patience, kindness, goodness, faith, meekness, temperance; against stories there is no law" (Galatians 5: 19-23). Although the power of the flesh was defeated on the cross, as believers we experience this only as we practice faith in the works of the Holy Spirit through Jesus, Mary, and Yahweh. Therefore, to be effective in denying the power of the sinful nature of the flesh, it is necessary for us to review the fruit of the Holy Spirit.

The Holy Spirit in his spiritual form is invisible to the natural eyes of man, but He is in the world today, actively continuing his work through Jesus and the Virgin Mary, reproving men and women of sin, drawing men and women to Christianity, equipping believers with power for spiritual warfare, guiding them, and witnessing to their infinite glory.

The Holy Spirit is the Alpha and the Omega, not only for being the beginning and the end, but for the first male (symbolized in the Alpha) and the first female (symbolized in the Omega). One of the names of the Holy Spirit is "I Am", by which it is meant that He had no beginning and no end, and for this reason He will always be present, for Him there is no past or future, everything happens in the same instant.

The Holy Spirit is the creator of the universe. For this to be possible, He exists before creating the world and his gender is feminine and masculine at the will of his omnipotence.

The Holy Spirit is the supreme power and authority over all things. Nothing can happen without the Holy Spirit separating and allowing it to happen by his omnipresence and omniscience.

The Holy Spirit reveals to us everything we know about Him. He is God and personally He makes Himself known through the different people of His Most Holy Trinity. Although we do not know everything that respects the Holy Spirit, each one of us can know a little about Him and each one of his divine personifications.

The Holy Spirit always knows why things happen, He always has a purpose for everything that happens in the universe.

"As the heavens are higher than the earth, so are my ways higher than your ways, and my thoughts more than your thoughts" (Isaiah 55: 9).

The Holy Spirit created the world only by giving the order for everything to exist. The Holy Spirit has no limitation of power. He knows all things. He is always present.

The Holy Spirit is unique, sinless, and completely different. The Holy Spirit has all moral perfection. In the Holy Spirit all goodness is represented.

The Holy Spirit goes beyond simply loving us; the Holy Spirit is love. Nothing He does is outside His love. It is because of this great love that he was incarnated in the Virgin Mary and in his Son Jesus in order to give his life to redeem us from our sins.

The purpose of redeeming humanity was to unite the fellowship that was broken by our sins. The Holy Spirit of God did not intend for the world to be as it is today, but He has provided the way to redemption.

The Holy Spirit has always wanted us to be a sinless people in our lives. During the years of the Old Covenant, the Holy Spirit instituted a temporary sacrifice so that people would receive forgiveness of their sins. Once a year the sins of the people were symbolically thrown into a lamb that was expelled from the community. This process had to be repeated annually. The priest listened as people confessed their sins. Later, he sacrificed an animal and offered that blood as a dispensation of the person's sins.

After Jesus left the New and Eternal Covenant instituted, constituting Himself the Lamb of sacrifice to God, "the Lamb of God who takes away the sins of the world ...", the animal sacrifice was repealed and the death of Jesus is the sacrifice permanent for our sins. The blood of Jesus brings forgiveness for our sins for all eternity.

The Holy Spirit wanted to restore his Covenant with humanity through his personality as Mother, in Mary, and through his personality as Son, in Jesus, since ancient times he had established his Covenant with the Patriarchs through of his personality as YHVH (Yahweh) "Who exists." The Holy Spirit fully forms these three divine persons, but it is also present in every human being, although to a much lesser degree, and it is in every man and woman to cultivate it to be more and more in the image and likeness of Him. This was the main teaching of Jesus and Mary, that every human being has the opportunity to develop spiritually until reaching divinity, since it is established that we were created in the image and likeness of God. Every man who succeeds in imitating Jesus and every Woman who succeeds in imitating Mary will be able to reach the heavenly dimension where the Beings of Light live.

Men have given many names to God, and the names given to name God are revealed in the Bible that reveal His Ministry to us while you are engaged in this great spiritual conflict. Indeed, Jews are forbidden to pronounce the real four-letter name of God (Yud-Hei-Vav-Hei). This is the reason why they call it "Hashem" which means "The Name." But in the different versions of the Bible we find that God is named by different names; as "Jehovah" in the evangelical Bibles and "Yahve" in the Catholic Bibles. But deep down it is not important to argue for the name of God in the Old Covenant. What is of great importance is that we live today under the Eternal Covenant established by Jesus and the Virgin Mary in the Holy Spirit, and therefore we must speak of God as Jesus spoke of Him; Jesus told us that the Holy Spirit is love. God is a "Father" who loves all his creatures and humans are his favorite children, since we were created in his image and likeness. Jesus Himself taught us that we must invoke God as "Our Father and Creator" (Matthew 6, 9). All the ancient original texts when speaking of God do so with neutral articles, so they do not establish a specific sexual gender for God. It is from the New Testament where it begins to call God with a masculine article, repealing the feminine part of the Holy Spirit.

For the traditional students of the Bible this explanation is a little difficult to assimilate, because we must understand some things of the Hebrew language, the language in which the Holy Spirit was manifested to Moses. The Old Testament Israelites used many names to refer to God. All these names expressed an intimate relationship of the Holy Spirit with humanity, as we can see below:

In Exodus 6:7 we find in the Hebrew text the name "Elohim", which in Castilian means: "The strong and powerful God."

In Psalm 94 we find "Edonay", which in English is "The Lord".

In Genesis 17:1 God is spoken of as "Shadday" meaning the God of the mountain.

In Isaiah 7:14 we speak of "Emmanuel" which means "God with us."

But the name most used in those times was "YHVH" (Yud-Hei-Vav-Hei) which is pronounced "Yahvéh" and which in English means: "I am the one that exists". In Exodus 3, 13-15 we can read the account of when the Holy Spirit appeared to Moses in the form of a burning bush and sent him to Pharaoh to speak on his behalf. Moses asked the Holy Spirit: "But if the Israelites ask me ¿What your name is, what am I going to answer them?" And the Holy Spirit of God said to Moses: "Yud-Hei-Vav-Hei" which in english means "I AM THE ONE THAT EXITS". This is how you will say to the Israelites: "THE ONE THAT EXISTS" sends me to you. This you will say to them: "THE ONE THAT EXISTS (YHVH), the One who was with Isaac and who was with Jacob sends me to you. This is my name forever."

The word "YHVH" (Yud-Hei-Vav-Hei) is a Hebrew word, Hebrew is the language of the Israelites or Jews of the Old Testament. In this language the vowels of a word were not written but only the consonants. It was quite difficult to read it correctly, because when reading a Hebrew text, one had to know by heart which vowels he had to pronounce in the middle of the consonants. The name of God: "I AM THE ONE THAT EXISTS" was written with these four consonants: YHVH that the Jews pronounced "Yud-Hei-Vav-Hei" but over time it degenerated until reaching the pronunciation of "Yahvéh", and in English it is pronounced "Yahweh" as the closest pronunciation of the original Hebrew to indicate the name by which the Own Holy Spirit was named as "I am the one who exists." It is important to clarify here that the Old Testament Jews never called God by the name "Jehovah" since that name was created by men in the Middle Ages.

The ancient Israelites had a deep respect for the name of the God: "YHVH" (Yud-Hei-Vav-Hei) was the most sacred name of God, because the Holy Spirit Himself had given this name The same; "I AM THE ONE THAT EXISTS." But over time the Israelites, out of respect for the proper name of the Holy Spirit, stopped pronouncing the name "YHVH" and when they read the name "YHVH" in the Bible, instead of saying "Yud-Hei- Vav-Hey" said another name to refer to God, this other name was "Edonay" which means "The Lord". But it turned out that after hundreds of years the Israelites completely forgot about the original pronunciation of "YHVH" (Yud-Hei-Vav-Hei) because they always said "Edonay". And it is in the Middle Ages, about 1,300 years after Christ, when religious analysts studied the ancient Hebrew language and began to put vowels between the consonants of the Hebrew language. And when it came to placing vowels in the Hebrew word YHVH the original name of the Holy Spirit of God they encountered many difficulties.

Not knowing the original pronunciation of the four consonants that correspond to YHVH in English letters and JHVH in Latin letters, and to remind the reader that out of respect he should say: "Edonay" instead of "JHVH", they put the three vowels (e, o, a) of the word Edonay; and the word "Jehovah" came out in Latin. That is, they took the 4 consonants of a word "JHVH" and simply inserted the 3 vowels of the word Edonay and thus formed a new word: "Jehovah." It is clear that the word "Jehovah" is an arrangement of two words in one, which later began to be written "Jehovah" for ease of pronunciation. Of course the word "Jehovah" has never existed in Hebrew; that is, the pronunciation "Jehovah" is a faulty pronunciation of the name "YHVH" or "Yahweh."

In the 1600s A.D. they began to translate the Bible into all languages, and since they found the word "Jehovah" as God's proper name in all the biblical texts of the Middle Ages, they copied this name "Jehovah" literally in the different languages. And from that time on, Catholics and Evangelicals began to pronounce the word "Jehovah" in english as the proper name of the Holy Spirit in the Old Testament.

Now, even Catholic Bibles use the name "Yahweh" and not "Jehovah." Since all the students of the Hebrew language believed that the original and primitive way to pronounce the name of the Holy Spirit should have been "Yahweh" and not "Jehovah."

Since "Yahweh" is a form of the verb "havah" (to be, exist) and means: "I am the one who exists" and "Jehovah" is not any form of the verb "to be", it is not even a real word that existed before the writers of the middle ages combined the consonants of JHVH with the vowels of Edonay to form the word "Jehovah", as I have explained above. So the Roman Catholic Church made the decision to use the original pronunciation it believed to be "Yahweh" instead of "Jehovah" and because the Israelites of Moses 'time as well as those of Jesus' time never knew the name "Jehovah."

We already know that "YHVH" is mispronounced "Yahweh" and that it means "I am the one who exists." But to understand this name we must think that all the peoples of that time were polytheists, that is, they believed in the existence of many gods. According to them, each nation, each city and each tribe had its own God or its own gods. In saying the Holy Spirit of God to Moses: "Yud-Hei-Vav-Hei" (I AM THE ONE THAT EXISTS), He wants to establish that He is the only and true God; and the other gods do not exist, the gods of the Egyptians, of the Assyrians, of the Babylonians do not exist. I am the only God that exists.

The prophet Isaiah explains well the meaning of the name of the Holy Spirit of God. God says through the prophet: "Yud-Hey-Vav-Hey" (I AM THE ONE THAT EXISTS), and no other. "Am I Yahweh the only one and nobody but me?" (Isaiah 45:18).

Another important point in which we must be clear is to know that Jesus and his apostles, according to the Jewish custom of that time, never pronounced the original name of God "YHVH" or "Yahweh," much less "Jehovah" (since as we saw previously the name Jehovah was created 1,300 years after Christ.) They always read the Bible saying: "Edonay -the Lord- to indicate the proper name of God. But as the entire New Testament was written in Greek, in it we find the word

Kyrios which means "the Lord," which is the Greek translation of "Edonay."

But Jesus also introduced a novelty in religious customs and named God "Father": "I praise you, Father, Lord of heaven and earth." "My Father continues to act and I also act." "That is why the Jews wanted to kill him: because he called God his Father making himself equal to God." "My Father and I are ourselves." "He who has seen me has seen the Father." (John 5:17-18).

Other names widely used in different versions of the Old Testament to cry out to God are:

> Yahweh: In the Hebrew language that the Old Testament was written in, the word "Yahweh" means God. This word is combined with other words to reveal more about the character of God. God is called:
>
> Yahweh Jireh: "The Lord who provides" (Genesis 22:14)
>
> Yahweh Nisi: "The Lord is a flag" (Exodus 17:15)
>
> Yahweh Shalom: "The Lord is peace" (Judges 6:24)
>
> Yahweh Sebaot: "The Lord of Hosts" (I Samuel 1: 3)
>
> Yahweh Macadeshem: "The Lord your Sanctifier" (Exodus 31:13)
>
> Yahweh Tzidkenu: "The Lord our Justice" (Jeremiah 23: 6)
>
> Yahweh Shamah: "The Lord is there" (Ezekiel 48:35)
>
> Yahweh Elohim Israel: "The Lord God of Israel" (Judges 5: 3)
>
> Qadosh Israel: "The Holy One of Israel" (Isaiah 1: 4)
>
> Yahweh Rapha: "The Lord your Healer" (Exodus 15:26)
>
> Jehovah: which means Lord. The Bible combines this word with other names of God:
>
> Jehovah-Rafa: "The Lord who heals" (Exodus 15:26).
>
> Jehovah-Nisi: "The Lord our flag" (Exodus 17: 8-15).
>
> Jehovah-Shalom: "The Lord our peace" (Judges 6:24).
>
> Jehovah-Raah: "The Lord my shepherd" (Psalms 23: 1).
>
> Jehovah-Tzidkenu: "The Lord our righteousness" (Jeremiah 23: 6).
>
> Jehovah- Jireh: "The Lord who provides" (Genesis 22:14).
>
> Jehovah-Shamah: "The Lord is there" (Ezekiel 48:35).
>
> Elohim: means God and is used wherever the creative power of God is present.

Father: Acts 17:28; John 1: 12-13.

Edonay or Adonai: means Lord or Master: Exodus 23:17; Isaiah 10:16, 33.

The: is frequently used in combination with other words for God:

Shadai: "The Lord who is sufficient for the needs of His people" (Exodus 6: 3).

Elolam: "The Eternal God" (Genesis 21:33).

The Elyon: "The highest God who is exalted above the so-called gods" (Genesis 14:18, 22).

The Lord of Hosts: In the Biblical record, these different names of God were used to request God to move in a specific way in favor of his people. For example, the name Jehovah-Rafa meaning "The Lord Who Heals" was used when seeking healing.

The specific name of God to be used in spiritual warfare (holy warfare) is "Yahweh Sebaot" which is translated as "The Lord of Hosts" in the King James Version of the Bible. When you claim that name in war, the battle is the Lord's and all the armies of heaven come to your aid.

The greatest and most important mystery of all this for humanity is in knowing and accepting the true composition of God. When the Bible was rewritten in the fourth century after Christ and the Creed of the Roman Catholic Apostolic Church was established, it created a dogma of faith, that is, a truth that we must believe: "There is one and only God, who is the Creator Father, Redeeming Son and Holy Spirit, Lord and Giver of Life and Sanctifier." This mystery of the Holy Trinity is one of the "mysteries hidden in God, -which as the Second Vatican Council says-, if they are not revealed, they cannot be known" And, even after the Revelation, it is the deepest mystery of faith, which the understanding alone cannot understand or penetrate. Instead, the same understanding, illuminated by faith, can in a certain way grasp and explain the meaning of dogma, to bring man closer to the mystery of the intimate life of the One and Triune God.

All Holy Scripture reveals this truth: "God is Love in the interior life of a single Divinity, as an ineffable communion of persons." They are three different Persons in a single Holy Spirit of God, as the catechism teaches.

The mystery of the Holy Trinity of the Holy Spirit is the greatest revelation made by Jesus Christ. The Jews worship the oneness of God and are unaware of the plurality of people in the oneness of substance. The other peoples adore the multiplicity of the gods. Christianity is the only religion that has discovered, in the revelation of Jesus, that God is one in three persons. Faced with this divine revelation of his intimate essence, we are left with nothing but to thank him for this trust and to adore the Three Divine Persons: Jesus (the Son), Mary (the Mother) and the Father in the Holy Spirit.

The Holy Spirit is the Giver of Life, Gifts and Holiness. The Holy Spirit of God is the Being that forms the Essence of everything that exists in the universe. He is the one from before the Beginning and will last after the End. He is the Alpha and the Omega. He is the Male and the Female. From Him we were made in the image and likeness. He can assume any image or figure known or unknown to humanity. He is the only omnipotent, omnipresent and omniscient. Everything else comes from Him. After Him came the Mother and the Father to beget the Son. And all three are part of their own essence. The Father is the Holy Spirit, the Mother is the Holy Spirit and the Son is the Holy Spirit. Three Divine Persons in a single Substance, in a single Spirit; the Holy Spirit of God. All three have the same divine origin and their way of coming to the human world was only to cover the appearances of something that could not be understood by the beings of ancient times.

We are in the presence of a divine phenomenon that we have called it by hundreds of different names trying to explain its mysteries, mysteries that are far beyond human understanding to this day. It is a Being that is one and all at the same time. A Being that has all the possible states of matter. A Being that none of the humans who have had contact with Him in any of their ways of presenting themselves has been able to give a logical description of what they have seen or felt. He manifested himself to the Patriarchs and Prophets in the form of a burning flame, then in Mary and Jesus in human form, to remain present first at Baptism and the Transfiguration of Jesus, and then on the day of Pentecost over the disciples and the apparitions. of the Virgin Mary in the peoples of the world. "It lives in the hearts of the faithful with the gift of charity." (Ephesians 4:30)

In the Gospel of Saint John, Jesus pleads with the Father for what is his great desire:

"May they all be one like You, Father, you are in Me and I am in You. Also be one in us: thus the world will believe that you have sent me." (John 17:21)

They are "subsistent" relationships, which by virtue of their vital impulse meet one another in a communion, in which the whole of the Person is open to the other.

It is this, the supreme paradigm of sincerity and spiritual freedom to which human interpersonal relationships, hitherto so distant from this transcendent model, must tend.

"Our Lord Jesus, when he pleads with the Father that - everyone be one, as we are also one - tries to make humanity aware that the perspective of human reason must be opened in order to be more in tune with the Holy Spirit, so that a certain similarity may arise between the union of divine persons and the union of the children of God in truth, in charity and in love. This similarity clearly alludes to the fact that man, the only earthly creature to The one that God has loved for himself cannot find its own fullness if it is not in the sincere dedication of himself to others." (Vatican Council II, Gaudium et spes, 24).

"Knowing the mystery of the Holy Trinity, involves us and commits us to acquire certain attitudes in human relationships: The most perfect unity of the three divine Persons is the transcendent vertex that illuminates all forms of authentic relationship and communion between us, beings. Human." (John Paul II," I believe in God the Father ", p.170)

It is not just that we want to understand the Mystery of the Holy Trinity, this is impossible. Jesus revealed this Mystery to us to show us the model of what the human relationships of Christians should be. The Model of the Divine Family; the Father, the Mother and the Son. The Father, the Mother - the Virgin Mary - and the Son - Jesus - all three are the Holy Spirit. But the universal Church taught us to "glorify" a mutilated and deformed Holy Trinity, as a manifestation of the celebration of the triumph of arrogant machismo that has kept the church hostage for more than two thousand years. Trying to hide that for perfection to exist in the church there must first be perfection in the family." The church is constantly fighting against same-sex couples families, but it has hidden the feminine part of God for ever and ever.

The Church dedicates the following Sunday after Pentecost to the celebration of the day of the Holy Trinity. The mystery of the Holy Trinity - One God in three different Persons - is the central mystery of faith and of the Christian life, since it is the mystery of the Holy Spirit in Himself. But, although it is a difficult dogma to understand, it was the first that the Apostles understood after the Resurrection, they understood that Jesus was the Savior sent by the Holy Spirit. And, when they experienced the action of the Holy Spirit within their hearts at Pentecost, they understood that the only God was the Holy Spirit and that He had worked as Father, Mother and Son; the example of the Divine Family. But over time and jealous knowing the role played by the Virgin Mary in the Holy Trinity and the role of Mary Magdalene as leader of the Apostles and connoisseurs of the ancient struggles between Moses and the religious leader Mirian, they decided that they should change the truth and make believe that the Holy Trinity was made up only of men and that only women were used as servants in their service in order to establish the maleness monarchy that has dominated the life of the Christian churches from the ascension of Jesus and Mary, until today.

Father, Mother and Son of God have the same nature, the same substance, the same divinity, the same eternity, the same power, the same perfection; they are one and the only god. Furthermore, we know that each of the Persons of the Holy Trinity of the Holy Spirit is totally contained in the others, since there is a perfect communion between them.

Nevertheless, the people of the Holy Trinity are different from each other, given the diversity of their mission: God the Mother - who gave birth to the One who created everything - is sent by the Holy Spirit, She is the Mother of all Creation. God the Son - by whom all things are - is sent by the Holy Spirit (whom He called God the Father and Creator), He is our Savior. The Holy Spirit (Father and Creator) - who contains all things - is the one sent by himself, he is all our Sanctifying essence.

4.- The Virgin Mary; Our Lady of the Holy Trinity of God

The Holy Spirit incarnated in Mary and Jesus fulfilling the proclamation made to the serpent in Eden.

"And I will put enmity between you and the woman, and between your offspring and her offspring; she will hurt your head, and you will hurt her in the heel." Genesis 3:15

Since humanity demonstrated that it could not control itself in the face of Satan's temptations, The Word became flesh, at the same time, in Mary and Jesus. The incarnation of the Virgin Mary had unique privileges, just like the incarnation of her Son Jesus. Mary, the Divine Being incarnated as Woman, is and will be pure, holy, with all the most precious divine graces. Mary has the Divine Grace of the Holy Spirit from before her incarnation and will have it forever, because they are one Being.

"Let us say - if it is allowed - a secret: the Father of All joined with the virgin who had descended and a fire illuminated him that day. He unveiled the great bridal chamber, and so his body — which originated that day — came out of the bridal chamber as one that has been begotten by husband and wife. And likewise, thanks to these, Jesus straightened the All in her, requiring each and every one of his disciples to enter their resting place." Philip's Gospel.

The composers of the Christian Bible describe in the gospel of Luke the Divine Conception of the Virgin Mary in the narrative framework of the Annunciation as the work of the Holy Spirit. They present the Virgin Mary as the central figure of the childhood gospel, linked to the birth of Jesus, but they do not recognize that She plays a leading role in the Christianization of humanity, and continues to do so through the apparitions in which She grants all kinds of miracles to people in need, which has helped to convert the Christian faith to many peoples of different parts of the world. Although this faith has been misused by the Roman Catholic Church, it is fair to recognize that unfortunately this is the only church that has welcomed it, at least as its patron saint of almost all populations.

In Juan, they describe the presence of the Virgin Mary in Cana, where he points her out as an active intervener in the first of the miracles performed by Jesus, and at the foot of the cross during his passion and death, together with María Magdalena and her sister Martha, but this miracle is one of the moments in which the divinity of the feminine part of the Holy Trinity of the Holy Spirit is tested. John himself points out that when the mother of Jesus said to him "Jesus has finished the wine", Jesus' answer was; "Mother, my hour has not yet come." This makes it very clear that Jesus was not act or prepared to perform such a miracle, therefore it can be inferred that said miracle was performed by Mary and not by Jesus. Unless you think, that Jesus said he couldn't, - because it wasn't his time -, and his mother made him to do it. But in either of the two situations an essential role of the feminine part of the divine trinity is demonstrated, that is to say, of Mary, at that moment, since the phrase "it is not my hour" means "I still do not have permission from the Holy Spirit to do that" So that performing a miracle without such authorization, at the request of a "simple servant" (as the church considers the Virgin Mary) tells of the real power of She. Which denotes in any way that one wants to see that the Holy Spirit is conformed by the Holy Trinity; of the Father, the Mother and the Son. And that as one and trill at the same time they have the same power. Although as parts, each one has a specific mission, both in creation and in the actions of the known and to be known world. (John 2: 1-12)

Some Christian erudites analyzed the participation of the Virgin Mary in the set of mysteries of salvation and in her relationship with Jesus Christ. Among them, Saint Ignatius of Antioch investigated the mystery of Jesus born of Mary, while Saint Justin defended the virgin conception of Mary, Saint Irenaeus proposed a parallelism between the meaning of the figures of Eva-Maria and Adam-Christ. In the middle of the 20th century, some texts written in the 2nd century by Santiago appeared where Mary's life is recounted, from her adoptive parents, Joaquín and Ana, until after the birth of Jesus. In other texts, the death of Mary and her assumption in body and soul to heaven were explained, but they never dared to say more of that for fear of punishment and mockery of a completely macho society. We are sure that there are ancient writings that prove the truths that are revealed today in this book about Mary and her divinity. When the time comes when humanity has access to all the hidden documents, all the truth revealed today will be confirmed.

For Christians in medieval times, the perpetual virginity of Mary and her personal holiness was a matter of discussion. Progressively the idea of a virginity came to prevail "before and after childbirth." Over the centuries under pressure from devotees and the fear of the Roman Catholic Church knowing that the truth was going to come out sooner or later, they assumed the dogma of the Immaculate Conception and the dogma of the Assumption or glorification of Mary, where the church states that Mary was assumed in body and soul to heaven after her death, without knowing the corruption of the grave mean to avoid revealing the True Mysteries of the Virgin Mary, thus keeping hidden that She is part of the Holy Trinity. Concealing that Mary was not conceived by any human being, but embodied by the work and grace of the Holy Spirit, God, her Own Being, only in this way could the Mother of Christ be, since both come from the Own Holy Spirit, both had a holy life and both by fulfilling their human mission on earth ascend They went to the firmament, to dwell at the right and left of the Holy Spirit.

Genesis 3:15 is the prophecy that Mary and Jesus would come to earth to defeat satan and redeem all humanity from all sin. This proclamation made by the Holy Spirit himself to the serpent immediately after he persuaded Adam and Eve to commit sin, is the faithful demonstration of how great is the mercy of God, who from the beginning has the intention of saving humanity, but without imposition, through salvation through faith.

Through the Blessed Virgin Mary, Jesus reigns in the Universe. The true mysteries of Mary's life were hidden by those who rewrote the Bible in the 4th century, this fact carried out by the bishops, scribes and the Roman emperor Constantine I. For which they devised the idea of calling it alma mater o Hidden and hidden mother. And to attribute to her infinite humility her supposed desire to hide herself and all creatures, to be known only to God. Under this assumption She asked God to hide her in her conception, birth and assumption. As Saint Louis put it: "Her own parents did not know her and angels, cherubs and seraphim frequently asked each other Who is this? Why did the Most High hide it from us? Or, if something manifested them about Her, it was infinitely more that covered them up." Something that shows the great ignorance of the most renowned representatives of the Christian Church, on the subject of the essence of the Divine Being, or their interest in hiding the true composition of the Supreme Being.

On April 12, 1947, in Tre Fontane, Rome, Our Blessed Mother announced, "I am the Virgin of the Apocalypse." Gobbi one of the most renowned priests of the Marian Movement, who is said to have received more revelations from Mary than anyone else, asserts that the Virgin Mary told him the following on April 24, 1980: "I am the Virgin of the Revelation: In Me, the Father's masterpiece is carried out in such a perfect way that He can shed the Light of His predilection on Me. The Word assumes his human nature in my virginal womb, and thus can come to you through me true role of Mother. The Holy Spirit draws me, like a magnet, towards the intimacy of the life of love between the Father and the Son, transforms me internally and assimilates me so much to Him that he makes me his Wife. I will take you to full understanding of Holy Scripture."

Here we can see that the Virgin Mary is the excellent masterpiece of herself; who has reserved to herself the knowledge and possession of Herself and Her Creation. Mary is the Mother and sublime Bride of her Own Being who is God. There are those who saw fit to humiliate her and hide her true origin, knowingly, and for so long. Those who, to promote maleness power, considered her as a simple woman, a simple servant of the Lord, as if she were a stranger, are the few times that she is mentioned in the Scriptures of the Bible that she was manipulated by order of the Emperor Constantine the Great and some bishops loyal to him. Pain will come in those who always knew that She was the most appreciated and loved person in the Infinite Universe and by egoism they have hidden her.

Mary is the sealed source, into which the Holy Spirit can only enter into the persons of the Father and the Son; as a faithful Husband or as a beloved Son. "Mary is the sanctuary and tabernacle of the Holy Trinity, where the Holy Spirit dwells, more magnificently and wonderfully than anywhere else in the universe, without excepting the cherubs, seraphim and other beings of the universe, be they of flesh or of spirit: no creature, pure as it may be, is allowed to enter there without special privilege", this was expressed by Saint Louis, the only Christian who tried to reveal his divinity, but was not allowed to reveal it to the world as we do in this opportunity, with the full conviction that the Virgin Mary is Our Lady of the Holy Trinity of God.

She elevates with her merits the Throne of the Holy Trinity of the Holy Spirit, to an inaccessible height. Her power and greatness extends even to herself, since She is her Creator. Although it seems incomprehensible, She is the Divine Energy of Creation itself made Woman, Mother and Wife of her Own Being; Creation does not exist without the Feminine Entity that Creates it, just as Adam has not existed without first being Eve. Many centuries passed from Eve before the century of Adam arrived.

As part of the Holy Trinity of the Holy Spirit, She has all the power, to act and perform miracles, but She always understood that she must let her Son fulfill the mission assigned by The Holy Spirit and only on some occasions She has flaunted her power on earth, her power as part of the divine trinity of the Supreme Being, her Own Being, her Own spawn.

The whole universe is full of her glory and many true Christians have forced with her devotion that She has been chosen as Patron of all nations, provinces, dioceses and cities around the world. Many Cathedrals have been consecrated to God under one of her multiple advocations. All Catholic churches have an altar in her honor. There is no region where some of her miraculous images are not worshiped, where all kinds of diseases are cured and all kinds of goods are obtained. Today there are many brotherhoods and congregations in her honor. Many religious institutes have been placed under her name and protection. Thousands of congregants in the pious associations and thousands of men and women religious in all Orders publish her praises and proclaim her mercy.

Since today, all living being of the earth must proclaim for the joy of all universe, the Divinity of the Virgin Mary. All angelic choirs, men and women, regardless of age or conditions, or religion, rich and poor, and even the contrary spirits, are forced by the evidence of the truth, to proclaim to the four winds that the Holy Mother is part of the Holy Trinity of the Holy Spirit; She is and forever will be "Our Lady of the Holy Trinity of God."

The work of the Virgin Mary teaches us to praise the Supreme Being for the graces that the Holy Spirit bestows on her and for the blessings that she showers on the world. We can entrust our needs to Her, because She has the power that emanates from the Holy Spirit, God, her Own Being. Many people have had the holy experience of being in contact with the Holy Spirit, in the presence of the Holy Trinity of Being and they have stated that the Supreme Being has spoken to them with the three voices; that of the Mother, that of the Father and that of the Son from a single entity of light, since They three make up the Holy Spirit. These people have stated that when the Virgin Mary speaks they hear a feminine voice of angelic goodness, when Jesus speaks they hear a manly voice of tenderness and patience, and when the Father speaks they hear a voice that rumbles and exults.

The Virgin Mary has kept coming to earth preparing the second coming of Our Lord Jesus Christ. To these visits in aid of human beings in need, is what we Christian-Marians call the Apparitions of the Virgin. These apparitions take place in different locations on earth and it is for this reason that so many different names have been given to her, depending on the place where she appears or the mystery she represents, the names have been given to her, but in reality the Virgin Mary is only one, although sometimes her face acquires the characteristic features of the population where she makes her appearance.

As revealed here, the Blessed Virgin Mary is part of the Holy Trinity of the Holy Spirit. Three different figurations of the same Supreme Being who are themselves, a single Being. Mary, Mother of God made woman is part of the divinity of the Supreme Being of the Holy Spirit. "Before the Son, the Mother came and before the Mother, the Father, and the three came by the grace and work of the Holy Spirit, of whom they three are a whole and a part." "And each one has his/her place assigned." Thus it was expressed: "SHe is there, but SHe is still here; if you wake up here, you will wake up there."

For true Christians, this revelation confirms and affirms the whole set of "Marian paradoxes" that have manifested themselves over time on the True Mysteries of Christianity. We can analyze how these paradoxes confirm that this revelation is true, since it refers to the extraordinary graces of which Mary was deposited during her incarnation, and in order to her divine motherhood. Because she is the mother of the Christ - considered the Incarnate Word, God Himself -, to conceive the Word, Mary must be the Word Himself, just as the Holy Spirit is the Word and there is only one Word.

The Virgin Mary, as a female part of the Holy Spirit is:

- *the one who engendered her Own Being,*
- *the one who begot the Being who begot her,*
- *the one that existed before all existence,*
- *the one who gave the Being to the Being creator of everything,*
- *the one who locked in her bosom the Immense and Infinite God,*
- *the one who locked up in her guts who does not fit in the whole world,*
- *the one who held in her arms the one who supports everything,*
- *the one who had the obligation to exercise vigilance over the one who all-seeing,*
- *the one who took care of the Being who cares for everyone,*
- *the one who touched the confines of one who has no end,*
- *the Word made Woman, to be Mother and Wife of God,*
- *the feminine part of the Word; which is Mother, Father and Son united in the grace of the Holy Spirit of God,*
- *Our Lady of the Holy Trinity of the Holy Spirit.*

Despite all the beliefs that have been instilled in us for thousands of years, we must be clear and not confuse things, each part of the Supreme Being have their mission. The mission of the redemption of the human being was entrusted to the God's Son, incarnated in Jesus Christ, but the beginning and the end of devotion for the salvation of true Christians is a mission that corresponds to Jesus and Mary in the Holy Spirit alike, since the three are in themselves one being. Mary is the one who creates the link between the God-Spirit and the God-Man. Jesus Christ is the connecting element between the Holy Spirit and the Human Being, through him we are united in the same Being. To reach the Supreme Being we need to imitate Jesus Christ in whom all fullness and grace remain, given to him, here on earth, by the Virgin Mary and the Holy Spirit. Through the Son one reaches the Father and through Christ we are to receive every blessing of the Holy Spirit. But to reach the Holy Spirit, which is the complementary union of the Holy Trinity of God, one must be in harmony with the three Divine Persons; the Father, the Mother and the Son.

The Holy Spirit, God, is one and triune at the same time, so that if you personally feel comfortable praying to the Father, you obtain the goodness of the three Divine Persons who are truly one Being, but if you feel identified with the Virgin Mary and in harmony with the Mother of the Being who is one, and if you pray to her your prayers will also be heard the same by all three, because they are the same Holy Spirit; And not to mention the Son, whenever you ask Jesus for something, you are also asking his Father and his Mother. And whenever you ask with devotion and faith you will receive with abundance all the grace that emanates from the Holy Spirit.

<San Pedro Nolasco founder of the Order of Santa María de la Merced, of the redemption of the captives, a religious community that has dedicated itself for centuries to helping prisoners and has had martyrs and saints, tells the story of one day being praying, asking God for help and, as a sign of divine mercy, the Virgin Mary responds by telling her to found a liberating order.> Clear proof that the Virgin Mary, like the Father and the Son, is God.

There has been a great blur in humanity throughout the course of time where the basic concept of the humanization of the Supreme Being has been lost. We have overlooked that the first example that the Holy Spirit taught us was to marry Mary and then make her mother by begetting her Son, her own incarnation, in order to make known to the world the essence of the Holy Spirit which is one and three at the same time. Forming the first example of family; in the name of the Father, the Mother and the Son. They wanted to set an example for this to come to us out of conviction and not imposition. Neither the Father nor the Son have seen with good eyes the vexation made by man to woman in the feminine person of the Holy Trinity of the Holy Spirit.

The Bible states that; "Men on earth have not been given another name, of human being, by which we can be saved," but that of Jesus, But the Holy Spirit has given us another foundation of salvation, perfection and glory, in the Virgin Mary. "Any building that is not built on firm rocks rests on quicksand and sooner or later it will fall infallibly." All these and many other expressions have been sources of confusion, but we must not allow ourselves to be confused with all these precepts that apply only to human being, not to the divinity of the Virgin Mary. Since as we have seen here, She is above everything. She is the only one who has engendered the being that created Her, in an action that lacks human logic but not so in the divine entities.

We must kneel before the Blessed Virgin Mary, to humbly ask her for her Divine Majesty, to forgive the ignorance of the vast majority of human beings, who have belittled the union that binds her to the Holy Trinity of the Holy Spirit, who is the same that unites the Father with the Son. We must also recognize that, through the Holy Spirit, Jesus is always with Mary, just as Mary is always with Jesus; Mary is so transformed into Jesus by the grace of the Holy Spirit, that She no longer lives and is nothing without Him, just as He is nothing without Her, and the same thing happens with the Holy Spirit. Under this great Divine Mystery, the Mother (Virgin Mary), the Father (Holy Spirit) and the Son (Jesus) are the same integrated being, in the Holy Spirit, and who lives with all the creatures of the macro Universe of all dimensions, and whose energy comes from himself/herself.

Today I am sure, my beloved Virgin Mary, that when all human beings recognize the glory and love that resides in the mysterious and admirable figure, who makes up the Holy Trinity of the Holy Spirit; Father, Mother and Son. We will all have different feelings than we have now, when we discover that She is united to the Father and the Son so firmly that it would be easier to separate the light from the sun, the heat from the fire, the cold from the ice, because they love her more ardently and glorify her with greater perfection than all the others creatures of the Universe.

It is not strange, Holy Celestial Mother! to see the arrogance of all men towards you, who have ignored you only because you are woman. But it is not only the pagans and heretics, also the Christians themselves have unknown you. These gentlemen very rarely speak of You, and others have never rendered you the worship that you deserve, supposedly for fear of offending the honor of God and Jesus. These average Christians, when they see someone speak with devotion to You, Blessed Virgin Mary! with effective and persuasive language, without pain and without fear, of an immaculate and imperfect path and of a wonderful secret that reveals to us that you are part of the Most Holy Trinity of the Holy Spirit, the feminine part of the Supreme Being, they argue thousands of falsehoods, which according to them prove that they should not talk so much about You, that you should only talk about Jesus or Jehovah of armies. Others even say that you are a servant who was only used by Jehovah for his purpose. How amazed everyone will be when they see you at the head of the Celestial Supreme Court commanding the stars.

I am aware, my beloved Virgin Mary, that the Rosary, the scapular and the crown as devotions themselves are not enough to praise you and adore your greatness. But many of these so-called Christians think that this is enough and many others even think that this is too much or that it is an abuse. In fact, when these knights find a devotee of your greatness praying the Rosary or practicing some devotion in your honor, they make great efforts to try to "purify" their spirit and cleanse their heart, advising their that instead of praying the Rosary, they should pray the seven penitential psalms. When the truth is that one prayer does not oppose the other, and on the contrary both complement and strengthen each other in the Holy Spirit. These gentlemen ask people only to pray to Jesus or the Father. But, in truth, will he please the Lord, who for fear of displeasing him, does not honor his beloved Mother; his own Self? Consecrating yourself to the Virgin Mary, instead of distancing you from Jesus brings you closer to Him. Because he who loves the Son must love the Mother, just as he who loves the Son loves the Father, since in the end he is the same being, a single Divine Spirit, the Holy Spirit.

The current reality is that most erudites, even Christians, think they wiser the further away they are from devotion to the Blessed Mother and show an absolute indifference towards her Divinity. Keep us from these feelings and this type of apathy towards your Divine Majesty, Divine Mother. Give us wisdom and help us share in the feelings of gratitude and love that you have for us, your sons and daughters, so that we can love and glorify you, and that love towards you make us more perfect and worthy of your kingdom heavenly.

Although no one else admits, Holy Virgin Mary, grant me the honor and grace of being able to love and adore you for the graces that you grant to the Holy Spirit. Grant me the grace to praise you with dignity, in spite of all your detractors, because he who offends the blessed Mother will not obtain divine mercy. Instead, whoever praises the Blessed Mother will already have the pass to reach the Son and the Father, in the bosom of the Holy Spirit. Because it is said here, to achieve the mercy of Jesus, a true devotion to his Blessed Mother is necessary, and even more so if it is spread with devotion and faith throughout the whole earth as it is to spread this book throughout the confines of the earth.

There is nothing among Christians that makes us belong more fully to Jesus Christ than the veneration and adoration of his Blessed Mother, accepted voluntarily. The man and woman who profess their love for the Virgin Mary will never be outside the grace of the Holy Spirit that is God. Christians are repeatedly called servants of Christ in the Bible, and I tell you that he who serves Christ serves the Supreme Being, thereby also serving Mary and the Holy Spirit at the same time. It has been shown that he who loves the Virgin Mary reaps the fruits of his good works and will never be deprived of the protection of the Holy Spirit.

As there is divinity in Jesus Christ, there is divinity in the Virgin Mary. Being She the inseparable companion of his life, glory and power in heaven and on earth, he granted her respect and Majesty with all the rights and privileges that correspond to Her by nature. All the Gifts that come from the Holy Spirit by work and grace, come from Mary by nature. It should be understood that they having the same people to protect, they also have the same subjects and servants to give the same glory, and they give it.

According to all these approaches, we can become servants of the love for the Divinity of the Virgin Mary, in order to be more perfectly of Jesus Christ. The Blessed Virgin is the means by which we must use ourselves to go to Him. For Mary is not like other creatures, who, if we cling to her, can separate us from God instead of approaching Him. The strongest inclination towards which crushed the serpent, is to unite us to Jesus Christ, his Son and his own Being; and the greatest desire of Jesus is that we go to Him through his Divine Mother.

Because not without reason has the Holy Spirit given us mediators before himself. So that we can identify more with the Supreme Being himself through one of his personifications. Since he knows our unworthiness and incapacity, he took pity on us and to give us access to his mercy he provided us with two powerful mediators before his greatness; the Virgin Mary and Jesus Christ. Because our soul is so corrupted that if we rely only on our own efforts we will not be able to reach the Supreme Being and much less we will be able to unite ourselves with Him and listen to us. Therefore, we recognize in Jesus Christ and the Virgin Mary the only mediators who can bring us directly to Divine Holiness.

Jesus Christ is our mediator of Redemption and the Virgin Mary our mediator of affliction; And both are before the Holy Spirit. For him/her we must pray together all humanity. Through him/her we have access to the Divine Majesty and, only supported by him, clothed in his/her merits, we must present ourselves before the Holy Spirit, with the humility and respect they deserve by having the highest investiture in the Universe, above all being, priest, minister, pope, ruler, president, king, lodge, sect, religion, belief, thought and science.

Jesus Christ is the main mediator before the Father, but the Virgin Mary is mediator before the Mediator himself, before the Father and before herself. Through her Jesus Christ came to us and through her we must go to him. This relationship is like the equilateral triangle; being in one of the vertices you can get to any of the other two that you have at the same distance, that are exactly the same and that only have different names to be able to differentiate them when you must call them separately, because in reality they are a single element that called an equilateral triangle. If you fear going directly to the Holy Spirit, because of his infinite greatness and your smallness or sins, implore with filial trust the help and intercession of the sweet and tender Virgin Mary, the Mother of Creation. She is tender and kind, she is the pure nature, there is nothing austere or terrible in her whole Being.

The Virgin Mary is so kind that she has never rejected any of those who implore her intercession, no matter how many sinners they may have been, because it has never been heard that anyone has been rejected by having come confidently and perseveringly to her. She is like the sun that with the brilliance of its rays illuminates the entire Universe and at the same time, beautiful and peaceful as the moon that takes those rays and accommodates them so that our views can appreciate the beauty of the dim light, without suffering any hurt. She is so pious that your requests will never be ignored, it is enough for her to present some request, so that She accepts it and receives and lets herself be lovingly overcome by the pleas of her beloved children.

To harmonize with our Creator God we have three possible ways: the first is the Holy Spirit as the Father; The second is the Holy Spirit as the Son, Jesus Christ; The third is the Holy Spirit the Mother, the Virgin Mary. To come to Jesus Christ we must go to Mary our Mediator of intercession. In order to reach the Father, we must go to the Son, who is our Mediator of Redemption, although one can also reach the Father directly through Mary, his beloved Bride and his Own Self. And each of the three can lead us to the Holy Spirit; Father, Mother and Son, if you manage to evolve until you reach the dimension where the Holy Trinity of the Holy Spirit lives.

It is practically impossible, under the normal evolution of the human being, given its smallness and fragility, to preserve the graces given by the Holy Spirit, to each man and woman at birth, since, although we are all made up of divine particles, these particles they cannot evolve at an accelerated rate while we are limited by our little faith, and by the minimal knowledge of the corruption of the matter of the human body that even science cannot reveal. Only when our mind and spirit reach beyond the high dimensions can we achieve harmony with the Holy Spirit. Human beings only have three ways to achieve this; Jesus Christ, Mary and the evolutionary process of the human being through the cosmic consciousness itself.

We carry in the blood and throughout the body the divine particles of the Creator Being, something more valuable than heaven and earth, together. But our body is corruptible, our soul is weak and fickle because of anything it disturbs and lowers us, leaving our spirit adrift. We create false demons, to justify our weakness and weakness. Beings that supposedly surround us to devour and rapture us in a moment, for a single sin, all the graces and merits achieved in many years. His malice and cunning must make us infinitely fear this misfortune. But the truth is that everything, the good and the bad, is in our divine particles, that is, within our own being, in such a way that the divine particles at the same time can be evil particles. And these will depend on what type of energy feeds our bodies. You turn to Mary to give you the strength and wisdom that will make you capable of preserving the attributes of creation. No one better than She as Mother and creator knows the essence of our being. If you feed your soul, your mind and your body with positive things, everything in you will be positive, while if you feed them with negative things, everything in you will be negative.

Nothing better than the admirable devotion to the Virgin Mary, to entrust our essence of life, since She will keep it for us as if it were her own. It is difficult to persevere in grace, because of the dreadful corruption of the world, in all times and ages. Corruption such that it becomes practically impossible for any man or woman to live without blemish and fear; fear for having failed or fear for fear of failure. Since it would be a miracle for a person to remain pure in the midst of this whirlwind of world corruption at all social levels, without being swept away by evil, vice, infidelity, greed, envy, immorality, etc. Only with a true devotion to the Virgin Mary, against whom the serpent could do nothing, and with a human advancement in Cosmic Consciousness, could this miracle be achieved in favor of all humanity.

> <*Sovereign Virgin Mary, Mother of Jesus, Living God, because you have given birth to her: Pray for all sinners to forgive us. Deliver us from the enemy that fights us and grant us eternal glory. Amen.*>

> <*Blessed Virgin, pray for me, you will always be praised and blessed. Pray for this sinner, your beloved Son, precious beauty of the Angels, of the Prophets and of the Patriarchs; crown of the Martyrs, the Apostles and the Confessors; Glory of the Seraphim, of the Cherubim and of the Virgins, deliver me from that dreadful figure when my soul leaves my body. Oh, Holy Source of piety and beauty of Jesus Christ, joy of glory, consolation of the clergy, remedy in the works! With you, most prudent Virgin, the angels rejoice. Praise my soul and that of all the faithful Christians; pray for us to your blessed son, and lead us to eternal paradise, where you live and reign for ever and ever; and there we will praise you eternally, Amen.*>

The Virgin Mary has kept coming to earth, preparing the human being for the coming of the Holy Spirit with all her Heavenly Court. These visits to the aid of peoples and needy human beings are what we call "the apparitions of the Virgin." These apparitions take place in different localities of the earth and it is for this reason that so many different names have been given to her, since depending on the place where She appears it has been given different names, but in reality there is only one Virgin Mary, Our Lady of the Holy Trinity of God.

We can group the majority of Marian invocations into various categories:

1) Relating to the mysteries or passages of the Virgin's life, such as the Annunciation, the Assumption, the Presentation, the Immaculate Conception, Divine Providence, etc.

2) Relating to abstract theological truths, such as Hope, Charity, Consolation, etc.

3) Relating to the physical or psychological states of the Virgin, such as Dolores, Solitude, etc.

4) Relating to her condition as mediator and protector of humanity, as Auxiliadora, Las Mercedes, los Remedios, La Sanación, etc.

5) Relating to fruits, flowers, birds ... used as symbols of their qualities, such as Pine, Granada, Dove, etc.

6) Relating to geographical features, generally coinciding with the places where their sanctuaries are, such as Carmen, the Sea, Fatima, Lourdes, etc.

7) Relative to her main mission on earth, the Virgin of Coatlaxopeuh term (Nahuatl / Aztec) which means "The one who crushed the serpent" and is pronounced in the native language "quatlasupe," a proclamation that the Spanish understood as "Guadalupe" by its great similarity.

Marian advocations are usually named with the formulas "Holy Mary of," "Virgin of" or "Our Lady of" But also, the advocations often give rise in many cases to feminine proper names, made up of the name Mary and her dedication: Mary of the Carmen, Mary of Dolores, Mary of Lourdes, etc.

Although the name is different regarding the attribute related to the Virgin Mary, it always refers only to her, even if several names are mentioned at the same time, the instance is the same, the Virgin Mary; Our Lady of the Holy Trinity of God.

Among the different advocations of the Virgin Mary we have: Mary Help of Christians, Our Lady of the Assumption, Our Lady of Hollywood, The Virgin of Regla, Our Lady of Altagracia, the Virgin of Charity of El Cobre, Our Lady of Guadalupe, the Virgin of the Mercedes, the Virgin of the Carmen, the Virgin of the Immaculate Conception, the Virgin of Divine Providence, Our Lady of Coromoto, Our Lady of the Angels, the Virgin of Fatima, Immaculate Heart of Mary, the Virgin of Covadonga, the Virgin of Montserrat, the Virgin of the Miraculous Medal, Our Lady of the Rosary, the Virgin of Lourdes, the Virgin of China, Our Lady of Paris, Our Lady of Syracuse, the Virgin of Rome, Our Lady of La Salette, the Virgin of Pontmain, the Virgin of Banneux, the Virgin of pellevoisin, Our Lady of Beauraing,

Our Lady of Knock, the Virgin of the Mystic Rose, Our Lady of Chiquinquirá, Our Lady of Perpetual Help, the Virgin of the Pilar, the Virgen of Candelaria, Our Lady of Loreto, Our Lady of Dolorosa del Colegio, Our Lady Aparecida, Our Lady of Luján, Our Lady of the peace, Our Lady of Suyapa, Our Lady of Tears, Our Lady of the Thirty-Three, Our Lady of Carmen del Maipú, Our Lady of Akita, Our Lady of Miracles of Caacupé, Our Lady of the Presentation of the Quinche, Holy Mary of the Antigua, Our Lady of Sorrows, Our Lady of Evangelization, Our Lady of "The Old Man", Our Lady of Schoenstatt, Our Lady of Czestochowa, Our Lady of Copacabana, Our Lady of Franquira, Our Lady of the Snows, Our Lady of the Forsaken, Our Lady of Rogation, Our Lady of the Arrixaca, Our Lady of Rosell, Our Lady of Azahar, Our Lady of the Peña, Holy Mary Mother of the Eucharist, Holy Mary Untie knots, among others.

4.1.- Our Lady of Altagracia; Advocation of the Virgin Mary.

Our Lady of Altagracia or Virgin of Altagracia (High grace): She is the Holy Protective Mother of the Dominican Republic. His patronal feast is celebrated on January 21 in that country where many faithful devotees of the Virgin Mary go from all over the Dominican national territory to her temple in the Basilica of Higuey to worship her. This devotion began in the country during the first colonial period, when the first trips of the Spanish, although it was also traveled to other regions of the world.

The brothers Alonso and Antonio Trejo were the ones who brought the image of the Virgin of Altagracia to the Dominican country; These came from the town of Siruela where the virgin appeared to a farmer on a tree, and hence its name "High Grace" lowered from the sky. It is also venerated in Garrovillas de Alconétar, another Spanish town, where legend has it that the Blessed Virgin appeared to a girl on a large rock. The Trejo Brothers were the first to found a sugar mill to produce sugar, which would later give way to the famous sugar mills of the Dominican Republic. The Trejos moved to the town of Higuey, and immediately gave the image of the Virgin of Altagracia, so that the entire community venerated her.

The image of the Virgin of Altagracia (High grace) represents the scene of the Birth of Jesus in the Manger of Bethlehem, where the maternity of the Virgin stands out. In the painting is the Star of Bethlehem, which has eight points and symbolizes heaven and has two rays extending towards the manger, in which the Holy Spirit is pointing to the two humanized divinities, in his son Jesus and in his mother Mary. Above the Virgin there are twelve stars and around it there is a glow, as if it were clad in the sun. The Virgin also wears a crown on her head that symbolizes that She is the Queen of the Universe, and a veil over her head that symbolizes the purity of the woman. In front of the Mother is the Child Jesus, asleep on straws and behind him, well removed from Her, is Joseph, dressed in a red cape and a candle in his left hand. In the image you can also see the figure of Mary in an attitude of worship, with her hands joined in the shape of an arch. A kind of white triangle is distinguished on his chest, an expression of the divine trinity represented at that time, which rises from the manger, where the child rests, to almost Maria's shoulders. Maria's face is serene, with a low profile, but without reflecting sadness, but rather joy and peace, in an attitude of meditation. Her head is covered with a dark blue, shoulder-length veil, and her cloak is dotted with sixteen little stars, eight on each side. Behind it is a column, as a sign that at that time that manger had become a sacred temple, because two of the three divine people were present there. The image of the Virgin of Altagracia is an icon. There is no element, color, or relationship that does not have its meaning. It is also one of the few paintings around the world that is stamped in pure gold.

The Virgin of Altagracia is venerated in Mexico, in the community of Zapopan, Jalisco, where She is Patroness, there is a chapel dedicated to Our Lady of Altagracia. The town of Altagracia, in the Province of Córdoba, Argentina, owes the origin of its name to the Virgin of Altagracia. In Spain, the Virgin of Altagracia is Patron Saint of Garrovillas de Alconétar, Cáceres, Siruela, and Badajoz. In Panama, the Virgin of Altagracia is Patron Saint of the community of Jobo Dulce, Los Santos, Panama. In Venezuela She is the Patron Saint of Curiepe, Miranda and Quibor, Lara.

4.2.- Our Lady of Guadalupe; advocation of the Virgin Mary.

The Sanctuary of Our Lady of Guadalupe is unique among the great centers of Marian devotion, because it has preserved and venerates the most beautiful image of the Virgin Mary, Mother of God, in the tilma of the humble Indian, Juan Diego, which It was painted with ink and brushes that are not from the world known to humans, at least until now.

Tradition has it that the Virgin Mary appeared to the Indian Juan Diego when he was on his way to the Tlaltelolco Convent to hear mass. At dawn he reached the foot of the Tepeyac, and suddenly he heard a melody coming from the trees. Surprised, he stopped and looked up at the hill and saw that it was illuminated with a light like sunbeams. The music stopped playing and immediately he heard a sweet voice coming from the top of the hill, saying: "Juanito; dear Juan Dieguito." For this reason he hurriedly climbed and upon reaching the summit he saw the Virgin Mary, in the middle of a rainbow, dressed in heavenly splendor. Her beauty and kind gaze filled his heart with infinite joy as he listened to the tender words She spoke to him. She told him that She was the Virgin Mary, Mother of God. He revealed his desire to have a temple there on the plain where, as a pious mother, She would show all her love and mercy to him and his family and to all those who acclaimed their help. The Holy Mother sent him to go to the house of the Bishop of Mexico and tell him that he was on behalf of the divine majesty of the Mother of God to request the construction of a Temple in her honor on the plain indicated by her. Tell him how much you have seen, heard and admired. And John bowed before her and said: "My Lady, I am going to fulfill your mandate; I take leave of you, I, your humble servant."

Juan went to Bishop Zumárraga's house and told him everything that the Mother of God had told him. But the Bishop doubted his words, and said that he did not have time to listen to him and asked him to return another day. Juan returned to the top of the hill and found the Virgin who was already waiting for him. And with tears of sadness She told him of her failure. She asked him to return to the Bishop's house the next day. Juan returned and this time he ran with better luck, this time the Bishop listened to him, but demanded that he bring him a sign. Juan returned to the hill, told Maria the Bishop's request and She assured her that he would give her the sign he asked for. But Juan was unable to fulfill this commission since an uncle of his, also named Juan, had become seriously ill. So Juan Diego rushed to find him a priest in the city, for which he took a different route to avoid seeing the Virgin Mary. But to her surprise, She came down and met him. Juan apologized to her for not having been able to fulfill his mission the day before. After hearing Juan Diego's words, She replied: "Hear and understand, my youngest son, that there is nothing that scares and afflicts you. Do not disturb your heart, do not fear this or any other disease or anguish, Am I not here, your mother? Are you not under my shadow? Am I not your health? What else do you lack? Do not grieve your uncle's illness, who will not die from it now, he is sure that he has healed. "Juan was happy to hear these words. He asked him to send him to see the Bishop to bring him some proof so that he would believe him. And She said to him: "Come up, my youngest son, to the summit where you saw me, you will find different flowers, cut them and bring them to me." He did so and brought them before the Virgin. She took the flowers in her hands, arranged them in the tilma and said: "My youngest son, here is the sign that you must take to the Lord Bishop. You will tell him in my name to see my will in her and that he has to You are my envoy and you are trustworthy. I strictly order you to display your tilma only before the Bishop. "When Juan Diego was before the Bishop, and he told him the details of the fourth apparition of the Blessed Virgin, he opened his tilma to show him the flowers, which fell to the ground. At that moment, to the immense surprise of the Bishop and his companions, the image of the Blessed Virgin Mary appeared, beautifully painted in the most beautiful colors on the coarse fabric of her cloak.

On the same day, the Blessed Virgin Mary appeared at the hut of Juan Bernardino, Juan Diego's uncle, to cure him of his deadly disease. His heart was filled with joy when She gave him the happy message that his portrait miraculously appeared in the tilma of Juan Diego, would be the instrument that would crush the idolatry of his brothers towards the serpent, through the teaching that the divine image contained. Te-coa-tla-xope in the Aztec language means "She will crush the stone serpent." The Spaniards heard the word from Juan Bernardino's lips. They understood that he said "de Guadalupe." Surprised, they wondered why this Spanish name, but the favorite children of America, knew the meaning of the phrase well in their native language. This is how the image and the sanctuary acquired the Guadalupe's name, a title that she has carried until now, and thus the proclamation of the prophets was fulfilled: "And God will send a woman whose descendants will crush the serpent and liberate the children of God."

Sacred Scripture tells us that in ancient times a great kite traveled the outer space. This comet had the appearance of a fire snake. For this reason the Indians of Mexico gave it the name of Quetzalcoatl which means a serpent with feathers, and for fear they made stone idols, in the form of a feathered serpent, which they began to worship and offer them human sacrifices. But after seeing the sacred image of the Virgin Mary, the Indians abandoned their false gods and embraced the Christian - Marian faith. Some nine million indigenous people converted to Christianity in the first seven years after the image of Our Lady of the Holy Trinity of God appeared.

The tilma of Juan Diego, where the image of the Blessed Virgin Mary appeared, is made of maguey fiber, which has a maximum ordinary duration of approximately twenty years. 195 centimeters long by 105 centimeters wide with a suture in the middle that goes from top to bottom. Printed directly on the canvas is the Divine image of Our Lady of Guadalupe. Her body is 140 centimeters tall. This image of the Blessed Virgin is the only authentic portrait of her. Its conservation in a fresh and beautiful state for more than four centuries is considered miraculous. The image is venerated in the Basilica of Our Lady of Guadalupe in Mexico City, where it occupies the place of honor on the main altar. Experts in digital images and photography assure that 13 images of people have been recorded in the eyes of the Virgin of Guadalupe, which have not yet been deciphered.

4.3.- Our Lady of Charity of Copper; advocation of the Virgin Mary.

The adoration of the Virgin Mary on the Island of Cuba began with the defeat of Alonso de Ojeda and the first conquerors of Cuba when they tried to impose themselves on the Indians. These faced them forcing the Spanish to flee through mountains and swamps to save their lives. Arriving at the Indian town of Cueibá in the Jobabo area, in very bad condition, so they had compassion for them and helped them. Out of gratitude, Alonso de Ojeda built a small hermitage with tree branches. And there he placed an Image of the Virgin Mary that was his precious property. Thus fulfilling the promise he had made to give the Image to whoever helped him out of that situation alive. He also taught the Indians to pray the "Ave Maria" which spread so quickly among the Indians that Cuba later became known as the "Ave Maria" island. Without knowledge of Christianity, the Indians of that place worshiped and prayed to the Image of the Virgin Mary and kept the hermitage with care when Ojeda and his men left.

When the exploitation of copper began in the mountains of the eastern region of the island of Cuba. Next to the mines, the Spanish established the Barajagua herd that had a lot of cattle. That is why the salt that prevented the corruption of the meat was necessary. One morning when three people went out to look for salt in the bay of Nipe, and while they were going through the salt, the appearance of the statue of the Virgin Mary occurred. These three men were called Juan de Hoyos, Rodrigo de Hoyos and Juan Moreno, known as "the three Juanes." This is how one of them recounted it years later: "... having ranched in the French key that is in the middle of the Bay of Nipe in order to go to the salt flats in good weather ..., being the calm sea one morning we left the French key before when the sun came up, the sayings Juan and Rodrigo de Hoyos and this declarant, embarked in a canoe for said salinas, and away from said French key, saw a white thing on the foam of the water, which we did not distinguish what it could be, and getting closer the more it seemed to us like a bird and dry branches. These Indians said "it looks like a girl," and in these speeches, when they arrived, they recognized and saw the image of Our Lady (of the Holy Trinity) with the Child Jesus in her arms on a small tablet, and in said little board, some large letters which said Rodrigo de Hoyos read, and She said: "I am the Virgin of Charity," and seeing their robes of clothing, they admired that it were not wet. They took the image and three third of salt and they came back to the Hato de Barajagua ..."

The administrator of the Real de Minas de Cobre district, Don Francisco Sánchez de Moya, ordered the erection of a hermitage to place the image and established Rodrigo de Hoyos as chaplain. One night Rodrigo went to visit the Virgin and noticed that She was not there. An unsuccessful search was arranged. The next morning, and to everyone's surprise, the Virgin was again at her altar, without being able to explain, since the door of the hermitage had remained closed all night. This fact was repeated two or three more times until the inhabitants of Barajagua thought that the Virgin wanted to change places. So they moved in procession, with great pain for them, to the Parish Temple of Copper. The Virgin Mary was greeted with the ringing of bells and great joy in her new house, where She was placed on the high altar. Thus it became known as the Virgin of the Charity of Copper.

But in The Copper the disappearance of the Virgin was repeated. They thought then that She wanted to be on the mountains of the Sierra Maestra. This was confirmed when a girl named Apolonia climbed up to the hill of the copper mines where her mother worked. The girl was chasing butterflies and picking flowers when, on the top of one of the mountains, she saw the Virgin of Charity. The news of little Apolonia caused quite a stir. Some believed, others did not, but the girl remained firm in her testimony. Therefore they took the Virgin to that place. Since the statue's appearance, devotion to the Virgin of the Charity spread with amazing speed throughout the island of Cuba. Over the years, a larger precinct was built, this new precinct welcomes the growing number of pilgrims who annually visit the sanctuary of the Blessed Virgin of Charity of copper, for the festivities of September 8. The Virgin of Charity was crowned by Pope John Paul II as Queen and Patroness of Cuba on Saturday, January 24, 1998, during the Holy Mass that he celebrated on his apostolic visit to Santiago de Cuba.

The first celebration of the Feast of the Virgin of Charity of Copper in exile was held on September 8, 1961, the same day that the image of the Blessed Virgin arrived in the city of Miami. This was the image that had been adored for a long time in the Guanabo Parish of Havana. This celebration was held with deep emotion, presided over by the Archbishop of Miami, and from that date a tradition was made that continues to this day. But the image of the Virgin was not only present at these celebrations, but also began a tour of the camps for exiled Cuban children who were without their parents. The Cubans organized to build a Hermitage to the Virgen de la Caridad in exile. The foundation stone of the provisional chapel was laid on May 20, 1967. On May 21, 1968, Archbishop Carrol of Miami, ordered the foundation of the Brotherhood of the Virgin of Charity to gather devotees to honor the Virgin. Mary and with her evangelize. Miami has citizens from all Hispanic countries. Since the 80s, in addition to the 126 Cuban municipalities, they also make an pilgrimage to the hermitage of the Virgin of the Charity of Copper in an organized way, all the countries of Hispanicity during the month of October.

The devotees of the Virgin have managed to spread not only the devotion to the Virgin of Charity, but also to make the Hermitage a center of evangelization of worldwide irradiation. The main instrument of the Virgin Mary for the work of the Hermitage was from the beginning Monsignor Agustín Román, with the help of the Sisters of Charity who minister in the Hermitage and the Archconfraternity. The image of the Virgin of Charity reflects that the Holy Spirit is above everything and everyone. In her right hand She holds the Cross, the only way of salvation, which must be embraced by all her children. With her left hand She holds her Son, the Child God. Thus She teaches us the importance of imitating her who was faithful, accompanying Jesus from the beginning of his life to the Cross. The Virgin Mary is our Mother and Creator. She, in a storm, came to save "the three Juanes". Like the Virgin Mary comes today to save us from the storms, plague and virus in our lives. Just as She accompanied the Apostles when they gathered full of fear at Pentecost. The Virgin Mary takes us into her maternal heart, a sanctuary of the Holy Spirit where She forges us in another Christ, radiating us with her divinity. The feminine part of the Supreme Being wanted to become a woman of flesh and blood to conceive in her womb the one who is God, her own self, in turn, setting an example for the human being that the path of light and truth leads to the Holy Spirit. She is the mother of all who keep the Word and of all who do not keep it too. The Virgin Mary teaches us the importance of Motherhood, the dignity of the woman who assumed such a great mission. Therefore, the respect it deserves. The Virgin Mary is the mother of all families, the Mother of Being, the Mother of the Word, the Mother of herself. By turning to her, the family is consolidated in the authentic charity that She represents.

The Virgin of Charity of Copper teaches us that the true homeland of every human being is the Universe regardless of language. The homeland of the earth is loved and built according to our human ideas and limitations. As your children do God's will in a country, that country is exalted. But the glory must be of every human being wherever he is, God sent to inhabit the whole earth and wherever we go the divine essence accompanies us. And although in each city or nation the Virgin has a different name, in truth there is only one, the Divine Virgin Mary. Mary teaches us that charity is patient, it is helpful; charity is not envious, it is not boastful; does not seek their interest; is not irritated; it does not take into account evil; is not happy with injustice; rejoices with the truth; Everything awaits with faith; It supports everything; Charity never ends.

4.4.- Our Lady of Coromoto; advocation of the Virgin Mary.

Our Lady of Coromoto in Guanare de los Cospes or Virgin of Coromoto is the patron saint of Venezuela and, since November 19, 2011, Principal Patron of the archdiocesan Church of Caracas after the Holy See approved her appointment. It is a Marian advocation, revered both in the city of Guanare, where it appeared 368 years ago, and throughout Venezuela.

When the town of Guanare was founded in 1591, the indigenous people who lived in the region, the Cospes, fled into the jungle in the north of the town. This hindered the evangelization that the Roman Catholic Church had undertaken. The apparition of the Virgin occurred in this jungle to which the natives had fled, on September 8, 1652, where the Virgin Mary appeared to the Cacique of the Cospes, the native Coromoto, and to his wife, saying in their own language: "Go to the whites' house and ask them to pour the water on their heads so they can go to heaven," with this phrase the Virgin asks him and his tribe to be baptized. According to oral tradition, the cacique related what had happened to his encomendero, Don Juan Sánchez, who asked him to be ready with the tribe in eight days to receive catechesis and baptism. Several Cospes Indians were converted and baptized, but not the chief, because he did not feel comfortable, since he was no longer the chief. The native Coromoto fled, the Virgin appeared to him again, and Coromoto, blinded by anger, raises his arm to grab her and disappears, the appearance materialized in a stamp made of tree fiber that was later sought and found the relic that it is venerated today in the National Shrine of Our Lady of Coromoto.

The account tells that Coromoto is bitten by a poisonous snake and returns to Guanare, wounded and about to die, he began to ask for baptism, he was administered by a Barinés, and when he was baptized, he became an apostle and begged the group of rebellious Indian cospes who was under his command, to be baptized. Later Coromoto, now with the Christian name of Ángel Custodio, died in good old age.

In 1950 Pope Pius XII declared her Patroness of Venezuela, Pope John Paul II crowned her on his visit to the Marian Shrine in Guanare, and Pope Benedict XVI elevated the National Shrine of Our Lady of Coromoto in 2006 to the category of Minor Basilica.

On the island of Tenerife (Canary Island, Spain) there are several replicas of the image of the patron saint of Venezuela, including:

- In San Cristóbal de la Laguna we find a neighborhood that owes its name to this Marian image, El Coromoto and where a replica of the image is found in a tiny chapel, the hermitage of Our Lady of Coromoto, the neighborhood celebrates the festivity of the image on the first weekends of September.
- In the municipality of Candelaria there is a replica of the Virgin of Coromoto in the Church of Santa Ana, near the Basilica and Royal Marian Sanctuary of the Virgin of Candelaria (Patroness of the Canary Islands).
- In the municipality of La Guancha there is an image of the Virgin of Coromoto in a small hermitage in the Guancha neighborhood below, whose festival is held on the last Sunday of May.
- In the Church of San Miguel Arcángel in the City of Villahermosa, Tabasco, Mexico, there is a replica of the Image of Our Lady of Coromoto brought by the Civil Association "Union of Venezuelans in Tabasco (UVETAB A.C.)."

We can also find it in the center of the town of Bolivar (Bolivar officially and according to the current Basque spelling) Vizcaya, Basque Country - Spain. There is the Church of Santo Tomás in whose portico it has kept since 1959 the chapel with a glass door dedicated to the Virgin of Coromoto Patroness of Venezuela.

In Madrid, in the San Antonio de Padua church (Calle Bravo Murillo, 150), in the first chapel is the altar of Our Lady of Coromoto. Above the Altar is read: "Our Lady of Coromoto, Patroness of Venezuela." The background of the altarpiece is a painting of heaven with angels surrounding the image of the Virgin of Coromoto. The painting is the work of Francisco Boira Castells and belongs to the year 1955.

4.5.- Our Lady of the Immaculate Conception; advocation of the Virgin Mary.

The dogma of the Immaculate Conception is a belief of Catholicism that maintains that Mary, mother of Jesus, unlike all other human beings, was not reached by original sin, but, from the first instant of its conception, it was free from all sin. This doctrine should not be confused with that of the virgin motherhood of Mary, who maintains that Jesus was conceived without male intervention and that Mary remained a virgin before, during and after pregnancy.

In developing the doctrine of the Immaculate Conception, the Catholic Church contemplates Mary's special position as mother of Christ, and maintains that God preserved Mary free from all sin and, even more, free from all stain or effect of original sin, that it was to be transmitted to all men because they were descendants of Adam and Eve, considering that She was going to be the mother of Jesus, who is also God. The doctrine reaffirms with the expression "you are full of grace" (Gratia Plena) contained in the greeting of the archangel Gabriel (Luca 1,28), and collected in the Hail Mary prayer, this aspect of being free from sin by the grace of God.

The definition of dogma, contained in the bull Ineffabilis Deus, of December 8, 1854, reads as follows:

> For the honor of the Holy Trinity, for the joy of the Catholic Church, with the authority of our Lord Jesus Christ, with that of the Holy Apostles Peter and Paul and with ours: We define, affirm and pronounce that the doctrine that sustains that the Blessed Virgin Mary was preserved immune from any original stain of guilt from the first moment of her conception, by the singular privilege and grace of God Almighty, in attention to the merits of Christ-Jesus, Savior of mankind, has been revealed by God and therefore must be firmly and constantly believed by all the faithful. Therefore, if anyone has the recklessness, which God does not allow, to

doubt in his heart what has been defined for us, know and understand that his own judgment condemns him, that his faith has been shipwrecked and that he has fallen from the unity of the Church and that is if they also dare to express in word or in writing or in any other external way what they feel in their hearts, they are therefore subject to the penalties established by law.

Pius IX, contemplating the rough sea of Gaeta, listened and meditated on the words of Cardinal Luigi Lambruschini: "Most Beatiful Father, you will not be able to heal the world except with the proclamation of the dogma of the Immaculate Conception. Only this dogmatic definition will be able to reestablish the sense of Christian truths and retract the intelligences from the paths of naturalism in which they are lost."

The historian Francesco Guglieta, expert in the life of Pius IX, points out that the theme of naturalism, which despised all supernatural truth, could be considered as the underlying question that prompted the Pope to proclaim dogma: The affirmation of the Immaculate Conception of Our Lady laid solid foundations to affirm and consolidate the certainty of the primacy of Grace and of the work of Providence in the lives of men. Guglieta points out that Pius IX, despite his enthusiasm, accepted the idea of consulting with the world episcopate, who expressed his positive opinion, and finally led to the proclamation of the dogma.

The doctrine of the Immaculate Conception is not accepted by members of the Protestant churches. Protestants reject the doctrine since they do not consider that the dogmatic development of theology is a referent of authority and that mariology in general, including the doctrine of the Immaculate Conception, is not taught in the Bible.

Protestants argue that, if Jesus needed a sinless womb to be born sinless, God also had to have intervened in the conception of the mother of Mary, in her grandmother, and so on throughout time. Catholicism's answer is that only Mary had to remain free of sin since She was going to directly conceive Christ, while her ancestors did not. In other words, Christ did need a sinless womb, but Mary did not.

Another argument supported by Protestants comes from the Gospels of Mark 10:18 and Luke 18: 9. When Jesus is named Good Shepherd (Mark 10:17), he replies "No one is good except God." They point out that with this phrase Christ teaches that no one is without sin, leaving room for the conclusion that he is God incarnate. Catholics point out that the entire Bible, and not an isolated phrase or sentence, manifests the true doctrine of Jesus Christ. Although the Bible says nothing about the extraordinary fact that Mary was born without sin.

Another argument against belief in the Immaculate Conception appears in the first epistle of Saint John 1: 8 "If we say that we have no sin, we deceive ourselves and the truth is not in us."

However, the initiator of the Protestant movement, Martin Luther, said:

It is sweet and pious to believe that the infusion of Mary's soul was carried out without original sin, so that in the very infusion of her soul She was also purified from original sin and adorned with the gifts of God, receiving a pure soul infused by God; so that from the first moment She began to live She was free from all sin.

Sermon: "On the day of the Conception of the Mother of God," 1527.

However, the law recorded in Leviticus 12: 1-8 mentions that the woman who gave birth to a man had to be unclean for seven days. Mary fulfilled this law, according to Luke 2: 22-24.

That does not indicate that Mary has sinned. From this point of view Jesus receives the baptism of John preached for the forgiveness of sins, not being Jesus himself a sinner. "Let me do it for now, because it is necessary for us to fulfill what God has ordained."

At the XI Council of Toledo, the Visigoth king Wamba was already entitled "Defender of the Immaculate Conception of Mary," opening a line of faithful devotees among the Hispanic kings. Monarchs such as Fernando III the Saint Jaime I the Conqueror, Emperor Carlos V or his son Felipe II were faithful devotees of the Immaculate Conception and carried their banner in their military campaigns.

King Carlos III, very fond of this Marian dedication, created an order in his name, the Order of Carlos III, and declared her patron of their states.

Since the 14th century, there have been references in Spain to brotherhoods created in honor of the Immaculate Conception. The oldest, in Gerona, dates from 1330. In the 16th century this fervor will be revitalized with a huge number of brotherhoods established under the title of the Pure and Clean Conception of Mary, brotherhoods dedicated to charitable work and social assistance. The Franciscans were very faithful to the belief in the Immaculate, and contributed to its roots and spread throughout the world.

The feast of the Immaculate was a feast of keeping in all the kingdoms of her Catholic Majesty, that is, in the entire Spanish Empire, since 1644; It was declared a feast of keeping throughout the Church from 1708 by order of Pope Clement XI.

Spain celebrates the Immaculate Conception as patron and protector since 1644, being on December 8 a national holiday. During the celebration of this festival, Spanish priests have the privilege of wearing blue chasuble. This privilege was granted by the Holy See in 1864, as thanks to Spain's defense of the dogma of the Immaculate Conception.

- The patron saint of the Spanish Infantry is the Immaculate Conception. This patronage has its origin in the so-called Miracle of Empel during the wars in Flanders.
- The vote for the Immaculate Conception was made for the first time in Spain in the town of Villalpando (Zamora), on November 1, 1466, in the church of San Nicolás, followed by the then Villa de Alcázar de San Juan, renewing the I vote every year. 13 towns did it (Villalpando, Quintanilla del Monte, Cotanes del Monte, Villamayor de Campos, Tapioles, Cañizo, Villar de Fallaves, Villardiga, Prado, Quintanilla del Olmo, San Martín de Valderaudey, Villanueva del Campo, Cerecinos de Campos). Two manuscripts, one on parchment and the other on paper, both from 1527, keep the texts of the Vow and the first two endorsements. This was first printed in 1668 by F. López de Arrieta, Villalpandino priest, in León. The 6 endorsements or renewals of the Vote (1498, 1527, 1904, 1940, 1954 and 1967) have been made in the main square of Villalpando as solemn notarial acts. The 5 "notaries of the Purísima" have been Diego Fernández de Villalpando (1466), Alonso Pérez de Encalada (1498, 1527), Manuel Salas Fernández (1904), Eloy Gómez Silió (1940) and Luis Delgado González (1954 and 1967).
- Puente Genil (Córdoba) was the first town in Andalusia to celebrate in honor of the Immaculate Conception. On October 26, 1617, the Cabildo agreed to hold a solemn feast in immaculist defense, but specifically, it made an official vote on May 8, 1650. In that

year, the same thing that happened in other towns in Andalusia in this century, the population of the old Don Gonzalo bridge suffered the consequences of a cholera epidemic that devastated the Villa causing numerous deaths in the neighborhood. Those neighbors, distressed by such scourge and clinging to a great faith, decided to entrust themselves with supplications and prayers to the protection of Our Lady of the Holy Trinity of God, so that by their divine intervention they would free them from the contagious disease, which is why They promised to keep, fulfill and always execute the Vow with which they acclaimed her for Patron Saint and which has been faithfully fulfilled annually until today. Through which it is promised to celebrate the day of its name day, December 8, with the renewal of the Vow and the celebration of the solemn procession of the Image to its sanctuary. It is the only population that has uninterruptedly renewed said Vote, and neither wars nor idioms have managed to extinguish it. It was an official initiative of the City Council, an institutional proposal and not particular as it happened in other cities, because brotherhoods made their defense vote and either have been extinguished or have been renewed sporadically and individually. Its iconography is somewhat peculiar given that it has the Infant Jesus in its hands.

- The most important temple in the city of Santa Cruz de Tenerife (Canary Islands), is dedicated to the Immaculate Conception (Iglesia Matriz de la Concepción). Also on the island of Tenerife, the Immaculate Conception of the city of San Cristóbal de la Laguna, is the Mayor of the city of La Laguna and Patron of the Spanish Red Cross in the city of La Laguna.
- The Official Colleges of Pharmacists and the Faculties of Pharmacy also have her as patron saint.
- The first temple dedicated to the Immaculate Conception in Spain was the Monastery of San Jerónimo in Granada.
- Patron saint of the town of Torrejoncillo (Cáceres), who prepares her throne every 30 November in the altarpiece of the church; on the 7th, at 10 at night La Encamisá (declared a Festival of National Tourist Interest), consisting of a rider carrying the banner of the Immaculate Conception, followed by two hundred riders dressed in white sheets, all cheered by the crowd.

- Patron Saint of the New Towns founded by King Carlos III, La Carlota, Fuente Palmera.
- In the city of La Línea de la Concepción (Cádiz) it is named Concepción in honor of its patron saint, in turn the city has the Sanctuary of the Immaculate Conception built in the 19th century. On the day of the patron saint, the image is processed through the streets of the city.
- She also receives special veneration in the Murcian town of Yecla, where she is the patron saint and in whose honor important festivals declared of National Tourist Interest are held.
- Patron saint of the municipality of Fortuna (Murcia), and owner of its parish church.
- Patron saint of the municipality of Segart (Valencia), and owner of its parish church.
- Patroness of the municipality of Torremejía (Province of Badajoz) and owner of its parish church
- Patron saint of the hamlet of La Punta (Valencia), and head of its parish church.
- She holds the patronage and ownership of the parish in the Murcian district of Palmar.
- Patroness of the Almería municipality belonging to the region of La Alpujarra, Alhama de Almería (Almería).
- In the Gran Canaria municipality of Agaete, she is the patron saint of the town.
- She is the patron saint of the municipality of Villanueva del Ariscal (Seville), whose flag reproduces the Conceptionist.
- She is the patron saint of the municipality of Arenales de San Gregorio (Royal City). On December 8 the solemn mass and traditional bonfires are celebrated in honor of the patron saint. Despite this solemnity being proper, the "Day of the Virgin" is celebrated with greater importance, which usually falls on the Saturday closest to May 9, on the occasion of the Fair and Festivities in honor of San Gregorio Nacianceno and the Immaculate Conception, both patterns of the locality.
- She has been the patron saint of Nava del Rey (province of Valladolid) since 1745, and since then a ninth anniversary has been held in her honor. For this reason, the Virgin descends processionally on November 30 from her hermitage to the

parish of Los Santos Juanes, where the novena is celebrated. After the liturgical acts, on December 8 the image returns to its hermitage acclaimed by the faithful. Both processions are known as the Los Pegotes festival, the name given to the torches with which the route is illuminated. Among other particularities, the processions are celebrated at night with the tour lit by bonfires; in addition the Virgin goes inside a horse carriage pulled by mules. The festival is declared of regional tourist interest.

- Horcajo de Santiago, (Cuenca) celebrates its Vitor festivities in honor of the Immaculate Conception, on December 7 and 8; declared of regional tourist interest.
- She is the patron saint of the illicit hamlet of Torrellano, in which the most important festivals are celebrated in her honor, in which a solemn procession of the patron's image takes place through all the streets of the hamlet.
- She is the patron saint of the diocese of Huelva.
- She is the patron saint of Torrevieja (Alicante).
- She is the patron saint of the diocese of Asidonia-Jerez.
- Argentina. December 8 is a national holiday.
- Brazil. December 8 is a holiday in several Brazilian cities, such as Angra dos Reis, Dourados, Itapura, Bragança Paulista, Jacareí and Mogi Guacu (patron saint of the city), Recife, Salvador, João Pessoa, Campina Grande, Nuevo Mundo, Belo Horizonte, Contagem, Conceição dos Ouros, Divinópolis, Porto Franco, Campos dos Goytacazes, Port Colborne, and so on.
- Chile. December 8 is a national holiday, and on the eve of that day each year thousands of pilgrims move mostly on foot or by bicycle to the Sanctuary of Lo Vásquez, located on Route 68 (in which the transit of motorized vehicles is interrupted), 85 km from Santiago and 34 km from Valparaíso.
- Colombia. It is a national holiday on whose eve or dawn Catholics, children and adults, gather with family or friends to light candles and lanterns on the sidewalks of the streets in honor of the Virgin Mary, a holiday also known as the day of Las Velitas, which traditionally begins the Christmas season.
- Sicily. National holiday, being the Virgin of the Immaculate Conception protecting her army.

- United States of America. In 1792, the Bishop of Baltimore, John Carroll, consecrated the newborn nation of the United States to the protection of the Immaculate Conception. In 1847, Pope Pius IX formalized this patronage.
- Guatemala. The procession of the Immaculate Conception runs through the streets from day 7. In ancient times, the streets were lit with bonfires for the passage of the procession that made its journey during the night. After the burning of the bonfires, it was called the Burning of the Devil, a tradition to purify the material prior to the Feast of the Immaculate Conception and begins the popular Christmas festivities in the country.
- Mexico. The Metropolitan Cathedral of Mexico City is consecrated to the Immaculate Conception of Mary. The town of Celaya, Guanajuato, from its foundation protected this dedication, being brought from Salamanca an image that is still considered today as the most beautiful in the Franciscan province of San Pedro and San Pablo. In the state of Tamaulipas, the Cathedral of Tampico is dedicated to the Immaculate Conception. In the state of Veracruz, the city of Cosamaloapan in the Papaloapan Basin, has as its patron saint the image of the "Our Lady of Cosamaloapan," belonging to the dedication of the Immaculate Conception, a figure carved in wood that according to tradition arrived to the people floating in the waters of the river in the year 1546. In the city of Chignahuapan in the state of Puebla the Basilica of the Immaculate Conception is erected, where there is a 14-meter-high image carved in wood, the which is registered as the largest in the world (2018). In the municipality of Mazatán (Chiapas), the virgin is celebrated under the name of Virgen Margarita Concepción, from November 29 to December 8 of each year. She is currently Queen of the Diocese of Tapachula.
- Nicaragua. From the end of the 18th century, the festival of "La gritería" began in the city of León on the night of December 7 of each year, the eve of its festivity. The Christian people overturned in the streets of the city visit the altars prepared in the rooms and porches of the houses and to the shout of joy "Who causes so much joy? The Conception of Mary!" typical

sweets are distributed. This national holiday is held from then until today.

- Panama. On December 19, 1988 with the Bull "Ad Perpetuam Rei Memoriam" of Pope John Paul II, the Diocese of Colón-Kuna Yala, Panama was created on the Caribbean coast. In addition, she is the patron saint of the diocese of Coclé and venerated in the Santiago Apóstol Minor Basilica of Natá de los Caballeros. It is a national holiday and officially Mother's Day.
- Paraguay. December 8 is a national holiday. The Immaculate Conception is venerated under the title of "Virgin of Caacupé." That day and in the previous ones, thousands of people make a pilgrimage to the city of Caacupé, located between the mountain ranges of the Cordillera de los Altos, about 54 km east of the Paraguayan capital.
- Peru. December 8 is a national holiday. In turn, in various regions including Ancash and Huayao, this day is celebrated, singing and dancing the traditional Carrera de Cintas dance, in which the Ancashinos celebrate the Virgin.
- Portugal. Nossa Senhora da Conceição is patron saint of Portugal, being a holiday that day.

The Immaculate Conception; Symbolism of Light and Fire:

- Fire, since the beginning of time, has awakened in men a very special feeling: leaving the darkness to enter the light, the truth and eternal life.
- The tradition of associating the lighting of candles with the Immaculate Conception has its own history (although the history of fire dates back to ancient times, it will only be discussed here with regard to its use in general in Christianity and in particular in the veneration of the Immaculate Conception).
- The first mentions of the use of candles or candles are found among the Etruscans, (15th century BC, a civilization that influenced the Romans), who apparently made them out of wax, tallow or fish, with wick of vegetable fibers such as papyrus or the junk. It was later custom in pagan Rome to light the shrines in their ceremonies, with wax candles, as happened in the so-called Feasts of Saturn or Saturnalia.

- However, in the first century of life of Christianity nothing suggests about the use of candles, except the use that had to be given to them at the time of the persecution. As Christians took refuge in dark, underground places, the need to light candles to celebrate the holy mysteries became a must: "Christians initially celebrated their mysteries in remote houses and caves at night; and from this came that they were called lucifugaces..." (Voltaire 1981: 184).

- Once the persecution was over, we could say that it could have started timidly and slowly to consolidate this tradition in the following centuries, which then evolved. From the 12th century, candles placed on the altars of certain churches began to appear, until the custom took root and spread definitively in the 15th and 16th centuries, which is precisely the time when America was invaded and colonized.

- Pre-Hispanic men had their own religious beliefs and practices, but it took far less than a century for the customs and culture of those aborigines to have been ostensibly disrupted. Spain was in the midst of a conquest fever, and was also going through a period of great religious upheaval, the one caused by Luther in 1519, which had triggered that lethal movement of the counter-reform, so that it also emigrated with the Spanish and marked with traces deep Andean religious experience.

- Actions such as establishing Courts of Holy Inquisition for Indians, initiating a "movement of extirpation of idolatries", expropriation of the lands of the Indians for the right thus granted by a papal bull, and other vexations (Bonilla, comp. 1992), undoubtedly they would end up curtailing the customs and beliefs of the natives, at the same time that they would adapt to the habits of the colonizers in a long road of miscegenation. And it is in a panorama like this that the custom of celebrating the day of the "Immaculate Conception" will begin in America, and what was once done with an American identity, became a religious syncretism, so the festivities of pre-Hispanic man became replaced by traditional Spanish. Specific case was the ancient Inti raymi festival (festival of the sun) that the Incas celebrated around the same time as the Corpus Christi solemnity.

- Now, the festivities especially helped the native to learn to integrate into the new lifestyle, and the playful element that stood out in any party was the light, so the lights were like the visible part of the joy in the villages, that in the middle of the night and the uproar acquired other connotations. Among the kinds of festivals that were celebrated, there were the "sudden ones" that consisted of a representation of Spanish power (a float carried the portrait of the king between cheers and cheers). The "solemn" ones corresponded to the Catholic calendar and included in them all the patron saint festivals, Easter and Corpus; in addition, the "patriotic" ones.

- Some historical records testify to the above in formidable detail. One of them tells of the arrival of the viceroy to the people of Lima, in the year 1556: "... rejoice as much as possible, and so they ordered that it be proclaimed later in the squares and streets of this city, that the first night all the residents and residents of this city put lights at the top of their houses on the first night and make fires at their doors ..." (Libros ... Lima, tome 10, p.128 quoted in López 1992: 66).

- And one of the most significant is the one celebrated in Puerto Rico in 1747 and which refers to the exaltation to the throne of Fernando VI: "Everyone demonstrated their joy with many lights, which they put on windows, balconies and streets. The royal fortress (governor's dwelling) was adorned with forty axes and more than two hundred candles, so symmetrically on balconies, corridors and roofs, that everyone wanted to see its beauty, forced by its extraordinary and abundant decoration, and in the same conformity it was adorned every day the festivities lasted, the neighborhood doing the same ..." (Bulletin ... Puerto Rico, Relation Veridica ..., p.165 cited in López 1992: 67).

- These evidences of the early use of candles in colonial times, suggest that their use had more meaning from the folkloric and festive than from the religious and symbolic. In this way we arrive then at the moment when it enters Colombia, the celebration of the Solemnity of the Immaculate Conception: "The feast that today begins the Christmas period, the Immaculate Conception on December 8, was imposed in Spanish America by ID card real in 1760, although said identity card arrived in Cauca in March 1762." (Miñana 1997: 23)

- And it is Popayán the city that takes the honor of welcoming, in the first place, this order that came through Pope Clemente, who decreed: "... that the Immaculate Conception was held, recognized and revered as the main and universal patron saint de las Españas (...) the custom of lighting the city on the night of December 7 was established, in what was the inevitable order of the lieutenant governor or the mayor." (Arboleda 1956: 310).

4.6.- Our Lady of Divine Providence; advocation of the Virgin Mary.

Our Lady of Divine Providence is a Marian advocation of the Catholic Church that originated in Italy in the 13th century. She currently has great veneration in Puerto Rico, in fact, She is the Patroness of Puerto Rico. His image is in a chapel in the Metropolitan Cathedral of San Juan in the Puerto Rican capital.

When the Catalan Gil Esteve y Tomás was appointed bishop of Puerto Rico, he brought with him to Puerto Rico this devotion that he knew in his years as a seminarian. This prelate had to place his entire diocese in the hands of Divine Providence, as he found the cathedral practically in ruins and the economy of the diocese in worse condition. The bishop's trust and his work quickly bore fruit and before the age of five he had already been able to rebuild the cathedral temple, where worship and devotion to the Virgin of Providence was established.

The original image revered by the Servants of Mary and other Italian religious orders, is an oil in which the Virgin appears with the Divine Child sleeping peacefully in her arms. The title "of Divine Providence" is due to Saint Philip Benicio, fifth superior of the Servants of Mary, who, invoking the protection of the Virgin on a day when his friars had no food, found two baskets outside the convent full of food without its origin being known.

The image sent to do by Don Gil Esteve was carved in Barcelona (Spain) according to the taste of the time. It is a sitting image, "of clothing," (that is, made to be dressed), and it was exposed to worship in the cathedral for 67 years, until in 1920 it was replaced by another carving, all made of wood, which is the image Our Lady of Divine Providence, more familiar and known to Puerto Rican communities.

Maria leans over the Child, who in a total attitude of confidence sleeps peacefully in her lap. The Virgin's hands are joined in prayer as she gently holds the Divine Infant's left hand.

Pope Paul VI declared Our Lady of Divine Providence, as the main patron saint of the island of Puerto Rico by means of a decree signed on November 19, 1969. In that document it was also decreed that the Solemnity of the Virgin should be transferred from the 2nd of January, the anniversary of his arrival on the island, on November 19, the day the island of Borinquén was discovered. The intention was to unite the two great affections of Puerto Ricans; love for her precious island and love for the Mother of God.

The oldest carving, dating from 1853, was the one chosen to be solemnly crowned during the meeting of the Latin American Episcopal Council held in San Juan de Puerto Rico on November 5, 1976. On the eve of the event this image was vilely burned in the Parish of Santa Teresita de Santurce. The burned image was sent to Spain to be restored. Currently, the construction of the projected great national sanctuary is waiting to be placed there.

4.7.- Our Lady of Perpetual Help; advocation of the Virgin Mary.

The Virgin of Perpetual Help is a Marian advocation. The original image is an icon from Crete and venerated in Rome in the Augustinian church, at the end of the 15th century, and since 1866 in the Roman church of San Alfonso. Dating the icon is difficult to pin down. Some place them between the 10th and 11th centuries, and others at the beginning of the 15th century. His feast day is celebrated on June 27.

The original icon is on the main altar in the church of San Alfonso, very close to the Basilica of Santa María la Mayor in Rome. The 21-by-17-inch icon of the Virgin, painted on wood, shows Mary with the Child Jesus. The Child observes two angels who show him the instruments of his future Passion while holding tightly with both hands that of his Mother, who holds him in her arms. The painting recalls the Virgin's divine motherhood and her care for Jesus from her conception until her death.

According to a tablet formerly placed next to the icon with the origins of the image, the cradle of this painting was the island of Crete, in the Aegean Sea. A merchant stole the icon from a church, hid it in his luggage, and sailed for other lands. During the crossing a great storm happened and the passengers entrusted themselves to God and the Virgin. Legend has it that the sea regained its calm and the passage arrived at a safe harbor.

Shortly after, the merchant arrived in Rome with the painting and, after some resistance from the family, the icon came to occupy a preferential place in the church of San Mateo, run by the Augustinians. It was the year 1499, in times of Pope Alexander VI. The church of San Mateo was a minor temple between the great basilicas of San Juan de Letrán and Santa María la Mayor. There the image of the Perpetual Help remained for three hundred years. The writers of the time widely recounted the miracles attributed to the image. The seventeenth century seems to be the most intense in the devotion and worship of the Virgin of Perpetual Help.

In February 1798, with the invasion of Napoleon, his troops seized Italy and destroyed more than thirty churches in Rome, including that of Saint Matthew. The Augustinian religious save the miraculous painting and take it with them. The icon has been forgotten for more than 88 years.

In 1855 the Redemptorists bought land next to Via Merulana, very close to Santa María la Mayor. It was called Villa Caserta and inside it one day the church of San Mateo was built. Through the father Miguel Marchi the whereabouts of the miraculous icon is discovered. The sons of San Alfonso María de Ligorio, the great singer of the Glorias de María, ask the pope to grant him the Perpetual Help. It is December 11, 1865, and on January 19, 1866 the image of Our Lady of Perpetual Help returns to the church of San Alfonso, in the same location where it had been for three centuries.

Restored, it occupies the center of the apse of the church of San Alfonso and its devotion and influence extends to the five continents. Hundreds of thousands of Perpetual Help icons are scattered throughout the churches, houses and roads of the world. Pius IX said, in the audience to the Superior General of the Redemptorists on December 11, 1865:

"Make it known to everyone." In referring to the origins of his priestly vocation, Saint John Paul II, in his autobiography "Gift and Mystery," affirms: "I cannot forget the Marian trajectory. The veneration of the Mother of God in its traditional form comes from the family and from the parish of Wadowice. I remember, in the parish church, a side chapel dedicated to the Mother of Perpetual Help to which, in the morning, before the beginning of classes, the students of the institute attended. Also, at the end of classes In the afternoon, many students came to pray to the Virgin."

The Virgin of Perpetual Help is patron saint of many places and institutions. In Spain it is closely linked to insurance brokers. She is the patron saint of Haiti. There are twenty religious institutes hosted by the Mother of Perpetual Help. Likewise, various health institutions, numerous publishers, books, magazines, radio stations maintain and spread their devotion.

Having this Marian dedication as the patron saint of their congregation, the Redemptorist Fathers took her to their missions in Haiti. A sanctuary was built there in Béle-Aire, near Port-au-Prince, the capital of Haiti.

In 1883 a terrible smallpox epidemic hit the country. The devotees went to the Virgin and made her a novena. The epidemic miraculously stopped and it was decided to name her patron saint of the country.

In 1993 the centenary of the miracle and the naming of the Virgin as patron saint of Haiti was celebrated with great rejoicing. Pope Saint John Paul II visited Haiti for this celebration and put the country under the protection of the Virgin of Perpetual Help.

4.8.- Our Lady of the Pillar; advocation of the Virgin Mary.

Our Lady of the Pillar or the Virgin of the Pillar, is a Catholic Marian advocation. On May 27, 1642, the municipality of Zaragoza proclaimed the patron saint of the city to the Virgin of the Pillar, patronage that in the Aragonese Courts of 1678 extended to the entire Kingdom of Aragon. Accumulates various patronages on the Corps of the Civil Guard (1913), Corps of Posts (1916), Corps of Secretaries, Interveners and Depositors of Local Administration (1928), Mariological Society (1940) and Superior Council of Missions (1948). She is also the patron saint of Hispanidad (not of Spain, although the National Holiday is celebrated that day). It is venerated in the Cathedral-Basilica of Zaragoza (Spain) to which it gives its name.

The legend about its origins dates back to the year 40, when, according to Christian tradition, on January 2 the Virgin Mary appeared to Saint James the Greater in Caesaraugusta. Maria arrived in Zaragoza "in mortal flesh" —before her Assumption — and as a testimony of her visit she would have left a jasper column popularly known as "the Pillar". It is said that James and the first seven converts of the city built a primitive adobe chapel on the banks of the Ebro. This testimony is collected by a 1297 manuscript of the Moralia, sive Exposition in Job, by Gregorio Magno, which is kept in the Pillar Archive. Marian devotion began at the dawn of the 13th century when the first pilgrimages to Santa María la Mayor begin.

On top of the pre-existing Mozarabic church, the Romanesque temple of El Pilar was erected shortly after the conquest of Zaragoza by Alfonso I el Batallador (1118), which was completed in the 13th century. At this time a primitive chapel to house the Pillar is documented in the temple, as transmitted by Diego de Espés in 1240. By 1293 the temple was in such poor condition that Bishop Hugo de Mataplana promoted the restoration of the temple and its conversion into Gothic-Mudejar collegiate church of Santa María la Mayor with resources from a bull of Bonifacio VIII that for the first time mentions the dedication of "the Pillar". Currently the only preserved vestige of the Romanesque temple of the Pillar is the tympanum of the church, which has been placed on the south façade of the Baroque basilica.

The carving of the Virgin in gilded wood measures thirty-eight centimeters high and rests on a jasper column, protected by a bronze and silver lining and covered by a cloak to the foot of the image, except on days two, twelve and twenty of each month in which the visible column appears on its entire surface. In the rear façade of the chapel the humilladero opens, where the faithful can venerate the Holy Column through an oculus open to jasper.

It is a sculpture of the late Franco-Burgundian Gothic style from around 1435 attributed to Juan de la Huerta, imager of Daroca. As for its iconography, Mary is seen crowned and in a robe and cloak, which she picks up with her right hand, contemplating Jesus the child who grasps the cloak of his mother with his right hand and a bird with his left. The Virgin's face is tender and the child may have been the subject of a careless restoration.

It was probably an image donated by Dalmacio de Mur with the patronage of the White Queen of Navarra, wife of Juan II de Aragón, as a result of the cure of a disease that afflicted the queen at the time.

The image represents the Virgin crowned and dressed in a buttoned Gothic dress. It is a garment belted by a belt with a buckle that reaches to the feet and allows you to discreetly observe the right rather than the left. A large piece of cloth covers the head and shows a wavy hairstyle. The right hand holds a fold of clothing, which covers his entire abdomen and most of his lower extremities. The Child Jesus is in the left hand and looks from behind. He appears naked and radiates innocence. Her figure turns to the left and her head points to the Virgin's belt. The Gothic factory sculpture was restored in 1990 by the Spanish Historical Heritage Institute, on the initiative of the Zaragoza Metropolitan Council.

The Holy Column is made of jasper, it is 1.70 meters high, with a diameter of 24 centimeters and a bronze and silver lining. The pilarista tradition affirms that its location has never changed since María's visit to Santiago.

On March 24, 1596, the gift of Felipe II was received at the Pillar sanctuary, which consisted of two silver angels - the work of Diego Arnal - who serve as a guard for the Virgin. They are the only elements of the Gothic-Mudejar collegiate church of Santa María la Mayor that are preserved in the current Baroque basilica.

The temple is divided into three naves, of equal height, covered with barrel vaults, in which domes and plate vaults are interspersed, resting on sturdy pillars. The exterior is facing brick, following the tradition of Aragonese brick construction, and the interior is plastered with stucco. The central nave is divided by the presence of the main altar under the central dome. The altar is presided over by the great main altarpiece of the Assumption, belonging to the Gothic-Mudejar collegiate church of Santa María la Mayor in Zaragoza, made by Damián Forment in the 16th century.

Under the other two elliptical domes of the central nave, the Holy Chapel of the Virgen del Pillar was arranged, and the choir and organ, which also came from the predecessor collegiate church. Currently the choir and organ are displaced to the next section, to provide more space for the sections of the main altar.

The Christian community of Caesaraugusta is one of the oldest in Spain, along with those of Mérita, León and Astorga. Towards 254 its existence in the epistolary of San Cipriano is documented. It is also recorded that Bishop Valerio was in the Council of Elvira at the beginning of the 4th century and that El Pillar was most likely the seat of the 380 anti-Priscilianist Council.

In the 4th century, canon VIII of the council of Antioch stands out - held in the second half of the 4th century -, which establishes the placement of religious images on columns or pillars. From which scholars such as Mariano Nougués Secall and Manuel Aramburu deduce that the fact could have been inspired by the knowledge of the appearance of Mary to Santiago, although this tradition was very popular in paganism. According to Francisco García Palacios, in this century Bishop Atanasio de Zaragoza, disciple of Santiago, already used the symbols of early Christianity as the agnus dei.

Around 1608, the tomb of a deacon named Lorenzo was discovered on a wall next to the medieval Holy Chapel the tomb would have been written in the late second century - the pillar chapel was actively operating in 196 and already had several ordained deacons. The underground communications of the Pillar church with various sites in the city of Cesaraugustana also date from the 2nd century. In 1718, when the original Plaza del Pillar was dismantled, communications were discovered between a private house and the temple. It is believed that they were built around 130 BC, when the Jews began to use the catacombs to practice their religion persecuted by the emperor Hadrian, a tactic that would soon be adapted by the early Christian communities.

To study the 3rd century there is a greater diversity of documents that provide information to the history of El Pillar. There is evidence that Bishop Valero of Zaragoza built a room attached to the temple known as the "Valerian room." The existence of the Pillar chapel during Diocletian's persecutions is also discussed, although numerous sources indicate that witnesses visited the temple during those years, such as Caledonio, bishop of Braga.

In November 380 a national council was convened in the city of Zaragoza, chaired by Bishop Valerio II of Zaragoza. The minutes of the council are signed by twelve bishops. It is inferred that this cathedral had represented, in painting or in bas-relief, twenty-four scenes from the Old Testament and the same number for the New Testament. On the border arch were the Pantocrator and the twenty-four elders.

Apparently, the late Roman poet Aurelio Prudencio wrote an ode to the martyrs of Zaragoza between 380 and 395. According to some interpretations, in one of the stanzas of his composition he alludes to the Pilar temple as "temple" and "house full of angels." However, Juan de Arruego, Antonio de Nebrija and Lupercio Leonardo de Argensola, each on their own, rejected this theory when they stated that Aurelio Prudencio was referring to the entire city of Zaragoza and not to the Pillar in particular. Whatever the case may have been, it is certain that by the fourth century the Pillar chapel had been enlarged and had enough space to house the eighteen martyrs who, according to tradition, died during the persecutions at the dawn of the fourth century.

Prudencio himself was commissioned to write simple glosses to some scenes of the temple, but when placing the explanation to the Holy Pillar he wrote something unusual: "the Column (tied) to which the Lord was flogged." Thanks to this testimony, authors such as Lupercio Leonardo de Argensola, Diego Murillo, Manuel Aramburu and José Félix de Amada speculated that the Holy Column could be the one that served to bind Christ in the flagellation or that it was even a portion of it. Lupercio wrote about it:

"They say that the Pillar that we see in the holy Chapel was brought by the angels. Being as the tradition assures, we must give some worthy cause that such ministers brought it and that the Virgin put herself on him; for what more plausible cause than to have been the one in which Our Lord Jesus Christ was scourged? I heard him preach as a child to Father Government." (Daniel Lasagabáster Arratíbel, History of the Holy Chapel of Our Lady of Pilar, Zaragoza (Reyes de Aragón, 5): D. Lasagabáster, 1999, p. 201. ISBN 84-605-8648-0.)

Another testimony about the veneration of the Virgin in the times of the low empire is one of the bas-reliefs of the sarcophagus of Santa Engracia, where the descent of the Virgin's skies to interview James is represented. It has been known since the 4th century.

With the arrival of the Visigoths in Hispania, numerous religious conflicts arose between the two main doctrines of the time: Arianism and Roman Catholicism. Thanks to the Councils of Toledo, the conversion of King Recaredo and martyrs like San Hermenegildo, the

Visigoth kingdom gradually experienced a unifying transition towards Catholicism.

The survival of the Pillar chapel in the 5th century has been questioned, due to the severe invasions suffered by Hispania at the time.

There are testimonies that affirm that in 542 the stole of San Vicente, sheltered in the Pillar, was carried in procession to Paris, where Chideberto requested it in gratitude for having raised the fence of the city. Likewise, it is related that in this century the denomination of "basilica of San Vicente" was very common for the Pillar temple.

In the 6th century, the use of the own mass of the Virgen del Pillar, who had used the Mozarabic missal since 368, is also attested. A document dated in 645 by Chindasvinto - a donation - where the Pillar temple is mentioned as founded by the apostle Santiago is also known. Finally, in this century the Zaragoza chair was held by Bishop San Braulio, documented as bishop between 626 and 651 and whose tomb was found in El Pillar in 1290. He is buried near the main altar.

During the last decades of Visigothic domination, the episcopal see of Zaragoza and the Pillar temple reached their greatest splendor. Braulio de Zaragoza is the leading figure of these years, although, according to Daniel Lasagabáster, there is some strangeness because Braulio never commented in his texts on the existence of the aedicule and the pillar tradition.

Duchesne put forward this argument against James' preaching. Z. García Villada applies it to the Virgin's Visit to Zaragoza. He considers it important since the fact of the appearance of Idacio, Orosio, Juan de Viclara, S. Isidoro de Sevilla, S. Ildefonso de Toledo, S. Braulio and Prudencio, which seems to have been recorded, is silent. And he adds: "It is strange that Braulio did not take advantage of any occasion to write something about an event as glorious as that of the Virgen del Pillar." Here is precisely the mistake of García Villada. In the 7th century the object of the pillar tradition was centered on an insignificant 4 x 2 m aedicule, located in an open area where rubbish was dumped, an inhospitable place outside the walls. What did Orosius have to say about this aedicule! Daniel Lasagabáster Arratíbel, History of the Holy Chapel of Nuestra Señora del Pilar, Zaragoza (Reyes de Aragón, 5): D. Lasagabáster, 1999, p. 189. ISBN 84-605-8648-0.

In 716 the Muslims captured Zaragoza and named it Saraqusta. Also, although they imported their religion and built the largest mosque in Saraqusta al Baida, "Zaragoza la Blanca", one of the oldest in Al-Ándalus, the Christian religion was allowed and the Pillar became one of its strongholds. During that time, according to the chronicles, the Brotherhood of the Blessed Virgin Mary of the Pillar was even formed. Arruego points out that in the 8th century, when Islamization began in Zaragoza, the cathedral passed to the Pillar temple.

In the 9th century, mention is made of the Senior Bishops, who transferred the corpse of Saint Vincent to the Pillar, and Eleca, a participant in numerous councils and a relevant figure in Spanish Christianity of that century.

It is here when Aimoino writes his History of the transfer of San Vicente, where he describes the Mozarabic church of El Pillar in the same location of the Baroque temple. The Christian community of Zaragoza was gathered around it.

Around 985, the Barcelona-born Moción, son of Froya, made a donation to the Mozarabic church of Santa María la Mayor and to the Santas Masas de Zaragoza. In his will he inherited one hundred salaries "ad Santa María". The parchment is kept in the archives of the Archdiocese of Barcelona. This testimony allows us to affirm that the pilarista temple existed from the Visigothic era, since, despite the Islamic religious tolerance, it was not allowed to build new churches.

The capitulations signed on December 18, 1118, after the conquest of Zaragoza, granted the Muslims certain concessions, including the period of one year to leave the city and settle outside the walls, and practicing their religion. Alfonso the Battler granted the patronage of the Pillar chapel to Gastón IV de Bearn, champion of the taking of Zaragoza. According to Lasagabaster, the fact that the two pillar managers after the conquest, Pedro de Librana and Gastón IV, were French, is proof that pilarista devotion was already well known in Europe.

Pedro de Librana was appointed Bishop of Zaragoza, and upon verifying the regrettable and dilapidated state of the Temple of Santa María, he issued the following letter:

"You have heard (audivistis) tell in sufficient detail that, with the help of heaven, reached with your prayers, and the courageous efforts of the combatants, the city of Zaragoza has been conquered by Christian weapons and that the church of the Blessed Virgin Mary, after having been held for a long time, oh pain! to the domain of the infidel Saracens. You know from yesteryear (novistis) that this church is prevalent (pollere), it precedes all of them because of its blessed and ancient name of sanctity and dignity. However, I must let you know that now, as a result of the previous sad captivity, it lacks everything necessary. Know that it is in a dilapidated state due to the lack of repairs during the long captivity and that it lacks everything. There are no means to restore its shattered walls and replace the ornaments. The clergymen who dedicate themselves day and night to divine service do not have housing or means of subsistence. We therefore appeal to your benevolence so that, if you cannot physically visit it, at least visit it with the generous offering of your alms. (...) To those who sympathize with this church, deprived of the most necessary resources and, sympathizing with the moans of its poverty, give a denarius, or what you can, for its restoration, we, confident in divine mercy On the authority of Pope Gelasio, the Archbishop of Toledo and all the bishops of Spain, we grant you plenary indulgence. The rest will obtain the remission of their sins in accordance with the amount of their alms and the merit of their good works. Those who offer hospitality to our archdeacon Miorrando and companions, bearers of our letter, obtain from God eternal life." (Daniel Lasagabáster Arratíbel, History of the Holy Chapel of Nuestra Señora del Pillar, Zaragoza (Reyes de Aragón, 5): D. Lasagabáster, 1999. ISBN 84-605-8648-0.)

Thus, between 1119 and 1120 the archdeacon Miorrando toured various dioceses in Spain, Italy and France in search of donations to restore the pillar chapel. According to the written testimonies, he must have obtained a generous sum that allowed Pedro de Librana to undertake the tasks that he had indicated as soon as possible.

It is in the 12th century when the Pillar receives numerous gifts that attest to the existence of the pilarista tradition during the Islamic domination. The most outstanding is the olfactory of Gastón IV de Bearn, donated by his widow Talesa de Aragón and housed in the Museo del Pillar. In 1138 the first Augustinian congregation will be founded. Six bulls of the popes Eugenio III, Alejandro III and Celestino III give importance to the Pillar de Zaragoza. Similarly, the temple was favored by the kings of Aragon —both of the House of Aragon and of the House of Trastamara— from Ramón Berenguer IV to King Fernando II, as well as Alfonso VII of León and Sancho II of Navarra. Thus, the Pillar becomes a prestigious and recognized temple of Marian worship.

Already in the thirteenth century the pillar tradition spread throughout Spain and soon after the first brotherhood was founded. It is important to point out that the Aragonese people already knew the Holy Chapel as "Santa María of the Pillar", although the temple in which it settled was called "de Santa María la Mayor". Until well into the fifteenth century the title of "Santa María la Mayor y del Pilar' will be used.

For 1261 strong floods severely damaged the structure of the Romanesque temple of Santa María. In 1291 the recently arrived Bishop Hugo de Mataplana decided to undertake the restoration of the church and its conversion to the Gothic style, so in vogue during those years. In March 1293 he ordered the worker canon to devise a solution to improve the state of the pillar temple. This fact is considered the end of the Romanesque temple and the beginning of the history of the Gothic-Mudejar collegiate church. In 1296 Hugo de Mataplana traveled to the Holy See to obtain the support of Pope Boniface VIII. Although Mataplana died while in Rome, the pontiff issued the bull Mirabilis Deus shortly after, to spur the people to collaborate in the restoration works of the Pilar de Zaragoza.

In 1318 a document from Juan XXII mentions Santa María la Mayor de Zaragoza as "built by Santiago in the year 40" and also states that this temple is the oldest in Spain. However, it incurs a fairly common mistake: to point out that the collegiate church was built in 40 when its construction dates back several centuries later. But this data allows us to know that for the canons the Holy Chapel and the Gothic temple were part of a single ensemble.

According to sources of the time, the White Queen of Navarra, wife of Juan II el Grande, experienced a miraculous cure attributed to the Virgin of the Pillar and in gratitude left for the sanctuary in July 1434.

Between 1434 and 1435, a fire originated in the cloister sacristy, which destroyed several jewels and the alabaster altarpiece of the temple. It is almost unanimously accepted the theory that the dressing room of the Virgin and the Holy Pillar were unscathed from the incident. There is no indication that the fire has reached the Gothic collegiate church. The image that is venerated today of the Virgin of the Pillar, made in the late Gothic style by an imager from Daroca, was most likely a donation from the White Queen and Archbishop Dalmau de Mur. In this century the concessions to the Pillar continued, granted by Juan II and his son Fernando II.

The faithful and the nobility of Aragon collaborated in the works to restore the damage from the fire. The walls were covered with bas-reliefs that represented the appearance of the Virgin to Santiago. The construction of a new altarpiece, "made of alabaster, one of the clearest and most transparent I have seen, was also undertaken, where there are some very well-carved figures of bulk, placed inside their niches and the assembly and the rest of the altarpiece made with great delicacy. All this is accompanied by other alabaster moldings and small figures, which are on the rest of the wall on one side and on the other."

Archbishop Alonso de Aragón, son of Fernando el Católico, was responsible for transforming the church into a Gothic style, and to him is the magnificent altarpiece carved by Damián Forment (1512-1518). In the 16th century the House of Austria came to rule in Spain and continued the tradition of the Aragonese dynasty of granting privileges and protections to the Pillar sanctuary. In 1530 Clemente VII's decision to exceed the episcopal jurisdiction of Pillar generated an internal conflict in the local archbishoprics. The Seo filed a lawsuit over the cathedral that was resolved until 1676, when Clemente X merged the Seo and Pilar councils, which gave rise to the Zaragoza Metropolitan Council.

Already entered the sixteenth century the Gothic church undergoes its transformation into the Mudejar style. In this century, events of significance for the temple occur, such as the construction of a starred flamed rib vault full of gleaming gold rosettes (1504-1515), similar to those that adorned the Aljafería Palace.

On March 29, 1640, the event known as Milagro de Calanda occurred, since the lame Miguel Pellicer affirmed that through the intercession of the Virgin of the Pillar his right leg was restored, which he had lost in an accident. The fact gained great relevance throughout the kingdom, and on April 27, 1641 it was ruled a miracle. Already on May 27, 1642, the municipality of Zaragoza proclaimed the patron saint of the city to the Virgin of the Pillar.

The devotion to the Virgin of the Pillar had spread throughout Spain, and in 1678 the viceroy Pedro Antonio de Aragón called Cortes in the name of King Carlos II, in order to declare the Virgin as the patron saint of Aragon.

1904 was the year declared by Pius X as "Marian jubilee". During this period several ladies from Spain began to invite the people to raise funds to solemnly crown the Virgin. On September 28, thanks to the intervention of the Countess of Guiomar, Pius X gave his support to the cause.

The crown was built in the Ansorena workshops in Madrid thanks to the sponsorship of a group led by Queen María Cristina de Habsburgo-Lorena. On April 28, 1905, the Archbishop of Zaragoza, Juan de Soldevilla, took the crowns to Rome to be blessed by the Pope.

May 20 was the day that the Virgin of the Pillar was crowned. Prelates from all over Spain and diplomatic representatives attended the ceremony, where a hitherto unusual number of pilgrims was also present. At twelve o'clock on the day the bishop crowned the Child and then the figure of the Virgin, in the middle of an atmosphere of general emotion. Days later the pilgrimages began, carried out by groups, since it was not possible to obtain accommodation in the city for all the pilgrims. In memory of the canonical coronation, every 20th of the month the Virgin does not wear a cloak.

The Virgin of the Pillar was the sixth Marian image of Spain to receive the Canonical Coronation after the images of the Virgin of Montserrat (1881), the Virgin of the Merced of Barcelona (1889), the Virgin of the Candelaria of Tenerife (1889, the Virgin of the Kings of Seville (1904) and the Virgin of Mercy of Reus (1904).

On the morning of August 3, 1936, during the Spanish Civil War, the republican trimotor Fokker dropped three bombs, of 50 kilograms each, on the towers of the Basilica of the Pillar. One of them was nailed to the Basilica of the Pillar, another pierced the ceiling and the last one managed to penetrate the vault of the coreto of the Virgin and cause serious damage to the golden frame of Goya's Adoration of the Name of God. None of them managed to explode or cause significant damage, a fact that was attributed to a miracle of the Virgin. The bombs were deactivated and today they are exhibited in pilasters near the Holy Chapel.

An International Mariological and Marian Congress was held in the Basilica in October 1979. Despite the fact that Pope Saint John Paul II did not attend, for this celebration, the domes and roofs of the temple were ordered to be remodeled.

Various miracles are attributed to the intercession of the Virgin of the Pillar, among which the amazing healing of Doña Blanca de Navarra, believed to be dead, and those of the blind, such as the boy

Manuel Tomás Serrano and the organist Domingo de Saludes o the so-called "Miracle of Calanda", by which the beggar Miguel Pellicer, born in Calanda, had his leg amputated in October 1637 restituted. This extraordinary event occurred on March 29, 1640 and was proclaimed a miracle on April 27, 1641 by Archbishop Pedro Apaolaza Ramírez, after a process in which three civil judges intervened and twenty-five witnesses were questioned. That same year, King Felipe IV sent Miguel Pellicer to the palace and kneeling before him kissed his leg. This prodigious fact determined that in 1642 the Virgin of the Pillar became the co-patron saint of Zaragoza together with San Valero. More mundane are other events attributed to him, such as prisoner releases, passing tests or economic and sports successes.

Among the military campaigns that Catholics consider the work of his intercession are the taking of Zaragoza from Muslim hands in 1118, the resistance against the French army during the Spanish War of Independence and the protection of the temple in the Spanish Civil War. The latter narrates the bombardment suffered by the temple on August 3, 1936, when four bombs were dropped on the Basilica of the Pillar that did not explode. The charges that fell in the temple are exposed on the sides of the Dressing room of the Virgin and make up the long list of miraculous events attributed to the Virgin Mary of the Pillar.

4.9.- Our Lady of Chiquinquirá; advocation of the Virgin Mary.

Our Lady of the Rosary of Chiquinquirá is one of the advocations with which the Virgin Mary is venerated in Catholicism. She is the patron saint and queen of Colombia, of the Zulia State in Venezuela and of the city of Caraz, in the department of Ancash in Peru.

In Colombia, the image rests in the Basilica of Our Lady of the Rosary of Chiquinquirá, where thousands of pilgrims go not only on the day of their patronal feast on July 9, but every Sunday, when masses and processions are celebrated. On July 3, 1986, Pope Saint John Paul II visited the sanctuary and prayed for peace in Colombia at the feet of the Virgin Mary. On July 9, 1999, the canvas last visited the city of Bogotá to preside over the prayer for peace. It is known by the name of the city of Chiquinquirá, where the first of its miraculous manifestations took place, and where the original canvas rests.

An image of the Virgin of Chiquinquira from Venezuela rests in the Basilica of Maracaibo. In that city, every year, on November 18, the traditional "Chinita Fair" is celebrated and masses and processions are held in honor of the Virgin.

The history goes back to the 16th century when the friars and Dominicans carried out evangelistic expeditions in the central region of the country. A knight from Spain, Antonio de Santana, in 1560 obtained the charge of the region to build a house endowed with different dependencies, appropriate for the administration of settlers, indigenous people and slaves; in addition it had to construct a chapel for religious offices in Suta. Later from Spain a friar collaborating in the missions arrives, Fray Andrés Jadraque who sees the need to equip the chapel with a canvas or picture of the Virgin of the Rosary, a dedication promulgated by the Dominican Order to which the religious belonged. In this way they went to a Spanish painter Alonso de Narváez who lived in the city of Tunja, Boyacá, close to the region, to ask him to paint the Virgin of the Rosary. They all agree to place their devotional saints, Saint Anthony of Padua and Saint Andrew, next to the Virgin for being the first patron of the encomendero who requested the image and the second, of the friar who had sent it to be made. By the year 1562, the painting made of indigenous cotton, measuring 125 cm wide by 111 high, was already in the chapel and remained there for more than a decade until approximately the year 1574. At that time, the chapel, which had a straw deteriorates due to humidity, to the point that the image was practically erased. The image was in such poor condition that it was brought within the same region to the town of Chiquinquirá, where it was left in a room that was rarely used as a chapel or oratory. It is said that even the canvas served to dry grains in the sun.

The historical chronicle (produced the year after the events) indicate that in 1586 María Ramos, a local woman, knowing that the canvas had kept the image of the Virgin Mary, decided to repair the old oratory and the battered canvas, granting her the best place in the chapel. He prayed daily and asked the Virgin of the Rosary to demonstrate, until on December 26, 1586, when Maria was leaving the oratory, an indigenous woman named Isabel, along with her little son, as they passed by the place, shouted to Maria: "Look, Look Lady ...", when he turned his gaze to the painting it shone with brilliance and the image, which was unrecognizable, had been restored with its original colors and brightness; the holes and scratches in the fabric disappeared. Since then the devotion to the dedication known as "Our Lady of the Rosary of Chiquinquirá" began.

The sanctuary was entrusted to the order of the Dominicans, who built a convent next to it, keeping the image until present times. After a strong earthquake, which occurred in 1785, the friars decided to build a new basilica in another part of the town and to transfer the image of the Virgin there. This generated protests by the residents of Chiquinquirá. Despite everything, the new church was built and the image was moved around 1823.

People's devotion to this image is evident in multiple events, ranging from traditional "pilgrimages" or major pilgrimages to the place, through popular music, to historical events featuring characters such as viceroys, bishops and politicians, beginning with Simón Bolívar himself, who not only received for his Liberation Campaign the treasures and jewels of the painting, but he himself went on several occasions to pray for the success of his company. Finally, the government of the Republic of Colombia decided in 1919 to consecrate the country to the Virgin of Chiquinquirá as its Queen and Patroness. On July 9, 1919, President Marco Fidel Suárez crowned the Virgin of Chiquinquirá as Queen of Colombia in a ceremony held in the Plaza de Bolívar in Bogotá in the presence of the Apostolic Nuncio and several bishops.

On some occasions the image has been transferred with great pomp, to the city of Bogotá (about 120 km to the south) in order to ask God for the end of wars, catastrophes or epidemics. The last transfer of this type occurred in 1999.

The story tells that a humble old laundress who lives in a humble neighborhood of Nueva Zamora in Maracaibo called El Saladillo, in the province of Venezuela, was doing her job on the shores of the Coquivacoa lagoon when a tablet came into her hands, without any particularity that made it special, but apparently it was collected by the laundress giving it the usefulness of a lid for the water jar. At the time the old woman seemed to recognize a very blurred image of a religious character on the tablet and perhaps out of reverence placed it on one of its walls. On Tuesday, November 18, 1709, she was absorbed in what she was doing, so she did not pay attention to a series of blows that were heard on the wall where the image hung. The thumping was heard again, but she did not move. However, the third time, she went astonished to the place where the blows came from and surprised, saw how the image of the Virgin of Chiquinquirá was clearly seen on the tablet and a brilliant light came out of it. The surprise of such a phenomenon led her to the street where she began to shout: "Miracle, miracle" and with this began the great devotion of the Zulia to the Mother of Jesus Christ. The image is presumed to have been released as dispossession in sea waters, of a looting by a pirate in the then Viceroyalty of New Granada (today Colombia) and it is unknown how long it could have been floating in the waters of the sea until reaching the Coquivacoa Lagoon (today Lake Maracaibo). The Virgin's gaze in the image is given to the left, as if to presume that she continues on her way to the then Province of Venezuela, becoming since then the most beloved "undocumented" in this country, perhaps also foreshadowing the great exodus of Colombians that have arrived in Venezuela. And after the portent similar to the one that occurred in the neighboring Viceroyalty, they wanted to transfer the Image to the Cathedral of Nueva Zamora de Maracaibo and in fact it was possible to do up to a certain section of the adjacencies to the temple, but when it arrived at a certain place the image began to get extremely heavy, to the point that it had to be lowered and left on the ground, after which it could not be lifted again. In view of the circumstances, it occurred to some of the residents that perhaps providence wished that the image not be in the main temple, along with the Mantuanos (the wealthy of the time) but in the hermitage under construction for that time of San Juan de Dios (more in agreement with the most deprived) towards the west of the city. The suggestion was taken into account and surprisingly the image recovered its original weight and arrived with honors at the aforementioned hermitage, today converted into a Minor Basilica dedicated to Our Lady of the Rosary of Chiquinquirá and San Juan de Dios, in which it has been venerated since then.

Festive cycle: framed in the celebration of the Fair, along with the formal and religious schedule of activities, other popular and mass events take place according to the beliefs of the faithful. Every November 18, Maracaibo and the Zulia State in general, have been celebrating the Chinita festival, as it is affectionately called in the country, a date that has become since then, on the occasion of parties for the faithful of the Zulia town and its surroundings. With the lighting of the Bella Vista avenue, to the sound of the bagpipe (music originated in the colonial era and which today is largely dedicated to the celebration of the Virgin festivities and protests of the Zulia people), fireworks that The Marabino sky lights up, chimbangueles (drum music) that resound, orchestral bands there is a party setting, accompanying the Virgin on her tour of the streets where the miracle of renewal is said to have happened, as it also happened in Chiquinquirá, Colombia.

The devotion to the Virgin of the Rosary of Chiquinquirá is very great in the city of Maracaibo and many favors are attributed to it, some of the most surprising have been exalted in beautiful stained glass windows in the same Basilica.

The Virgin of the Rosary of Chiquinquirá is the formal patron saint of the City of Maracaibo, the Zulia state and of the National Guard of the Bolivarian Republic of Venezuela, she was canonically crowned with gold offerings along with precious and semi-precious stones such as rubies, sapphires and emeralds that his people have given him since the colony. This crown is supported by four silver angels. In Hispanic times the table was covered on its edges with a gold embossing, certain ornaments on the image such as crowns for the Virgin and child, the halo, etc., which have been mostly removed except for the crown. The image has a scepter of gold, sapphires and emeralds; The image also has a crown made with stones called "tumas", a gift from the Guajira ethnic group.

The image of Our Lady of the Rosary of Chiquinquirá has been transferred on several occasions to multiple sites; One of the most remembered was when he visited the capital of the Republic and more frequently he has been walked through the different parishes of the state of Zulia, moving in boats by the lake and rivers, in land vehicles and even by helicopter. Today these visits continue, but making use of a replica to protect the original image.

The celebrations in honor of the Virgin of the Rosary of Chiquinquirá, ceased to be the modest patron saint festivals of the past to acquire international characteristics of celebration of great complexity where religious and popular events converge, all gathered under the name of the International Fair of Chinita.

In it the famous bullfights, dances in public and private places of the city, piper sunrises, baseball games, the great beauty gala, (beauty contest that allows to choose the sovereign who will be the queen of the fair throughout the year, the parade of floats and troupes, plus many other activities.

November 18 is an important day when all the marabinos (natives of Maracaibo) pay homage to the Virgin of Chiquinquirá. That day is known and celebrated as (La Feria De La Chinita) and is celebrated with great enthusiasm, joy, faith and fidelity by all the inhabitants of the city. At the same time, the Copa la Chinita baseball game takes place, a sport activity very frequented by the Zulia fanatic, who meets (after a long night of partying) to give encouragement and support to the baseball team of the Águilas del Zulia. The following week the Aurora procession takes place and the image is walked from the basilica at 3:00 in the morning, so that together with his people he receives the day on the street. Finally, the following Sunday the image is returned to his dressing room.

In Spain: Since 2004 in Madrid (Spain) they venerate the Virgin of Chiquinquirá and the Chinita fair is celebrated in the same way as in Maracaibo (Venezuela) thus celebrating the day of the patron saint in Spain, the celebration is held on 17, November 18 and 19, thus starting the celebration every year of the fair to the patron saint of Spain, Colombia and Venezuela and in December there are also activities of the fair in Spain the special day of the patron saint is the same day that It is celebrated in Maracaibo with a mass and then a bagpipe serenade with the group between sticks and happiness and also the bagpiper group Madrid is bagpipes.

4.10.- Our Lady of the Angels; advocation of the Virgin Mary.

Our Lady of the Angels is an invocation of the Virgin Mary in the Roman Catholic Church. This cult originates from Spain, in Getafe, near Madrid, and was brought to America by the Spanish conquistadors.

The Virgin of the Angels was declared Patroness of Costa Rica and protector of the Americas by Pope Saint John Paul II.

The celebration of Our Lady of the Angels is held in the city of Cartago, Costa Rica, since the end of the 19th century there is a pilgrimage to the sanctuary every August 2, in the Basilica of the Angels.

There are also temples to the same dedication in Italy, Spain, Mexico, the United States and Argentina.

In 2005 this image was taken to the Vatican, in Rome. Pope Benedict XVI blessed her, and they placed her in the Basilica Santa María de la Luz, to which many immigrants make pilgrimages.

In the Colonial Period, Cartago was the main city for Spaniards in Costa Rica and its provincial capital. Around it were several towns for native Indians. In 1635, mulattoes lived scattered east of the city, as Spanish laws prohibited free or brown mulattos from passing the Cruz de Caravaca.

History says that on August 2, 1635, a young mulatto girl named Juana Pereira, was going to wash clothes as usual, and she found a small statue, of a doll with a baby in her arms, similar to the Virgin Mary, in the middle of the forest, on a rock, near a spring, in the place called "La Puebla de los Pardos". She decided to take it home with her, where I keep it in a drawer wrapped in a cloth. The next day, Juana returned to the site of the first find, she found a stone doll the same as the one found the previous day, she did the same, took it to her house, to keep it next to the other, but when she came to look for it, He realized that it was not there, so he kept the image found again, the same thing happened on the third day, but this time he took it to the local priest, Alonso de Sandoval, who kept it in a box, and forgot about it. The next day he opened the box and, to his surprise, he was gone. Juana Pereira returned to the place of the apparitions and found the image there, so she took it to the priest and he kept it inside the tabernacle. The next day he opened the tabernacle and did not find it, so he declared that this was a message from the Virgin Mary, she wanted to be in the forest, on the rock, so they built a small temple in her honor, where she is currently he finds the Basilica of the Angels, and around him the pardos began to gather.

The small image of 20 centimeters was baptized with the name of Virgin of the Angels, because on August 2 the Franciscans celebrate the feast of Our Lady of the Angels (Getafe). For this reason, it is certain that the discovery occurred that day, but the exact date was not. It is estimated that it was before 1639 although some take it for a fact that it was in 1635.

The young woman who had the honor of finding the image of Our Lady of the Angels seems to have been lost in the history of Costa Rica. It is known that it existed because the writings of the time and of the Church prove it, however, it was not followed up after the discovery of "La Negrita" (the little black girl).

The second Archbishop of San José, Monsignor Víctor Sanabria Martínez, tried to recover data on that mulatto. In his investigations, he found that the majority of women in that area were called Juana and had the surname Pereira. When he did not find the identity of this girl, he called her "Juana Pereira" as a tribute to all the mulattos who met the true young woman who found the image of Our Lady of the Angels. They sought to extend this honor to the entire indigenous and Afro-descendant culture of Costa Rica.

According to other sources, at that time religious imagery was very popular in the Central Valley of Costa Rica. There is a lot of documentation on teachers, officers and apprentices who specialized in making images in wood or stone, to sell them in the local market. The administration of the Spanish Governor Gregorio de Sandoval Anaya y González de Alcalá, the Spanish Bishop Fernando Núñez and the parish priest of Cartago, Alonso de Sandoval, in the years of the discovery, was characterized by establishing several churches in "Pueblos de Indios" in the surroundings Carthage, and the hermitage of "Puebla de Pardos" was his work.

The statuette was made with the technique of chiseled in jade (indigenous technique inherited through miscegenation), volcanic stone at the base, and graphite to color it.

The composition of "La Negrita", it has been said, consists of three different stones: graphite, jade and volcanic rock. Archaeologists are very interested in this composition because it is very difficult, almost impossible, to join the three stones; However, they coincide in pointing out that the image of the Virgin has characteristics of all of them.

There are investigations that at that time there was no graphite in Costa Rica, only in Europe, while in the Old Continent the other two rocks were not available. Based on that reality, it could be concluded that the image has characteristics of the two continents. It is 20 cm high, they call it "La Negrita" despite the fact that its true color is a greenish-gray. The features of the Virgin are mestizo, specifically mulatto. She sees the front, while her Son sees her directly in the eyes, and with her little hand touches her heart.

Some agree that this narration describes the Virgin Mary as assuming heaven in body and soul. It is for this reason that the Valle Family, the Virgin's personal jewelers, built her a very special throne. It's all in gold with precious stones, most donated by worshipers grateful for a favor. In total, the structure is one meter high. It is easily observable that the image of the virgin of Los Angeles, fulfills the description of the Apocalypse, in verse 12: 1: "A great sign appeared in the sky, a woman dressed in gold with twelve stars on her head and the moon under your feet." At the highest point of the glow stands out the pectoral (cross worn by the bishops on his chest) that was donated by the Archbishop of San José, Monsignor Otón Castro. At the base of the structure the Costa Rican shield was placed, which was a gift from the then president, Daniel Oduber. To the national emblem were added some rings that Monsignor Rodríguez donated to remember his mother in the Image of "La Negrita".

The Church rose with the contribution of the residents, many of whom had cocoa farms. By 1777 the elaboration of the current altar begins, which is why the carvings with stylized leaves are found surrounding a carving of a large cocoa pod and underneath this one is incipient or growing. On both sides are carved fruit baskets that are an allegory to the abundance of favors, miracles and food for their parishioners. The dome is, in fact, a huge crown on which the anagram of the Virgin Mary is seen and whose final cap is the image of Saint Michael the Archangel, who defeats the devil.

The Basilica of the Angels is currently located there, a place of devotion and pilgrimage for the Costa Rican and Central American Catholic people. Between July 25 and August 2 of each year, the Plaza de la Basilica receives approximately 2,500,000 people (unofficial figure, since data from the UCR have shown that pilgrims reach maximum numbers of 800,000), national and foreign, to show their devotion to the Virgin, who mostly arrive walking from rural places such as Guanacaste and San Vito, or from the city of San José, this tradition is called ROMERÍA and they started from July 25. Next to the Basilica is a holy water spring, the faithful who come to the Basilica collect the water in bottles in the shape of the virgin, and some wash parts of their body or the whole body to ask for a favor or to be healed. In the Basilica is the room for votive offerings, where the faithful leave a medal in the shape of the part of the body that the Virgin healed or a memory of the miracle. There are many favors that the Virgin has done and that is why Costa Ricans want her as their queen and mother.

4.11.- Our Lady of Mercedes; advocation of the Virgin Mary.

The Blessed Virgin Mary appeared to Saint Peter Nolasco in 1218, recommending that he found a religious community dedicated to helping the captives who were taken to distant places. In this way, this Marian dedication was born in Spain and then spread throughout the rest of the world.

San Pedro Nolasco, inspired by the Blessed Virgin Mary, founded an order dedicated to mercy. His mission was mercy towards captive Christians in the hands of Muslims. Many of the members of the order exchanged their lives for that of prisoners and slaves. He was supported by King Jaime the Conqueror and advised by San Raimundo de Peñafort.

Saint Pedro Nolasco and his very devoted friars of the Virgin Mary, took her as patron and guide. Her spirituality is based on Jesus the liberator of humanity and on the Blessed Virgin, the liberating Mother. The Mercedarians wanted to be knights of the Virgin Mary at the service of their redemptive work. That is why they honor her as Mother of Mercy or Virgin Redemption.

In 1272, after the founder's death, the friars officially take the name of The Order of Santa María de la Merced, from the redemption of the captives, but they are better known as Mercedarians. Father Antonio Quexal in 1406, being general of the Mercy, says: "Mary is the foundation and head of our order."

This religious community has dedicated itself for centuries to helping prisoners and has had martyrs and saints. His religious rescued many captives who were imprisoned in the hands of the fierce Saracens.

Father Gaver, in 1400, relates how the Virgin calls San Pedro Nolasco and reveals his desire to be liberating through an order dedicated to liberation.

Nolasco asks God for help and, as a sign of divine mercy, the Virgin Mary responds by telling him to found a liberating order.

From the year 1259 the Mercedarian parents began to spread the devotion to Our Lady of Mercy (or of the Mercedes) which is spread throughout the world.

Mercedarians reach the American continent and soon the devotion to the Virgin of the Merced spreads widely. In the Dominican Republic, Peru, Argentina and many other countries, the Virgin of the Merced is well known and loved.

In the last centuries of the Middle Ages, the Arabs had in their possession the south and the east of Spain and their lives on edge. The Turks and Saracens had infested the Mediterranean, and attacked the ships that landed on the coasts taking captives; to much.

A charitable soul, raised by God, in favor of the captives, was San Pedro Nolasco, from Barcelona, called the Consul of Liberty. He wondered how to remedy such a sad situation and he begged God earnestly.

Soon he began to act in the purchase and rescue of captives, selling what he had. On the night of August 1, 1218, Nolasco was in prayer, the Virgin Mary appeared to him, encouraged him in his attempts and transmitted the mandate to found the Religious Order of Mercy for the redemption of captives. A few days later, Nolasco was fulfilling the mandate. The Mercedarians undertook a fourth vow: to free others more cebilistic in the faith, remaining as hostages, if necessary.

In this way, through the members of the New Order, the Virgin Mary, Mother and Coredemptrix, Mediatrix of all graces, would relieve her captive children and all those who yearned for her, moaning and crying in this valley of tears. He would give everyone the favor of his favor.

The Virgin Mary will now have the title of Mercy, or even more beautiful in the plural: Our Lady of Mercy, thus indicating the countless abundance of her graces.

Our Lady of Mercedes would grant her children the mercy of liberation. Alfonso X the Wise said that "taking men out of captivity is something that is very pleasing to God, because it is the work of Mercy."

Under the protection of Our Lady of Mercy, the Mercedarian friars carried out enormous work. As enormous were the sufferings of San Pedro Nolasco, San Ramón Nonato and San Pedro Armengol. And there were no lack of martyrs like San Serapio, San Pedro Pascual and many others.

The cult of Our Lady of Mercy soon spread throughout Catalonia and throughout Spain, France and Italy, from the thirteenth century. In 1265 the first Mercedarian nuns appeared. The Mercedarians were among the first missionaries in America. In Hispaniola or the Dominican Republic, for example, Fray Gabriel Tellez (Tirso de Molina) missioned.

Barcelona glories in having been chosen by Our Lady of Mercy as the place of her appearance and considers her to be the heavenly patron saint. "Princess of Barcelona, protegiu nostra Ciutat."

In the Valencia museum there is a painting by Vicente López in which several figures turn their faces towards the Virgen de la Merced, as if imploring him, while the Virgin opens her arms and extends her cloak, covering them all with love, thus reflecting her title of Santa María de la Merced.

The Argentine city of Tucumán was founded by Don Diego de Villarroel in 1565, but on the day of Our Lady of the Mercedes in 1685 it was transferred to the current site.

The Cabildo in 1687 named Our Lady of the Mercedes as Patroness and Lawyer of the city, for the many favors that the Virgin gave to the tucumanos.

The Argentine victory in the battle of Tucumán on September 24, 1812, is credited to Our Lady of the Mercedes. In it the fate of the United Provinces of the Río de la Plata was decided. The Spanish were about three thousand and the Argentines scarcely eighteen hundred. Belgrano, the Argentine general, put his trust in God and in Our Lady of the Mercedes, whom he chose as Patron of his Army.

On the morning of September 24, 1812, the day of the battle, General Belgrano spent a long time praying before the altar of the Virgin. The Argentine army obtained the victory. In the part that he transmitted to the Government, Belgrano emphasized that victory was obtained on the day of Our Lady of the Mercedes, under whose protection the troops had been placed.

The party says verbatim: "The homeland can boast of the complete victory that their weapons have had on the 24th of this month, the day of Our Lady of the Mercedes under whose protection we put ourselves."

General Belgrano placed his command staff in the hands of the image of the Virgin. The delivery was made during a solemn procession with the entire army, which ended in the racing field, where the battle had been fought.

Belgrano went to the platforms where the image of Our Lady of the Mercedes was led, and gave him the cane he was carrying, putting it in the hands of the Virgin and proclaiming her as General of the Army.

Upon learning of these acts of devotion, the nuns of Buenos Aires sent four thousand scapulars of Our Lady of the Merced to Belgrano for distribution to the troops. The Tucuman battalion gathered before leaving for Salta, in front of the atrium of the Merced temple, where they were handed the scapulars, both the chiefs and officers and troops placed them on their uniforms.

On February 20, 1813, the Argentines who were seeking their independence again faced the Spanish in Salta. Before going into combat, Belgrano reminded his troops of the power and courage of Mary Most Holy and exhorted them to put their trust in her. He also made the vow to offer him the trophies of victory if through his intercession he obtained it.

With the help of the Mother of God they again defeated the Spanish, and of the five flags that fell into Belgrano's power, one was destined for Our Lady of Mercedes de Tucumán, two for the Virgin of Luján and two for the Cathedral of Buenos Aires.

From the year 1812, the cult of Our Lady of the Mercedes acquired great solemnity and popularity. In 1813, the Cabildo de Tucumán asked the ecclesiastical government for the declaration of the vice-patronage of Our Lady of the Mercedes "to be venerated in the Church of their religión" and ordered on their part that the public powers celebrate their feast annually on September 24. The Ecclesiastical Authority, by special Decree, declares September 24, 1813, a holiday in honor of Our Lady of the Mercedes.

After August 31, 1843, She was officially declared Vice Patron, swearing her day as a holiday and arranging for a solemn Mass to be celebrated every year with the assistance of the Magistrate and that in the afternoon the image of the Blessed Virgin be taken in procession, as evidence of gratitude for the benefits provided.

On the centenary of the battle and victory of Tucumán, the image of Our Lady of the Mercedes was solemnly crowned, in the name of Pope Saint Pius X, in 1912.

On June 22, 1943, the President of the Republic, General Pedro P. Ramírez, by decree approved the previous day with his ministers, ordered by Article 1:

"They are recognized with the rank of General of the Argentine Army: the Blessed Virgin Mary, under the dedication of Our Lady of the Mercedes, and the Blessed Virgin Mary, under the dedication of Our Lady of Carmen."

Articles 2,3 and 5 refer to the imposition of the band and belt that corresponds to the generals of the nation. The Argentine government thus solemnly proclaims to the world its religiosity.

In 1945, the National Government appointed Our Lady of the Mercedes as the Patron Saint of Military Aeronautics.

In Santa Fe the image is venerated in the Temple of the Miracle, Paraná is venerated in the cathedral, in Córdoba in the Church of the Mercedarian Fathers, and so on in many other places.

In the Dominican Republic one of the images of great devotion, and the oldest is that of Our Lady of the Mercedes.

In March 1495 Christopher Columbus, accompanied by a few Spaniards, had to face a growing number of Indians led by a cacique. They raised a trench and next to it placed a large wooden cross.

The Indians managed to evict the Spanish, who immediately retreated to a hill. Meanwhile the Indians set fire to the cross and with axes tried to destroy it, without being able to do so. Given the aggressiveness of the Indians, Colón and the majority of the troops decided to withdraw from the place. However, the mercedarian Fray Juan Infante, confessor of Columbus, who carried with him an image of Our Lady of Las Mercedes, exhorted the Spanish to continue fighting and promised victory in the name of the Virgin.

The following day, Columbus's forces won an incredible victory against the Indians. The story goes that in the middle of the battle the Virgin of the Merced appeared and the Indians, even though they were winning the battle, fled and scattered across the mountains. After this event, a sanctuary was built for Our Lady of the Mercedes on the very top of the hill where Columbus and his men fought the battle against the rebel Indians.

In Peru, devotion to Our Lady of Mercedes dates back to the time of the founding of Lima. It is recorded that the Mercedarian Fathers, who arrived in Peru together with the conquerors, had already built their primitive convent church around 1535, a temple that served as the first parish of Lima until the construction of the Main Church in 1540.

The Mercedarios not only evangelized the region, but were managers of the development of the city by building the beautiful temples that today are preserved as valuable historical, cultural and religious heritage.

Along with these friars came his heavenly patron saint, the Virgin of the Merced, a 13th century Marian dedication.

This Order of Mercy, approved in 1235 as a military order by Pope Gregory IX, managed to liberate thousands of Christian prisoners, later becoming one dedicated to missions, teaching and work in the social field. The Mercedarian friars took their habit from the garments that the Virgin wore in the apparition to the founder of the order.

The image of the Virgin of the Merced wears totally white; on his long robe he wears a scapular on which the shield of the order is printed at chest height. A white cloak covers her shoulders and her long hair is veiled by a fine lace mantilla. In some images she is represented standing and in others sitting; sometimes it is shown with the Child in the arms and other times it has them extended showing a real scepter in the right hand and in the other some open chains, symbol of liberation. This is the appearance of the beautiful image that is venerated in the Basilica de la Merced, in the capital of Lima, which was enthroned at the beginning of the 17th century and has been considered the patron saint of the capital.

It was proclaimed in 1730 "Patroness of the Fields of Peru"; "Patroness of Arms of the Republic" in 1823; and on the first centenary of the nation's independence, the image was solemnly crowned and received the title of "Great Marshal of Peru" on September 24, 1921, solemnity of Our Lady of Mercy, since then declared a feast national, occasion in which every year the army honors its high military hierarchy of "Mariscala". The image bears numerous decorations awarded by the Republic of Peru and its rulers and national institutions. In 1970 the Lima council awarded him the "Keys to the city" and in 1971 the President of the Republic imposed the Peruvian Grand Cross on Naval Merit, gestures that demonstrate Peru's love and devotion to this dedication considered by many to be its National Patron.

4.12.- Virgin Mary Help of Christians; advocation of the Virgin Mary.

The ancient Christians in Ephesus, Constantinople, Jerusalem, Athens, Greece, Turkey, Egypt, Antioch and Alexandria called the Blessed Virgin Mary with the name of Help of Christians, in Greek "Boetéia", which means "The one who brings aid from the sky". The two titles that are most read in the ancient monuments of the East are:

Theotocos and Boetéia, that is, Mother of God and Help of Christians. The great orator Proclus said, in the middle of the fifth century: "The Mother of God is our Help because she brings us help from above." Sabas de Cesarea, a century later, called the Virgin "Help of those who suffer" and narrates the fact of a very serious patient who, along with an image of the Virgin Mary, recovered health and that image of the "Help of the sick" became extremely popular with the people of his time. The great poet Greco Romano Melone, in that same century, calls the Virgin Mary "Help of those who pray and help of those who are weak" and asks us to pray that she is also "Help of those who rule" and thus fulfill what Christ said: "Let us give the ruler what belongs to the ruler" and with what Jeremiah said: "Let us pray for the nation where we are living, because their good will be our good." The nations of Asia Minor celebrate the Feast of Mary Help of Christians on October 1. In Europe and America it is celebrated on May 24. Sofronio, Archbishop of Jerusalem said: "Mary is Help of those on earth and the joy of those in heaven." Juan Damasceno, famous Christian preacher, is the first to spread the famous phrase: "Mary Help of Christians pray for us." And he repeats: "The Virgin is a helper to achieve salvation. Help to avoid danger, Help in the hour of death. Germán, Archbishop of Constantinople, said: O Mary, You are Powerful Help of the poor, courageous Help against the enemies of faith. Helper of the humble people who need your help."

The Basilica of Virgin Mary Help of Christians was consecrated on June 9, 1868, in the city of Turin, Italy. Its construction was in charge of San Juan Bosco, a peasant of humble origin who was orphaned after three years. That to study he had to ask for alms. The Blessed Virgin Mary appeared to him in dreams and commanded him to acquire "knowledge and patience", since the Holy Spirit had destined him to educate many poor children. As a man, the Virgin Mary appeared to him again and asked him to build a temple for her and to invoke her with the name of Help of Christians. The temple work began with three twenty-cent coins. But there were so many miracles that Mary Help of Christians began to do for her devotees, that in just four years the great Basilica was finished. The saint used to repeat: "Every brick in this temple corresponds to a miracle of the Blessed Virgin." From that sanctuary, devotion to the Mother of God began to spread throughout the world under the title of Auxiliadora, and there are so many favors that the Virgin Mary grants to those who invoke her with the title of Auxiliadora, that this devotion has become a one of the most popular in the world. Saint John Bosco said: "Spread devotion to Mary Help of Christians and you will see what miracles are" and he recommended repeating this little prayer many times: "Mary Help of Christians, pray for us". (History of the Devotion to Mary Help of Christians. Aciprensa.com)

4.13.- Our Lady of Lourdes; advocation of the Virgin Mary.

The Catholic dedication of Our Lady of Lourdes refers to the eighteen apparitions of the Virgin Mary that Bernadette Soubirous (1844-1879) claimed to have witnessed in the Massabielle grotto, on the banks of the River Gave, on the outskirts of the town of Lourdes, France, in the foothills of the Pyrenees, in 1858.

In Bernadette's lifetime, many Catholics believed in the apparitions of the Virgin Mary as a vehicle of the grace of the Holy Spirit, her own Self, and Pope Pius IX authorized the local bishop to allow the veneration of the Virgin Mary at Lourdes in 1862, some seventeen years before Bernadette's death.

Bernadette Soubirous was proclaimed a saint by Pope Pius XI on December 8, 1933. Since then, the dedication of the Virgin Mary as Our Lady of Lourdes has been the cause of great veneration, and her sanctuary is one of the most visited in the world.

The Christians of the Catholic Church invoke Our Lady of Lourdes as patron saint of the sick.

Bernadette Soubirous, a poor and illiterate fourteen-year-old adolescent, claimed to have seen the Virgin Mary 18 times in a grotto in the Massabielle area, west of the town of Lourdes between February 11 and July 16, 1858.

In the third appearance, the girl spoke to the Lady in Gascon, an Occitan dialect used in the area, who addressed her using the courtesy "you" (voi) and asking: "Would you do me a favor? come here for fifteen days?" (Boulet aoue was grace of bié aci pending fifteen days?). Bernadette promised her she would. In turn, the Lady announced that she did not promise to make her happy in this world, but in the other.

In successive appearances, the message took shape:

- Invitation to Penance and to prayer for sinners (February 21).
- Invitation to live a more evangelical poverty.
- Request that processions take place to the grotto and a chapel be erected there (March 2).

On February 25, as Bernadette testified, the Virgin told her to go drink water from the fountain and eat from the plants that grew freely there. She interpreted that she should go and drink water from the nearby Gave River and headed there. But the Lady taught her with her finger to dig in the ground. When digging in the mud and trying to drink, Bernadette dirtied her face, and her gestures and appearance were cause for skepticism on the part of many of the more than 350 people present, since the spring did not manifest itself immediately. However, shortly afterwards a water source emerged that, to this day, is a destination for pilgrimages by many Catholics and has witnessed numerous miracles. The spring that flowed that February 25, 1858 produces one hundred thousand liters of water per day, continuously from that date to the present day.

Before Bernardette's repeated request to reveal her name, on March 25, 1858 (in her sixteenth appearance) the Lady told her: "That I am the Immaculate Councepciou" ("I am the Immaculate Conception") the Immaculate Conception of the Virgin Mary had been solemnly proclaimed three years earlier on December 8, 1854. The expression was alien to Bernadette's vocabulary and, in principle, it was a matter of confusion, both in Father Peyramale himself - parish priest of Lourdes - as in other ecclesiastical and civil authorities. However, Bernadette Soubirous maintained a consistent calm attitude during all the incisive interrogations that were made to her, without changing her history or her attitude, nor pretending to have a knowledge beyond what has been said regarding the visions described.

The last interrogation before the ecclesiastical commission, chaired by the Bishop of Tarbes, Laurence, was on December 1, 1860. The old bishop ended up excited, when Bernadette repeated the gesture and the words that the Virgin made on March 25, 1858: "I am the Immaculate Conception."

On January 18, 1862, the elderly Bishop of Tarbes published the pastoral letter with which he declared that "the Immaculate Mother of

God has truly appeared to Bernadette." In that same year, Pope Pius IX authorized the local bishop to allow the veneration of the Virgin Mary at Lourdes. Since then the various pontiffs have supported devotion and pilgrimage to the sanctuary in various ways. Pope Pius X extended the celebration of memory to the entire Church. Pope Pius XI definitively ratified the celebration of Our Lady of Lourdes by beatifying Bernadette Soubirous on June 6, 1925, and canonizing her in the Solemnity of the Immaculate Conception of the Holy Year of Redemption, on December 8, 1933. In 1937, Pius XI himself appointed Eugenio Pacelli as Papal Delegate to personally visit and venerate the Virgin Mary in Lourdes. On September 8, 1953, in commemoration of the centenary of the dogma of the Immaculate Conception, Pope Pius XII, decreed in his Encyclical Letter Fulgens Corona the celebration of a Marian Year (the first in the history of the Catholic Church) throughout the world, while describing the events of Lourdes in the following words:

"And it seems as if the Blessed Virgin had wanted to confirm in a prodigious way the opinion that the Vicar of her divine Son on earth, with the applause of the whole Church, had pronounced. For not even four years had passed when about a village of France, in the foothills of the Pyrenees, the Blessed Virgin, dressed in white, covered with candid cloak and girded her waist with a blue sash, appeared with a youthful and affable appearance in the cave of Massabielle to an innocent and simple girl, to which, as she insisted on knowing the name of the person who had deigned to appear, she, with a soft smile and raising her eyes to heaven, replied: "I am the Immaculate Conception." They understood this, of course, the faithful, who in almost innumerable crowds, coming from all parts in pious pilgrimages to the grotto of Lourdes, revived their faith, stimulated their piety and strove to adjust their lives to the precepts of Christ." (Pius XII, Encyclical Letter Fulgens Corona, No. 3-4)

The apparitions were private and not public revelations, which is why the Catholic Church does not consider them articles of faith - they did not incorporate new material as an object of faith of the Catholic Church, nor are their faithful required to believe in them. In the faith of the Catholic Church, God chooses who to heal and by what means, because "your thoughts are not mine, nor are your ways my ways, says the Lord" (Isaiah 55, 8). In Blaise Pascal's saying, "God has his reasons that our reason does not know."

Furthermore, the authorities of the Catholic Church have explicitly expressed their devotion to Our Lady of Lourdes in different ways. On March 25, 1958, the centenary of that apparition in which the "Lady" appeared with the words "I am the Immaculate Conception", Cardinal Angelo G. Roncalli, later Pope and Blessed John XXIII, consecrated the great underground Basilica of Saint Pius X. At the closing of the centenary of the appearances of Lourdes, he put it this way: "The Church, by the voice of her popes, does not stop recommending Catholics to pay attention to the message of Lourdes."

The Catholic liturgical calendar celebrates the "Feast of Our Lady of Lourdes" on the day of the first apparition, that is, on February 11. In 1992, Pope Saint John Paul II instituted the celebration of the "World Day of the Sick" to be held on February 11 of each year, in liturgical memory of Our Lady of Lourdes.

In 1983 and 2004, Saint John Paul II personally visited Lourdes, as would his successor Benedict XVI on September 15, 2008, in commemoration of the 150th anniversary of the 1858 apparitions.

Today, the Sanctuary of Our Lady of Lourdes is one of the main Catholic pilgrimage sites in the world. With a population of approximately 15,000 inhabitants, Lourdes is currently visited by some 6,000,000 pilgrims per year.

The image of the Virgin of Lourdes that the Catholic faithful venerate generally follows Bernadette's description of Our Lady:

- Young.
- Dressed in white with a blue ribbon around the waist.
- With hands together in a prayerful attitude.
- With a rosary hanging from his arm.
- With a golden rose on each foot.

The Catholic Church always considered the Virgin Mary as a figure intimately close to all human suffering, from that moment described by the Gospel according to Saint John:

"Next to the cross of Jesus were his mother and his mother's sister, Martha, wife of Cleopas and Mary Magdalene. Jesus, seeing his mother and next to her the disciple whom he loved, says to his mother: "Woman, There you have your son." Then he says to the disciple: "There you have your mother." And from that hour the disciple took her into his house." John 19, 25-27

Based on the events witnessed by Bernadette Soubirous, the Catholic Church considered the Virgin Mary, in her dedication to Our Lady of Lourdes, the patron saint of the sick.

It is important to point out that both the appearances of Lourdes and the existence of events "not scientifically explainable by natural laws" do not constitute articles of faith - the latter included in the creed.

"Le Bureau des Constatations Médicales" and "Le Comité Médical International" de Lourdes, which govern the scientific analysis of the cures produced in Lourdes, do it in a very strict way. Of the approximately 7,000 healing records recorded since the apparitions, only 67 cases have been recognized by the Church as miracles in a century and a half. "The Church has always been very careful about cures," said French physician Patrick Theillier, director of the medical office. "He'd rather not recognize a true miracle than proclaim one where it doesn't exist." Indeed, such is the degree of rigor expressed in this matter that the cure of Marie Bailly, afflicted with late-stage tuberculosis peritonitis (the famous "Dossier 54" of the Archives of "Le Bureau des Constatations Médicales" de Lourdes), and Attested by the very - and then skeptical - Dr. Alexis Carrel (Nobel Prize in Physiology or Medicine in 1912), it is not included among the cases considered "miraculous" by the Catholic Church, simply because of insufficient confirmation of the psychic state of the patient prior to healing.

The youngest person considered to have received this grace was a 2-year-old boy: Justin Bouhort, from Lourdes (France), who suffered from chronic post-infectious hypotrepsy with delayed motor development. The most recent recognition of a miracle by the Catholic Church occurred in 2005. Likewise, it was recognized that 6 miracles took place through the intercession of Our Lady of Lourdes without the sick traveling to Lourdes. Most miracles occurred through contact with Lourdes water (49 miracles out of 67). In order for a cure to be considered "miraculous", a series of requirements must be met, including:

- That the disease is incurable, from a scientific point of view.
- That the total ineffectiveness of the medications or protocols used in their treatment has been revealed.

- That the healing has happened suddenly and not gradually.
- That the cure has been absolute, with lasting effects, and not just a remission.
- That the healing is not the result of an interpretation derived from the psychic state of the person.

Some of 67 cases of healing considered "miraculous" by the Catholic Church are the following:

- Jeanne Fretel, from Rennes (France). He visited Lourdes on May 10, 1948, at age 31. She had tuberculous peritonitis, with extreme weakness and fever. She was brought to Lourdes in a comatose state. He was given a tiny fragment of the Eucharist and woke up. She was reported to have been "immediately and permanently healed" that night as she lay in her wheelchair next to the spring. She had not yet bathed in the spring, nor drunk of its water. His cure was officially recognized on November 11, 1950.
- Brother Léo Schwager, from Friborg (Switzerland). He visited Lourdes on April 30, 1952, at the age of 28. He suffered from multiple sclerosis from the age of 5. His cure was officially recognized on December 18, 1960.
- Alicia Couteault, from Bouille-Loretz (France). He visited Lourdes on May 15, 1952, at the age of 34. He had suffered from multiple sclerosis for three years. His cure was officially recognized on July 16, 1956.
- Marie Bigot, from La Richardais (France). He visited Lourdes twice, on October 8, 1953 and October 10, 1954, at the age of 31 and 32, respectively. He suffered from arachnoiditis at the level of the posterior fossa (cause of his blindness, deafness and hemiplegia). His cure was officially recognized in Rennes on August 15, 1956.
- Ginette Nouvel, from Carmaux (France). He visited Lourdes on September 21, 1954 at the age of 26. He suffered from Budd-Chiari Syndrome (thrombosis of the main branches of the suprahepatic veins). His cure was recognized on May 31, 1963 in the diocese of Albi.
- Elisa Aloi, then Elisa Varcalli, from Patti (Italy). He visited Lourdes on June 5, 1958, at the age of 27. He suffered from

osteoarticular tuberculosis and fistulas at various sites of the right lower limb. His cure was recognized on May 26, 1965 in the Diocese of Messina (Italy).

- Juliette Tamburini, from Marseille (France). He visited Lourdes on July 17, 1959, at the age of 22. He suffered from femoral osteoperiostitis with fistulas and epistaxis. His cure was recognized on May 11, 1965 in the diocese of Marseille.

- Vittorio Micheli, from Scurelle (Italy). He visited Lourdes on June 1, 1963, at the age of 23. He suffered from sarcoma (cancer) of the pelvis. His cancerous tumor was so large and terrible that it dislodged his left thigh, leaving his left leg paralyzed. After being bathed in the waters of the spring, he broke free from pain and was able to walk. The decrease in tumor size occurred immediately, although the final verification was carried out in February 1964, the date on which not only the tumor had completely disappeared, but also the union with the hip had been recalcified, Vittorio having returned to your normal life. The cure was recognized on May 26, 1976 in the Diocese of Trento.

- Serge Perrin, from Lion d'Angers (France). He visited Lourdes on May 1, 1970 at the age of 41. He suffered from recurrent hemiplegia on the right side, with eye injuries, due to bilateral carotid artery thrombosis. The symptoms, which included headache, impaired speech and vision, and partial paralysis of the right side, began without warning in February 1964. For the next six years, he lived in a wheelchair, almost blind. In 1969 he traveled to Lourdes, returning in the same alarming state. During his pilgrimage to Lourdes in 1970, he felt a sudden warmth from head to toe, returning his vision and his ability to walk without help. He returned from Lourdes with medical confirmation that he was cured. His cure was officially recognized on June 17, 1978 in the Diocese of Angers.

- Delizia Cirolli, then Delizia Costa, from Paternò (Sicily, Italy). He visited Lourdes on December 24, 1976 at the age of 12. He suffered from Ewing's Sarcoma on the right knee. Doctors suggested amputation as the progression of the disease could prove fatal, but her parents refused. The mother took the girl to Lourdes. Upon his return to Italy, the tumor showed a rapid regression until all evidence of it disappeared. The tumor left her tibia angulated, requiring a corrective operation (osteotomy). The girl began to walk, eat, and live normally. His cure was recognized on June 28, 1989 in the diocese of Catania (Italy). She became a nurse.

- Jean-Pierre Bély, from La Couronne (France). He visited Lourdes on October 9, 1987, at the age of 51. He suffered from multiple sclerosis since 1972 and his condition deteriorated year after year. When he left on a pilgrimage to Lourdes on October 5, 1987, he had been recognized by the French health system with a degree of total disability. In Lourdes, after receiving the anointing of the sick on the esplanade of the Shrine, she experienced deep inner peace. Suddenly, he regained tactile sensitivity and was able to move again. On the spot, he didn't dare stand up. The next night, an inner voice repeated, "Get up and walk," which he did. As he himself liked to emphasize: "The Lord has healed my heart first, and then my body." The attending physician, Dr. Patrick Fontanaud, an agnostic, openly acknowledged that what happened is scientifically inexplicable. After 12 years of medical research, his cure was officially recognized on February 9, 1999 in the Angoulême diocese. A canonical commission declared that this healing was "an effective sign of Christ the Savior, who was consummated through the intercession of Our Lady of Lourdes." Here you can see that the Virgin and Christ are the same divine entity, which work within the Holy Spirit.

- Anna Santaniello from Salerno (Italy). Born in 1911, she suffered from severe heart disease derived from acute rheumatic fever, known in the scientific environment as Bouillaud's disease. As a result of her illness, she had difficulty speaking, was unable to walk, and had severe asthma attacks, cyanosis on her face and lips, and edema in her lower limbs. On August 16, 1952, at the age of 41, he made a pilgrimage to Lourdes with the Italian organization UNITALSI (Italian National Union for the Transport of the Sick to Lourdes and the International Shrine). She made the trip to Lourdes by train on a stretcher. During his stay he found asylum in Notre-Dame, precursor of the current House of Our Lady, in the Sanctuary, being constantly monitored. On August 19, 1952, she was taken to the pool at Lourdes on a stretcher, leaving the water under her own power. That same afternoon, he participated in the Marian torchlight procession. The International Medical Committee of Lourdes described the healing of women as "extraordinary" in 1961. On September 21, 2005, the miraculous cure of Anna Santaniello was officially recognized by Monsignor Gerardo Pierro, archbishop of the diocese of Salerno (Italy), when she was 94 years old. Anna Santaniello later confided that, being ill, she did not pray for herself in the Lourdes grotto, but for a young man of twenty, Nicolino, who had lost the use of his legs after an accident. She remained unmarried and, in the exercise of the profession of pediatric nurse, treated since her return to Italy hundreds of disadvantaged children.

For Catholic believers, scientific or not, the focus is not on the surprising or extraordinary of the events that occurred, but on the Holy Spirit, whose authority emanates the power to carry them out. Like Jesus in the Gospels, "whose discretion minimizes the risk of a possible magical interpretation," believers are called to live these events in a simple way, distrusting the great words.

An extraordinary cure is a challenge, but it would certainly be unfortunate to pose it as a "challenge to science." It is rather a challenge for the human spirit. In Lourdes, the Catholic Church considers that, through the intercession of the Virgin Mary, there have been many more changes of life than cures of the body. Although it was not an abrupt but a gradual conversion, Alexis Carrel's is perhaps the best known, being a scientist who won the Nobel Prize for Physiology or Medicine in 1912.

It is not appropriate to try to elucidate the mystery that contains all conversion, but it is possible to approach the convert, describe his trajectory before and after his encounter with the mystery, study the context and highlight what is significant for our days.

Dr. Alexis Carrel came from a devout Catholic family and was educated by the Jesuits. However, at the time of entering the University, he no longer practiced his religion. He was a second-year medical student when French President Marie Francois Sadi Carnot was assassinated by an anarchist in Lyon in 1894. The anarchist's knife had severed a major artery, causing the president to die after two days of agony.

In those days, suturing a large blood vessel was still an issue with no sure solution. The young medical student Carrel decided to solve the problem. Julius H. Comroe, Professor Emeritus at the Cardiovascular Research Institute (University of California at San Francisco) wrote: "Carrel won the Nobel Prize in Physiology and Medicine in 1912, and did not win it for some obscure and esoteric research, but in recognition of his work in vascular suturing and in transplantation of blood vessels and organs." Between 1901 and 1910, Alexis Carrel, using experimental animals, carried out all the actions and developed all the techniques known today in vascular surgery."

Six years after his beginnings, already a physician and assistant in the Anatomy Department, Carrel read his scientific work published in the Lyon Society of Medicine on May 12, 1902. That scientific work made history and catapulted him to fame. Decade later, as Carrel sensed he would. Two weeks later he found himself on the train that took Marie Bailly to Lourdes. What happened from then on for the next five days was later written by Carrel, although the manuscript was published in 1948 under the title "Le voyage de Lourdes, suivi de fragments de journal et de meditations," four years after his death. in November 1944. In 1950, it was published in an English translation as "The Voyage to Lourdes."

A colleague of Alexis Carrel's and a former classmate asked him to take his place as a doctor in charge of a train that took sick people to Lourdes. Carrel was interested in Lourdes, but not to assess the "authenticity" of miracles. At those times, he did not believe in miracles. He was interested in personally appreciating the speed with which the healing of various illnesses or injuries reported in Lourdes occurred. Gifted with a fine sense of observation, his friends said of him that he had "an eye on his back ..."

Among the sick, Dr. Alexis Carrel turned his attention to a dying young sick woman, Marie Bailly (whom he called with the pseudonym "Marie Ferrand" in his writings - published posthumously under the title "A Journey to Lourdes" -). Marie Bailly was afflicted with late-stage tuberculosis peritonitis, a truly fatal disease at the time.

Marie Bailly's story is well known in the medical field. His entire family had died of tuberculosis. She had had tuberculous ulcers, lesions of the lungs, and then peritonitis, diagnosed by both a general practitioner and a renowned Bordeaux surgeon, Bromilloux. His condition was very serious and he could die at any time. The doctor had expressed that the only way she could be cured was with a miracle.

Removing the covers, Marie's body was exposed again. The abdomen was swollen as before, but somewhat more pronounced on the left side ... "I'm afraid it will die in my hands ...", Carrel would have declared. When the train arrived in Lourdes, young Marie Bailly was semi-conscious, but when she arrived at the Lourdes Hospital proper, she was conscious. Carrel had such a pessimistic view of the young woman's condition that she promised to "become a monk" if she came to the Grotto alive, just 400 meters from the hospital. At Marie Bailly's insistence, a jug filled with water from the Lourdes spring was poured three times over the young woman's certainly swollen abdomen. Half an hour later, the young woman's pulse began to drop and her hitherto swollen belly flattened. During that time, Marie Bailly remained fully conscious. Carrel was puzzled: the scientist who ruled his interior refused to accept the possibility of a miracle, but his mind also failed to reach an empirical and pragmatic conclusion.

Marie Bailly's sudden healing was widely publicized in Lyon, along with the fact that Carrel was present during her healing. A newspaper published an article, implying that Carrel refused to believe in the miracle. Consequently, Dr. Carrel was compelled to post an answer that was not to anyone's liking. He criticized believers for too easily taking something unusual as if it were a miracle. And, on the other hand, he reproached those who refused to look at the facts every time it seemed to be a miracle (involving to a large extent the members of the medical community).

Half a year later, Dr. Carrel had to leave the Faculty of Medicine. He first went to Paris, thence to Montreal, thence to the University of Chicago, and from there, through a lecture at Johns Hopkins University, the Rockefeller Institute. The Marie Bailly case became big news in France only after 1913, after Alexis Carrel, with the halo of the 1912 Nobel Prize in Physiology / Medicine, returned to France.

The most precise details on the important facts that constitute the backbone of the "Bailly case" can be obtained from "Dossier 54", in the archives of "Le Bureau des Constatations Médicales", an organization that, together with "The International Medical Committee", governs the scientific analysis of the cures produced in Lourdes. Dossier 54 is also found in the introduction written by Stanley L. Jaki (winner of the

1987 Templeton Prize) on the occasion of a re-edition of Carrel's book "A Journey to Lourdes."

Marie Bailly was born in 1878. Both her father, an optician, and her mother died of tuberculosis. Of his five brothers, only one did not suffer from this disease. She was twenty years old when the symptoms of pulmonary tuberculosis first became apparent. A year later, he was diagnosed with tubercular meningitis, from which he suddenly recovered when he used Lourdes water. Two years later, in 1901, he suffered from tuberculous peritonitis. Soon after, she was no longer able to withhold food. In March 1902, doctors in Lyon refused to operate on her for fear that she would die on the operating table.

On May 25, 1902, she begged her friends to "smuggle" her onto a train that was carrying the sick to Lourdes. She had to be the object of illicit transit since, as a general rule, it was forbidden to carry dying people on these trains. The train left Lyon at noon. At 2 the next morning, she was dying. Alexis Carrel was called. He gave her morphine in the light of a kerosene lamp and stayed with her. Three hours later, he diagnosed that case as tuberculous peritonitis and said quietly that he was not going to make it to Lourdes alive. Immediate diagnosis at that time depended heavily on a palpation procedure.

At Lourdes, Marie Bailly was examined by various doctors. On May 27, she insisted on being taken to the Grotto, although the doctors (including Carrel) were afraid that she would die on the way. The "File 54" ("Dossier 54") of the Medical Office File contains the immediate statements made by three doctors, including Carrel himself, and the testimony of Marie Bailly, who wrote in November and gave it to Carrel, who forwarded it duly to the Lourdes Medical Office. The highlights of Marie Bailly's own testimony are as follows:

Upon reaching the baths adjacent to the grotto, he was not allowed to dive. He asked for a little water from the baths to spill onto his abdomen. This caused a throbbing pain throughout his body. Still, she asked for a repeat. The second time, she felt much less pain. When the water poured over his abdomen the third time, it gave him a very pleasant feeling. Meanwhile Carrel was behind her, a notepad in her hands. He marked the moment, pulse, facial expression and other clinical data, as an eyewitness. The abdomen, hugely swollen and very hard, began to flatten out and within 30 minutes the swelling had completely disappeared. No type of body discharge was observed.

She was taken first to the Basilica and then to the Medical Office, where she was re-examined by various doctors, including Carrel. At night, she sat on her bed and ate dinner without vomiting. The next morning, she got up on her own and was already dressed when Carrel saw her again.

Carrel couldn't help but register that she was cured. "What are you going to do with your life now?" Asked Carrel. "I will join the Sisters of Charity to spend my life caring for the sick," was Marie Bailly's response. The next day, Marie Bailly got on the train on her own and, after a 24-hour journey in hard banks, arrived in Lyon refreshed. There she took the tram and went to the family home, where she would have to "prove" that she really was Marie Bailly, the same one that only five days before had left Lyon in a critical condition.

Carrel continued to take a great interest in her. She asked a psychiatrist to test her every two weeks, which took four months. She was regularly examined for traces of tuberculosis. In late November, she was declared in good health, both physically and mentally. In December, she entered the novitiate in Paris. Without having a relapse, she lived the hard life of a Sister of Charity until 1937.

Carrel had a problem before him. If anyone knew the facts of the case, it was he who humanly knew what happened to Marie Bailly. However, he dared not believe that more than just natural forces had intervened in Marie Bailly's sudden recovery. He continued to return to Lourdes so that he could see other sudden healings. He hoped in this way to perceive some purely natural force that would produce so-called "miraculous" healings and that would do so through the power of prayer, which he considered a purely natural psychic force. The proof of this is in his famous book "L'homme, cet inconnu" ("The Unknown Man - The Man, That Unknown"), which appeared published for the first time in French in 1934, then in English, and later, in thirty languages. Reference is made there, precisely in this sense, to several of Lourdes' miracles.

By then, thirty-two years had passed since Carrel had been behind Marie Bailly's gurney. In all those years, he had interviewed priests over and over again. He met with theologians, or rather, some theologians sought him out, hoping that Carrel would give them "scientific" confirmation of the miracles. None of this seemed to have brought him closer to the faith of his childhood. So Marie Bailly died in 1937 at the age of 58.

The following year, Carrel ran into a priest, Rector of the Major Seminary in Rennes, with whom he quickly developed a relationship. The Rector suggested that he see a Trappist monk, Alexis Presse. Father Alexis had spent a decade restoring and reopening ruined abbeys throughout France. In 1939 he began work at a dilapidated abbey in Bouquen, just an hour's drive from Carrel's summer residence in Brittany. On the way to his wife, Carrel grumbled, saying, "Meeting with priests does more harm than good." Upon reaching the ruins, a monk, Father Alexis, looked at Carrel, who began to feel "something strange running through him". Four years later, in November 1944, Carrel died in Paris. The message was sent to Father Alexis in Brittany. The monk boarded a military train carrying bananas from America to troops who were still fighting the Germans beyond Paris. It arrived just in time. Carrel asked for the sacraments before dying, on November 5, 1944. Eduardo de la Hera made a description of the converts that perhaps corresponds to that of Alexis Carrel, a convert of "Our Lady of Lourdes":

"The converts are those people who, after having lived on the fringes of all religious faith, one unforgettable day took such an intense turn in the trajectory of their lives that they changed course. And they began, if I may say so, to" take God seriously. "God turned their lives upside down. In a sense, they made it difficult for them. Someone could see them suggesting, hallucinating or alienated beings. But no, they did not leave this world: theirs and everyone's, the only one we have. (...) They did not become religious fanatics either. They simply knew how to be consistent with their truth and respectful of the truth of others." Eduardo de la Hera

This is the essence of what really happened in Lourdes to that man awarded with the Nobel Prize. The entirety of the famous "Dossier 54" provides only half of the answer to the question: What really happened? The other half is not so much about medicine, but is framed on the plane of the Catholic faith.

Incidentally, this healing was not recognized as "miraculous" by the Church. The case of Marie Bailly was discussed on several occasions at different levels by the Lourdes Medical Office and, finally, in Paris, at its highest level, by the International Committee. It was 1964. The decision was made against the miraculous nature of the cure. The reason?

Because the first physicians who treated her had not considered the possibility of a psychological pregnancy (pseudociesis) - for which more psychological and psychiatric reports prior to healing would be required - the International Committee decided to rule against the recommendation of consider the healing of Marie Bailly for ecclesiastical approval as a "miracle". It could be assumed that this was a wild assumption. Could so many doctors misdiagnose such a case? Could all doctors be wrong to feel the heavy mucus from the abdomen? This, because Marie Bailly's peritonitis did not produce liquid, but heavy mucus. Palpation can easily establish the presence of that dense, heavy mucus, especially when it occurs in large amounts. Furthermore, where had all that heavy mucus gone in just 30 minutes? Finally, Marie Bailly had successfully passed all of the psychological tests after her healing. She turned out to be a balanced person, with common sense and hardly impressionable.

However, the ruling was against, in order to exclude the slightest possibility of error in the certification of that fact as "miraculous". That, although the one who signed on behalf of medical science that it was an inexplicable fact was a Nobel Prize in Physiology or Medicine.

In a sense, the contributions of Dr. Alexis Carrel in the field of medicine did not last in the recognition that they should be due, not even from his scientific colleagues. In the aforementioned article, Julius H. Comroe noted: "In 1974, before I started a talk to a group of cardiovascular scientists at their annual meeting, I gave each of them a card that had this requisite on top:" No consult no one, please write below each person's name (mentioned), the one you consider to be your greatest contribution to biomedical science. "They followed four names, one of which was Alexis Carrel. When the answers were tabulated, I found that only 7 of the 111 who returned their cards knew of his great contributions to vascular surgery, 33 only knew of his latest work on organ cultures, and 71 wrote after Carrel's name: NOADE - I never heard of him -. 11 However, Alexis Carrel's spiritual rebirth became one of the most recognized examples of conversions in Lourdes.

In his posthumous book "Journey to Lourdes", the protagonist carries the pseudonym Dr. "Lerrac", which is his last name in reverse, Carrel. There, Alexis Carrel wrote:

"And he went to the grotto, to contemplate attentively the image of the Virgin Mary, the crutches that, like ex-votes, filled the walls illuminated by the glow of the tapers, whose incessant smoke had blackened the rock ... Lerrac took a seat in a chair next to an old peasant and he remained immobile for a long time with his head in his hands, rocked by the nightly chants, while from the bottom of his soul this prayer arose: "Holy Virgin, help from the unfortunates who humbly implore you, Save me. I believe in you, you have wanted to answer my question with a great miracle. I do not understand it and I still doubt. But my great desire and the supreme object of all my aspirations is now to believe, passionately and blindly believe without arguing or criticizing anymore. Your name is more beautiful than the morning sun. Welcome the restless sinner, whose heart is troubled and his forehead furrowed by wrinkles, he runs after the chimeras. Under the deep and hard advice of and my intellectual pride lies, unfortunately still drowned, a dream, the most seductive of all dreams: to believe in you and love you as the monks of pure soul love you ..." It was three in the morning and Lerrac thought it that the serenity that presided over all things had also descended on her soul, flooding her with calm and sweetness. Everyday worries, hypotheses, theories, and intellectual concerns had disappeared from his mind. He had the impression that, under the Virgin's hand, he had reached certainty and even thought he felt her admirable and pacifying sweetness in such a profound way that, without the slightest concern, he removed the threat of a return to doubt." Alexis Carrel

Perhaps the total number of healings declared as miracles is only anecdotal, since the importance of "Our Lady of Lourdes" is given by the spiritual rebirth of those who come to her.

"Our inquiries will never elucidate the mystery of a spiritual rebirth and of the ways of grace. However, one can pretend to see how it fits into its time, how it shapes and is shaped by it." Romano Guardini

On September 24, 2008, Archbishop of Canterbury and Primate of the Anglican Communion Rowan Williams made a pilgrimage to the Shrine of Our Lady of Lourdes himself to honor the Immaculate Conception, preaching before 20,000 people in the International Eucharist. In his homily he highlighted:

"Mary presents herself to us here as the first missionary," the first messenger of the Gospel, "as the Bishop of Lourdes, Perrier, called her: the first human being who brought the good news of Jesus Christ to someone else; which she does simply by bringing Christ within herself. She reminds us that the mission begins not with the delivery of a message made of words but on the way to another person with Jesus in the heart. She testifies the paramount importance of simply carrying Jesus, even before that there are words or actions to show and explain to him (...) When Maria appeared to Bernadette, the first time she did so as an anonymous figure, a beautiful woman, a mysterious "thing", not yet identified as the Immaculate Mother of the Lord. And Bernadette - uncultivated, lacking doctrinal instruction - jumped for joy, recognizing that there was life, that the cure was there. Remember her narrations in which she speaks of her movements graceful and light at the orders of the Lady; as if she, like Juan in Isabel's womb, began to dance following the music of the Incarnate Word carried by her Mother. Only little by little will Bernadette find the words for the world to know; only little by little, we could say, discover how to listen to the Lady and refer to what she has to say to us. (...) The neighbors, teachers, and clergy of Bernadette's parish knew what they thought they needed to know about the Mother of God, but they had to be surprised by this helpless, insignificant, expressionless teenager who had jumped from I am glad to acknowledge having found Mary as mother, sister, carrier of her Lord and Redeemer. (...) Here today, with Isabel and Bernadette, we say with grateful amazement: "What have I done to deserve that the mother of my Lord has come to me?" And we recognize that our heart's desire has been satisfied and the depths of our being have been brought to a new life." Rowan Williams, Archbishop of Canterbury and Primate of the Anglican Communion

This fact was considered very significant in terms of Christian unity and was followed by the historic visit of Pope Benedict XVI to the Anglican primate on September 17, 2010, on the occasion of the 50th anniversary of the first meeting of a Pope and an Archbishop of Canterbury in modern times, that of John XXIII and Archbishop Geoffrey Fisher, in December 1960. This in turn was followed by Benedict XVI's reception of Rowan Williams at the Vatican on November 18, 2010, shortly after Five Anglican bishops announced their passage to the Catholic Church, taking advantage of the new ordinariate created for this purpose by the Holy See. On that occasion, Pope Benedict XVI and Rowan Williams prayed together. In the sentiment of the Church, Our Lady of Lourdes constitutes a way to overcome divisions among Christians, in order to fulfill the mandate of Jesus: "May they all be one." John 17:21.

4.14.- Our Lady of the Rosary; advocation of the Virgin Mary.

Our Lady of the Rosary or Virgin of the Rosary is a Marian advocation venerated in the Catholic Church, which is why it celebrates on October 7 the feast of the Blessed Virgin Mary of the Holy Rosary.

Legend has it that the Virgin Mary appeared in 1208 to Santo Domingo de Guzmán in a chapel of the monastery of Prouilhe, France, with a rosary in his hands, taught him to pray it and told him to preach it among men; In addition, he offered different promises regarding the rosary. The saint taught it to the soldiers led by his friend Simon IV of Montfort before the Battle of Muret, whose victory was attributed to the Virgin. For this reason, Montfort erected the first chapel dedicated to this dedication.

An increasing number of men joined the apostolic work of Santo Domingo and, with the approval of the Holy Father, Domingo formed the Order of Preachers (better known as Dominicans). With great zeal they preached, taught, and the fruits of conversion grew. As the order grew, they spread to different countries as missionaries for the glory of God and the Virgin Mary.

The rosary remained the favorite prayer for almost two centuries. When the devotion began to decrease, the Virgin Mary appeared to Alano de la Rupe and told him to relive that devotion. The Virgin Mary also told him that immense volumes would be needed to record all the miracles accomplished through the rosary and reiterated the promises given to Santo Domingo regarding the rosary.

The Promises of Our Lady, Queen of the Rosary, taken from the writings of Blessed Alano:

1. Whoever constantly prays my Rosary will receive whatever grace they ask of me.
2. I promise my very special protection and great benefits to those who devoutly pray my Rosary.
3. The Rosary is the shield against hell, destroys vice, frees from sins and lowers heresies.
4. The Rosary makes the virtues germinate so that souls can obtain divine mercy. It replaces in the hearts of men the love

of the world with the love of God and elevates them to desire heavenly and eternal things.

5. The soul entrusted to me by the Rosary will not perish.

6. He who devoutly prays my Rosary, considering its sacred mysteries, will not be oppressed by misfortune, nor will he die of unfortunate death, he will be converted if he is a sinner, he will persevere in grace if he is just and, in any case, he will be admitted to the eternal life.

7. The true devotees of my Rosary will not die without the Sacraments.

8. All those who pray my Rosary will have the light and fullness of grace in life and death and will be partakers of the blessed merits.

9. I will soon liberate the devout souls to my Rosary from Purgatory.

10. The children of my Rosary will enjoy a singular glory in heaven.

11. Anything you ask me through the Rosary will be achieved quickly.

12. I will help those who spread my Rosary in their needs.

13. I have asked my Son for the grace that all the confreres and devotees have in life and in death as brothers all the blessed of the heavenly court.

14. Those who pray the Rosary are all my beloved children and brothers of my Only Begotten Jesus.

15. Devotion to the Holy Rosary is a manifest sign of predestination of glory.

In these promises made by the Virgin Mary, it is not necessary to be very erudite to see that we are facing the demonstration that She is the Own Supreme Being. Here at no time does she say I am going to come before God for whom the rosary prays, she assumes in first power "I will help", "I will deliver", etc., so that we are in the presence of one of the divinities of Being Supreme, of the Holy Spirit; we are in front of the feminine person of the Holy Trinity of God; Our Lady of the Holy Trinity.

In the 15th century, devotion to the Holy Rosary had declined, so once again the image of Our Lady of the Holy Trinity of God appeared to Blessed Alano de la Rupe, asked him to revive her, to collect in a book all the miracles performed by the rosary and reminded him of the promises he gave to Santo Domingo centuries ago.

In the 16th century, Saint Pius V established its date on October 7, the anniversary of the victory in the Battle of Lepanto, where the Christian forces defeated the Turks who invaded Europe (attributed to the Virgin), calling it Our Lady of Victories; In addition, he added to the litany of the Virgin the title of Help of Christians. His successor, Gregorio XIII, changed the name of his festivity to that of Our Lady of the Rosary. Because of the victory at the Battle of Temesvár in 1716, attributed by Clement XI to the image, the pope ordered that his feast be celebrated by the universal Church. Leo XIII, whose devotion to this dedication caused him to be nicknamed "the Pope of the Rosary", wrote some encyclicals referring to the rosary, dedicated the month of October to the rosary and included the title of Queen of the Holy Rosary in the litany of the Virgin.

As anecdotes, both the Virgin of Lourdes in her appearance in 1858 and that of Fatima in 1917 asked their apparitions to pray the rosary. Many of the popes of the 20th century were very devoted to this dedication, and Saint John Paul II declared in 1978 that the rosary was his favorite prayer.

She is the patron saint of many cities and towns throughout the world, as well as of Christian battles:

Europe and with it all Christendom was in serious danger of extinction. The Muslims intended to make Christianity disappear at the point of the sword. They had already taken the Holy Land, Constantinople, Greece, Albania, North Africa, and Spain. In these vast regions Christianity was persecuted, and many martyrs shed their blood, many dioceses completely disappeared. After 700 years of fighting for the reconquest, Spain and Portugal were able to break free from Muslim rule. That fight began at the feet of the Virgin of Covadonga and culminated in the conquest of Granada, when the Catholic kings, Fernando and Isabel, were able to definitively expel the Moors from the peninsula in 1492. This victory was of incalculable importance since in that same year the discovery of America occurred and the Christian faith began to spread in the new continent.

In the time of Pope Pius V (1566 - 1572), the Muslims controlled the Mediterranean Sea and prepared the invasion of Christian Europe. Europe's Catholic kings were divided and seemed unaware of the impending danger. The Pope asked for help but little attention was paid to him. On September 17, 1569, he asked that the Holy Rosary be prayed. Finally in 1571 a league was established for the defense of Europe. On October 7, 1571, the Christian and Muslim fleets were found in the Gulf of Corinth, near the Greek city of Lepanto. The Christian fleet, made up of soldiers from the Papal States, from Venice, Genoa and Spain and commanded by Don Juan of Austria, entered into battle against an enemy much larger in size. The whole was at stake for the whole. Before the attack, the Christian troops prayed the holy rosary with devotion. The battle of Lepanto lasted until late in the afternoon but, in the end, the Christians were victorious.

In Rome, the Pope was reciting the rosary while the decisive and miraculous victory for the Christians had been achieved. The power of the Turks at sea had been dissolved forever. The Pope left his chapel and, guided by an inspiration, very calmly announced that the Blessed Virgin Mary had granted victory. Weeks later, the message of victory came from Don Juan, who from the beginning attributed the triumph of his fleet to the powerful intercession of Our Lady of the Rosary. Grateful to Our Mother, Pope Pius V instituted the feast of Our Lady of Victories and added the title of "Help of Christians" to the Litany of the Blessed Virgin. Later, Pope Gregory III changed the party to that of Our Lady of the Rosary.

The Turks remained powerful on land and, in the following century, invaded Europe from the East and, after taking huge territories, besieged Vienna, the capital of Austria. Once again, the enemy troops were far superior. If they conquered the city, all of Europe became very vulnerable. The emperor put his hope in Our Lady of the Rosary. There was great fighting and bloodshed and the city seemed lost. Relief came on the feast day of the Holy Name of Mary, September 12, 1683, when the King of Poland, leading a rescue army, defeated the Turks.

Prince Eugene of Savoy defeated a Turkish army twice as large as his own on Temesvar (in modern Romania) on August 5, 1716, which at that time was the feast of Our Lady of the Snows. Pope Clement XI attributed this victory to the devotion manifested to Our Lady of the Rosary. In thanksgiving, he ordered that the feast of the Holy Rosary be celebrated by the universal Church.

A great apostle of the family rosary is Father Patrick Peyton, who made the first plans for a worldwide family rosary crusade at Holy Cross College, Washington DC, in January 1942. He made this crusade in thanks to Most Holy Mary for restoring her health. In a wonderful way, the crusade spread throughout the world with the motto: "The family that prays together stays together."

Throughout the centuries the Popes have fostered the pious devotion to the recitation of the rosary and have granted him indulgences.

Our Lord said: "Where two or three are gathered in my name, there am I in the midst of them" (Matthew 18:20). The rosary in family is something wonderful. It is a practical way to strengthen the unity of family life. It is a prayer within everyone's reach. The Popes, especially the most recent ones, have placed great emphasis on the importance of the rosary in the family.

The Dominican Pope, Saint Pius V (1566 - 1572) gave the charge to his congregation to propagate the holy rosary. Many Popes have been great devotees of the rosary and have spread it with deep conviction and confidence.

His Holiness Leo XIII wrote twelve encyclicals referring to the rosary. He insisted on the recitation of the rosary as a family, dedicated the month of October to the rosary and inserted the title of "Queen of the Most Holy Rosary" in the Litany of the Virgin. For all this he deserved the title of "The Pope of the Rosary."

His Holiness Saint John Paul II insisted on the prayer of the Holy Rosary. Pray as a family, in groups. Pray in private. Invite everyone to pray. Don't be afraid to share the faith. Nothing more important. The world is in crisis. Our human forces are not enough. Victory will come once again for the Virgin Mary.

The Virgin Mary loves the rosary. It is the prayer of the simple and the great. It is so simple that it is within everyone's reach; you can pray anywhere, anytime. The rosary honors God and the Blessed Virgin in a special way. The Virgin had a rosary in her hand when she appeared to Bernadette in Lourdes. When he appeared to the three little shepherds in Fatima, he also had a rosary. It was in Fatima where she identified herself with the title "The Lady of the Rosary".

4.15.- Our Lady of Fatima; advocation of the Virgin Mary.

The Virgin Mary appeared six times in 1917 to three children; Lucía, 10 years old, Francisco, 9 years old, and Jacinta, 7 years old.

At the time they were taking the sheep to the hills that belonged to Lucia's father known as Ensenada de Irene. It was there that the Blessed Virgin Mary under the name of Our Lady of the Rosary appeared to them six times in 1917, with the exception of a seventh time in 1920 in which she only appeared to Lucia. In this 1917 the world was receiving the ravages of the First World War and in Russia the revolution was brewing that would overturn the social and economic system of many countries on earth, and in which almost half of the planet's inhabitants submerged. It is under this situation that the Virgin of Fatima intercedes for the human being to alleviate moral and social ills, through her message.

When Our Lady of Fatima appeared to the children, she was dressed in an extraordinarily white cloak, with a gold trim that fell to her feet. In his hands he carried the Rosary that looked like shining stars, with a crucifix that was the most radiant gem above all others. He told Lucia that She came from heaven not to fear. The presence of the Virgin Mary brought him happiness and confident joy.

In the first apparition the Divine Mother told the children to return to this same place every thirteenth of each month for six months at the same time for Her to reveal her desire. And then I would come back a seventh time. Lucia tells that while the Virgin Mary spoke these words, she opened her hands, and they were covered by a heavenly light that came directly from her hands and this light that penetrated their souls and hearts made them understand that somehow it came from the Holy Spirit himself. God. And the light made them feel embraced by Her. Then by an impulse of Divine Grace they fell to their knees repeating from the depths of their hearts: **"O Most Holy Trinity, we adore you. My God, my God, I love you in the Blessed Sacrament."**

<This is another fact that demonstrates and confirms the revelation we make in this book about the divinity of the Virgin Mary, the Mother of God. She is the Self Supreme Being, the female personification of the Holy Trinity of God.>

The children remained on their knees in the torrent of this wonderful light source, until Our Lady of the Holy Trinity of the Holy Spirit spoke again. She told him about the war in Europe, of which these children had no notion. The Blessed Virgin Mary asked him to pray the Rosary every day, to bring peace to the world with the end of the war. After saying this, the Divine Mother began to rise slowly to the east, until it disappeared into the sky. The light that surrounded her was confused between the stars, as if the sky were absolving her.

Lucia had asked the other children to keep everything a secret, knowing the difficulties they would experience if these events were known. However, Jacinta could not contain her enthusiasm, and she promptly forgot her promise and revealed everything to her mother, who listened patiently but did not believe her, thinking it was an invention of the girl. Among the entire family, only his father was inclined to accept the story as true. He believed in the honesty of his daughter, and having some appreciation of the works of God, he became the first believer in the appearances of the Virgin Mary at Fatima.

When Lucia's mother, when she was finally told what had happened, believed that her own daughter was the instigator of a fraud, or even more so of blasphemy. Lucia quickly remembered what the Virgin Mary had told her about the fact that they would suffer a lot. María Rosa, Lucía's mother, was unable to retract her, even under threats. Finally he took her to the parish priest, to unsuccessfully try to get her to back down. On June 13, when the children were with the Virgin, they revealed that she had few believers, and many against in the communities of Aljustrel and Fatima. On this occasion when they arrived they saw that there was a small crowd waiting for them and for which they prayed the Rosary together with the crowd that was present. When the Virgin arrived they saw the reflection of the light that was approaching her and then Our Lady of the Rosary on the edge of the oak. And the Divine Virgin said to him: I want you to come here next month. I want you to continue saying the Rosary every day. After each mystery, my children, I want you to pray as follows; "Oh my good Jesus, forgive our sins, deliver us from the fire of hell. Take all souls to heaven, especially those most in need of your Divine Mercy." I want you to learn to read and write, and then I will tell you what I want most from you. I also want you to know that I will soon take Jacinta and Francisco to heaven, but you Lucia will stay here a while longer, since Jesus wants you to make me known and loved on earth. He also wants you to establish worldwide devotion to my Immaculate Heart. But you will not be alone, my daughter, do not feel sad because I will be with you always and my Immaculate Heart will be your consolation and the path that will take you to God."

The Divine Virgin Mary having said these last words, opened her hands, and transmitted to them as the first time, the reflection of that intense light that made her feel that they were immersed within the same God. Jacinta and Francisco seemed to be in the part of the light that rose towards the Heavens, while Lucia was in the part that spilled onto the earth. In front of the palm of Our Lady of the Rosary's right hand was a heart surrounded by thorns that seemed to dig into it. This made him think that this was the Immaculate Heart of the Virgin Mary offered for the sins of humanity, eagerly wanting healing. This second appearance ended as on the first occasion, with Our Lady rising to the east and disappearing into the vastness of the sky.

The appearance of the Virgin Mary on July 13 became the most controversial of the Fatima message, providing a three-part secret that the children jealously guarded. In the first two parts, the vision of hell and the prophecy of Russia's future role and how to prevent it, were not revealed until Lucia wrote them in her third diary, in obedience to the bishop, in 1941. The third part, commonly known as the Third Secret was later communicated to the bishop, who sent it without reading to Pope Pius XII. In this apparition the Holy Virgin said to the children; "I want you to come here on the thirteenth of next month. I want you to continue praying the Rosary every day in honor of Our Lady of the Rosary, to obtain world peace and the end of the war, because only She can obtain it. **You must come here every month, and in October I will tell you who I am and what I want from you. Then I will perform a miracle for all to believe ...**"

<Look here, of course, where the Virgin Mary says to the children: "... continue to pray the Rosary every day in honor of Our Lady of the Rosary ... because only She can obtain world peace and the end of the war." I go back and emphasize: "Only She can do it", that is, no one else can. It is clear that at this moment the Virgin Mary is revealing her power and authority above all things, something that only being in Her Own Supreme Being, the Own Holy Spirit of God, could do.>

"... And I will heal some people that you ask of me but I will not heal others."

<Here we see how at no time does the Virgin say that God or Jesus will intercede before to heal some people. She here establishes Her Own Authority, affirming categorical; "I will HEAL some people, but I will not

heal others," that is, She will heal, not that She will ask another entity to heal.>

The Virgin Mary continues to tell the children; **"... I also want you to make sacrifices for sinners, and say often, especially when you make a sacrifice: Oh Jesus, this is for the love of You, for the conversion of sinners, and in reparation for the offenses committed against the Immaculate Heart of Mary."**

<Here clearly the Virgin Mary is claiming for the offenses committed by men against her Divine Majesty by not having recognized her as one of the divine persons of the Holy Spirit.>

And Lucia continues narrating: "while Our Lady of Fatima said these words She opened her hands once more, as She had done in the previous two months. The rays of light seemed to penetrate the earth, and they saw as if it were a sea of fire. Immersed in this fire were demons and souls in human forms, like transparent burning tails, all black or burnt bronze, floating in the fire, now lifted up into the air by the flames coming out of themselves together in great clouds of smoke, they fell everywhere like sparks between enormous fires, without weight or balance, between screams and moans of pain and despair, which horrified us and made us tremble with fear. Demons could be distinguished by their terrifying and disgusting similarity to fearful unknown animals, black and transparent as burning coals. Horrified and as if asking for help, we looked towards Our Lady, who said to us, so kindly and sadly: "You have seen hell, where the souls of poor sinners go. It is to save them that God wants to establish in the world a devotion to my Immaculate Heart. If you do what I tell you, many souls will be saved, and there will be peace. This war will stop, but if men do not stop offending God, another more terrible war will begin very soon. When you see a night that is illuminated by a strange and unknown light, you will know that this is the sign that God will give you that will indicate that you are about to punish the world with war and famine."

The Divine Virgin Mary of Fatima came to the world on these dates and in this place to ask that Russia be consecrated to her Immaculate Heart, and to ask that on the first Saturdays of each month communions be made in the name of the Virgin of the Rosary for the forgiveness of all the sins of the world. If these wishes are fulfilled, Russia will be converted and there will be peace, if not, Russia will spread its errors around the world, bringing new wars and persecutions to the Church, the righteous will be martyred and the Pope will have to suffer a lot, certain nations will be annihilated. But in the end the Immaculate Heart of Mary will triumph. The Pope will consecrate Russia to the Virgin Mary, and she will be converted and the world will enjoy a period of peace. In Portugal the faith will always be preserved. Then, like all the previous times, Our Lady of the Rosary began to ascend towards the east, until it finally disappeared in the immense darkness of the sky.

The possession of the Secret proved to be a great test for the three young children. His families, his neighbors, devotees and believers in the apparitions, and the clergy, tried unsuccessfully to have it revealed. Finally, as the day of the apparition approached the civilian government, which was secular and poisonously anti-clerical, alarmed by the number of people who were taking an interest in the events of Fatima, they attempted to snatch them away and somehow demonstrate that everything was a fraud. Under the pretext of providing them with their own car, so that the children could safely move in the midst of the crowd surrounding their homes, the civil administrator or mayor of the district in which the town of Fatima was located, arrived in Aljustrel on the morning of the August 13. In an unsuccessful attempt to ignore the truth, on August 11, Arturo Santos, an influential official, planned a trap for the children to remain in his custody to force them to reveal everything. The latter offered to take the three children and their parents to see the parish priest, but when he arrived at the parish house he abandoned the parents, taking the children alone to the district headquarters in Vila Nova de Ourem. Here he tried to persuade them, threatened them with death and locked them in a cell with different criminals to make them retract their history, without any results. Despite their ages, their faith in the Virgin Mary and their courage were unflappable.

In Cova at noon on August 13, the characteristic external signs of the apparition of the Virgin Mary became visible to the crowd, the largest crowd so far. After these signs ended, the crowd dispersed, unaware of the children's trial, which lasted two days. Thus, on the feast of the Assumption on August 15, the Administrator led the children back to the town of Fatima and left them in front of the rectory. Here they were seen by people leaving Mass trying to find out with Lucia's father where the children had been. This was the only serious effort on the part of the authorities to intervene with Our Lady of Fatima.

This situation caused the Virgin's plans to be delayed a little. On Sunday the 19th Lucia, her brother Juan and Francisco were herding their sheep in a place called Valinhos. It was around 4 in the afternoon, sensing that the Virgin was about to appear, Lucia offered Juan a few pennies to go find Jacinta. While she and Francisco waited they saw the typical light. As soon as Jacinta arrived, the Virgin Mary appeared. And he told them; "Come to Cova da Iria again on the thirteenth of next month, and continue to pray the Rosary every day. On the last day I will perform a miracle for all to believe. With the offerings that the people are leaving here I want them to make two platforms - to carry statues - for the feast of Our Lady of the Rosary. I want Lucia and Jacinta to carry one of them with two more girls. You two will wear white. And I also want Francisco, with three children, to load the other one. Children should also wear white. What remains of the offerings will help build the chapel to be built here.

Despite the ridicule caused by the secular and atheistic press, thousands of people gathered in Cova for the appearance of the month of September. Now as the Rosary was prayed the crowd could see the children stand up facing east and see how their faces changed amazingly. The other people could not see the Virgin, but this time people who were close to Lucia heard her ask: What do you want from me? But they could not hear the Virgin's answer; "Continue saying the Rosary, my children. Say it every day to stop the war. In October Our Lord will come, as well as Our Lady of Perpetual Help and Our Lady of Mount Carmel. Saint Joseph will appear with the Child Jesus to bless the world. God likes their sacrifices, but He does not want them to put their shoelaces on at night to go to sleep. Just wear them during the day.

Lucia was concerned that many people believed that she was an impostor and a fraud, so they asked that she be hung or burned. So the Virgin Mary promised him that in October he would perform a miracle to be believed.

During the night of October 12-13, it had rained all night, drenching the ground and the thousands of pilgrims who traveled to Fatima from everywhere to see the apparition of Our Lady. On foot, by car and floats they came, entering the Cova area on the road to Fatima, until they reached the site of the apparitions where the chapel and statue of Our Lady of the Rosary of Fatima were built. As for the children, they managed to reach Cova between the flattery and the skepticism that the people showed them. When they arrived they found critics who questioned its veracity and the punctuality of the appearance, who had promised to arrive at noon. It was already past twelve according to the official time of the country. However, when the sun had reached its peak Our Lady appeared as she had said. And he told them; "I want a chapel built here in my honor. I want you to continue saying the Rosary every day. The war will soon end, and the soldiers will return to their homes." On this occasion the Virgin Mary told him; "I am the Lady of the Rosary." As for your requests, I must tell you that some will be granted, and others I must deny. People must rebuild their lives and ask forgiveness for their sins. They should no longer offend Our Lord, they have already offended Him too much.

As Our Lady of the Rosary rises to the east, She turned her palms to the dark sky. Although the rain had given way, dark clouds continued as the sun darkened, which suddenly escapes between them and looks like a smooth silver disk. At this time two different appearances could be seen, the phenomenon of the sun witnessed by some 70,000 spectators and the one that was seen only by children. After the Virgin disappeared into the immense distance from the sky, the figure of Saint Joseph and the Child Jesus was seen making the sign of the cross with their hands. Then when this apparition ended they saw Our Lord Jesus Christ and the Virgin Mary with the aspect of the Sorrowful. Our Lord Jesus Christ seemed to bless the world just as Saint Joseph did. When this apparition disappeared, Our Lady was seen again, this time with the appearance of Our Lady of Mount Carmel.

As Lucia continues narrating in her diary; "At one o'clock in the afternoon, solar noon, the rain stopped, the pearly gray sky illuminated the vast arid region with a strange light. The sun had like a transparent gauze veil that made it easy to stare at him. The mother-of-pearl greyish hue that turned into a silver foil that snapped when the clouds opened and the silver sun wrapped in the same veil of gray light, was seen to spin and move in the circle of open clouds. A moan was heard from every mouth and people fell to their knees on the muddy ground."

... And Lucia continues, "the light turned into a beautiful blue, as if it were going through the stained glass window of a cathedral and spread its rays over the people who were on their knees with outstretched arms. The blue slowly faded, and then the light seemed to pierce a yellow crystal. The yellow light tinted the white scarves, the women's dark skirts. The same thing happened in the trees, the stones and in the mountains. People cried and prayed with their heads uncovered in the presence of the miracle they had hoped for. The seconds seemed like hours, that's how intense they were."

According to Sister Lucia, that afternoon in Fatima, everyone could easily look at the sun, which for some reason did not blind them. The Sun seemed to flicker first one way and then another. Its rays spread out in many directions and painted everything in different colors, the trees, the people, the air and the earth. But the most extraordinary thing was that the sun did not hurt his eyes. Everything was calm and quiet and everyone looked up at the sun, which suddenly began to move and dance in the sky, until it seemed to detach itself from its place and fall on those present. It was extraordinarily amazing. The sun transformed everything in different colors - yellow, blue and white, then it shook and trembled, it looked like a wheel of fire falling on people. They began to shout "He is going to kill us all!, Others cried out to Our Lord to save them. When at last the sun stopped jumping and moving, everyone breathed with relief. They were still alive, and the miracle predicted by the children was seen by all.

It was by then around 2 in the afternoon. The sun a few moments before had appeared among some clouds, which hid it and shone clearly and intensely, attracting all eyes. It looked like a disk with a clearly marked ring, bright and shiny, but that did not harm the eyes of those present. The light was a bright, light orange color that had some of the luster of a pearl. It was not at all like the moon on a clear night because when you saw and felt it seemed a living body. It was not a sphere like the moon nor did it have the same color or hue. It perished like a crystal wheel made of the mother of all pearls. It could not be confused with the sun seen through the haze as there was no haze at the time, because it was not opaque, diffuse, or veiled. That afternoon, in Fatima, it gave light and heat and looked like a clear chest with a well-defined arch.

This was the last appearance at Fatima for Jacinta and Francisco. But not for Lucia to whom Our Lady of the Rosary appeared a seventh time in 1920, as the Virgin Mary had promised in May. This time Lucia was in prayer, before leaving Fatima to go to a girls' boarding school. Our Lady of the Rosary came to ask her to dedicate herself entirely to God.

Saint John Paul II the only pope who made real attempts to recognize the divinity of the Virgin Mary, as queen of the court of heavenly stars. He was also the only pope who tried to redirect the Roman Catholic Church along the path of true Christianity, in his vain effort he recognized the power of the feminine part of the Holy Spirit and the role of Mary Magdalene as Apostle of the Apostles. On Youth Day he placed "The Mary of the New Advent" as special and divinely associated with World Youth Day, which Saint John Paul II promoted for several years. It was worshiped all night at the prayer vigil of the pilgrims who met with the most Christian pope of the era of the Roman Catholic Church. This time, in his talks, Saint John Paul II at times personally addressed the Virgin Mary in heaven. The pope began his speech by saying: "With my heart full of praise for the Queen of Heaven, the sign of hope and the source of comfort on our pilgrimage of faith to the heavenly Jerusalem, I greet all of you who are present in this solemn liturgy. In this liturgy I present to you, Mary, as the woman clothed with the sun, oh woman clothed with the sun, the youth of the world greets you with so much love.… In Mary the final victory of life over death is already a real lity." It is evident, here, that Pope Saint John Paul II makes an effort to highlight something that the Roman Catholic Church has hidden throughout the history of humanity of the Christian era, the True Majesty and Divinity of Mary in heaven and the Earth.

The churches of the world are uniting on common points of faith, thanks to the kind intervention of the Virgin Mary. She, despite knowing that the bearers of the faith, do not carry a true faith because in the past everything was distorted, she clings to her infinite goodness with hope in the man and woman of the beginning of time. The beginning of the Christian-Marian era of the Holy Spirit that marked its beginning on January 13, 2013. Where what seemed to draw you closer to God, will draw you away and what seemed to draw you away from God, will draw you closer. We must recognize that Louis Grignon de Montfort was the great pilgrim who for the first time dedicated his life and ministry to worshiping the Virgin Mary. When he was a seminarian, he won a special trip to a Shrine of the Virgin Mary that was granted to the most outstanding of his classes. And when he reached the sanctuary he remained eight hours in a row, motionless, praying on his knees. This shows at the same time the patience and devotion of Saint Louis, who was the first Christian to recognize the divinity of Mary. He came to know Mary more than any other mortal. For him, his two best friends were Jesus and Mary. He wanted to celebrate his first Mass on an altar of the Virgin Mary, and for many years the Cathedral of Our Lady of Paris was his preferred temple and his refuge.

During his life, Pope Saint John Paul II claimed to have prayed to the Virgin Mary every day, to whom he attributed having saved his life. "At a certain time on May 13, 1981, during an open-air papal audience in St. Peter's Square, in the presence of 75,000 people and before the sight of some 11 million viewers, Pope Saint John Paul II spotted a girl carrying a small portrait of Our Lady of Fatima. Just as he bent over to lightly caress the girl, the murderer Mehmet Ali Agca, fired two shots precisely in the direction of where he had aimed the pope's head moments before the shots to the head of the pope failed because the pope bent at that moment to revere the image of the Virgin Mary. As two pilgrims fell to the ground slightly wounded, two more shots were heard, and this time the blood of Saint John Paul II stained his white papal cassock, but his wounds were not fatal On May 13, 1991 and again on the same date in 1994, Saint John Paul II went to Fatima and thanked Our Lady of Fatima for saving him life in the 1981 assassination attempt. Pope Saint John Paul II was the most convinced man, after Saint Louis, of the divinity of the Virgin Mary. And no man today has been more devoted to the feminine part of God. Saint John Paul II dedicated himself and his pontificate to Our Lady the Virgin Mary, wearing the M of Mary on his coat of arms; His personal motto, embroidered in Latin on the inside of his cloaks, is "totus tuus sum María" which means "Mary, I am all yours."

Saint John Paul II was fully convinced, as thousands of others are, that it was Mary who ended communism throughout Europe. Their faith is firmly based on the famous prophecies that Mary pronounced at Fatima in 1917. According to Sister Lucia, who was part of the group of boys and girls who claimed to have seen her. The Virgin predicted the rise of Soviet totalitarianism long before this became a reality. In a subsequent vision, she directed the pope and his bishops to dedicate their Immaculate Heart to Russia in order to end communism. The papacy's efforts to carry out this commission failed in 1942, 1952, and 1982. It was Saint John Paul II who finally carried out the order in 1984, a year later Mikhail Gorbachev came to power who initiated the fall of the Soviet empire. The world will recognize in due course that the defeat of communism was the result of the intercession of the divine power of Our Lady of the Holy Trinity of God.

Investigating the revelations in this book I was able to find great similarity in some analyzes of the authors of "The Thunder Of Justice" regarding the vision that Mary refers to herself as the one who "would crush the serpent," in the end times, since she is the "woman" of Genesis 3:15. By carefully examining this biblical passage we see that this interpretation is correct. In Genesis 3:15 it says: "And I will put enmity between you and the woman, and between your seed and her seed; this one will hurt your head, and you will hurt her in the heel." This verse is a prophecy and at the same time a promise that one day a woman would come, and "this will hurt your head, and you will hurt her in the heel." As it can be interpreted clearly it says that the woman you will hurt the serpent, in any case would defeat the enemy with a fatal blow to the head at the end of time. This prophecy was complemented in Revelation 12 and fulfilled with the apparitions of the Virgin of Fatima: "A great sign appeared in heaven: a Woman, clothed with the sun, with the moon under her feet and a crown of twelve stars on her head." If we analyze the stories of the boys and girls who interacted in these apparitions, we can identify Our Lady of Fatima as the biblical representation of the Woman clothed with the sun.

But there is another neuralgic point in which some revelations of the old testament, of the new testament, and of some seers of different times coincide, and that was an order given by Our Lady of Fatima to the ecclesiastical hierarchy through Lucia, in "the third secret" of the Virgin of Fatima given to children, which no Pope has dared to fulfill since 1960. This point is the establishment, or rather the transfer, of the church's headquarters to the sanctuary of the Virgin of Fatima in Portugal. This request was clearly specified by Lucia, and for which she asked that the letter containing "the third secret" be opened only after 1960. Our Lady of Fatima even asks that the cornerstone covering Peter's tomb, the first Holy Father, be transferred to the Sanctuary of the Virgin of Fatima. This year 2020, 100 years have passed since the request of the Holy Spirit of God through the Virgin, but it is also 60 years since this request had to be executed. Five Popes have passed, and six with the current one, who have postponed the execution of transferring the leadership of the Christian church to the Basilica of the Virgin Mary in Fatima.

4.16.- Our Lady of Carmen; advocation of the Virgin Mary.

The oldest devotion to the Virgin Mary, with more than twenty centuries. The name of Carmen comes from Mount Carmel or "vineyard of God" that is in the Holy Land. According to the Book of Kings, the Prophet Elijah lived there with a group of young people dedicated to prayer. The year was 300 BC, and a great drought devastated the region; the Prophet went up to the mountain to ask for rain and he saw a cloud of luminous whiteness from which the abundant water gushed out; he understood that the vision was a symbol of the arrival of the expected Savior, who would be born of an immaculate maiden to bring a shower of blessings. Since then, that small community has dedicated itself to praying for what would become the Mother of the Redeemer, thus beginning the devotion to Our Lady of Mount Carmel.

Many events have happened over time in this locality, but the prayers continued to rise from Carmel: it is that men and institutions pass, but the works of the Holy Spirit of God remain because they share a little of their eternity. Thus she incarnated the feminine part of the Holy Spirit of God in the Virgin Mary and became the Mother of the Savior: according to tradition she visited the monks and encouraged them to continue their prayers. Then came passion and death, followed by the resurrection and march to Heaven of Jesus, and later of his Mother. Then came the Muslim invasions, but Carmel's prayers are not interrupted, but the monks decide to move to Europe. There we find them in the 13th century: their Superior, Saint Simon Stock, was in prayer, worried about new persecutions, when the very Mother of God appeared to him to say: "Beloved son, receive the Scapular of my order so that whoever died would carry it piously, do not suffer eternal fire." Pope Gregory XIII declared this appearance true after serious studies, and based on the favors received by those who used the Scapular. This apparition was also recognized by Pope John XXII, who received a new apparition from the Virgin Mary, in which he promised to bring his devotees out of purgatory on the first Saturday after his death.

This devotion spread throughout Europe and included Saints of the stature of San Juan De la Cruz and Santa Teresa; it is not strange that it came to America and accompanied the awakening to the faith of our indigenous people who venerated it since the mid-sixteenth century. Already in the eighteenth century, the image that is venerated there today is found in Mendoza, Argentina, since Don Pedro de Núñez "knight of great fortune and devotion, donated the image and everything necessary for the cult of the Virgen del Carmen." First, he was in the temple of the Jesuit Fathers, when the Brotherhood was founded. In 1776, following the expulsion of the Order, the image was transferred to San Francisco, from where he would preside over one of the most beautiful days in history. The year 1814 arrived, when San Martín made the peaceful inhabitants of Cuyo heroic soldiers forging freedom, but they needed a Mother to protect them and make sense of so much sacrifice. It is known the deep devotion that the Liberator professed to the Virgin Mary and that made him appoint her General of his Army, overcoming the human respects of a time when liberalism had imposed the idea that "religion is a private matter." He gave so much importance to the subject, that he decided with his General Staff, according to Espejo in his work El Paso de los Andes: "devotion to the Virgen del Carmen was deeply rooted in Cuyo and almost all the soldiers wore their scapular, that's why it was she who had preference, "he says, and later describes the brilliant ceremony (January 5, 1817) during which San Martín gives him his baton, names it Generala, and also makes the Andes Flag bless," greeted by targets and the band with boxes and bugles, while breaking a salvo of twenty-one gunshots, before the great gala army and all the people of Mendoza." Later, after his triumphs, he will definitely hand over his cane, this time in the silence that accompanies everything great and leaving that well-known letter: "the protection that the Patron Saint and General Virgin of Carmen have given to the Army of the Andes are too visible..." Both relics, the staff and the letter, are preserved today in the dressing room of the Virgin Mary, as silent witnesses of the part that she had in the greatness of the soul of the Liberator. Being General of the Argentine Army, along with the band, our flag accompanies the image, as well as the flags of Peru and Chile, being this patron saint of the 2 neighboring countries.

By concern of Fray Leonardo Maldonado, Pope Pius X, decreed: "that the Sacred Image of the Virgin Mary under the title of Carmen venerated in the Church of San Francisco in Mendoza, be with a solemn vote crowned with a golden Crown." He supported his resolution on the "sufficient evidence that exists of the popular veneration of the image, of its fame and celebrity as well as admirable and heavenly graces, gifts abundantly granted by it." The crown, an offering of his devotees, was imposed on him in a memorable ceremony on September 8, 1911 and is a reminder of such solemnity that it was decreed on that day as the Provincial Patronal Festival and on that day, since 1950, it is also honored very especially the Blessed Virgin of Carmen de Cuyo, in the schools of Mendoza, as Patron Saint of the Primary School, instituted in such capacity by superior decision; and education at its three levels by decree of 08-30-80. In 1982 she was declared Patron of the 8th Mountain Brigade. (The Virgin of Carmen, users.advance.com)

In the words of Benedict XVI, (15, VII, 06): "Carmel, a high promontory that stands on the eastern coast of the Mediterranean Sea, at the height of Galilee, has on its slopes numerous natural grottos, favorites of the hermits The most famous of these men of God was the great prophet Elijah, who in the 9th century BC bravely defended the purity of faith in the one true God from the contamination of idolatrous cults, the contemplative Order of the "Carmelites" emerged, a religious family that counts among its members great saints, such as Juan de la Cruz, Teresa de Ávila, Teresa del Niño Jesús and Teresa Benedicta de la Cruz. The Carmelites have spread devotion to the Blessed Virgin of Mount Carmel among the Christian people, pointing her out as a model of prayer, contemplation and dedication to God. Mary, in fact, before and in an insurmountable way, believed and experienced He imitated that Jesus, the Incarnate Word, is the culmination, the summit of man's encounter with God. Fully accepting the Word, "he happily reached the holy mountain" (Prayer of the Collection of Memory), and lives forever, in soul and body, with the Lord. Today I wish to entrust to the Queen of Mount Carmel all the communities of contemplative life scattered throughout the world, especially those of the Carmelite Order, among which I remember the Quart monastery, not far from here (Valle d'Aosta). May Mary help each Christian to find God in the silence of prayer.

The Scapular was used as a symbol of union with a religious order and its spirituality since before the 10th century, even though living ordinary life in the middle of the world. They consisted of a strip of cloth equal to the habit of the religious, which was inserted through the head falling forward and behind the shoulders, hence its name that comes from the Latin "scapulae" which means "shoulders." Originally it was an overlay dress that falls from the shoulders and was worn by the monks during their work. With time they reduced its size to the present and it was given the sense of being the cross of each day that, as disciples of Christ we carry on our shoulders. For Carmelites in particular, it went on to express special dedication to the Blessed Virgin and the desire to imitate her life of dedication to Christ and to others. But the most important thing is that it is not an amulet or something with magical powers. It is a sacramental sign that makes present the Virgin's love for those who are good children of God, live in her friendship, that is, grace, and fulfill her law. Today it is substituted for daily use by the corresponding medal, both receive the same indulgences and can be worn by those who do not belong to the Brotherhood.

The Scapular is an external, sacramental sign that presupposes a life of grace. The convenient preparation consists of:

1 - Being very devoted to the Blessed Virgin Mary, especially under the dedication of Carmen de Cuyo.
2 - Participate in all the ceremonies that are performed in his honor.
3 - Know that it is a commitment for life, an Alliance between Our Lady and the one who receives it.
4 - Behave according to the norms and laws of the Church.
5 - One of the primary conditions imposed by the Blessed Virgin of Carmen is the permanent use of this scapular, or the medal that replaced it. This should be with the image of the Virgin and the Sacred Heart on the back.
6 - All the people who make up the Brotherhood of Carmel, promise to pray the Holy Rosary daily or at least 3 Hail Marys in honor of their Patron Saint.

The scapular of the Blessed Virgin Mary is imposed all the 1st Wednesday of the month, on July 16 and during the ninth, to people who wish to receive it. The promise of the Virgen del Carmen to Saint Simón Stock was that whoever died with the scapular would not suffer from eternal fire. In another appearance to Pope John XXII, he promised to remove souls who died piously from purgatory, with the scapular, on the Saturday following his death.

"The devotion of the scapular of Carmen has sent down upon the world a copious rain of spiritual and temporal graces." (Pius XII, 6-VIII-1950)

The Carmelite scapular is a sacramental, that is, a religious object that the Church has approved as a sign that helps us live holy and increase our devotion. The sacramentals must move our hearts to renounce all sin, even venial.

The scapular, being a sacramental, does not communicate graces to us as the sacraments do, but they dispose us to love God and the true contrition of sin if we receive them with devotion.

Human beings communicate by symbols. As well as we have flags, shields and also uniforms that identify us. Religious communities wear their habit as a sign of their consecration to God.

The laity cannot wear a habit, but those who wish to associate with the religious in their quest for holiness can use the scapular. The Virgin gave the Carmelites the scapular as a miniature habit that all devotees can wear to signify their consecration to it. It consists of a cord that is worn around the neck with two small pieces of brown fabric, one on the chest and the other on the back. Used under clothing, along with the rosary and the miraculous medal, the scapular is one of the most important Marian sacramentals.

Saint Alphonsus Ligorio, doctor of the Church, declares: "Just as men are proud that others wear their uniform, so Our Lady of the Holy Trinity of God is satisfied when her servants use her scapular as proof that they have dedicated themselves to their service, and they are members of the family of the Mother of God."

In 1246 they named Saint Simón General Stock of the Carmelite Order. He understood that without the intervention of the Virgin Mary, the order had little time left. Saint Simón resorted to Mary putting the order under his protection, since they belonged to him. In his prayer he called it "The flower of Carmel" and the "Star of the Sea" and begged for protection for the entire community. In response to this fervent prayer, on July 16, 1251, the Virgin appeared to Saint Simon Stock and gave him the scapular for the order with the following promise:

"This should be a sign and privilege for you and for all Carmelites: whoever dies using the scapular will not suffer eternal fire."

Although the scapular was given to the Carmelites, many lay people over time felt the call to live a life more committed to Carmelite spirituality and thus the brotherhood of the scapular began, where many lay people were added through devotion to the Virgin. Mary and the use of the scapular. The Church has extended the privilege of the scapular to the laity.

The Blessed Virgin Mary appeared to Pope John XXII in the fourteenth century and promised to those who fulfilled the requirements of this devotion that "as Mother of Mercy with my prayers, prayers, merits and special protection, I will help you, free as soon as possible from their sorrows, (...) their souls be transferred to bliss."

Since then, many popes, saints and Catholic theologians have explained that, according to this promise, whoever has the devotion to the scapular and uses it, will receive from Holy Mary at the time of death, the grace of perseverance in the state of grace (without mortal sin) or the grace of contrition (repentance). On the devotee's part, the scapular is a sign of his commitment to living the Christian life following the perfect example of the Blessed Virgin.

The scapular has 3 meanings:

1- Mary's love and maternal protection: The sign is a small cloth or cloak. We see how Mary when Jesus is born wraps him in a cloak. The Mother always tries to shelter her children. Wrapping her cloak is a very maternal sign of protection and care. Signal that wraps us in her motherly love. He makes us his. It covers us from the ignominy of our spiritual nakedness.

2- Belonging to Mary: We carry a brand that distinguishes us as her chosen children. The scapular becomes the symbol of our consecration to Mary. Consecration means belonging to Mary, that is, recognizing her maternal mission over us and surrendering ourselves to her in order to be guided, taught, shaped by her and in her heart. Thus we can be used by Her for the extension of the Kingdom of her Son.

3- The soft yoke of Christ: "Load my yoke on you and learn from me, because I am patient and humble of heart, and thus you will find relief. For my yoke is soft and my burden is light." (Matthew 11: 29-30)

In 1950 Pope Pius XII wrote about the scapular: "May it be your sign of consecration to the Immaculate Heart of Mary, which we are particularly in need of in these dangerous times." In these words of the Pope we see once again devotion to the Virgin of the Carmen is devotion to the Immaculate. Whoever wears the scapular must be aware of his consecration to God and the Virgin and be consistent in his thoughts, words and deeds.

<The scapular symbolizes that yoke that Jesus invites us to carry but that Mary helps us carry. Whoever wears the scapular must identify himself as a Catholic without fear of the rejections and difficulties that the yoke brings.>

The scapular is a sign of our Christian - Marian identity, intimately linked to the Virgin Mary with the purpose of living fully according to our baptism. It represents our decision to follow Jesus through Mary in the spirit of the religious, but adapted to our own vocation. This requires that we be humble, chaste, and obedient out of love for God.

By constantly using the scapular we make a silent request for continued assistance to the Blessed Mother. The Virgin Mary teaches and intercedes for us to receive the graces to live like her, open to the Lord with our hearts, listening to His Word, praying, discovering God in daily life, and close to the needs of our brothers. The scapular is also a reminder that our goal is heaven and everything in this world is happening.

In moments of temptation, we take the scapular in our hands and invoke the assistance of the Our Lady of the Holy Trinity of God, determined to be faithful to the Lord. She directs us to the Sacred Heart of her Divine Son and the demon is forced to retreat defeated.

Imposition of the Scapular:

- The imposition is preferably done in community.
- It is necessary that in the celebration the spiritual meaning of the graces united to the Scapular of the Virgin of the Carmen and the commitments assumed with this sign of devotion to the Blessed Virgin be well expressed.
- The first scapular must be blessed by a priest and imposed by him while saying the prayer:

"Receive this blessed scapular and ask the Blessed Virgin to take it without any stain of sin on its merits and to protect you from all evil and take you to eternal life."

Once the first scapular is blessed, the devotee does not need to ask for the blessing for later scapulars.

Worn scapulars, if blessed, should not be thrown away. They can be burned or buried as a sign of respect.

For its part, the medal-scapular has on one side the image of the Sacred Heart of Jesus and the image of the Blessed Virgin Mary on its reverse. In 1910, Pope Pius X stated that a person validly invested in his cloth scapular could wear the medal-scapular instead, provided he had legitimate reasons to substitute his cloth scapular for the medal-scapular. This concession was made at the request of missionaries in the countries of the tropics, where cloth scapulars soon deteriorate. Now, Pope Pius X and his successor, Pope Benedict XV, expressed their deep desire that people continue to wear the cloth scapular whenever possible, and that they do not substitute the cloth scapular for the scapular medal without first mediating reason enough. Vanity or fear of professing your faith in public cannot be reasons that satisfy Our Lady. These people risk not receiving the promise of Carmen's scapular. ("Give great importance to your scapular" from the World Apostolate of Fatima, Washington, NJ 07882-0976 USA).

The Popes and Saints have warned many times about not abusing our mother's promise as if we could save ourselves by wearing the scapular without conversion. Pope Pius XI warns us: "although it is true that the Virgin Mary loves in a special way those who are devoted to her, those who wish to have her as an aid at the time of death, must in life earn this privilege with a life of rejection to sin and living to give honor."

Living in sin and using the scapular as an anchor of salvation is committing a sin of presumption since faith and fidelity to the commandments is necessary for all who seek the love and protection of Our Lady of the Holy Trinity of God.

Saint Claude de la Colombiere warns: "Your questions: What if I wanted to die with my sins? I answer you, then you will die in sin, but you will not die with your scapular."

The Sabbath Privilege is a promise of the Virgin that consists in the liberation from purgatory, the first Saturday (day that the Church has dedicated to the Virgin), after death through a special intercession of the Virgin. It originated in a bull or edict that was proclaimed by Pope John XXII on March 3, 1322 as a result of an appearance he had of the Virgin in which he promised for those who fulfilled the requirements of this devotion that "as Mother of Mercy, With my prayers, prayers, merits and special protection, I will help you so that, as soon as possible, free from your sorrows, your souls may be transferred to bliss."

Conditions for this privilege to apply:

1) Use the scapular with fidelity.
2) Observe chastity according to the state of life.
3) I pray the office of the Virgin (prayers and readings in honor of the Virgin) or pray 5 decades of the rosary daily.

Pope Paul V confirmed in an official proclamation that all believers could be taught about the Sabbath privilege.

It is evident that the Virgin Mary wants to reveal to us in a special way the scapular. Lucia (seer of the Virgin of Fatima, later converted to Sister Mary of the Immaculate Heart) reports that, in the last appearance (October, 1917, day of the miracle of the sun), the Virgin Mary came dressed in the Carmelite habit and with the scapular in hand and remembered that his true children carried it with reverence. She also asked that those who consecrate themselves to it use it as a sign of that consecration.

Pope Pius XII frequently spoke of the Scapular. In 1951, the 700th anniversary of the appearance of Our Lady to Saint Simon Stock, the Pope before a large audience in Rome urged that the Scapular be used as "Sign of Consecration to the Immaculate Heart of Mary" (as requested by the Virgin at Fatima.) The Scapular also represents the sweet yoke of Jesus that Mary helps us to bear. And finally, the Pope continued, The Scapular marks us as the chosen children of Mary and becomes for us, as the Germans call it, a "Dress of Grace."

The same day that Saint Simon Stock received the Scapular and the promise from Mary, he was called to assist a dying man who was desperate. When he arrived he put the Scapular over the man, asking the Virgin Mary to keep the promise she had just made to him. Immediately the man repented, confessed and died in God's grace."

Blessed Pope Gregory X was buried with his scapular only 25 years after the Vision of the Scapular. 600 years later when his tomb was opened, his scapular was intact.

Saint Alfonso Ligorio and Saint Juan Bosco had a special devotion to the Virgin of the Carmen and used the Scapular. When Saint

Alphonsus Ligorio died they buried him with his priestly garments and his Scapular. Many years later when they opened his grave they found that his body and all the clothes were in dust, however, his Scapular was intact. The Scapular of Saint Alphonsus is on display at his Monastery in Rome.

Saint Alphonsus Ligorio tells us: "Modern heretics mock the use of the Scapular. They discredit it as a vain and absurd insignificance."

Saint Peter Claver, became a slave to slaves for love. Every month a ship with slaves arrived in Cartagena, Colombia. Saint Peter strove for the salvation of each one. He organized catechists, prepared them for baptism, and invested them with the Scapular. Some clerics accused the saint of indiscreet zeal. However, he continued his work until he had more than 300,000 converts.

Saint Claudio de Colombiere (spiritual director of Saint Margaret Mary) stated: "I wanted to know if Mary had really taken an interest in me, and in the Scapular She has given me the most palpable security. I just need to open my eyes, She has given her protection to this Scapular: "Whoever dies clothed in it will not suffer eternal fire." And I add; "Because all the ways of loving the Blessed Virgin and the different ways of expressing that love cannot be equally pleasing to her and therefore do not help us to the same degree in reaching heaven, I say this without hesitation for a moment, The Carmelite Scapular is his favorite! And he continues saying; "No devotion has been confirmed with more authentic miracles than the Carmelite Scapular."

"A Chicago priest was called to go and assist a dying man who had been away from his faith and the sacraments for many years. The dying man did not want to receive him or speak to him. But the priest insisted and taught him the Scapular that He was wearing. He asked if he would let him put it on. The man accepted as long as the priest left him alone. An hour later the dying man called the priest because he wanted to confess and die in grace and friendship with God."

The demon hates the Scapular. One day Venerable Francisco Yepes dropped the Scapular. As he put it on, the demon howled: "Take off the habit that takes so many souls from us!"

A Carmelite missionary from the Holy Land was called to supply the anointing of the sick in the year 1944. He noticed that as he walked, his feet sank deeper and deeper into the mud until, trying to find firm ground, he slipped into a well mud in which it sank towards death. He thought of the Virgin and kissed her habit which was Scapular. He then looked towards the Carmel Mountain shouting: "Holy Mother of Carmel! Help me! Save me!". A moment later he found himself on solid ground. He later testified: "I know that I was saved by the Blessed Virgin through her Carmelite Scapular. My shoes disappeared into the mud and I was covered in it, but I walked the remaining two miles, praising Mary."

In the summer of 1845 the English ship, "King of the Ocean" was in the midst of a fierce hurricane. The waves whipped him mercilessly and the end seemed near. A Protestant minister named Fisher accompanied by his wife and children and other passengers went to the deck to beg for mercy and forgiveness. Among the crew was Irishman John McAuliffe. Looking at the gravity of the situation, the young man opened his shirt, took off the Scapular and, making the Sign of the Cross on the furious waves, threw it into the ocean. Just then the wind died down. Only one more wave reached the deck, bringing with it the Scapular that was deposited at the boy's feet.

During the events, the minister had been carefully observing McAuliffe's actions and witnessed the miracle. When questioning the young man, they were informed about the Blessed Virgin and her Scapular. Mr. Fisher and his family resolved to enter the Catholic Church as soon as possible and thus enjoy the great protection of the Scapular of Our Lady of the Holy Trinity of God.

In May 1957, a Carmelite priest in Germany published an extraordinary story of how the Scapular had freed a home from fire. An entire row of houses had caught fire in Westboden, Germany. The pious residents of a two-family house, upon seeing the fire, immediately hung a Scapular on the front entrance door. Sparkles flew over and around her, but the house remained intact. In 5 hours, 22 homes had been burned to ashes. The only construction that remained intact, in the midst of destruction, was the one with the Scapular attached to its door. The hundreds of people who came to see the place that the Scapular had saved are eyewitnesses to the power of the Scapular and the intercession of Our Lady of the Holy Trinity of the Holy Spirit.

In October 1952, a Texas Air Force officer wrote the following: "Six months after I started using the Scapular, I experienced a remarkable change in my life. Almost immediately, I began attending Mass every day. During Lent I lived fervently like never before. I was initiated into the practice of meditation and found myself making weak attempts on the path of perfection. I have been trying to live with God and I credit the Scapular of Mary." (GARMENT OF GRACE - e-Catholic 2000)

Let us remember that the scapular is a powerful sign of the love and maternal protection of Mary and of her call to a life of holiness and without sin. Wearing the scapular is a response of love to the Mother who came to give us a gift of her mercy. We must use it as a reminder that we belong to her, that we want to imitate her and live in grace under her protective cloak. Plenary indulgence can be gained:

- the day the scapular is received
- on May 16, at the Feast of San Simón Stock.
- on July 16, at the Solemnity of the Blessed Virgin of Carmen,
- on July 20, at the Feast of the Prophet Saint Elias.
- on October 1, on the Feast of Saint Therese of the Child Jesus.
- on October 15, at the Feast of Saint Teresa of Jesus.
- on November 14, at the Feast of All Saints of the Order.
- on December 14, at the Feast of San Juan De La Cruz.

5.- The Virgin Mary in the Holy Spirit in this new millennium

Father Nicolás Schwizer maintains that today, more than ever, our journey as Christians costs a lot. Infidelity, doubt, disorientation and insecurity, even in the midst of the Church itself, hinder our Christian life. According to him, we need more clarity and security, we look for a light to be able to orient ourselves in the darkness of our time. This light for us is the Virgin Mary. She is the vital model and intuitive teaching for the life of all human beings and especially for the life of believers in the Holy Trinity of the Holy Spirit.

The Virgin Mary is our vital model, she is the light that guides us through the darkness that covers the world today. She is the only vaccine that can save humanity from this terrible pandemic that plagues the world. Father Nicolás Schwizer highlights her as a reverse of Eve, as a new Eve. We know that Eve is Adam's companion and helper in original sin, in the ruin of mankind. Mary is also not merely a passive instrument, but a companion and helper of the Holy Spirit and Jesus Christ for the salvation of the world. Eve's disobedience and unbelief are offset by Mary's obedience and faith. Eve brought death, Mary brings life. Thus the Immaculate Virgin, the new Eve reveals herself to us as the Supreme Being. In this world of evil, the Holy Spirit preserves the original idea of purity and holiness of paradise in the person of the Virgin Mary. Conceived by the Holy Spirit, His Own Being, without sin, to join the Father and the consubstantial Son in the bosom of the Holy Trinity of God.

The Blessed Virgin Mary represents the perfection of the work of the Holy Spirit and it is in her that the essence of the redemption of Christ in all its fullness is conjugated. The Bible does not express in its content the true greatness of the divine personality of Mary as the feminine part of the Trinity of the Holy Spirit. She, although incarnated in a human figure, has always been part of the Supreme Being, like her Son, Jesus Christ and the Holy Spirit.

Therefore, the angel Gabriel declared that She is "full of grace". Although in truth, her whole person is fully filled with all the gifts of the Holy Spirit, since all perfection and redemption comes from Her Own Being. From her incarnation She came with the perfect harmony between her body, soul and holy spirit. When we look at the image of the Virgin Mary, great feelings of desires and hopes awaken in us.

Before the creation of the world, the Holy Spirit chose us to have the opportunity to be part of Him. All human beings were created in the image and likeness of the Holy Spirit and we all have the opportunity to become new men and women. The Holy Spirit infused us through baptism with the divine life of Mary and of Christ and we should all aspire to maintain this gift throughout our lives.

Through the baptism in the Holy Spirit we are all called to become new human beings, in the image of Christ and the Virgin Mary. We must all imitate Mary and Jesus, and seek to fulfill the mission of "Thy will be done in me" to achieve harmony with the Holy Spirit. And so see the new man born and grow in us, whom we so admire in Jesus and the new woman we admire in Mary.

"The Blessed Virgin Mary is a model of renewal and hope, but also, Mother and Educator of new men and women. Her womb, in which God was formed, is the best mold to forge human beings in the image of the Holy Spirit. The Church fathers called her not only a creature of paradise, but also the door to paradise. Door to paradise because it attracts and educates us towards that ideal, and introduces us to paradise." (Father Nicolás Schwizer, catholic.net)

5.1.- The Virgin Mary; a sure path to salvation.

We must not be confused, there is no risk in the Marian cult: Many mistakenly argue that Mary apart from Christ, who makes her "competition", and who is placed as "screen" between God and us. At the origin of this fear are usually negative experiences, caused by deviant practices of the Mariana cult, or false approaches to the person of Mary. But such fears do not correspond to the reality willed by the Holy Spirit and so it is proclaimed by the Christian Marian Church of the Holy Spirit in its life and in its doctrine.

The Trinity of the Holy Spirit is the true center of our faith, it is the true reason for our trust, it is the last end of our love. Jesus Christ and the Virgin Mary are the means arranged by the Holy Spirit to help the human being to achieve a harmonious harmony with Him. In the triune God, Jesus and Mary, both are part of the central mysteries of the Christian-Marian faith. Jesus represents the masculine part of the Being and Mary the feminine part, and both were formed into a single "Divine Entity" called the Holy Spirit.

"Do whatever he tells you" are the last words of the Virgin Mary preserved in the mutilated Gospel of the Bible. And more than the wedding servants, they are words addressed to men and women of all time. It is regrettable that many other words expressed by Her at transcendental moments of the birth of our era were not included in these important stories to know more deeply all the longing, the experience and the mission of Mary in her ministry. Today, it is difficult to recognize that Mary is the true center of the Christian faith. She, by her leading role in the general history of salvation and in creation, is by obligation the center of focus of the men and women of the new times.

Saint John Paul II said: "Mary was truly united to Jesus. Many of his words have not been preserved in the Gospel; but those who are left take us back to their Son and to his word. In Cana of Galilee he addressed the servants with these words: "Do whatever he tells you.""

Today, the Virgin Mary continues to repeat those same words "Do what he tells you" which is the same as "do what I tell you" or "do what the Holy Spirit says."

The Virgin Mary is for us the normal path to salvation through the Trinity of the Holy Spirit. Since, if the path by which Jesus reached the human being is Mary, then, precisely, Mary is the path by which we can reach Christ. When we give Mary a privileged place in our hearts, and we commit ourselves to her education, then we are on the way to her Son, who is her own being. Then She leads us to Christ in the Holy Spirit. She is aware of this truth that Pope Pius X said: "Mary is not only the normal way to Christ but also the easiest, shortest and safest way to Christ," and continues saying about her: "The Divine Virgin Mary gives a vital knowledge of Christ."

Devotion to the Virgin Mary is one of the great gifts that the Holy Spirit or God has given to the people: it is demonstrated by the great enthusiasm with which the image of the Virgin has been received in all places. And the more we love the Virgin, the more we love Christ Jesus. Since they are in themselves, a single Being in the Holy Spirit.

The divinity of Mary represents the feminine and maternal divinity of the Trinity of the Holy Spirit. She gives us familiarity with the supernatural world and makes the Marian Christian faith a similarity between life in the Church and in the home, of men and women forming families like mothers, fathers, sons, daughters, brothers and sisters. The power of Mary explains the strength and roots of Marian devotion in the people, despite the fact that the intentions of the men of Christianity have been to relegate her to a simple role as a servant, despite being the true Queen of the Universe.

By studying a little about the main Saints of all times we can realize that each one of them, each of them, prove with their lives the truth and the importance of Mary on the path of Christianity. They have been almost without exception men and women with great Marian devotion. Many of them have even consecrated themselves to the Virgin and She, without fail, has led them to the Trinity of the Holy Spirit. This shows that all the love that we give to the Divine Virgin Mary, She takes it to the bowels where the Most High is born. This is how our love finds, through Mary, the easiest, shortest, safest and most fruitful way to the Holy Spirit.

The life of the Virgin Mary, by its very origin, is complemented in the composition of the Holy Spirit with the life of Our Lord Jesus Christ. The Virgin Mary is divine, holy and full of all the Grace of her Creator Spirit. She is the beginning of her own infinity. She represents the first moment of the existence of the Being. She is called tabernacle, tabernacle, sanctuary of the Holy Spirit. Mary cohabitates in the Holy Spirit or God in a totally unique and superior way. The Spirit of holiness works in and through the Virgin Mary.

The Holy Spirit has always acted together with the Virgin. Through their union, Jesus Christ, "the Son of God," was born. The Holy Spirit and Mary are the Father and the Mother of Jesus Christ, and the three form in themselves a single Divine Being. The Feminine Part of the Holy Spirit that is God incarnated in the human figure of the Blessed Virgin Mary in a totally voluntary and free way, to surrender to the Holy Spirit, and through this relationship to give an example of family union and sacrifice as the First Family of the Universe.

The Holy Spirit wanted to give an example of wife, mother and sister through his incarnation in the Virgin Mary, and to give example of father, son and brother in the person of Jesus Christ. Each one of them had to go their own way for the creation of faith. And when the great Hour of sacrifice arrived, on Mount Calvary, Mother's natural wants and needs were controlled in Her. At that moment, everything was subject to the will of the Holy Spirit. How difficult it was for Her to bear the crucifixion of her Son in her presence, and although they both had the power to change the situation, it was also her own and voluntary decision that all these events happened the way they happened. Both were sure that everything should be consummated in this way for them to be able to enter in a more perfect way, giving an example of life and sacrifice to humanity.

Despite her divinity, Mary has been an example of human goodness. Despite the fact that we human beings had not known how to recognize her true position in creation, she has not bothered with us and has supported the needy of the world.

In the beginning of Christianity, Mary showed signs of being the main instrument of faith by becoming the Spirit of Pentecost. On that occasion, Mary led the apostles and disciples to the Upper Room, conveyed to them her deep longing for them to carry out the will of the Holy Spirit and gave them the strength of the Most High to work on the whole Church in such a way.

At Pentecost the light of the Holy Spirit was filled with Mary. There she was completely absorbed and transformed in Him. Already in her life she had a spiritualized human body, that is, the Spirit transformed into a body of flesh and blood, which could not be destroyed since it was not corruptible. After Pentecost it was prepared for the ascension in body and soul towards its origin; the Holy Spirit, in the bosom of the Holy Trinity. She and her son, Jesus, gave us an example of how we can also insert ourselves in the Holy Spirit.

The best of the gifts of the Holy Spirit to humanity, after its creation is the incarnation of Mary to father her son Jesus. Jesus dying on the cross, despite being dispossessed of everything, still possessed the most precious Treasure in the universe, His Divine Mother. Which gave us so that in her departure She would continue to protect us. John 19: 25-27 tells us about this episode of Jesus in his last minutes on the cross, and the strength of his mother standing before him without weakness despite the pain that tore her soul, devoid of all divinity. In this narration it is noted that the three women most loved by Jesus were present at the time of the distribution of the garments and the draw of the Savior's robe. Juan makes it very clear here that this robe was the work of Mary, the mother of Jesus, and that it is precisely this draw that makes the memories sprout in the dying person's head and what prompts him to focus his attention on the group of disciples who They stood guard at the foot of the cross. Since the group of onlookers had moved away to their different chores. Only the guard soldiers and the small group of faithful women remained, since all the other male Apostles, out of fear, were not at that important moment next to the crucified Messiah.

The group of faithful women was led by Mary, the mother of the Son of God, who lay dying hanging on the cross. But She was not alone, there were two other women by her side: Martha, the sister of her Mother and Maria Magdalena, a faithful follower. As John the Evangelist narrates, they were there by the cross: "Mary, his mother; Martha, the sister of his mother, the wife of Cleopas; and María Magdalena." The three women approached the cross, to try to perceive the last breath of Jesus, since no law prevented the relatives from approaching the condemned. The soldiers guarded the crosses to prevent any possible form of manifestation of the multitudes following Jesus; but they did not remove the curious who came to see in small groups. There really was little the guards could fear from those three defenseless women. The soldiers themselves must have had compassion on that condemned man whom so many people followed and at the moment of truth, only three faithful women remained.

We know that these three women were standing by the cross and that they stood firm until the last breath of Jesus. Mary had a moment of fainting within her human condition, since she had been stripped of her divinity at those moments, and of her own free will, to be able to suffer, "in her own flesh", along with her son, those terrible moments of the crucifixion. But the divine Mother always had the support of Mary Magdalene, who from that day on became her daughter at the request of Jesus himself, who among his last words said to them both: "Mother, here is your daughter; Daughter, here is your mother." This transcendental fact, the manipulators of the word of God, when writing the Bible attributed it to John, although the evangelist himself clearly describes that the disciple that Jesus loved the most was Mary Magdalene.

The Virgin Mary is much more than a simple devotion, more than a flag, more than a patron saint, She is the true origin of life, the origin of the Creator. We must recognize the divinity of Mary, and place it in its just dimension together with the Holy Spirit and his Son Jesus. Mary is the genuine representation of the synthesis between faith and life, between the divine and the human. Modifying a little the words of Father José Kentenich we would say: Whoever wants to be a builder and collaborator for today's world, must be linked to Mary. All humans, regardless of peoples, races or cultures, must be linked to Her so that She may lead them to the Holy Trinity of the Holy Spirit.

Mary teaches us, with her being and her actions, that all perfection and redemption comes from the Holy Spirit, in which She and Jesus Christ are fully condensed. In Mary the Holy Spirit can document the perfection of her work. Mary, as a human person, is the one who most fully realizes the ideal of the human being as Christians in this new millennium. With her we can find the lost paradise, of desires and hopes, and achieve the perfect harmony between the body, the soul and the spirit.

All Christians are converted into new human beings on the day of our baptism. At that moment, the Holy Spirit infuses into our souls the divine lives of Christ and Mary. What for the holy Mother and her Son is a gift, for us it is a lifelong struggle. Therefore, all of us are called to become new men and women, in harmony with the image of Christ and of Mary. We are all invited to imitate Jesus and the Virgin Mary in the Holy Spirit, and to open ourselves to his will, making our lives according to his wishes. The Word became flesh in Mary and Jesus, and today it continues to become flesh in the men and women devoted to Mary and Jesus in the Holy Spirit.

Mary is the fullness of love. His life and actions today prove that this is true. Because what most characterizes her life is that she lives in full communion of love not only with the Holy Spirit, but also with human beings. This is how the Virgin Mary appears from the first scenes of the Gospel to the present day with her glorious and generous appearances. She lives linked by deep bonds of love for human beings of all times.

The Holy Spirit is always in Mary, and Mary is always the Holy Spirit. From the very moment she was incarnated, he created her fully with all his own gifts. That is why Mary is also called "the Immaculate," the sinless one. To sin, it is necessary not to fulfill the mandate to love God and neighbor, which She fully fulfills since She is herself God in her feminine part.

Salvation through Jesus Christ, as it happens through Mary, begins with liberation from sin and return to a life full of love. This is achieved through the opening of the heart to the Divine Being and to all our fellow human beings, while at the same time we cast out selfishness and pride. Let us ask the Virgin Mary to help us free ourselves from everything that is in the heart against love. Let us ask him for the strength to overcome in ourselves the pride and selfishness that separate us more and more from each other. Let us ask him to open our hearts to love for God and other human beings. He who opens his heart to love, by living in communion with the Holy Trinity of the Holy Spirit and with his fellows, is already saved, and freed from the petty feelings that self-destruct the human being.

The Virgin Mary teaches us that love helps us to be caring and compassionate. She shares within the Holy Spirit with the Father and the Son, his divine greatness and his mission. His love and compassion have become a communion of life and work, and a communion of joy and sorrow.

Our Lady of the Holy Trinity of God has a charism, a special gift to unite hearts and open them to love, to make us brothers and sisters. She wants to make us understand that all the happiness of the Gospel of her Son is summed up in these simple words: living in communion with the Holy Spirit and with our fellow men. Our Lady wants us human beings to live in an environment of unity and love. It asks us to create, cultivate, and refine it permanently in our homes, our workplaces, our neighborhoods, and our groups, as well as through social media and the internet. She invites us, at the same time, to build all together; rulers and ruled, rich and poor, employers and employees, priests and laity, a fairer, more humane, more supportive society that expresses its real help to those who suffer, to those who depend on us and to those who come to us.

All these situations are the reality of the modern world in which we have had to live and which we must leave as an inheritance to our sons and our daughters. For this reason it is necessary, today more than ever, to give life, to give light, to give hope, making known the greatness of the Holy Spirit, in his three divine persons; Father, Mother and Son. The only one who can redeem all the sins of the world, restore our worth and dignity, and give us abundant life for all eternity. In these precise moments of the third millennium we must experience a new advent, a new wait for the manifestation of the Holy Trinity of the Holy Spirit in a world that so much needs to find its origin, which we can only achieve by tuning ourselves to the Holy Spirit through one of his human personifications: Yahweh, Jesus or the Virgin Mary.

Two elements were needed for Jesus to come into the world: the incarnation of the feminine part of the Holy Spirit, in Mary, and the Work and Grace of the Holy Spirit Himself in the divine womb of Mary. In this way it was established that every advent of Christ for the world requires the joint action of the Trinity of the Holy Spirit, in the Divine Persons of the Holy Spirit (the Father), the Virgin Mary (the Mother) and the Jesus himself (the Son).

We need to establish the true composition of the Trinity of the Holy Spirit to ask for a new outpouring of the Holy Spirit on a new Pentecost in which all of us faithful recognize the real personality of the Virgin Mary in the Holy Spirit. Together all united without sectarianism to prepare a new Advent, a new era of faith and hope.

The union of the Holy Spirit as the Father and the Holy Spirit as the Mother, incarnated in Mary, resulted in the holy birth of the Holy Spirit as the Son, who is called Jesus Christ. But the wonderful thing about this mission is that it is not limited to that precise moment, but that it is a mission that is eternally manifested in souls, to promote that, by the divine union of both, Christ is born in every heart that opens to him day after day. All graces come to us from the Holy Spirit as the Father through the merits of the Holy Spirit as the Mother and the Holy Spirit as the Son. They are distributed through the work of Mary, not only as a reflection of her holiness, but also as a central part of the Supreme Divinity that She holds. As the wife of the Holy Spirit as the Father and due to her intimate and close relationship with Him, Mary collaborates freely and consciously in the work and work of sanctification of the Holy Spirit, her Own Being.

It is proven that Mary is not the simple human instrument of the Holy Spirit, she is the reflection of her own work in the process of sanctification of souls. She brings to all souls the graces earned by her own Self, in Jesus Christ, the Lamb of God sacrificed on the Cross. We see how the presence of Mary, inevitably attracts the outpouring of the Holy Spirit in the Church, since in herself is her own Being. Mary is the feminine Part of the Supreme Being in the Holy Spirit that is God. Mary has always remained among us, but today more than ever, Mary has been visiting the world, in a way never seen before, possibly waiting for us to become aware of her divinity before her bringing a new Pentecost on the Church and the world. Mary is acting in the Holy Spirit to bring a new advent of Christ to the Church and to the world, as a continuation of the passage of the visitation and that of Pentecost.

We have seen in the Church in the last 50 years a great manifestation of the Holy Trinity of the Holy Spirit that seems to be a sign of the times that reveals to us the first fruits of advancing to a new Pentecost where all human beings will have a total and complete knowledge on Jesus Christ and the Virgin Mary in the Holy Spirit. As we can see in the words of Pope Paul VI: What need, first and last, do we see for this our blessed and beloved Church? What do you really need? We must say it, trembling and in prayer, because it is its mystery, it is its life: it is the Holy Spirit, animator and sanctifier of the Church, its divine breath, the wind of its sails, its unifying principle, its interior source of light and of energy, his support and his comforter, his wellspring of charisma and songs, his peace and joy, his pledge and prelude to blessed and eternal life. The Church needs a perennial Pentecost: it needs fire in the heart, word on the lips, prophecy in the gaze. The Church needs to be a temple of the Holy Trinity of the Holy Spirit, that is, of total cleanliness and interior life. The Church and the world need more than ever for the prodigy of Pentecost to continue in history, like Paul VI said in 1972.

The Church needs a new Pentecost and to achieve this we must unite in prayer to get in touch with Jesus Christ and the Virgin Mary in the Holy Spirit, and allow ourselves to be guided, formed and shaped by their being. The recognition of the divinity of Mary in the Holy Spirit, wonderfully renews our era of faith by giving rise to a new Pentecost, and grants that the new Christian - Marian Church of the Holy Spirit, keep praying perseveringly and insistently as one heart and one mind, together with Jesus Christ and the Virgin Mary in the Holy Spirit, thus promoting the divine reign of the true Holy Trinity of God, a kingdom of justice, love and peace.

Through these prayers the Holy Spirit is revealing to us the relevant role of Mary, and just like the first coming of the Messiah was through the incarnation of Mary and the power of the Holy Spirit, this new advent or re-emergence of the body Mystical, it is developing through the Virgin Mary in the Holy Spirit. It has been shown that Mary plays an indispensable role in this preparation of the Christian – Marian Church so that together we may cry out to the Holy Spirit, "Come, Lord," "Come and Queen, doing your will in the heart of every man and woman."

The Holy Spirit has manifested in these times to reveal to us the true divinity of Mary, since in the past the meanness of men kept her hidden from this world at a lower point than the most insignificant woman. But today the Holy Spirit wants to make us see that God Himself is a masterpiece of his own hands and that is why He wants to be praised and glorified through our contemplation of the wonders that the Virgin Mary is doing today in humanity.

Mary is the way that our Lord Jesus Christ came to us the first time, and it is still the way that we can get to Him. She is the surest way and the direct way to find Jesus Christ and find Him perfectly. In such a way that, if the salvation of the world began through the incarnation of Mary, it is through her that we must reach the fullness of the Holy Spirit in her Son. She shines in these moments, more than ever, in mercy, power and grace.

As Pope Saint John Paul II will put it: "It is precisely because the Holy Spirit wants to powerfully reveal and manifest Mary in these times of great difficulty for the Church, that the specific strategy for the victory of the Church over the Prince of Darkness It is the consecration to the Immaculate Heart of Mary. Victory if it comes, it will come through Mary ... Christ will overcome through Her, because He wants the victories of the Church in the contemporary world and in the future world to be united to Her." (John Paul II; Crossing the threshold of Hope).

In the same way we could see in the stories about the Virgin of Fatima that She said to the girl Lucia: "In the end my Immaculate Heart will triumph." For this reason we must be confident and with high faith that this triumph of the Immaculate Heart of Mary and the triumph of the Holy Trinity of the Holy Spirit in this new Pentecost are the same triumph; the triumph of "Jesus Christ and Virgin Mary in the Holy Spirit."

This great joint triumph of Jesus Christ and Virgin Mary in the Holy Spirit, in the Church and the world, will bring with it a new advent of Christ, in an era in which, as Pope Saint John Paul II said, humanity seems having lost his consciousness and his heart. It is in these precise moments in which we most need the immaculate heart of Mary and Jesus, today that man increasingly hardens his heart, narrowing the barrier between good and evil, being unable to deliver true love, not to be greed and worldly.

The Holy Spirit became a fruitful woman, in Mary with Her, in Her and of Her he produced his masterpiece, which is Himself, made man, in Jesus Christ. For this reason, the more involved we are with Mary, the more powerful and fruitful the Holy Spirit will be by placing his gifts on each of us to reproduce the great work of Jesus Christ.

The Holy Spirit not only wants the divinity of Mary to be known, but has made it a condition to establish her new reign, with a new spiritual presence of Jesus Christ and Virgin Mary, at a new Pentecost. In such a way that her Church, her people and nations are consecrated to the Immaculate Heart of Mary, so that as She reigns over our hearts, she leads us on the safe path and prepares us for the Reign of the Immaculate Heart of Jesus.

Now, the grace of the Holy Spirit is and will be forever Christ; he is the sole revealer and bearer to man of the Creator's love. And this leads us to discover the true mystery that Mary assigned herself. She, from the first moment of her incarnation, is of Christ. In other words, from the first moment of her existence, she participates in advance of the redemptive and sanctifying action that would be carried out by her eternal Son and by the Holy Spirit, the same who, through the Incarnation, became her own son. Mary is the Mother of the same Being who engendered Her. Saint John Paul II correctly expressed this mystery when he said: "Mary receives the life of him to whom she herself gave life." (Redemptoris Mater, 10).

The divine motherhood of Mary was an absolutely unique and unrepeatable fact: the Holy Spirit became man in the bowels of the Virgin Mary, her Own Being. With the relationship between the Holy Spirit the Father and the Holy Spirit the Mother, represented in Mary, the son of God was begotten. The action of the Holy Spirit in Mary, her own Being, was the first Pentecost, and it is here when the Holy Spirit burst upon all believers, just as Mary does today, in her different advocations around the world.

María de todas las Vírgenes

Nuestra Señora de la Santísima Trinidad de Dios

"Ave María Purísima, sin pecados concebida."
Dios te salve María,
llena eres de gracia,
el Señor es contigo.
Bendita tú eres entre todas las mujeres, y
Bendito es el fruto de tu vientre, Jesús.

Santa María, Madre de Dios,
ruega por nosotros, los pecadores,
ahora y en la hora de nuestra muerte.

Santa Madre de Dios, glorificada junto al Hijo, en el Espíritu Santo.
Amén.

ÍNDICE

1.0.- Introducción

Durante el transcurso de la historia de la humanidad han surgieron grandes controversias sobre el tema de Dios. La mayoría de los pueblos de la antigüedad creían en la existencia de multiples dioses, pero el pueblo hebreo desde muy temprano logró establecer la creencia en la existencia de un solo y único Dios verdadero. Luego de la vida, obra, muerte y resurrección de Nuestro Señor Jesucristo esta creencia fue fortalecida por la iglesia cristiana, agregando la confesión sobre la existencia de la Santísima Trinidad de Dios; en una composición consustancial de Dios Padre, Dios Hijo y Dios Espíritu Santo, en un solo Ser como la conocemos hasta hoy.

Los grandes eruditos cristianos han debatido profundamente sus diferentes pensamientos e ideas acerca de la trinidad de Dios, pero, ya sea por error o por omisión, ninguno ha tenido el privilegio de revelar la verdadera composición de la *Santísima Trinidad del Dios* como lo hacemos ahora, en este libro.

Con un lenguaje directo y sencillo, apoyado en la Fe, conduciré a mis lectores hacia el camino de las revelaciones de la verdadera composición de la *Santísima Trinidad de Dios*. Veremos como El *Espíritu Santo* se revela en la Biblia, asi como las diferentes interpretaciones que se han hecho del *Espíritu Santo*, los dones y características del *Espíritu Santo,* siguiendo con la Verdadera Composición de la *Santísima Trinidad del Espíritu Santo y* las diferentes personas o figuraciones humanas asumidas por el *Espíritu Santo* durante el transcurso de la historia de la humanidad.

En nuestro análisis comenzamos con El *Espíritu Santo* como "El Padre", luego con el *Espíritu Santo* como "El Hijo", Jesucristo, para concluir con la revelación de *la Virgen María procedente y asumida en el Espíritu Santo*; su encarnación, su misión en la tierra antes y después de su Asunción, y sus Obras y Milagros a través de sus diferentes advocaciones, con lo cual se demuestra que ella posee Poder Divino como el Espíritu santo, Padre e Hijo, y que los tres, a la vez, son un mismo y único Ser llamado *Espíritu Santo* que es el Dios verdadero, el Dios Creador eterno y omnipotente.

Para guiar al lector en la búsqueda de esta verdad haremos un amplio uso de referencias bíblicas, de diferentes evangelios y de algunos libros de diferentes analistas que han tratado el tema de una u otra forma, para reforzar nuestros argumentos y hacer de este libro un documento valioso para el estudio de la verdadera composición de la *Santísima Trinidad del Espíritu Santo*, colocando a *la Virgen María* en su justo lugar de Madre y Esposa del *Espíritu Santo, su Propio Ser.*

Hemos titulado este libro *"María de todas las Vírgenes;* Nuestra Señora de la Santísima Trinidad de Dios", para sentar las bases del desarrollo de un importante debate acerca de la verdadera composición de la *Santísima Trinidad del Espíritu Santo*; su persona, su composición y su obra. Ya que haciendo consciencia de la verdadera composición del *Espíritu Santo* podemos conocer más acerca de las formas y los medios a través de los cuales actúa sobre cada individuo del Universo.

La primera parte del titulo del libro; "María de todas las Vírgenes" deja claro que, aunque hay muchas advocaciones con diferentes nombres y diferentes rostros físicos, solo existe una Virgen María, Madre de Dios. La segunda parte del titulo; "Nuestra Señora de la Santísima Trinidad de Dios" establece que la Virgen María forma parte consustancial e indivisa en el Espíritu Santo, con "el Padre" y "el Hijo"; los tres son uno en el Espíritu Santo que es el Dios de la creación.

Los eruditos cristianos plantean que "El *Espíritu Santo* es la tercera persona de la indivisa trinidad de Dios; que eternamente procede del Padre y del Hijo; verdadero Dios con ellos, de majestad y gloria co-igual; como ellos eterno, omnipotente, omnipresente, omnisciente, justo, misericordioso; que junto con el Padre y el Hijo es el Santo, el Señor de los ejércitos. Como tal puede hacer la obra que él, según el consejo de Dios, debe hacer — la santificación de la humanidad pecaminosa, trayendo a los pecadores a la fe en su Salvador, preservando y fortaleciéndolos en esta fe, capacitándolos para demostrar su fe con buenas obras, y finalmente reuniéndolos en los graneros celestiales." (*Abiding Word*, Barbara Reid and Cardinal Francis George, Vol. I, p. 57).

Como se puede ver en la anterior cita durante el transcurso de la historia del cristianismo los grandes analistas han considerado al Espíritu Santo como la tercera persona de la divinidad de Dios, sin embargo, en esta oportunidad les vamos a demostrar a nuestros lectores y al mundo que todas las teorías expuestas hasta ahora son incorrectas o incompletas, ya que el *Espíritu Santo* es en realidad el *Espíritu de Dios*, es decir, el Espíritu Santo es la esencia divina de "Aquel Todo" llamado Dios y personificado en el Padre "Dios", en Jesucristo "el Hijo de Dios" y la Virgen María "la Madre y Esposa de Dios." De forma que, el *Espíritu Santo* es el Padre, el *Espíritu Santo* es el Hijo y el *Espíritu Santo* es la Madre y la Esposa de Dios a la misma vez, y los tres son un único e indiviso Ser llamado Espíritu Santo que es el Dios eterno.

< *"La tierra era un caos total, las tinieblas cubrían el abismo, y contra un fondo frío, oscuro, sin vida, el Espíritu de Dios (el Espíritu Santo) se movía sobre la faz de las aguas."* (Génesis 1:2)>

En este libro demostraremos que *la Virgen María* no es un simple ser humano, no es una simple sierva, más que eso, Ella es la Viva Expresión que originó el "Ente Divino de la Creación", Ella es consustancial con el Padre y el Hijo en el *Espíritu Santo, por lo cual, Ella es, en Sí, Aquel Infinito que por no tener comienzo tampoco tendrá fin.*

El único Dios verdadero, el Espíritu Santo, que es eterno, omnipotente, omnipresente, omnisciente, inmesurable, justo, misericordioso, …; Como tal para realizar sus obras con la humanidad, se ha revelado cronológicamente en diferentes figuraciones personales temporales; como el Padre Creador, a los Antiguos Patriarcas, como el Hijo Redentor a través de Jesús, y en la época moderna como el Espíritu de la Virgen María en sus apariciones en los diferentes pueblos del mundo. El Espíritu Santo es el elemento y el todo del universo, es la verdadera esencia que conjuga toda la creación, es el Padre que se engendró en Sí mismo como el Hijo, en la eternidad del Divino Vientre de su Propio Ser.

Pero antes de entrar en los detalles que demuestran nuestro planteamiento, pasemos primero a analizar, en nuestro Marco Teológico, los diferentes planteamientos de los eruditos cristianos y las diferentes teorías e interpretaciones que se han dado sobre el Espíritu Santo durante el transcurso de la historia de la humanidad.

2.0.- Marco Teológico

Es necesario que nuestra generación se preocupe e interese por el estudio de la Obra del *Espíritu Santo*. Durante su ministerio Nuestro Señor Jesucristo habló abundantemente acerca del ministerio pleno y variado del Espíritu Santo. En Hechos encontramos detalles específicos de los resultados benditos del ministerio del Espíritu Santo en las vidas de individuos y congregaciones. También las Epístolas de Pablo de Tarso contienen abundantes referencias sobre la Obra del Espíritu Santo, "cuando la gente se hizo consciente del Espíritu Divino, cuando vivían y andaban en el Espíritu Divino, la iglesia se fortaleció y se extendió."

El Espíritu Santo tiene las características plenas de una persona – Isaías 11:1-2 – tiene sabiduría, por encima de toda imaginación humana; Romanos 8:27 – tiene una mente ultra o sobre humana; 1 Corintios 12:11 – posee voluntad; actúa y reacciona como una persona – Génesis 6:3 – pierde la paciencia con el aumento de la maldad; Juan 15:26 – sirve como un instructor; Efesios 4:30 – se entristece por la vida impía; Hechos 5:3-10 – se le puede mentir con consecuencias fatales; tiene pronombres que indican que es una persona – Juan 16:13,14.

No hay ningún asunto más importante en la religión cristiano - mariana que el del Espíritu Santo. A menos que sea entendido en forma apropiada, una gran porción de la Biblia, y especialmente el Nuevo Testamento, permanecerá indescifrable. Por otra parte, una revisión justa del tema ayudará más que una ilustración de cualquier otro tópico particular para dar armonía, claridad y consistencia de lo que pudiera ser aprendido de todos los otros asuntos presentados en la Palabra de Dios.

Pero a pesar de su importancia para entender las Escrituras como un todo, hay mucha confusión y superstición en las mentes de muchas personas en lo relacionado con el Espíritu Santo y su Santísima Trinidad.

En primer lugar, las Sagradas Escrituras establecen que Cristo es eterno (Juan. 1:1–3, 15, 30; 8:58; Mateo. 23:37; 12:41; 17:5, 24; Isaías 44:6; 48:12–16; Col. 1:15–17; Apocalipsis 1:8, 17) Es decir, nunca tuvo un comienzo y nunca tendrá fin, siendo eternamente Dios (Juan. 1:1; He. 1:8; Col. 2:9), compartiendo la esencia de la deidad con el Padre y con el Espíritu Santo (Juan. 10:30–33; 1 Co. 3:16; Romanos. 8:9; Juan. 14: 16–23), iguales en valor y en sustancia.

Miqueas 5:2, Pero tú, Belén Efrata, aunque eres pequeña entre las familias de Judá, de ti me saldrá el que ha de ser gobernante en Israel. Y sus orígenes son desde tiempos antiguos, desde los días de la eternidad.

Juan 1:1, En el principio existía el Verbo, y el Verbo estaba con Dios, y el Verbo era Dios.

Colosenses 1:17, Y Él es antes de todas las cosas, y en Él, todas las cosas permanecen.

Hebreos 13:8, Jesucristo es el mismo ayer y hoy y por los siglos.

El propio Jesús afirma y confirma que Él es eterno:

En Juan 8:57-58, Los sacerdotes del Templo le dijeron: "Aún no tienes cincuenta años, ¿y has visto a Abraham? Jesús les dijo: En verdad, en verdad os digo: antes que Abraham naciera, yo soy."

En Juan 17:5, cuando dice "Y ahora, glorifícame tú, Padre, junto a ti, con la gloria que tenía contigo antes que el mundo existiera."

En Juan 17:24, al aclamar "Padre, quiero que los que me has dado, estén también conmigo donde yo estoy, para que vean mi gloria, la gloria que me has dado; porque me has amado desde antes de la fundación del mundo."

En Apocalipsis 2:8, le ordena a Juan, "Y escribe al ángel de la iglesia en Esmirna: "El primero y el último, el que estuvo muerto y ha vuelto a la vida, dice esto…""

Isaías 44:6,8, Así dice el SEÑOR, el Rey de Israel, y su Redentor, el SEÑOR de los ejércitos: "Yo soy el primero y yo soy el último, y fuera de mí no hay Dios…"

Ya vimos como las Santas Escrituras revelan al Espíritu Santo con atributos que solo puede poseer una persona. Por ejemplo, Él habla claramente; en 1 Timoteo 4:1, Hechos 8:29, Hechos 10:19-20, Hechos 13:1-4. Él enseñó todas las cosas a los apóstoles, según Juan 14:26. Él iba a testificar sobre Jesús como se puede leer en Juan 15:26-27. Jesús siempre se refirió a Él como persona, usando el pronombre personal "él", según Juan 14:16-17. Él llevaría adelante y completaría la obra empezada por Jesús, según se lee en Juan 16:12-13. Él previno a Pablo y a sus compañeros de ir a ciertas áreas de Asia; Esto lo hizo "prohibiéndoles", y no "permitiéndoles" a pesar de sus esfuerzos iniciales, según Hechos 16:6-7.

El Espíritu Santo mismo intercede por nosotros, como nos dice Pablo en Romano 8:26, igual como Cristo "intercede por nosotros," según Romano 8:34. Y Romano 8:27 nos dice que Él tiene una mente, por lo cual tiene pensamientos propios. Él "sabe las cosas de Dios," 1 Corintios 2:11. En Romano 15:30, Pablo habla de "el amor del Espíritu," Corintios 12:11 nos dice: "Pero todas estas cosas las hace uno y el mismo Espíritu, repartiendo a cada uno en particular como él quiere." Fue el Espíritu Santo quien decidió que persona recibió tales dones. Él sufre los desaires e injurias "no contristéis al Espíritu Santo," Efesios 4:30. Él Puede ser entristecido por medio de nuestra negligencia voluntaria. Atribuir sus acciones al trabajo de Satanás, es "pecado imperdonable," Mateo 12:31-32. Alguien que ha "pisoteado al Hijo de Dios" también ha "afrentado al Espíritu de gracia," Hechos 10:29. Hay quienes le mienten al Espíritu Santo, como Ananías y su esposa Safira fueron culpados de hacerlo; "Por qué llenó Satanás tu corazón para que mintieses al Espíritu Santo?" Hechos 5:3.

Tertuliano fue el primero en usar el término Trinidad (trinitas), en el año 215 d. C., aunque anteriormente, Teófilo de Antioquía ya había usado la palabra griega τριάς (tríada) en su obra *A Autólico* (c. 180) para referirse a Dios, su Verbo (*Logos*) y su Sabiduría (*Sophia*). Tertuliano diría en *Adversus Praxeam II* que "los tres son uno, por el hecho de que los tres proceden de uno, por unidad de sustancia."

La fórmula fue adquiriendo forma con el paso de los años y no fue establecida definitivamente hasta el siglo IV: La definición del Concilio de Nicea, sostenida desde entonces con mínimos cambios por las principales denominaciones cristianas, fue la de afirmar que el Hijo era consustancial con el Padre (ὁμοούσιον, *homousion*, literalmente de la misma sustancia que el Padre). Esta fórmula fue cuestionada y la Iglesia pasó por una generación de debates y conflictos, hasta que la "fe de Nicea" fue reafirmada en Constantinopla en el año 381 d.C.

En el Concilio de Nicea (325 d.C.) toda la atención fue concentrada en la relación entre el Padre y el Hijo, inclusive mediante el rechazo de algunas frases típicas arrianas mediante algunos anatemas anexados al credo; y no se hizo ninguna afirmación similar acerca del Espíritu Santo ocultando completamente la parte femenina de Dios.

En el Concilio de Constantinopla (381 d.C.) se indicó que el Espíritu Santo es adorado y glorificado junto con el Padre y el Hijo (συμπροσκυνούμενον καὶ συνδοξαζόμενον), sugiriendo que era también masculino y consustancial a Ellos. Esta doctrina fue posteriormente ratificada por el Concilio de Calcedonia (451 d.C.), sin alterar la sustancia de la doctrina aprobada en Nicea.

La doctrina cristiana está basada en el monoteísmo; la existencia de un solo Dios. Por lo cual, en el Concilio de Nicea se hizo necesario hacer los ajustes necesarios a lo que decía la Escritura con respecto al Padre, al Hijo y el Espíritu Santo. Los teólogos cristianos que estructuraron los libros que fueron incluidos en la Biblia elaboraron explicaciones confusas que generaron varias corrientes de pensamiento y una intensa polémica. Esta polémica se acentuó teniendo el emperador Romano, Constantino I, que tomar cartas en el asunto para llegar a un consenso y es a partir de esta situación cuando los dirigentes de la Iglesia comenzaron a contar con el apoyo imperial y es el emperador quien precisó cuál sería la doctrina unificadora compartida por las diversas comunidades cristianas, naciendo así la Iglesia Católica Romana. Es así como frente a esta posición algunos teólogos plantearon que, si estas tres personas compartían diferentes cualidades y características divinas exclusivas de Dios: señorío, eternidad, omnipotencia, omnisciencia, omnipresencia, santidad, etc., se tendría que utilizar la fórmula matemática 1x1x1=1 en vez de 1+1+1=3, ya que ésta rompe el monoteísmo de Dios y se convierte en politeísmo o henoteísmo. El emperador romano, Constantino I, fue quien decidió que las tres divinas personas serian Padre, Hijo y Espíritu Santo, sellando así la exclusión de la parte femenina de Dios y en su lugar colocando la figura del Espíritu Santo, cuando en realidad el Espíritu Santo es el todo, el Dios Eterno y Omnipotente, que se personifica en multiples figuraciones humanas, según su voluntad. Es decir, todos son uno y uno son todos.

2.1.- La Trinidad del Espíritu Santo; Perspectivas bíblicas de Dios.

En la Biblia se encuentran alusiones al Padre, al Hijo y al Espíritu Santo que se han presentado como menciones implícitas de la naturaleza trinitaria de Dios.

• Citas del Tanaj (Antiguo Testamento judío) en las que aparecen referencias a Dios en plural:

- o "Dios (el Espíritu Santo) dijo: "**Hagamos** al hombre a **nuestra** imagen, según **nuestra** semejanza..."" (Génesis 1:26)
- o "El hombre ha llegado a ser como uno de **nosotros** en el conocimiento del bien y del mal." (Génesis 3:22).
- o "Y dijo Yahvé: "Veo que todos forman un solo pueblo y tienen una misma lengua. Si esto va adelante, nada les impedirá desde ahora que consigan todo lo que se propongan. Pues bien, **bajemos** y **confundamos** ahí mismo su lengua, de modo que no se entiendan los unos a los otros"". (Génesis 11:6-7)
- o "Yo oí la voz del Señor que decía: "¿A quién enviaré y quién irá por **nosotros**?". Yo respondí: "¡Aquí estoy: envíame!"". (Isaías 6:8).
- o También se presenta como argumento la utilización de la palabra Elohim, que es plural, para referirse a Dios (Génesis 20:13 y 2 Sam 7:23).

- • Citas del Nuevo Testamento en las que se identifica a Jesús como Dios:
  - o El inicio del Evangelio de Juan: "En el principio existía el Verbo y el Verbo estaba con Dios, y el Verbo era Dios" (Juan 1:1);
  - o El reconocimiento de Tomás hacia Jesús con la expresión: "Señor mío y Dios mío". (Juan 20:28);
  - o El reconocimiento de la omnisciencia de Jesús, atributo de Dios (Juan 21:17; Juan 16:30);
  - o "El que me ha visto a mí, ha visto al Padre" (Juan 14:9);
  - o "Yo estoy en el Padre y el Padre está en mí" (Juan 14:11);
  - o "Todo lo que tiene el Padre es mío" (Juan 16:15);
  - o La acusación de los judíos de hacerse Jesús igual a Dios (Juan 5:18);
  - o La capacidad de Jesús de perdonar los pecados (Marco 2:5-10).

- • Citas del Nuevo Testamento en las que se menciona a las tres entidades:
  - o El bautismo en el nombre del Padre y del Hijo y del Espíritu Santo (Mateo 28,19);

○ El saludo paulino: "La gracia del Señor Jesucristo, el amor de Dios y la comunión del Espíritu Santo sean con todos vosotros". (2 Corintios 13,13).

○ Fuera de los libros considerados canónicos, la fórmula trinitaria está presente en la Didaché, documento cristiano datado del siglo I por la mayoría de los estudiosos contemporáneos: "Os bautizaréis en el nombre del Padre y del Hijo y del Espíritu Santo en agua viva. Pero si no tienes agua corriente, entonces bautízate en otra agua [...]. Pero si no tienes ni una ni otra, entonces derrama agua sobre la cabeza tres veces en el nombre del Padre y del Hijo y del Espíritu Santo". (Did 7,1-3). (Santísima trinidad, Wikipedia, 2013)

○ Además de la polémica sobre la naturaleza de Jesús —si era humana, divina, o ambas a la vez—, de su origen —si eterno o temporal— y de cuestiones similares relativas al Espíritu Santo, el problema central del dogma trinitario es justificar la división entre "sustancia" única y triple "personalidad". La mayoría de las iglesias protestantes, así como las ortodoxas y la Iglesia Católica, sostienen que se trata de un misterio inaccesible para la inteligencia humana.

2.2.- Perspectivas de las iglesias cristianas sobre la Trinidad del Espíritu Santo.

Según the Catholic Encyclopedia, la Santísima Trinidad de Dios es un dogma y a la vez un misterio, por lo cual plantea que: *"Un dogma tan misterioso presupone una revelación divina"*.

Para la Iglesia Católica Apostólica Romana "La Trinidad de Dios es el término con que se designa la doctrina central de la religión cristiana [...] Así, en las palabras del Símbolo Quicumque: "el Padre es Dios, el Hijo es Dios y el Espíritu Santo es Dios, y sin embargo no hay tres Dioses, sino un solo Dios". En esta Trinidad [...] las Personas son co-eternas y co-iguales: todas, igualmente, son increadas y omnipotentes. [...]". (The Catholic Encyclopedia).

Para la Iglesia Ortodoxas Griega la Trinidad es lo siguiente: "Dios es trino y uno. El Padre es totalmente Dios. El Hijo es totalmente Dios. El Espíritu Santo es totalmente Dios". (Our Orthodox Christian Faith)

Las Iglesias Cristianas Evangélicas plantean que dentro de la unidad de un Único Dios existen tres distintas personas; el Padre, el Hijo y el Espíritu Santo. Los tres comparten los mismos atributos y la misma naturaleza, por lo tanto, estos tres constituyen el único Dios.

Según todas estas doctrinas:

- El **Padre**. Es increado y no engendrado.
- El **Hijo**. No es creado sino engendrado eternamente por el Padre.
- El **Espíritu Santo**. No es creado, ni engendrado, sino que procede eternamente del Padre y del Hijo (según las Iglesias Evangélicas y la Iglesia Católico Romana) o sólo del Padre (según la Iglesia Católica Ortodoxa).

Según el Dogma católico definido en el Primer Concilio de Constantinopla (381 d.C.), las tres personas de la Santísima Trinidad son realmente distintas, pero son un solo Dios verdadero. Esto es algo posible de formular pero inaccesible a la razón humana, por lo que se le considera un misterio de fe. Para explicar este misterio, en ocasiones los teólogos cristianos han recurrido a símiles. Así, Agustín de Hipona comparó la Trinidad con la mente, el pensamiento que surge de ella y el amor que las une. Por otro lado, el teólogo clásico Guillermo de Occam afirma la imposibilidad de la comprensión intelectual de la naturaleza divina y postula su simple aceptación a través de la fe.

El Apostol Felipe dice, en su evangelio: "Algunos dicen que María ha concebido por obra del Espíritu Santo: éstos se equivocan, no saben lo que dicen. *¿Cuándo jamás ha concebido una mujer de otra mujer?* María es la virgen a quien ninguna Potencia ha manchado. Ella es un gran anatema para los judíos, que son los apóstoles y los apostólicos. Esta virgen que ninguna Potencia ha violado, (... mientras que) las Potencias se contaminaron."

Si analizamos este párrafo por parte veremos que Felipe aquí se está refiriendo a que María es en sí el Espíritu Santo "...jamás ha concebido de mujer una mujer", esto quiere decir que Felipe tenía pleno conocimiento de que el Espíritu Santo es de género femenino, más claro aún, Felipe en sus limitados conocimientos sabía que el Espíritu Santo tenía una personificación femenina, pero no llego a comprender que en realidad el Espíritu Santo tenía ambas personificaciones, tanto femenina como masculina. De aquí podemos colegir que el Espíritu Santo "es una sustancia única" que a voluntad se presenta a la humanidad en multiples e infinitas figuraciones o personalidades siendo las tres principales Yahweh, Jesus Cristo, y la Virgen María en sus diferentes advocaciones.

Jesús es Dios y eterno, esto deja una concluyente afirmación de que María también es Dios y eterna. De forma tal, María es la personificación femenina del Espíritu Santo hecha mujer para ser Madre. El Espíritu Santo parte masculina engendró en María, su parte femenina, a su propio ser, en un proceso divino e incomprensible para el conocimiento humano hasta la actualidad. Dios es varón y hembra al mismo tiempo y su Divino Ser puede estar junto como un solo o reproducido, en uno o ambos sexos, en tantas veces como la mente humana no puede imaginar.

> "El Espíritu Santo encierra todo en sí mismo —ya sea "hombre", ya sea "mujer", ya sea "ángel", ya sea "animal", ya sea "árbol", ya sea "roca", ya sea "viento" … ya sea "misterio"—, incluso Padre, Madre e Hijo a la vez, y Ellos a la vez lo encierran a Él, ya que todos forman un solo Ser, el Espíritu Santo que es Dios." Evangelio de Felipe

"*El Espíritu Santo* es el Dios verdadero, el Dios de Abraham, y se encuentran de hecho en todas partes: arriba, abajo, en lo secreto y en lo manifiesto. El Espíritu Santo está en lo revelado, abajo, en lo secreto y arriba. *El Espíritu Santo* es el Padre de *Jesús*: "*Jesús* fue concebido por obra y gracia del *Espíritu Santo* en *María*". *Jesús* es el *Espíritu Santo* encarnado como hombre para ser el hijo de Dios, *María* es el *Espíritu Santo* encarnado como mujer para ser la madre de Dios. El *Espíritu Santo* dijo a los Profetas de la antigüedad "… enviare una mujer la cual aplastará las descendencias de la serpiente del mal", y ¡he ahí a María!

> "Las Potencias malignas están al servicio de los santos, después de haber sido reducidas a ceguera por el *Espíritu Santo* para que crean que están sirviendo a un hombre, siendo así que están operando en favor de los santos. Por eso, (cuando) un día un discípulo le pidió al Señor una cosa del mundo, Él le dijo: "Pide a tu madre y ella te hará partícipe de las cosas ajenas." Evangelio de Felipe.

"Los apóstoles dijeron a los discípulos: "que toda nuestra ofrenda se procure sal a sí misma". Ellos llamaban "sal" a (la Sofía), (pues) sin ella ninguna ofrenda (es) aceptable." "La Sofía es estéril, (sin) hijo(s); por eso se la llama (también) "sal". El lugar en que aquéllos (…) a su manera (es) **el Espíritu Santo**; (por esto) son numerosos sus hijos." Evangelio de Felipe.

"El **Espíritu Santo** apacienta a todos y ejerce su dominio sobre (todas) las Potencias, lo mismo sobre las dóciles que sobre las (indóciles) y solitarias, pues él (…) las recluye para que (…) cuando quieran." Evangelio de Felipe.

"Mientras éramos hebreos, éramos huérfanos: teníamos (sólo) nuestra madre. Pero al hacernos cristianos surgieron un padre y una madre para nosotros." Evangelio de Felipe

"Si alguien —después de bajar a las aguas— sale de ellas sin haber recibido nada y dice "soy cristiano", este nombre lo ha recibido (sólo) en préstamo. Más si recibe al *Espíritu Santo*, queda en posesión de (dicho) nombre a título de donación. A quien ha recibido un regalo nadie se lo quita, pero a quien se le da un préstamo, se le reclama. Evangelio de Felipe.

Aquí vemos como el apóstol Felipe plantea que es más importante recibir al *Espíritu Santo* que decir que se es cristiano por el simple hecho de haber recibido el agua bautismal.

"Nosotros somos —es verdad— engendrados por el ***Espíritu Santo***, pero re-engendrados por Cristo. En ambos (casos) somos asimismo ungidos por el **espíritu (santo)**, y —al ser engendrados— hemos sido también unidos." Evangelio de Felipe.

"Digamos —si es permitido— un secreto: el Padre del Todo se unió con la virgen que había descendido y un fuego le iluminó aquel día. Él dio a conocer la gran cámara nupcial, y por eso su cuerpo —que tuvo origen aquel día— salió de la cámara

nupcial como uno que ha sido engendrado por el esposo y la esposa. Y asimismo gracias a éstos enderezó Jesús el Todo en ella, siendo preciso que todos y cada uno de sus discípulos entren en su lugar de reposo." Evangelio de Felipe.

En el párrafo anterior el apóstol Felipe establece claramente que la Virgen María no fue engendrada, sino que descendió aquel día con la iluminación del *Espíritu Santo*, Su Propio Ser. Y al propio tiempo deja claro que el Padre, la Madre y el Hijo son una misma persona, y que las tres entidades tuvieron cuerpo, aquel mismo día; proviniendo los tres de una misma sustancia llamada Espíritu Santo.

El Espíritu Santo es el Ente Divino de la Creación, fue Él quien se le apareció en cada ocasión a los Patriarcas del Antiguo Testamento, fue Él quien le entregó los Mandamientos a Moisés, fue Él quien se encarno en la figura de María, fue Él quien engendró a su Hijo Jesús en el vientre de su Propio Ser en un proceso a través del cual Él entregó su vida por nosotros. Es Él el verdadero y único Dios. Él es quien personifica la divinidad del Padre, de la Madre y del Hijo en Sí mismo.

2.3.- El Ministerio de Jesús está basado en su esencia en el Espíritu Santo.

Veamos algunas afirmaciones bíblicas acerca del Espíritu Santo que corroboran con este razonamiento:

"Él es el Espíritu Original (…) Existe (…) sólo Él, único (…). Él ha existido desde toda la eternidad, y Su existencia no tendrá ningún fin. Él no tiene a nadie igual ni en el Cielo ni en la Tierra. (*El Apócrifo de Juan,* 4:35; 5:10,15).

Los secretos del universo están en las manos del Espíritu Santo. Porque el mundo, antes de que apareciera, existió ya en la profundidad del pensamiento Divino; se hizo material y visible por la voluntad del Espíritu Santo para quien no hay espacio ni tiempo.

"Cuando ustedes se dirijan a Él, vuélvanse de nuevo como los niños, pues ustedes no conocen ni el pasado ni el presente ni el futuro, mientras Dios (el Espíritu Santo) es el Amo de todo el tiempo." (*La Vida de San Issa,* 11: 12-15).

El Espíritu Santo es una Monocracia con nada por encima de Ella. Él es Dios y Padre de todo, el Espíritu invisible, Quien está por encima de todo, (…) Quien está en pura luz, quien ningún ojo puede ver.

> "Él es el Espíritu Santo. No es correcto pensar en Él como en dioses o algo similar. (…) Todo existe en Él. (…) Él es ilimitado, debido a que no hay nada anterior a Él que lo limite. (…) Él es inmensurable, debido a que no hubo nadie antes que Él, que lo midiera a Él. (…) Él es eterno (…). Él existe eternamente (…). No hay ninguna manera de decir Su cantidad (…). Él no está contenido en el tiempo (…). Evangelio de Felipe

> "El Gran Creador no ha compartido Su Poder con ningún ser viviente, (…) Él es el único Quien posee omnipotencia" (*La Vida de San Issa,* 5:16-17).

> "El Eterno Legislador es uno; no hay ningún otro Dios más que Él. Él no ha dividido el mundo con nadie, tampoco Él ha informado a nadie de Sus intenciones". (*La Vida de San Issa,*6:10)

> "(…) El Señor nuestro Dios es todo-poderoso, omnisciente y omnipresente. Es Él Quien posee toda la sabiduría y toda la luz. Es a Él, a Quien deben dirigirse para ser consolados en sus dolores, ayudados en sus obras y curados en sus enfermedades. Quienquiera que recurra a Su Santísima Trinidad su petición no será negada." (*El Apócrifo de Juan,* 2:25-4:25).

> "Él es la Vida Que da la vida. Él es el Bendito Que da la bendición. Él es la Sabiduría Que da la sabiduría. Él es el Amor Que da salvación y amor." (*El Apócrifo de Juan,* 2:25-4:25).

"Él es inamovible; Él reside en tranquilidad y en silencio. (…) Él dirige Sus deseos dentro de Su flujo de Luz. Él es la Fuente de este flujo de Luz (el Espíritu Santo)" (*El Apócrifo de Juan*, 2:25-4:25).

"Éste es el mensaje que hemos oído de Jesús, y lo manifestamos a ustedes: Dios es Luz, y en Él no hay ninguna oscuridad en absoluto" (1 Juan 1:5).

"(…) El bienaventurado y único Soberano (…) Quien exclusivamente tiene la Inmortalidad y mora en la Luz (…)" (1 Timoteo 6:15-16).

"Ahora al Rey eterno, inmortal, invisible, al único Dios sabio, sea el honor y la gloria por siempre jamás. Amén" (1 Timoteo 1:17).

La mayoría de estas palabras de Jesús no fueron incluidas en el Nuevo Testamento por los líderes de la iglesia del siglo IV, cuando por orden del emperador Constantino I se preparó el compendio de la Biblia. La mayoría de los cristianos se han olvidado de Dios el Padre, aunque Él y el Camino a Él eran la esencia de las prédicas de Jesús. Pero más aun, se distorsionó la esencia que encierran estas palabras en las que se deduce claramente que Jesús llama "Padre" al Espíritu Santo. Los términos "Dios es Luz"; "Dios es espíritu"; "Dios es invisible"; "Dios tiene la Inmortalidad y mora en la Luz"; "Dios dirige Sus deseos dentro de Su flujo de Luz"; "Dios es la Fuente de este flujo de Luz"; "Dios es el Espíritu… Todo existe en Él"; *"Contra un fondo frío, oscuro, sin vida, el Espíritu de Dios se movía sobre la faz de las aguas."* y muchos otros que seguiremos tratando en este libro, demuestran no solo que el **Espíritu Santo es Dios,** *sino, que ese Ser Supremo que nosotros llamamos* **Dios es en Sí el Espíritu Santo.**

De forma tal, Jesús está en el Padre y en María; El Padre está en Jesús y en María; María está en el Padre y en Jesús. El Padre es el Espíritu Santo; Jesús es el Espíritu Santo; María es el Espíritu Santo. El Espíritu Santo se presenta en una de las tres personalidades divinas por separado, pero en algunas ocasiones se ha presentado a algunas personas como la Santísima Trinidad del Espíritu Santo, en un Ente de Luz con movimiento del cual han salido tres diferentes voces: la del Padre, la de la Virgen María y la de Jesucristo, cada voz con su timbre y tono peculiar que permite identificar quíen esta hablando en cada momento.

La Santísima Trinidad del Espíritu Santo es el único *Ente Divino, el Ser Supremo o Dios,* por tanto, existe un solo y único *Ser Divino* llamado *"Espíritu Santo" o Dios,* el cual está compuesto por las tres divinas personas, que son: el *Padre,* la *Madre* y el *Hijo.* El Espíritu Santo *(Padre) se auto llamó* YHVH (que en el idioma antiguo de los judíos significa –"El que Existe"- y se pronuncia *Yahwéh y en castellano se adaptó la pronunciación a Jehová y Yahvé,* la *Madre* es llamada *Virgen María,* y el *Hijo* es llamado *Jesucristo.* De forma tal, tenemos tres personas en un mismo y único Ser, que por su divinidad, omnipotencia, omnisciencia y omnipresencia pueden actual juntos y/o por separado y al mismo tiempo cada uno de Ellos puede asumir diferentes figuraciones sin importar tiempo ni espacio.

3.0.- El Espíritu Santo; sexo, origen y procedencia

El vocablo "espíritu" proviene del griego "πνευμα" (pneuma) y el hebreo "ruaj o ruach". Se trata de una traducción incompleta ya que "ruaj" y "pneuma" también se traducen como "aire" (de ahí proviene la palabra "neumático"). Aire y espíritu son cosas distintas para nosotros hoy día, pero aparecían relacionadas entre sí, en el griego y el hebreo antiguos. Lo que actualmente es una doble acepción era en esos idiomas una identidad de conceptos.

Sobre la procedencia del *Espíritu Santo*, existe cierta unanimidad entre las diferentes confesiones cristianas. A excepción de la interpretación triteísta, que asume al *Espíritu Santo* como un ser increado e independiente de Dios, las otras interpretaciones consideran que procede de Dios, aunque se diferencian en la forma. Por ejemplo; en el modalismo, procede como fuerza, en el arrianismo como criatura y en el trinitarismo como persona. El trinitarismo aborda, además, una cuestión adicional propia de su marco teológico, distingue entre la procedencia del Padre y la procedencia del Hijo, cuestión conocida como cláusula filioque.

El único Dios verdadero y eterno, el Espíritu Santo, se ha revelado cronológicamente en tres diferentes Personalidades temporales; como Padre Creador en el Antiguo Testamento, como Hijo Redentor durante la vida de Jesús, y actualmente a través de las diferentes advocaciones de la Virgen María en los diferentes pueblos del mundo.

Hasta ahora, ninguna teoría había tratado sobre la parte femenina del *Espíritu Santo*, es decir, sobre ***"La Virgen María"*** *como parte consustancial en la Santisima Trinidad de Dios.*

La *Virgen María* debe ser glorificada como parte consustancial del *Espíritu Santo*, junta con el Padre y el Hijo (συμπροσκυνούμενον καὶ συνδοξαζόμενον), modificando la doctrina ratificada por el Concilio de Calcedonia (451 d.C.). Cumplan este mandato antes de que sea tarde.

3.1.- Naturaleza del Espíritu Santo.

En la teología cristiana, el *Espíritu Santo* (o sus equivalentes, Espíritu de Dios, Espíritu de verdad o Paráclito: acción o presencia de Dios, del griego παράκλητον *parakleton*: aquel que es invocado, y que proviene del latín Spiritus Sanctus) es una expresión bíblica que se refiere a una compleja noción teológica a través de la cual se describe una realidad espiritual suprema, que ha tenido múltiples interpretaciones en las diferentes confesiones cristianas y escuelas teológicas.

De esta realidad espiritual se habla en muchos pasajes de la Biblia, con las expresiones citadas, sin que se dé una definición única. Este fue el motivo de una serie de controversias que se produjeron principalmente a lo largo de tres periodos históricos: el siglo IV como siglo trinitario por excelencia, las crisis cismáticas de oriente y occidente acaecidas entre los siglos IX y XI y, por último, las distintas revisiones doctrinales nacidas de la reforma protestante.

En torno a la naturaleza del *Espíritu Santo* los eruditos sostienen básicamente cuatro interpretaciones que señalamos aquí a grandes rasgos para más adelante abundar sobre cada una de ellas, para luego concluir con la real y verdadera composición de la *Santísima Trinidad del Espíritu Santo*:

- Para los modalistas, el *Espíritu Santo* es una *fuerza o cualidad divina* tal como la sabiduría, la belleza, el amor o la bondad. La teoría del unitarismo, si bien guarda diferencias teológicas básicas con la del modalismo, comparte esta visión de un *Espíritu Santo* impersonal que actúa siendo el Poder o Fuerza Activa de Dios. En todo caso, ambas corrientes comparten la visión de que el *Espíritu Santo* no es "alguien" sino *"algo"*.

- Según las interpretaciones de carácter arriano, el *Espíritu Santo* es una *entidad espiritual* o naturaleza angélica de carácter excelso, muy cercana a la divinidad, pero diferente a ella por su condición de criatura.

- Según las interpretaciones de carácter triteísta el *Espíritu Santo* es *otro Dios*, quizá de carácter inferior al Dios principal, pero que comparte con él la cualidad de ser increado.

- Las interpretaciones de carácter trinitario consideran al *Espíritu Santo* como una *persona divina*, noción con la que se asume la divinidad del *Espíritu Santo*, manteniendo, sin embargo, la unicidad del principio divino. Esta es la doctrina del cristianismo católico, del cristianismo ortodoxo y de algunas denominaciones protestantes.

Como hemos podido ver desde los primeros siglos de la iglesia cristiana los teólogos han tenido grandes confusiones acerca de la *Santísima Trinidad del Espíritu Santo*. Oriente y Occidente han tenido diferentes puntos de vista; por un lado, se ha proclamado fuertemente la distinción del Padre, Hijo y *Espíritu Santo*, por el otro se mantuvo firme la proclama de que Dios es uno. Tanto Oriente como Occidente luchaban por evitar lo que para ellos es el error del Triteísmo, o la doctrina falsa de que haya tres dioses.

Hacia fines del siglo II como resultado de estas luchas por encontrar la verdad, comenzó una doctrina conocida como el monarquianismo en el Oriente y se extendió a Occidente. Fue un intento de proclamar la unidad de Dios, que desafortunadamente destruyó la Trinidad. Una forma de esta doctrina buscaba preservar la unidad de Dios, la deidad de *Cristo* y la deidad del *Espíritu Santo*, enseñando que el Hijo y el *Espíritu Santo* sólo eran modos o manifestaciones de Dios Padre. Se llamaba el monarquianismo modalista, (modal, que aparece en diferentes papeles, monarca, un ser principal). Otro nombre fue el Patripasionismo, porque insistía que el Padre sufría en su papel como Hijo.

Otra doctrina monarquiana distinta, el monarquianismo dinamista, también intentó preservar la unidad de Dios, pero lo hizo negando la deidad de *Cristo* y del *Espíritu Santo*. Especuló que Dios, el único gobernante, levantó a *Jesús* a un nivel casi divino, llenándolo de poderes, llamados "el logos" y "el espíritu".

Además, una tercera conclusión destructiva acerca de la Trinidad especulaba que el único Dios verdadero es el Padre y que las otras dos personas divinas sólo son manifestaciones temporales, algo inferiores, que fluyen del Padre. Esta doctrina llegó a conocerse como el subordinacionismo.

"En el tiempo de estas controversias había muchas opiniones diferentes acerca del *Espíritu Santo* quien fue identificado por algunos teólogos como una energía, una criatura o un ángel. Sin embargo, podemos estar seguros basándonos en las afirmaciones sencillas del Credo Apostólico que la iglesia antigua creía en la personalidad y la deidad del

Espíritu Santo. "Pero no fue hasta el siglo IV que la personalidad y la divinidad del *Espíritu Santo* se hicieron prominentes." (E. H. Klotsche, The History of Christian Doctrine, Grand Rapids, MI: Baker Book House, 1979, p. 69; Neve, A History of Christian Thought, The United Lutheran Publication House, 1943, vol. 1, p. 119;)

Cerca de 150 d.C. ciertas personas en la parte griega de la iglesia que querían evitar lo que a su consideración era la herejía del triteísmo declararon que Jesucristo no es Dios, pero es casi Dios. Dijeron que el Logos, que se hizo carne en Jesucristo, estuvo en un nivel inferior al Padre.

Orígenes de Alejandría en Egipto pulió algunas de las asperezas de este pensamiento conocida como subordinacionismo (del latín, teniendo una naturaleza inferior). Luchando contra los monarquianistas, insistió en que el Padre, el Hijo y el Espíritu eran tres personas eternamente distintas, pero no los creía iguales. Su concepto de la Trinidad era de tres círculos concéntricos que formaban un triángulo invertido, y se extiende de Dios al hombre. Orígenes razonaba que "puesto que todas las cosas han llegado a existir por medio del Logos, sigue que el Espíritu Santo es el primero de los espíritus engendrados del Padre mediante el Hijo." Enseñó que las tres personas tienen la misma esencia, pero no la misma existencia. Jesús y el Espíritu Santo eran parte de un puente que descendía entre el cielo y la tierra. El papel del Espíritu Santo fue proceder del Padre mediante el Hijo para santificar a los hombres. (Neve, op. Cit. vol. 1, p. 87)

Así, según Orígenes, el Hijo y el Espíritu Santo estaban subordinados al Padre y el Espíritu Santo también estuvo subordinado al Hijo. Esta distorsión que alcanzó amplia distribución, no fue claramente corregida hasta el Concilio de Nicea en 325 d.C.

Teodoto de Bizancio intentó preservar la unidad de Dios de otra manera. Él planteaba que Cristo y el Espíritu Santo no son iguales a Dios Padre, sosteniendo que el hombre Jesús fue elevado a un nivel similar a Dios cuando recibió un *dínamis,* un poder que procedía de Dios. Cerca de fines del siglo II Teodoto se trasladó a Roma llevando consigo su teoría que llegó a ser conocido como el monarquianismo dinamista o el adopcionismo. Según esta doctrina, "como resultado de la morada del Logos y del Espíritu Santo, Jesús fue "adoptado" como el Hijo de Dios, recibió el poder de hacer milagros, y finalmente alcanzó una unidad permanente con Dios." (Pieper, Francis D.D., Christian

Dogmatics, St. Louis, MO: Concordia Publishing House, 1951, Vol. 1, p. 383.)

Las confesiones luteranas en los Artículos Principales de la fe, artículo 1, de Dios, condenan la enseñanza de los samosatenses por negar la personalidad y deidad del Logos y del Espíritu Santo. Rechazan también la de los samosatenses, antiguos y modernos, que sostienen que sólo hay una persona y aseveran sofísticamente que las otras dos, el Verbo y el Espíritu Santo, no son necesariamente personas distintas, sino que el Verbo significa la palabra eterna o la voz, y que el Espíritu Santo es una energía engendrada en los seres creados."

Atanasio, obispo de Alejandría, declaró, en el concilio general de los obispos orientales de Nicea en 325 d. C., que el Padre y el Hijo son un Dios, que tienen la misma sustancia o naturaleza, lo cual resumio usando la palabra homoousios. También defendió el homoousios del *Espíritu Santo* en el sínodo de Alejandría en 362 d.C., enseñando que el *Espíritu Santo* es Dios, porque solamente un *Espíritu divino* podía hacer a personas "participantes de la naturaleza divina". Atanasio estuvo convencido de que la fórmula para el Bautismo revela la naturaleza divina del Espíritu Santo. Si el Espíritu fuera solamente una criatura no estaría incluida bajo el mismo nombre con el Padre y el Hijo. (Eerdman's Handbook to the History of Christianity, Grand Rapids, MI: Wm. B. Eerdmans Publishing Co., 1977, p. 164)

Hasta entonces no se había dicho mucho acerca de la tercera persona de la Trinidad, pero en los años siguientes se dio mucha más atención a la identidad del *Espíritu Santo*. El obispo Macedonio de Constantinopla se opuso a la posición de Atanasio e insistía que el *Espíritu Santo* es una criatura subordinada al Hijo.

Pero el sínodo de Alejandría de 362 d.C., impulsado por el tratado de Basilio de Cesarea sobre el *Espíritu Santo*, condenó tanto el arrianismo como la enseñanza similar de los pneumatomaquianos (del griego, los que luchan contra el *Espíritu Santo*), que también fueron llamados los macedonios. Basilio fue el primero en formalizar la terminología aceptada para la Trinidad: una sustancia (ousia) y tres personas (hupostaseis).

El amigo de Basilio, Gregorio Nacianzeno, notó la distinción bíblica entre las tres personas de la Trinidad, es decir, que el Padre es no engendrado, el Hijo es engendrado, y el *Espíritu Santo* procede del Padre por el Hijo. Esta distinción útil fue aceptada por la iglesia en un sínodo celebrado en Roma en 380 d.C. Un año más tarde, en Constantinopla, la iglesia siguió un paso más adelante afirmando la plena deidad del *Espíritu Santo*, declarando que él era el Señor y dador que procede del Padre, adorado y glorificado con el Padre y el Hijo. En 451 d.C., en Calcedonia, las partes oriental y occidental de la iglesia formalmente adoptaron esta expresión en el Credo Niceno. (J. L. Gonzalez, A History of Christian Thought, Nashville, TN: Abingdon Press, 1970, vol. 1, p. 323)

Tertuliano luchó contra la teoría modalista, enseñando correctamente que el Padre, el Hijo y el *Espíritu Santo* son tres personas distintas, eternas, que coexisten, que juntos conforman el único Dios trino. Para expresar su pensamiento utilizó la palabra trinitas (Trinidad). Tertuliano, sin embargo, no estuvo sin errores. Sostenía una subordinación del Hijo y del Espíritu al Padre. Para ilustrar esto sacó analogías de la naturaleza. El Padre, el Hijo y el Espíritu Santo están relacionados uno al otro como un manantial, una ribera, y un río. El Padre es toda la sustancia, mientras el Hijo y el Espíritu descienden del Padre. (Neve, op. Cit., tomo 1, p. 107; Klotsche, op. Cit., p. 54)

Agustín agregó un énfasis nuevo a la relación de las tres personas de la Trinidad 200 años más tarde, cuando formó la costumbre de decir que el Espíritu procede de ambos, el Padre "y el Hijo", (latín, filioque). Cuando habló de la procesión del Espíritu, hablaba de la eterna procesión del Espíritu del Padre y el Hijo, no solamente el enviar al *Espíritu Santo* en Pentecostés. Agustín razonó que si el Espíritu Santo procede del Padre también tiene que proceder del Hijo, porque tienen la misma naturaleza divina.

Pero Agustín también contribuyó a la confusión de la teología moderna cuando trató de explicar lo inexplicable. Para hacer una distinción entre la "generación" del Hijo del Padre, y la "procesión" del *Espíritu Santo* del Padre y del Hijo, expresó la teoría de que el *Espíritu Santo* es una sustancia misteriosa, eterna, común tanto al Padre y al Hijo, que también se puede llamar una "amistad" o "vinculo de amor". En su gran obra La Trinidad escribió: "Por tanto el *Espíritu Santo*, sea lo que sea, es algo común tanto al Padre y al Hijo, pero esa comunión misma es consustancial y coeterna, y si se puede llamar amistad con propiedad, que así se le llama, pero más aptamente se llama amor. Y eso también es una sustancia, ya que Dios es una sustancia, y Dios es amor, como está escrito." (González, op. Cit., pp 340-341)

En 589 d. C., en el tercer concilio de Toledo en España, se encuentra la primera evidencia de que el filioque se ha hallado en una versión occidental del Credo Niceno. Esto se hizo para refutar a los arrianos. La iglesia española estaba perturbada por un grupo de arrianos, que negaban la plena deidad del Hijo, pero esos arrianos estaban dispuestos a decir que *el Espíritu Santo* era Dios. Eso hizo a sus opositores contestar que Jesús también tiene que ser Dios, porque el Espíritu procede del Padre y del Hijo, filioque, y Dios sólo puede proceder de Dios. Esto no significa que el término filioque fue ampliamente aceptado en ese tiempo. De hecho, el filioque fue resistido tanto en occidente y oriente por generaciones. Los teólogos de occidente sabían que la iglesia oriental no había aceptado el concepto. El Papa León III, por ejemplo, rehusó permitir agregar la frase durante su vida. De hecho, ordenó inscribir el Credo en latín y griego sin filioque en dos platos de plata para adornar las paredes de la Basílica de San Pedro en Roma. Lo hizo a pesar de que él estuvo de acuerdo con el filioque en cuanto a doctrina.

Los teólogos orientales, que temían que el filioque enseñaba el sabelianismo, insistían que sólo podía haber un Dios que es el Padre, y que el Padre tiene que ser la fuente de ambos; del Hijo y del Espíritu Santo.

Cuando el Papa Benito VIII declaró oficialmente que la afirmación del filioque sería parte del Credo que se confesaba en la misa latina en 1014 d. C., ofendió profundamente a los líderes de la iglesia oriental. Cuarenta años más tarde, en 1054 d. C., después de varios siglos de controversia acerca de la doctrina y la práctica con relación a éste y otros asuntos, sucedió una ruptura entre la iglesia romana de occidente y la iglesia ortodoxa de oriente que perdura hasta la actualidad.

Entrada la época moderna el teólogo Robert W. Jensen considera que tiene una misión de enmendar la doctrina recibida hasta el momento. Según él, Espíritu era un término que la teología bíblica suplió para describir lo que precede de un encuentro entre Dios y el creyente. El "Espíritu" es "el conocimiento de Dios por la fe". Éste sostuvo que: "En verdad, la Trinidad es sencillamente el Padre y el hombre Jesús y su Espíritu como el Espíritu de la comunidad creyente." Llama al "Espíritu" un "dinamismo" que captó la iglesia cuando esperaba el futuro regreso de Jesús. Ya que cree que el Espíritu Santo no es una persona de la Trinidad, sino un poder que proviene de Dios, Jensen es un ejemplo moderno del monarquianismo dinámico. Pieper, a su vez, escribe que "la mayoría de los unitarios ingleses, norteamericanos y alemanes son monarquianos dinámicos." (Braaten y Jensen, editores, Christian Dogmatics, Philadelphia, PA: Fortress Press, 1984, tomo 1, p. 93, 108, 155, 156, 400; Pieper, op. Cit., p. 383)

La teología moderna, con su rechazo de la autoridad de la Escritura, presenta la especulación humana acerca de la Trinidad. Los académicos liberales niegan abiertamente la deidad del Hijo y del Espíritu Santo. Usan las palabras Padre, Hijo y Espíritu Santo, pero las explican como tres operaciones divinas de una persona divina, lo cual denota un monarquianismo modalista. (Braaten y Jensen, editores, Christian Dogmatics, Philadelphia, PA: Fortress Press, 1984, tomo 1, p. 400)

El teólogo reformador prusiano, Schleiermacher, recomendó que el nombre Padre se usara para el Dios verdadero, y que los nombres Hijo y Espíritu Santo se usaran para representar las maneras temporales en las que el Padre se revelaba. "El Espíritu Santo era solamente el espíritu de la comunidad creyente que procede de Cristo, una fuerza espiritual activa" que según él tenía la tendencia de estar de acuerdo con Imanuel Kant quien pensaba que no se puede conocer a Dios. Sugirió que dar el Espíritu en Pentecostés significaba solamente que el Cristo resucitado había causado el comienzo de una entidad organizada que se conoce como la iglesia. (Neve, op. Cit., tomo 2, p. 113; Justo González, A History of Christian Thought, New York, NY: Abingdon Press, tomo 3, p. 329)

Más tarde, en el siglo IXX Alberto Ritschl, un agnóstico, repitió y modificó un poco la doctrina de Schleiermacher al decir que el Espíritu Santo era un poder impersonal que emanaba de Dios y moraba en la iglesia. (Neve, op. Cit., tomo 2, p. 151)

El modalismo moderno intenta hacer la doctrina de la Trinidad razonable diciendo: "Dios es amor. El Padre es el amor que se ha dado en el pasado, el Hijo es el amor manifestado en el presente y el Espíritu es el amor que se extiende al futuro."

También hay subordinacionistas modernos, que incluyen algunos arminianos, que arguyen que el Hijo es más joven que el Padre, y que el Espíritu Santo es más joven que ambos porque procede de ellos. En contraste, el Credo Atanasiano dice: "Y en esta Trinidad ninguno es primero o postrero; ninguno mayor o menor; sino que todas las tres personas son coeternas juntamente y coiguales."

En este libro sustentamos que el Ente Creador, el Ser Supremo, el Dios único que existe y da vida es el Espíritu Santo, y Éste se ha revelado a los seres humano en diferentes figuraciones o expresiones humanas. Las expresiones o figuraciones personales, mas connotadas, que el Espíritu Santo de Dios ha asumido durante el transcurso de la historia de la humanidad son: la de La Virgen María, como Mujer y Madre, y la de Jesús, como Hombre e Hijo. Cuando Jesús hablaba de Su Padre estaba hablando del Espíritu Santo de Dios.

Dios en esencia es Espíritu, energía inmesurable, como lo dice la Sagrada Escritura: "… Jesús fue engendrado por Obra y Gracia del Espíritu Santo en el vientre de María". En un hecho sin precedente y fuera de toda lógica del conocimiento humano actual: María es Madre y compañera a la vez y ambos entraron al umbral de la encarnación humana al mismo tiempo como lo establece Felipe en su Evangelio: "Digamos —si es permitido— un secreto: el Padre del Todo se unió con la virgen que había descendido y un fuego le iluminó aquel día. Él dio a conocer la gran cámara nupcial, y por eso su cuerpo —que tuvo origen aquel día— salió de la cámara nupcial como uno que ha sido engendrado por el esposo y la esposa. Y asimismo gracias a éstos enderezó Jesús el Todo en ella, siendo preciso que todos y cada uno de sus discípulos entren en su lugar de reposo." Evangelio de Felipe.

El Espíritu Santo en su omnipotencia y omnipresencia se hizo mujer y hombre a la misma vez. Lo que para el ser humano pareció suceder en tiempos distantes, en realidad sucedió en un mismo instante de vida. Desde antes de la creación y por toda la eternidad; La Virgen María es el Espíritu Santo, Jesús es el Espíritu Santo y el Padre es el Espíritu Santo en una única y absoluta esencia consustancial y coeterna llamada Santísima Trinidad del Espíritu Santo.

3.2.- El Espíritu Santo; Cualidades, Nombres, Dones y Frutos.

En lo referente a las cualidades del *Espíritu Santo*, los teólogos cristianos asumen que es portador de dones sobrenaturales muy diversos que pueden transmitirse al hombre por su mediación. Si bien la enumeración de los dones puede variar de unos autores a otros y entre distintas confesiones, existe un amplio consenso en cuanto a su excelencia y magnanimidad.

La mayor parte de las iglesias cristianas, y entre ellas las principales, se declaran trinitarias. Existen también iglesias no trinitarias que confiesan alguna de las otras modalidades interpretativas.

Los textos judío-cristianos contienen un conjunto de expresiones que aluden a una "realidad divina" en la que creen el judaísmo y el cristianismo, las principales son: Espíritu Santo, Espíritu de Dios, Espíritu de la Verdad, Espíritu de Santidad, Espíritu Recto, Espíritu Generoso, Espíritu de Adopción, Mente de Cristo, Espíritu del Señor, Señor mismo, Espíritu de Libertad, Dedo de Dios y Paráclito. De todas estas, "Espíritu Santo" es la expresión principal, la más conocida y la que más se usa en el cristianismo.

En el judaísmo y el cristianismo se cree que el *Espíritu Santo* puede acercarse al alma y transmitirle ciertas disposiciones que la perfeccionan. Estos hábitos se conocen como los "Dones del *Espíritu Santo*." La relación de dones varía entre las diferentes denominaciones cristianas. En la Biblia existe una cita del profeta Isaías en donde se enumeran los "Dones del *Espíritu Santo*", estos son: *Espíritu de sabiduría, inteligencia, consejo, fuerza, ciencia, piedad y temor de Dios. (Isaías 11:2)*

Estos dones se complementan con los "7 frutos del Espíritu" que aparecen en la Epístola a los gálatas: *"Más el fruto del Espíritu es: caridad, gozo, paz, tolerancia, benignidad, bondad, fe, mansedumbre, templanza; contra tales cosas no hay ley." (Gálatas 5:22-23)*

Todos estos nombres, dones o frutos van implícitos en la expresión *"Espíritu Santo"* y enriquecen toda noción teológica. Sin embargo, a pesar de esta diversidad de nombres, en la teología cristiana se dice que no existe más que un solo y único Espíritu: *El Espíritu Santo*, el cual se expresa a través de diferentes personalidades divinas: Jehová o Yahvé, la Virgen María y Jesucristo.

3.3.- Personalidad del Espíritu Santo.

La forma como fue definida la verdad escritural de que Dios el Padre subsiste o existe en tres Personas - el Padre, el Hijo y el *Espíritu Santo* -, fue erróneamente reconocida por la gran mayoría de las congregaciones cristianas. Basando su definición en su interpretación de La Escritura plantean que el *Espíritu Santo* es una Persona tanto como Dios el Padre y Dios el Hijo, y que como se ve en el estudio de la doctrina de la Trinidad, las tres Personas forman un Dios y no tres. El error de esta interpretación está en que se considera al *Espíritu Santo* como una persona y al Padre como otra persona, pero no se hace mención de la personalidad femenina del *Espíritu Santo*. Sin embargo, cuando analizamos el Evangelio de Felipe nos damos cuenta que la realidad trinitaria es que el *Espíritu Santo* encarnó a la misma vez como mujer en María para ser la Madre de Dios y en Jesús para ser el hijo de Dios. De forma tal, El *Espíritu Santo* es "el todo" que contiene las partes que conforma las tres realidades conocidas por el cristianismo: el Padre, que es Espíritu Santo, la Madre (la Virgen María), que es Espíritu Santo, y el Hijo (Jesucristo) que es Espíritu Santo, y los tres son en sí un solo Ser llamado *Espíritu Santo*.

En la interpretación de las verdades fundamentales relativas al *Espíritu Santo* debemos hacer un énfasis especial sobre el hecho de su personalidad. Ya que el *Espíritu Santo* no habla de sí mismo; según Juan 16:13 y Hechos 13:2, Él habla lo que Él oye, y Juan 16:14 dice que Él ha venido al mundo para glorificar a Cristo, de tal forma también glorifica al Padre y a la Virgen María. En cambio, la Escritura solo representa al Padre y al Hijo, hablando de sí mismos con autoridad final y en una eminente conversión, el uno con el otro. Pero la verdad es que nada de esto tiende a hacer menos real la personalidad del *Espíritu Santo de Dios*. El hecho de que Él no hable de sí mismo está en que Él prefirió hablar con Su Obra a través de la *Virgen María* y de *Jesús* que son a la vez Él mismo, y a través de los verdaderos portadores de la fe que son inspirados a escribir en su Glorioso Nombre.

3.4.- El Espíritu Santo; fundador y cabeza principal del cristianismo.

El *Espíritu Santo* creó el cristianismo miles de años antes de su encarnación humana como *Jesús*, cuando inspiro a los profetas y patriarcas de la antigüedad a propagar y escribir acerca de la venida del Cristo, el Mesías, el Hijo de Dios, el Hijo de sus propias entrañas, aquel que daría su vida para salvar la humanidad. Es decir que antes de *Jesús* venir al mundo humano ya tenía seguidores, personas que seguían todas las señales dadas acerca de la forma y lugar en que éste llegaría al mundo, entres éstos estaban los reyes o magos de oriente y los esenios.

Esto es lo dicho por el profeta Joel: *"Y en los postreros días, dice Dios, Derramaré de mi Espíritu Santo sobre toda carne, Y vuestros hijos y vuestras hijas profetizarán; Vuestros jóvenes verán visiones, y vuestros ancianos soñarán sueños; Y de cierto sobre mis siervos y sobre mis siervas en aquellos días derramaré de mi Espíritu, y profetizarán. Y daré prodigios arriba en el cielo, y señales abajo en la tierra, ... antes que venga el día de que Yo demuestre a los incrédulos Que existo, grande y manifiesto; y todo aquel que invocare mi Nombre, será salvo".*

Todos los que profetizan estan entre aquellos siervos que son iluminados, gracias al *Espíritu Santo*. Utilizando la Escritura como su herramienta, el *Espíritu Santo* nos induce a proclamar el "misterio que se ha mantenido oculto desde tiempos eternos," que Jesucristo, el Cordero de Dios, es el Salvador de la humanidad. Él es el Salvador que todo el mundo necesita conocer y en quien necesita confiar para librarse del juicio venidero del Espíritu Santo. El Espíritu Santo es el Espíritu de Dios, el Espíritu de YHVH "El que existe", el Espíritu del Padre, el Espíritu de Jesús, el Espíritu de María y el Espíritu de la fe en "El único Dios que existe".

El *Espíritu Santo* es quien da la vida, es quien crea nuestra fe en lo divino, es quien nos bautiza, es quien convierte el pan y el vino en el cuerpo y la sangre de Cristo, es quien consagra todos los sacramentos, es quien guía nuestras vidas en la fe como creyentes y quien nos da poder para nuestra actividad de proclamar a Jesús como nuestro Salvador, a Jehová o Yahvé como nuestro Padre celestial y a la *Virgen María* como *Nuestra Señora de la Santísima Trinidad*, todos los milagros hechos sobre la faz de la tierra son realizados por Obra y Gracia del *Espíritu Santo*.

El apóstol Pedro hizo un anuncio importante que está escrito en el libro de Hechos. Al describir el milagro que sucedía en Jerusalén en Pentecostés, declaró el principio de la venida especial del *Espíritu Santo*. Esto había sido prometido a los profetas del Antiguo Testamento como una señal de los últimos días antes del glorioso advenimiento final de Cristo. Pero este relato fue manipulado por los hombres del comienzo de la era cristiana, para ocultar la verdadera procedencia de la *Virgen María*. En realidad, el día de Pentecostés, cuando todos los Apóstoles estaban reunidos con miedo e incrédulos acerca del poder de *Jesús*, la *Virgen María* se le presentó a ellos y les reveló que Ella es el *Espíritu Santo* encarnado en la figura de una simple mujer y que *Jesús* es el *Espíritu Santo* encarnado en la figura de un hombre aparentemente mortal, que los tres son un solo Ser, y que aunque *María y Jesús* lucían como de carne y huesos en realidad sus cuerpos no poseían elementos de corrupción como los del cuerpo humano.

El día de Pentecostés *María* revestida del *Espíritu Santo* es quién da los dones que inspiran y dan la fuerza suficiente a los Apóstoles para salir a predicar el evangelio después de la asunción de *Jesús*. Y es Ella que ha seguido inspirando a millones de hombres y mujeres a mantener y fomentar la fe de la Iglesia Cristiana por todo el mundo, a través de sus diferentes advocaciones como la Virgen de La Altagracia, la Virgen de Guadalupe, la Virgen de las Mercedes, la Virgen de la Caridad del Cobre, la Virgen del Rosario, la Virgen de Fátima, la Virgen de Pellevoisin, la Virgen de Regla, la Virgen de Lourdes, la Virgen del Carmen, la Virgen del Pilar, la Virgen de La Salette, la Virgen de Roma, la Virgen de Paris, la Virgen de Syracuse, la Virgen de Knock, la Virgen de Pontmain, la Virgen de Beauring, la Virgen de Banneux, la Virgen de Hollywood, la Virgen de la Milagrosa, la Virgen de Kibeho, la Virgen de Caacupé, la Virgen de Chapi, la Virgen de Czestochowa, la Virgen de China, la Virgen de Akita, la Virgen de la Vang, la Virgen de Sufanieh, la Virgen de Velankanni, entre muchas otras advocaciones, que no son mas que las diferentes formas de nombrar a la personificación femenina del *Espíritu Santo* en La Virgen María.

La Biblia testifica en 2 Pedro 1:21 acerca de nuestro Salvador Jesucristo solamente porque los escritores de la misma fueron "impulsados" a hacerlo por el *Espíritu Santo*, como barcos impulsados por el viento. El *Espíritu Santo* fue quien enseñó a los profetas y a los apóstoles que decir y que escribir. El *Espíritu Santo de Dios* es el verdadero autor de los reales Libros Sagrados, lo cual también se revela en dichos libros, aunque éstos fueron manipulados por el hombre con el transcurso de los tiempos, lo que ha dado como resultado las diferentes versiones de la Biblia que tenemos hoy, que tienen muchas alteraciones de la Palabra del *Espíritu Santo que es Dios*.

> *"Dios no es autor de confusión."* (1 Corintios 14:33) La manipulación que los hombres malvados han hecho en las escrituras para su propio provecho ha creado la confusión. Cuando Jesús se refería al Padre estaba hablando del *Espíritu Santo*. La propia Biblia dice: *"María* (la Madre de Dios) concibió a su *Hijo Jesús* (el Hijo de Dios) por Obra y Gracia

del Espíritu Santo." Aquí queda claro que "Dios Padre" es el propio Espíritu Santo.

Las primeras oraciones de Génesis proveen una introducción dinámica al *Espíritu Santo,* cuando dice: ***"Contra un fondo frío, oscuro, sin vida, el Espíritu de Dios (el Espíritu Santo) se movía sobre la faz de las aguas."*** (Génesis 1:2; Romanos 16:25). El Génesis no se refiere aquí a Jehová, Yahweh, Yahvé ni al Padre, sino que aquí se expresa claramente que el *Espíritu Santo es el Ente de la Creacion y existe desde siempre.*

Una y otra vez, siete veces más, el Pentateuco revela el poder del Espíritu Santo, diciendo que dio habilidad y conocimiento excepcional a ciertas personas escogidas (una vez más debemos resaltar que se está hablando del *Espíritu Santo*). A veces los dotó de manera física, pero con más frecuencia los bendijo espiritualmente en asuntos de la fe. Entre ellos están Josué, Gedeón, Sansón y Saúl quienes se convirtieron en líderes sobresalientes de Israel bajo la influencia del *Espíritu Santo.* David, el rey que escribió los Salmos, explicó su don lírico diciendo: "El Espíritu de Dios (el Espíritu Santo) ha hablado por mí, y su palabra ha estado en mi lengua." El Espíritu también recibe el crédito por poner en la mente de David los planes para el templo futuro. El Antiguo Testamento dice repetidamente que el Espíritu de Dios, o el Espíritu del Señor, vino sobre los profetas, guiando sus pensamientos, palabras y acciones. El *Espíritu Santo* recibe alabanza y la bendición a través de toda la época del Antiguo Testamento. (Génesis 41:38; Éxodo 31:3, 35:31; Números 11:17, 11:25,26; 27:18 y 34:9 los setenta ancianos; Jueces 3:10; 6:34; 13:25; 14:6,19 y 15:14; 1 Samuel 10:6,10; 11:6 y 19:23; 2 Samuel 23:2).

"Así como en un principio, antes de que hubiera vida en el mundo, ya el Espíritu Santo estaba "moviéndose sobre las aguas", así también cuando llegó el cumplimiento del tiempo, el omnipotente, omnipresente y omnisciente encarnó en *María Virgen para ser Madre y en Jesucristo* para ser Hijo, como esencia de su propia esencia, sustancia de su propia sustancia. Desde mucho antes del comienzo de ese gran evento, el *Espíritu Santo* hizo que una persona tras otra testificara acerca de *Jesús,* su propio Yo encarnado. Comenzó con los Profetas y Patriarcas de la Antigua Alianza y luego con Elizabeth, Zacarías y los magos y siguió con los pastores, Simeón y Ana. Luego el *Espíritu Santo* ungió al propio *Jesús*, su Propio Yo encarnado, para predicar las buenas nuevas a los hombres de buena voluntad. Después de la ascensión del Mesías el *Espíritu Santo* derramó sus dones sobre sus discípulos, a través de la divina persona de la *Virgen María*, para que entendieran las Escrituras y la predicaran por todo el mundo, y les dio potestad para que perdonaran los pecados en su nombre. El *Espíritu Santo* eliminó las barreras de las lenguas, disolvió temores, y preparó a los creyentes para dar testimonio de *Jesús* como nuestro Salvador. Lo que comenzó a hacer en Pentecostés, el *Espíritu Santo* ha seguido haciéndolo por toda la eternidad a través de la Virgen *María*; *"El Espíritu Santo vendrá sobre ti, y el poder del Altísimo te cubrirá con su sombra." "El Espíritu del Señor está sobre mí, Por cuanto me ha ungido para dar buenas nuevas a los humildes"; "Esto dijo el Espíritu que habían de recibir los que creyesen en él; pues aún no había venido el Espíritu Santo, porque Jesús y la Virgen María no habían sido aún glorificados."; "Pero cuando venga el Espíritu de verdad, él os guiará a toda la verdad." "Sopló, y les dijo: Recibid el Espíritu Santo. A quienes remitiereis los pecados, les son remitidos; y a quienes se los retuviereis, les son retenidos."* (Lucas 1:35; 4:18; Juan 7:39; 16:13; 20:22,23; Hechos 2:1; 1 Corintios 12:11)

3.5.- El Espíritu Santo tiene nombres y atributos divinos.

Las Escrituras revelan que el *Espíritu Santo* es Dios, acreditándole nombres, obras y atributos divinos. Ya vimos que la palabra espíritu literalmente significa aire, "aliento" o "viento" y que proviene del hebreo (ruaj o *ruach*) y del griego (*pneuma*). La palabra "espíritu" en sí no da a entender la divinidad, de igual forma que las palabras Padre e Hijo tampoco insinúan en sí la divinidad. Pero el hecho de que a este Espíritu con frecuencia se le llama Espíritu Santo claramente indica que él es Dios. Las traducciones de la Biblia por lo general lo reconocen, poniendo la palabra Espíritu en mayúscula cuando el contexto revela que está hablando del *Espíritu Santo.* (Salmo 99:9 "Exaltad a YHWH nuestro Dios, y postraos ante su santo monte, porque YHWH nuestro Dios es santo." Isaías 6:3 "Santo, santo, santo, Yahweh de los ejércitos; toda la tierra está llena de su gloria.")

El apóstol Pablo dio los nombres "Señor" y "Dios" al Espíritu Santo cuando escribió de dones espirituales: "Hay diversidad de dones, pero el Espíritu es el mismo. Y hay diversidad de ministerios, pero el Señor es el mismo. Y hay diversidad de operaciones, pero Dios, que hace todas las cosas en todos, es el mismo... Pero todas estas cosas las hace uno y el mismo Espíritu (el Espíritu Santo)." (1 Corintios 12:4; 6:11). San Pablo también dijo en 1 Corintios 6:19, "Vuestro cuerpo es templo del *Espíritu Santo*, el cual está en vosotros", es decir que el cuerpo del cristiano es un templo de Dios ya que el Espíritu habita en él.

El Credo Niceno alaba al *Espíritu Santo* como *"el dador de vida"*. Es una descripción apropiada de la actividad divina del *Espíritu Santo* durante la creación del mundo. También merece esta alabanza porque el don de la vida se puede transmitir de una generación a otra. Como dijo Job, "El *espíritu de Dios* me hizo, Y el soplo del Omnipotente me dio vida." Pero aun más importante que el don de la vida física es el nuevo nacimiento, la vida espiritual que el *Espíritu Santo* obra mediante el Evangelio en el Sacramento del Santo Bautismo y mediante el Evangelio en sí. Dios "nos salvó... por el lavamiento de la regeneración y por la renovación en el *Espíritu Santo*." "Dios os ha escogido desde el principio para salvación, mediante la santificación por el Espíritu y la fe en la verdad, a lo cual os llamó mediante nuestro evangelio, para alcanzar la gloria de nuestro Señor Jesucristo." (Génesis 1:1,2; Job 33:4; Tito 3:4,5; 2 Tesalonicenses 2:13,14).

Además, el *Espíritu Santo* también preserva la vida de su pueblo orando por ellos: "Y de igual manera el Espíritu nos ayuda en nuestra debilidad; pues qué hemos de pedir como conviene, no lo sabemos, pero el Espíritu mismo intercede por nosotros..." (Romanos 8:26) Esas actividades de creación y de preservación afirman que el *Espíritu Santo*. Como Dios, el *Espíritu Santo* también nos convence del pecado, nos testifica de Cristo, nos conduce a la fe en nuestro Salvador y nos preserva nuestra fe.

Se debe notar que las tres personas que conforman el *Espíritu Santo*; el Padre, la Madre y el Hijo de Dios, hacen en común todas estas obras divinas. Las tres personas tienen la misma naturaleza divina y juntas están activas en todas las obras divinas que se hacen hacia el exterior del *Espíritu Santo*, para la creación, la preservación y la evolución de la creación. El mundo está lleno de milagros hechos por las tres divina personas del *Espíritu Santo*.

Cuando se instituyó el bautismo, se nombró a las tres personas que conforman el Espíritu Santo, pero el machismo de la época eliminó la parte femenina del Ser Supremo y para lograrlo duplicaron las menciones Espíritu Santo como tal y como Padre. En Mateo 28:19 se lee; "bautizándolos en el nombre del Padre, y del Hijo, y del Espíritu Santo." Según los teólogos, el hecho de que se nombró al Espíritu Santo de último no indica que tenga una posición inferior, o que se originó en otro tiempo. Tampoco el hecho de que cada una de las tres personas se nombre por separado quiere decir que cada una tenga su propia naturaleza divina. La naturaleza divina del *Espíritu Santo* no está separada de la naturaleza divina del Padre, de la Madre y del Hijo. La Escritura enseña que hay un Dios, con una naturaleza divina. Las palabras apropiadas son: "Te bautizo en el nombre del Espíritu Santo como Padre, Madre e Hijo". Ya que no hay tres dioses con tres naturalezas divinas, hay un solo *Espíritu Santo* que ha poseído tres figuraciones diferentes para llevar a cabo acciones diferentes. Cada una de las tres personas asumidas por el *Espíritu Santo* posee una única e indivisible esencia divina en su totalidad. Porque en verdad existe un solo Dios que recibe el nombre de *Espíritu Santo* y que éste se ha hecho presente entre los humanos en tres personas o figuraciones divinas; *el Padre, la Virgen María y Jesús*, y que cada cultura los ha llamado por diferentes nombres. De hecho, los hebreos, antes de la venida de *María y Jesús, llamaban la parte femenina de Dios con el nombre de Asherah a la cual rendían tributos como la esposa de Dios. Pero todo esto fue editado de la biblia.*

"A veces leemos una referencia en plural al *Espíritu Santo* en la Biblia. Eso puede tener referencia a las características séptuples del *Espíritu Santo* que fueron dadas a Cristo como el profeta Isaías predijo: "Y reposará sobre él el *Espíritu de Jehová; espíritu de sabiduría y de inteligencia, espíritu de consejo y de poder, espíritu de conocimiento y de temor de Yahweh.*" (Apocalipsis 1:4; 3:1; 4:5; 5:6; Isaías 11:2; Lucas 4:18)

"El *Espíritu Santo* fue dado a la naturaleza humana de Jesús "sin límite". Por esta razón y también porque *Jesús* y el *Espíritu Santo,* uno solo es, con la misma naturaleza divina, a Jesús se le puede llamar, *"el Señor que es el Espíritu Santo."* La perfecta cooperación y unidad divina de estas dos personalidades del Ser Divino no cambia el hecho de que las dos personas son distintas y separadas en espacio y tiempo. El Hijo está en el Espíritu Santo y el Espíritu Santo está en el Hijo, lo propio pasa con la Madre, *la Virgen María*. Las Tres divinas personas; Padre, Madre e Hijo, están en el *Espíritu Santo* tanto como el *Espíritu Santo* está en cada uno de ellos. El *Espíritu Santo* es como un triangulo equilátero formado por el Padre, la Virgen maría y Jesús en donde ellos son el todo y las partes al mismo tiempo.

"Porque el Señor es el Espíritu; y donde está el Espíritu del Señor, allí hay libertad. Por tanto, nosotros todos, mirando a cara descubierta como en un espejo la gloria del Señor, somos transformados de gloria en gloria en la misma imagen, como por el Espíritu del Señor." En este pasaje las palabras "el Señor", la gloria del Señor" y "la misma imagen" tienen referencia a Jesucristo. "El Espíritu" tiene referencia al Espíritu Santo. De manera semejante, el Hijo es el Padre, y el Padre es el Hijo, ya que Jesús dijo: "Yo y el Padre uno somos", y "El que me ha visto a mí, ha visto al Padre." (Juan 3:34; 10:30 y 14:8-11; 2 Corintios 3:17.18). Cuando Jesús habla del Padre se está refiriendo a El en *sí* mismo.

> *"Porque el que Dios envió, las palabras de Dios hablan; pues Dios nos da el Espíritu por medida."*

La Escritura advierte en contra de ofender al Espíritu Santo. Cuando el Rey Saúl se apartó de Dios, "el Espíritu de Dios" se apartó de él. Cuando el Rey David reconoció que su pecado y falta de arrepentimiento había contristado al Espíritu Santo, se arrepintió con todo su corazón. Dios advirtió al Israel impenitente que eran "rebeldes, e hicieron enojar su santo espíritu" y que por eso "les volvió enemigo, y él mismo peleó contra ellos." Un juicio terrible cayó sobre Ananías y su esposa Safira cuando rehusaron arrepentirse o inclusive admitir que habían mentido al Espíritu Santo.

De la misma manera los hebreos fueron advertidos: "Porque si pecáremos voluntariamente después de haber recibido el conocimiento de la verdad, ya no queda más sacrificio por los pecados, sino una horrenda expectación de juicio, y de hervor de fuego que ha de devorar a los adversarios. El que viola la ley de Moisés, por el testimonio de dos o de tres testigos muere irremisiblemente.

¿Cuánto mayor castigo pensáis que merecerá el que pisoteare al Hijo de Dios, y tuviere por inmunda la sangre del pacto en la cual fue santificado, e hiciere afrenta al Espíritu de gracia? Pues conocemos al que dijo: Mía es la venganza, yo daré el pago, dice el Señor. Y otra vez: El Señor juzgará a su pueblo. ¡Horrenda cosa es caer en manos del Dios vivo! (1 Samuel 16:14; Salmo 51:1-11; Isaías 63:10; Hebreos 10:26-31).

El Espíritu Santo merece la adoración y el respeto del pueblo de Dios. El pecado lo entristece, la vida santificada lo honra. (Efesios 4:30-31 "Y no contristéis al Espíritu Santo, con el cual fuisteis sellados para el día de la redención. Quítense de vosotros toda amargura, enojo, ira, gritería y maledicencia, y toda malicia").

¿O ignoráis que vuestro cuerpo es templo del Espíritu Santo, el cual está en vosotros, el cual tenéis de Dios, y que no sois vuestros? Porque habéis sido comprados por precio; glorificad, pues, a Dios en vuestro cuerpo y en vuestro espíritu, los cuales son de Dios. (1 Corintios 6:19-20)

Ya que el Espíritu Santo provee el poder para la vida santificada solamente mediante el evangelio en palabra y sacramento, le damos honra manteniéndonos en contacto con estos medios de gracia, para que no apaguemos el fuego del Espíritu siendo negligentes del evangelio.

3.6.- La verdadera dinámica del Espíritu Santo.

En la iglesia cristiana antigua, un grupo de cristianos judíos conocido como los ebionitas sostenían la creencia de que el Espíritu Santo era la persona femenina en la Divina Trinidad. Un teólogo moderno cuyos escritos han aparecido últimamente en el internet también especula acerca del género femenino del Espíritu Santo. Luego procede a desarrollar su propio sistema teológico, sugiriendo que un Espíritu Santo hembra explica la caracterización femenina de la "sabiduría" en Proverbios 8:12:31. También algunos teólogos feministas modernos prefieren adorar a Dios como *Sophia*, una diosa, tienen la misma opinión heterodoxa. (Neve, op. Cit., tomo 1, p. 51; www.theology.edu/pneumato.htm)

Estas creencias se suman a todas las anteriores las cuales se han basado en muchos conceptos erróneos sobre la identidad del Espíritu Santo. Entre sus grandes confusiones algunos ven al Espíritu Santo como una fuerza mística. Otros entienden al Espíritu Santo, como el poder impersonal que Dios pone a disposición para los seguidores de nuestro Señor Jesucristo.

Hemos visto que la Biblia dice de manera clara y precisa que el *Espíritu Santo es Dios*. También nos dice que el *Espíritu Santo es una Persona*, un Ser con una mente, emociones, y una voluntad. El hecho de que el *Espíritu Santo*, es visto claramente en muchas partes de las Escrituras, incluyendo Hechos 5:3-4. En este versículo, Pedro confronta a Ananías por haber mentido al Espíritu Santo, y le dice que él "no había mentido a los hombres sino a Dios". Es una clara declaración de que mentir al *Espíritu Santo* es mentir a *Dios*, es decir que ambos son una misma esencia. También podemos saber que el *Espíritu Santo es Dios*, porque El posee los atributos o características de Dios. Por ejemplo, como ya pudimos ver anteriormente, el hecho de que el Espíritu Santo es omnipresente, en Salmos 139:7-8 "¿A dónde me iré de tu Espíritu? ¿Y a dónde huiré de tu presencia? Si subiere a los cielos, allí estás tú; y si en el Seol hiciere mi estrado, he aquí, allí tú estás". Luego, en 1 Corintios 2:10 vemos la característica de la omnisciencia del Espíritu Santo. "Pero Dios nos las reveló a nosotros por el Espíritu; porque el Espíritu todo lo escudriña, aún lo profundo de Dios". Porque ¿quién de los hombres sabe las cosas del hombre, sino el espíritu del hombre que está en él? Así tampoco nadie conoció las cosas de Dios, sino el Espíritu de Dios."

Podemos conocer que el *Espíritu Santo* es en verdad más que una Persona, "Es El Que existe" Aquel que ordenó y entregó los Mandamientos a Moisés, porque El posee una mente, emociones y una voluntad. "El Espíritu Santo piensa y sabe" (1 Corintios 2:10). "El Espíritu Santo puede ser afligido" (Efesios 4:30) "El Espíritu Santo intercede por nosotros" (Romanos 8:26-27). El Espíritu Santo hace decisiones de acuerdo con Su voluntad (1 Corintios 12:7-11). *El Espíritu Santo es Dios*. Como Dios, el Espíritu Santo puede funcionar verdaderamente como Consejero y Consolador, tal como lo prometió a través de Jesús. (Juan 14:16, 26; 15:26).

Con todo lo que hemos visto hasta ahora acerca de Las Divinas Personas que conforman la Santísima Trinidad del *Espíritu Santo* debemos colegir que en realidad YHVH (Yahvé), Jehová y el Padre, son exactamente nombres con los cuales se le ha llamado a la expresión masculina del *Espíritu Santo*; cuando Jesús está hablando de Su Padre se está refiriendo precisamente al *Espíritu Santo como padre*. El *Espíritu Santo* nunca ha encarnado como "El Padre"; encarnó como Mujer para ser Madre, en *María*, para a través de Su encarnación femenina encarnar a la misma vez como Hombre e Hijo en Jesucristo Nuestro Señor. Si se estudia con detenimiento y objetividad las escrituras que confirman y hablan de la naturaleza de Dios no habría ninguna posibilidad de confusión. De tal forma que no ha sido por confusión que los jerarcas eclesiásticos han mantenido mal informada a la humanidad acerca de esta materia, más bien lo han hecho cegados por el egoísmo machista que ha arropado las diferentes iglesias durante todo el transcurso de la historia de la humanidad. "Y Jesús, después que fue bautizado, subió enseguida del agua, y en ese momento los cielos fueron abiertos, y se vió la manifestación femenina del Espíritu Santo que descendía como paloma y se posaba sobre su propio Ser hecho Hombre. Y en ese momento se oyó la voz del Espíritu Santo decir: Este es mi Hijo amado, en quien tengo complacencia." (Mateo 3:16-17).

Si se analizan con detenimiento los pasajes de la Biblia en donde Dios ha hecho contacto con algún humano se comprobará que nunca se ha presentado con una figura de Padre, siempre lo hizo en forma de *zarza ardiente, fuego, fuente de luz y viento.* Las únicas partes en donde se habla del Dios Padre es cuando Jesús se está refiriendo a su Padre, al Padre Creador, el Templo de mi Padre, la casa de mi Padre, etc., si esto lo unimos con la parte de la Biblia que habla de su forma de venir al mundo humano, la cual dice: "Fue engendrado por Obra y Gracia del Espíritu Santo…", entonces está claro que el Padre de Jesús es el Espíritu Santo, al tiempo que Jesús es también el Espíritu Santo; "Mi Padre y Yo uno somos," "Quien me ha visto a mi ha visto a mi Padre." Jesús también dijo: "Yo me iré, pero siempre estaré con ustedes." Más adelante, en otro pasaje de la Biblia dice: Antes del regreso al cielo después de su ministerio en la tierra, Jesús habló de la venida del Espíritu Santo.

"Pero cuando venga el Consolador, a quien yo os enviaré del Padre, el Espíritu de verdad, el cual procede del Padre, él dará testimonio acerca de mí" (Juan 15:26). Si consideramos que Jesús dijo: "Yo y el Padre uno solo somos." Y agregó "el que me ha visto a mi ha visto al Padre". De forma tal que Jesús aquí está prometiendo volver Él mismo, enviado por Él mismo, aunque está enfatizando que su regreso será en una forma diferente, en una expresión diferente de su propio Ser Divino, la cual es precisamente la forma y esencia del Espíritu Santo que a la vez que es su Padre es Él mismo.

"Y yo rogaré al Padre y os dará otro Consolador, para que esté con vosotros para siempre: el Espíritu de verdad, al cual el mundo no puede recibir, porque no lo ve ni lo conoce; pero vosotros lo conocéis, porque vive con vosotros y estará en vosotros" (Juan 14:16-17). Quién más que el *Espíritu Santo en la Virgen María para consolar los Creyentes.* "Pero cuando venga el Consolador, a quien yo os enviaré del Padre, el Espíritu de verdad, el cual procede del Padre, él dará testimonio acerca de mí' (Juan 15:26).

"Manifiestas son las obras de la carne, que son: adulterio, fornicación, inmundicia, lujuria, idolatría, hechicerías, enemistades, pleitos, celos, iras, contiendas, divisiones, herejías, envidias, homicidios, borracheras, orgías, y cosas semejantes a estas. En cuanto a esto, os advierto, como ya os he dicho antes, que los que practican tales cosas no heredarán el reino de Dios. Pero el fruto del Espíritu es amor, gozo, paz, paciencia, benignidad, bondad, fe, mansedumbre, templanza; contra tales cosas no hay ley" (Gálatas 5:19-23). Aunque el poder de la carne fue derrotado en la cruz, como creyentes experimentamos esto sólo en la medida que practicamos la fe en las obras del *Espíritu Santo* a través de Jesús y la Virgen María. Por lo tanto, para ser efectivo en negar el poder de la naturaleza pecaminosa de la carne, es necesario que nos revistamos del fruto del Espíritu Santo.

El Espíritu Santo en su forma espiritual e invisible para los ojos naturales del hombre, pero está en el mundo hoy, continuando su obra a través de la Virgen María activamente, redarguyendo a los hombres y las mujeres de pecado, atrayendo a los hombres y las mujeres al cristianismo, equipando a los creyentes con poder para la guerra espiritual, guiándolos, y testificando sobre la gloria infinita que emana de su propio Ser.

El *Espíritu Santo* es el Alfa y la Omega, no solo por ser el principio y el fin, sino por ser varón (Alfa) y hembra (Omega). "...Y los creó a su imagen y semejanza. Varón y Hembra los creo." Uno de los nombres del *Espíritu Santo* es "Yo Soy", con lo cual se quiere significar que Él no tuvo principio ni tendrá fin, y por tal razón Él siempre será presente, para Él no existe pasado ni futuro, todo sucede en un mismo instante.

El *Espíritu Santo* es el creador del universo. Para que esto sea posible, Él existió antes de crear al mundo y su género es femenino y masculino a la voluntad de su omnipotencia.

El *Espíritu Santo* es el poder y la autoridad suprema sobre todas las cosas. Nada puede ocurrir sin que el *Espíritu Santo* lo sepa y permita que eso ocurra por su omnipresencia y omnisciencia. Una hoja no cae de un árbol si su aprobación.

El *Espíritu Santo* nos revela todo lo que sabemos de Él. Él es Dios y personalmente se deja conocer a través de las diferentes personas de su Santísima Trinidad. Aunque no sabemos todo lo que respecta al *Espíritu Santo*, cada uno de nosotros puede conocer un poco de Él y de cada una de sus divinas personificaciones, si honramos su nombre.

El *Espíritu Santo* siempre sabe por qué las cosas ocurren, Él siempre tiene un propósito para todo lo que ocurre en el universo.

"Como son más altos los cielos que la tierra, así son mis caminos más altos que vuestros caminos, y mis pensamientos más que vuestros pensamientos" (Isaías 55:9).

El *Espíritu Santo* creó el mundo solamente con dar la orden para que cada cosa existiera. El *Espíritu Santo* no tiene limitación de poder. Él conoce todas las cosas. Él está siempre presente.

El *Espíritu Santo* es único, sin pecado y completamente diferente. El *Espíritu Santo* tiene toda perfección moral. En el *Espíritu Santo* toda bondad es representada.

El *Espíritu Santo* va más allá de simplemente amarnos; el *Espíritu Santo* es amor. Nada de lo que Él hace está fuera de su amor. Debido a ese gran amor es que se encarnó en la *Virgen María* y en su Hijo *Jesús* con la finalidad de dar su vida para redimirnos de nuestros pecados.

El propósito de redimir a la humanidad fue unir la comunión que fue rota por nuestros pecados. El *Espíritu Santo* no tenía la intención de que el mundo fuera como es actualmente, pero Él ha proveído el camino hacia la redención.

El *Espíritu Santo* siempre ha querido que seamos un pueblo sin pecado en nuestras vidas. Durante los años de la Antigua Alianza, el *Espíritu Santo* instituyó un sacrificio temporal para que las personas recibieran el perdón de sus pecados. Una vez al año los pecados del pueblo eran simbólicamente echados en un cordero que era expulsado de la comunidad. Este proceso debía repetirse anualmente. El sacerdote escuchaba mientras las personas confesaban sus pecados. Luego, él sacrificaba un animal y ofrecía esa sangre como dispensación de los pecados de la persona.

Luego de Jesús dejar instituida la Alianza Nueva y Eterna, constituyéndose Él mismo en el Cordero de sacrificio a Dios, "el Cordero de Dios que quita los pecados del mundo…", el sacrificio de animales quedó derogado y la muerte de Jesús es el sacrificio permanente por nuestros pecados. La sangre de Jesús trae perdón por nuestros pecados por toda la eternidad.

El *Espíritu Santo* quiso restaurar su Alianza con la humanidad a través de su personalidad como Madre y Mujer, en María, y de su personalidad como Hijo y Hombre, en Jesús, ya en la antigüedad había instaurado su Alianza con los Patriarcas a través de su personalidad como YHVH (Yahvé) "El que existe". El *Espíritu Santo* forma a plenitud estas tres divinas personas, pero también está presente en cada ser humano, aunque en mucho menor grado, y está en cada hombre y mujer cultivarlo para ser cada vez más a imagen y semejanza de Él. Esta fue la principal enseñanza de Jesús y María, que todo ser humano tiene la oportunidad de desarrollarse espiritualmente hasta alcanzar la divinidad, ya que establecido está que fuimos creados a imagen y semejanza de Dios. Todo hombre que logre imitar a Jesús y toda Mujer que logre imitar a *María* podrá alcanzar la dimensión celestial en donde habitan los Seres de Luz.

Los hombres le han dado muchos nombres a Dios, y en La Biblia se recogen los nombres dados para nombrar a Dios que nos revelan Su Ministerio mientras estás comprometido en este gran conflicto espiritual. En verdad los judíos tienen prohibido pronunciar el nombre real de Dios de cuatro letras (Yud-Hei-Vav-Hei). Esta es la razón por la cual ellos le llaman "Hashem" que significa "El Nombre". Pero en las diferentes versiones de la Biblia encontramos que a Dios se lo nombra por diferentes nombres; como "Jehová" en las Biblias evangélicas y "Yahvé" en las Biblias católicas. Pero en el fondo carece de importancia discutir por el nombre de Dios en la Antiguo Alianza. Lo que si reviste de gran importancia es que nosotros vivimos hoy bajo la Eterna Alianza establecida por Jesús y la Virgen María en el Espíritu Santo, y por tanto debemos de hablar de Dios como Jesús hablaba de Él; Jesús nos dijo que el *Espíritu Santo* es amor. Dios es un "Padre" que ama a todas sus creaturas y los humanos somos sus hijos predilectos, ya que fuimos creados a su imagen y semejanza. *Jesús* mismo nos enseñó que debemos invocar a Dios como "Nuestro Padre y Creador" (Mateo 6, 9). Todos los textos originales antiguos al hablar de Dios lo hacen con artículos neutros, con lo cual no le dejan establecido un género sexual específico a Dios. Es a partir del Nuevo Testamento donde se comienza a llamar a Dios con artículo masculino, derogando la parte femenina del Espíritu Santo.

Para los tradicionales estudiosos de la Biblia esta explicación es un poco difícil de asimilar, porque debemos comprender algunas cosas del idioma hebreo, la lengua en la cual el Espíritu Santo se manifestó a Moisés. Los israelitas del Antiguo Testamento empleaban muchos nombres para referirse a Dios. Todos estos nombres expresaban una relación íntima del *Espíritu Santo* con la humanidad, como podemos ver más adelante:

En Éxodo 6:7 encontramos en el texto hebreo el nombre "Elohim", que en castellano significa: "El Dios fuerte y Poderoso".

En el Salmo 94 encontramos "Edonay", que en castellano es "El Señor".

En Génesis 17:1 se habla de Dios como "Shadday" que quiere decir el Dios de la montaña.

En Isaías 7:14 se habla de "Emmanuel" que significa "Dios con nosotros".

Pero el nombre más empleado en aquellos tiempos era "YHVH" que se pronuncia "Yahvé" y que en castellano significa: "Yo soy el que existe". En Éxodo 3:13-15 podemos leer el relato de cuando el Espíritu Santo de Dios se apareció a Moisés en forma de zarza ardiente y lo mandó al Faraón a hablar en su nombre. Moisés le preguntó al Espíritu Santo: "Pero si los israelitas me preguntan cuál es tu nombre, ¿qué voy a contestarles?". Y el Espíritu Santo dijo a Moisés: "YO SOY EL QUE EXITE". Así les dirás a los israelitas: "EL QUE EXISTE" me manda a ustedes. Esto les dirás a ellos: "EL QUE EXISTE (YHVH), Aquel que estuvo con Isaac y que estuvo con Jacob me manda a ustedes. Este es mi nombre por siempre".

La palabra "YHVH" (Yud-Hei-Vav-Hei) es una palabra hebrea, el hebreo es el idioma de los israelitas o judíos del Antiguo Testamento. En este idioma no se escribían las vocales de una palabra sino únicamente las consonantes. Era bastante difícil leerlo correctamente, porque al leer un texto hebreo, uno mismo debía saber de memoria qué vocales tenía que pronunciar en medio de las consonantes. El nombre de Dios: "YO SOY EL QUE EXISTE" se escribía con estas cuatro consonantes: Y H V H que los judíos pronunciaban "Yud-Hei-Vav-Hei" pero con el tiempo fue degenerando hasta llegar a la pronunciación de "Yahvéh", y en castellano se pronuncia "Yahvé" como la pronunciación más apróximada del hebreo original para indicar el nombre por el cual se nombró el Propio Espíritu Santo como "Yo soy el que existe". Es importante aclarar aquí que los judíos del Antiguo Testamento nunca llamaron a Dios por el nombre de "Jehová" ya que ese nombre fue creado por los hombres en la Edad Media.

Los israelitas de la antigüedad tenían un profundo respeto por el nombre del *Espíritu Santo de Dios:* "YHVH" (Yud-Hei-Vav-Hei) era el nombre más sagrado de Dios, porque el *Espíritu Santo* mismo se había dado este nombre Él mismo; "YO SOY EL QUE EXISTE". Pero con el tiempo los israelitas, por respeto al nombre propio del *Espíritu Santo,* dejaron de pronunciar el nombre de "YHVH" y cuando ellos leían en la Biblia el nombre de "YHVH", en vez de decir "Yud-Hei-Vav-Hei" decían otro nombre para referirse a Dios, este otro nombre era "Edonay" que significa "El Señor". Pero resultó que después de cientos de años los israelitas se olvidaron por completo de la pronunciación original de "YHVH" (Yud-Hei-Vav-Hei) porque siempre decían "Edonay". Y es en la época de la Edad Media, unos 1,300 años después de Cristo, cuando los analistas religiosos estudiaban el idioma hebreo antiguo y empezaron a poner vocales entre las consonantes del idioma hebreo. Y cuando les tocó colocar vocales en la palabra hebrea YHVH el nombre original del Espíritu Santo encontraron muchas dificultades.

Por no conocer la pronunciación original de las cuatro consonantes que en las letras castellanas corresponden a YHVH y en letras latinas a JHVH, y para recordar al lector que por respeto debía decir: "Edonay" en vez de "JHVH", pusieron las tres vocales (e, o, a) de la palabra Edonay; y resultó la palabra "Jehovah" en latín. Es decir, tomaron las 4 consonantes de una palabra "JHVH" y metieron simplemente las 3 vocales de la palabra Edonay y formaron así una nueva palabra: "Jehovah". Está claro que la palabra "Jehovah" es un arreglo de dos palabras en una, que más tardes se comenzó a escribir "Jehová" por facilidad de pronunciación. Por supuesto la palabra "Jehová" nunca ha existido en hebreo; es decir, que la pronunciación "Jehová" es una pronunciación defectuosa del nombre de "YHVH" o "Yahvé".

En los años 1600 d.C. comenzaron a traducir la Biblia a todas las lenguas, y como encontraron en todos los textos bíblicos de la Edad Media la palabra "Jehová" como nombre propio de Dios, copiaron este nombre "Jehová" literalmente en los distintos idiomas. Y desde aquel tiempo empezaron a pronunciar los católicos y los evangélicos como nombre propio del Espíritu Santo del Antiguo Testamento la palabra "Jehová" en castellano.

Ahora bien, aun las Biblias católicas usan el nombre de "Yahvé" y no el de "Jehová". Ya que todos los estudiosos del idioma hebreo creían que la manera original y primitiva de pronunciar el nombre del Espíritu Santo debía haber sido "Yahvé" y no "Jehová". Ya que "Yahvé" es una forma del verbo "havah" (ser, existir) y significa: "Yo soy el que existe" y "Jehová" no es ninguna forma del verbo "ser", ni siquiera es una palabra real que existiera antes de que los escritores de la edad media hicieran la combinación de las consonantes de JHVH con las vocales de Edonay para formar la palabra "Jehovah", como lo he explicado más arriba. Por eso la Iglesia Católica Romana tomó la decisión de usar la pronunciación que creía era la original "Yahvé" en vez de "Jehová" y porque los israelitas del tiempo de Moisés así como los del tiempo de Jesús nunca conocieron el nombre "Jehová."

Ya sabemos que "YHVH" se mal pronuncia "Yahvé" y que significa "Yo soy el que existe". Pero para comprender este nombre debemos pensar que todos los pueblos de aquel tiempo eran politeístas, es decir, creían en la existencia de muchos dioses. Según ellos, cada nación, cada ciudad y cada tribu tenía su propio Dios o sus propios dioses. Al decir el Espíritu Santo a Moisés: "Yud-Hei-Vav-Hei" (YO SOY EL QUE EXISTE), Él quiere dejar establecido que Él es el único y verdadero Dios; y los otros dioses no existen, los dioses de los egipcios, de los asirios, de los babilonios no existen. Yo soy el único Dios que existe.

El profeta Isaías explica bien el sentido del nombre del *Espíritu Santo*. Dice Dios por medio del profeta: "Yud-Hei-Vav-Hei" (YO SOY EL QUE EXISTE), y ningún otro". "¿Soy yo Yahvé el único y nadie mas que yo?" (Isaías 45, 18).

Otro punto importante en el cual debemos estar claros es saber que Jesús y sus apóstoles, según la costumbre judía de aquel tiempo, nunca pronunciaban el nombre original de Dios "YHVH" o "Yahvé" y mucho menos "Jehová" (ya que como vimos anteriormente el nombre Jehová se creó 1,300 años después de Cristo). Siempre leían la Biblia diciendo: "Edonay" -el Señor- para indicar el nombre propio de Dios. Pero como todo el Nuevo Testamento fue escrito en griego, en el encontramos la palabra Kyrios que significa "el Señor", la cual es la traducción al griego de "Edonay".

Pero Jesús introdujo también una novedad en las costumbres religiosas y nombró a Dios "Padre": "Te alabo, Padre, Señor del cielo y de la tierra". "Mi Padre sigue actuando y yo también actúo". "Por eso los judíos tenían ganas de matarlo: porque El llamaba a Dios Padre suyo haciéndose igual a Dios". "Mi Padre y yo uno mismo somos". "El que me ha visto a mi, ha visto al Padre". (Juan 5, 17-18).

Los libros originales del Nuevo Testamento hablan de Dios como "Padre" o "Señor", pero nunca como "Jehová" ni como "Yahvé". Pero cada una de las religiones que han escrito sus propias versiones de la Biblia sí mencionan estos nombres cientos de veces. Desconociendo así una vez más la gran revelación de Jesucristo que fue la de anunciarnos al Padre, a la Madre y al Hijo formando la *Santísima Trinidad en el Espíritu Santo*, donde los tres son uno mismo.

Otros nombres muy utilizados en las diferentes versiones del Antiguo Testamento para clamar a Dios son:

> Yahweh: en el idioma hebreo que es en el que el Antiguo Testamento se escribió, la palabra "Yahweh" significa Dios. Esta palabra es combinada con otras palabras para revelar más sobre el carácter de Dios. Dios es llamado:
>
> Yahweh Jireh: "El Señor que provee" (Génesis 22:14)
>
> Yahweh Nisi: "El Señor es bandera" (Éxodo 17:15)
>
> Yahweh Shalom: "El Señor es paz" (Jueces 6:24)
>
> Yahweh Sebaot: "El Señor de los Ejércitos" (I Samuel 1:3)
>
> Yahweh Macadeshem: "El Señor tu Santificador" (Éxodo 31:13)
>
> Yahweh Tzidkenu: "El Señor nuestra Justicia" (Jeremías 23:6)
>
> Yahweh Shamah: "El Señor está allí" (Ezequiel 48:35)
>
> Yahweh Elohim Israel: "El Señor Dios de Israel" (Jueces 5:3)
>
> Qadosh Israel: "El Santo de Israel" (Isaías 1:4)
>
> Yahweh Rapha: "El Señor tu Sanador" (Exodo 15:26)
>
> Jehová: que significa Señor. La Biblia combina esta palabra con otros nombres de Dios:
>
> Jehová-Rafa: "El Señor que sana" (Éxodo 15:26).
>
> Jehová-Nisi: "El Señor nuestra bandera" (Éxodo 17:8-15).
>
> Jehová-Shalom: "El Señor nuestra paz" (Jueces 6:24).
>
> Jehová-Raah: "El Señor mi pastor" (Salmos 23:1).
>
> Jehová-Tzidkenu: "El Señor nuestra justicia" (Jeremías 23:6).
>
> Jehová- Jireh: "El Señor que provee" (Génesis 22:14).
>
> Jehová-Shamah: "El Señor está allí" (Ezequiel 48:35).
>
> Elohim: significa Dios y es usado en dondequiera que esté presente el poder creador de Dios.

Padre: Hechos 17:28; Juan 1:12-13.

Edonay o Adonai: significa Señor o Amo: Éxodo 23:17; Isaías 10:16, 33.

El: es frecuentemente usado en combinación con otras palabras para Dios:

El Shadai: "El Señor que es suficiente para las necesidades de Su pueblo" (Éxodo 6:3).

Elolam: "El Dios Eterno" (Génesis 21:33).

El Elyon: "El más alto Dios que es exaltado por encima de los llamados dioses" (Génesis 14:18, 22).

El Señor de los Ejércitos: en el registro bíblico, estos diferentes nombres de Dios fueron usados para solicitarle a Dios que se mueve de una manera específica a favor de su pueblo. Por ejemplo, el nombre Yahweh-Rafa significando "El Señor que sana" fue usado cuando se buscaba sanidad.

El nombre específico de Dios que será usado en la guerra espiritual (guerra santa) es "Yahweh Sebaot" el cual es traducido como "El Señor de los Ejércitos" en la versión de la Biblia del Rey Jacobo. Cuando clamas ese nombre en la guerra, la batalla es del Señor y todos los ejércitos del cielo vienen en tu ayuda.

El misterio más grande e importante de todo esto para la humanidad está en conocer y aceptar la verdadera composición de Dios. Cuando la Biblia fue reescrita en el siglo IV después de Cristo y se estableció el Credo de la Iglesia Católica Apostólica Romana, en el mismo se creó un dogma de fe, es decir una verdad que debemos creer: "Hay un solo y único Dios, que es el Padre Creador, Hijo Redentor y Espíritu Santo, Señor y Dador de Vida y Santificador." Este misterio de la Santísima Trinidad, es uno de los "misterios escondidos en Dios, -que como dice el Concilio Vaticano II-, si no son revelados, no pueden ser conocidos" Y, aun después de la Revelación, es el misterio más profundo de la fe, que el entendimiento por sí solo no puede comprender ni penetrar. En cambio, el mismo entendimiento, iluminado por la fe, puede en cierto modo, aferrar y explicar el significado del dogma, para acercar al hombre al misterio de la vida íntima del Dios Único y Trino.

Toda la Sagrada Escritura revela esta verdad: "Dios es Amor en la vida interior de una única Divinidad, como una inefable comunión de personas." Son Tres Personas distintas en un solo Espíritu Santo, como enseña el catecismo.

El misterio de la Santísima Trinidad del Espíritu Santo es la revelación más grande hecha por Jesucristo. Los judíos adoran la unicidad de Dios y desconocen la pluralidad de personas en la unicidad de la sustancia. Los demás pueblos adoran la multiplicidad de los dioses. El cristianismo es la única religión que ha descubierto, en la revelación de Jesús, que Dios es uno en tres personas. Ante esta revelación divina de su íntima esencia, no nos queda otra cosa que agradecerle esta confianza y adorar a las Tres Personas Divinas: Jesús (el Hijo), María (la Madre) y el Padre en el Espíritu Santo.

El *Espíritu Santo* es el Dador de Vida, Dones y Santidad. El *Espíritu Santo* es el Ser que forma la Esencia de todo lo que existe en el universo. Es el que está desde antes del Principio y perdurará luego del Fin. Él es el Alfa y la Omega. Él es el Varón y la Hembra. De Él fuimos hechos a imagen y semejanza. Él puede asumir cualquier imagen o figura conocida o desconocida por la humanidad. Él es el único omnipotente, omnipresente y omnisciente. Todo lo demás proviene de Él. Luego de Él provino la Madre y el Padre para engendrar el Hijo. Y los tres forman parte de su propia esencia. El Padre es el Espíritu Santo, la Madre es el Espíritu Santo y el Hijo es el Espíritu Santo; Tres Personas Divinas en una sola Sustancia, en un solo Espíritu; el Espíritu Santo que es Dios. Los tres tienen la misma procedencia divina y su forma de venir al mundo humano solo fue para cubrir las apariencias de algo que no podía ser entendido por los seres de la época antigua.

Estamos ante la presencia de un fenómeno divino que le hemos llamado por cientos de nombres diferentes tratando de explicar sus misterios, misterios que están muy por encima de la comprensión humana hasta nuestros días. Es un Ser que es uno y todo a la vez. Un Ser que posee todos los estados posibles de la materia. Un Ser que ninguno de los humanos que han tenido contacto con Él en cualquiera de sus formas de presentarse ha podido dar una descripción lógica de lo que ha visto o ha sentido. Él se manifestó a los Patriarcas y Profetas en forma de llama ardiente, luego en María y Jesús en forma humana, para seguir presente primero en el Bautismo y en la Transfiguración de Jesús, y luego el día de Pentecostés sobre los discípulos y en las apariciones de la Virgen María en los pueblos del mundo. "Habita en los corazones de los fieles con el don de la caridad". (Efesios 4:30)

En el evangelio de San Juan, Jesús ruega al Padre por lo que es su gran deseo:

*"Que todos sean uno como Tú, Padre, estás en Mi y Yo en Tí.
Sean también uno en nosotros: así el mundo creerá que tú me
has enviado"*. (Juan 17, 21)

Son relaciones "subsistentes", que en virtud de su impulso vital salen al encuentro una de la otra en una comunión, en la cual la totalidad de la Persona es apertura a la otra.

Es esto, el paradigma supremo de la sinceridad y libertad espiritual a la que deben tender las relaciones interpersonales humanas, hasta ahora tan lejanas a este modelo trascendente.

"Nuestro Señor Jesús, cuando ruega al Padre que - todos sean uno, como nosotros también somos uno – trata de hacer consciente a la humanidad de que debe abrirse perspectiva de la razón humana para poder estar más en sintonía con el Espíritu Santo, de forma que pueda surgir cierta semejanza entre la unión de las personas divinas y la unión de los hijos de Dios en la verdad, en la caridad y en el amor. Esta semejanza hace clara alusión al hecho de que el hombre, única criatura terrestre a la que Dios ha amado por sí misma, no puede encontrar su propia plenitud si no es en la entrega sincera de sí mismo a los demás". (Concilio Vaticano II, Gaudium et spes, 24).

"Conocer el misterio de la Santísima Trinidad del Espíritu Santo, nos involucra y compromete para adquirir ciertas actitudes en las relaciones humanas: "La perfectísima unidad de las tres Personas divinas, es el vértice trascendente que ilumina toda forma de auténtica relación y comunión entre nosotros, los seres humanos". (Saint Juan Pablo II, "Creo en Dios Padre", p.170)

No se trata solo de que queramos entender el Misterio de la Santísima Trinidad del Espíritu Santo, esto es imposible. Jesús nos reveló ese Misterio para mostrarnos el modelo de lo que deben ser las relaciones humanas de los cristianos. El Modelo de la Familia Divina; el Padre, la Madre y el Hijo. El Padre, la Madre - la Virgen María – y el Hijo – Jesús – los tres son el Espíritu Santo. Pero la Iglesia universal nos enseño a "glorificar" a una Santísima Trinidad mutilada y deformada, como manifestación de la celebración del triunfo del machismo arrogante que ha mantenido secuestrada la iglesia por casi dos mil años. Tratando de ocultar que para que exista la perfección en la iglesia debe primero existir la perfección en la familia." La iglesia mantiene una lucha constante en contra de las familias formadas por parejas del mismo sexo, pero ha ocultado la parte femenina de Dios por los siglos de los siglos.

La Iglesia dedica el siguiente domingo después de Pentecostés a la celebración del día de la Santísima Trinidad del Espíritu Santo. El misterio de la Santísima Trinidad - Un sólo Dios en tres Personas distintas- es el misterio central de la fe y de la vida cristiana, pues es el misterio del Espíritu Santo en Sí mismo. Pero, aunque es un dogma difícil de entender, fue el primero que entendieron los Apóstoles después de la Resurrección, comprendieron que Jesús era el Salvador enviado por el Espíritu Santo. Y cuando experimentaron la acción del Espíritu Santo dentro de sus corazones en Pentecostés, comprendieron que el único Dios era el Espíritu Santo y que Éste había obrado como Padre, Madre e Hijo; el ejemplo de la Familia Divina. Pero con el tiempo, los hombres, celosos al saber el papel desempeñado por la Virgen María en la Santísima Trinidad y el papel de María Magdalena como líder de los Apóstoles y conocedores de las luchas antiguas entre Moisés y la líder religiosa Mirian, decidieron que debían cambiar la verdad expresada por los apóstoles e hicieron creer que la Santísima Trinidad estaba compuesta solo por varones y que solo utilizaron las mujeres como siervas a su servicio para así poder instaurar la monarquía machista que ha dominado la vida de las iglesias cristianas desde la ascensión de Jesús y María, hasta nuestros días.

Padre, Madre e Hijo tienen la misma naturaleza, la misma divinidad, la misma eternidad, el mismo poder, la misma perfección; son un sólo Dios. Además, sabemos que cada una de las Personas de la Santísima Trinidad del *Espíritu Santo* está totalmente contenida en las otras, pues hay una comunión perfecta entre ellas.

Con todo, las personas de la Santísima Trinidad son distintas entre sí, dada la diversidad de su misión: Dios Madre – quien dio a Luz al que Creo todo – es enviada por el Espíritu Santo, es la Madre de toda la Creación. Dios Hijo - por quien son todas las cosas - es enviado por el Espíritu Santo (a quien Él llamó Dios Padre y Creador), es nuestro Salvador. El Espíritu Santo (Padre y Creador) - quien contiene todas las cosas - es el enviado por sí mismo, es toda nuestra esencia Santificadora.

4.0.- La Virgen María; Nuestra Señora de la Santísima Trinidad del Espíritu Santo

El *Espíritu Santo* encarnó en *María y Jesús* cumpliendo con la proclamación hecha a la serpiente en el Eden.

"Y pondré enemistad entre tú y la mujer, y entre tu descendencia y la descendencia de ella; ella te herirá en la cabeza, y tú le herirás en el calcañar." Genesis 3:15

Ya que la humanidad demostró no poder controlarse ante las tentaciones de satanas, El Verbo se hizo carne, a la misma vez, en *María y Jesús*. La encarnación de la *Virgen María* tuvo privilegios únicos, igual que la encarnación de su Hijo *Jesús*. *María*, el Ser Divino encarnado como Mujer, es y será pura, santa, con todas las gracias divinas más preciosas. *María* tiene la Gracia Divina del Propio *Espíritu Santo* desde antes de su encarnación y la tendrá por siempre, porque ellos son un solo Ser.

"Digamos —si es permitido— un secreto: el Padre del Todo se unió con la virgen que había descendido y un fuego le iluminó aquel día. Él dio a conocer la gran cámara nupcial, y por eso su cuerpo —que tuvo origen aquel día— salió de la cámara nupcial como uno que ha sido engendrado por el esposo y la esposa. Y asimismo gracias a éstos enderezó Jesús el Todo en ella, siendo preciso que todos y cada uno de sus discípulos entren en su lugar de reposo." Evangelio de Felipe.

En Lucas la Concepción Divina de la Virgen María se describen en el marco narrativo de la Anunciación como obra del *Espíritu Santo*. Lucas presenta a la Virgen como figura central del evangelio de la infancia, unida al nacimiento de Jesús. Pero no reconocer que Ella jugó un papel principal en la cristianización de la humanidad, y sigue haciendolo a través de las apariciones en las cuales concede todo tipo de milagros a personas necesitadas, lo cual ha ayudado a convertir a la fe cristiana a muchos pueblos de diferentes partes del mundo. Aunque esta fe ha sido mal encausada por la Iglesia Católica Romano, es justo reconocer que lamentablemente es esta la única iglesia que la ha acogido, al menos como su patrona de casi todas las poblaciones.

Juan describe la presencia de la Virgen María en Caná, donde la señala como interventora activa en el primero de los milagros realizados por Jesús, y al pie de la cruz durante su pasión y muerte, junta con María Magdalena y su hermana Martha. Pero este milagro es uno de los momentos en los cuales se prueba la divinidad de la parte femenina de la Santísima Trinidad del *Espíritu Santo*. El propio Juan señala que cuando *María* –la madre de Jesús- le dijo: "Jesús se ha acabado el vino", la repuesta de Jesús fue; "madre todavía no ha llegado mi hora". Esto deja bien claro que Jesús no estaba acto ni preparado para hacer dicho milagro, por lo cual se puede colegir que dicho milagro fue hecho por *María* y no por Jesús. A menos que se piense, que Jesús dijo que no podía, - porque no era su hora -, y su madre lo obligó a hacerlo. Pero en cualquiera de las dos situaciones se demuestra un papel esencial de la parte femenina de la divina trinidad, es decir de María, en ese momento, ya que la frase "no es mi hora" quiere decir "aun no tengo permiso de mi Padre", de forma que realizar un milagro sin dicha autorización, por la petición de una "simple sierva" (como la considera la iglesia) dice del real poder de la *Virgen María*. Lo cual denota de cualquier forma que se quiera ver que el *Espíritu Santo* está conformado por la Santísima Trinidad; del Padre, de la Madre y del Hijo. Y que como uno y trino a la vez tienen el mismo poder. Aunque como partes, cada uno tiene una misión específica, tanto en la creación como en el accionar del mundo conocido y por conocer. (Juan 2:1-12)

Algunos eruditos cristianos analizaron sobre la participación de la *Virgen María* en el conjunto de misterios de la salvación y en su relación con Jesucristo. Entre ellos, San Ignacio de Antioquía indagó en el misterio de Jesús nacido de María, mientras que San Justino defendió la concepción virginal de María, San Ireneo propuso un paralelismo entre el significado de las figuras de Eva-María y Adán-Cristo. A mediados del siglo XX aparecieron unos textos escritos en el siglo II por Santiago donde se cuenta la vida de María, desde sus padres adoptivos, Joaquín y Ana, hasta después del nacimiento de Jesús. En otros textos se explicaba la muerte de María y su asunción en cuerpo y alma a los cielos. Pero nunca se atrevieron a decir más de eso por miedo al castigo y a la burla de una sociedad completamente machista. Estamos seguros que existen escritos antiguos que prueban las verdades que hoy se revelan en este libro acerca de María y su divinidad. Cuando llegue el tiempo en que la humanidad tenga acceso a todos los documentos ocultos, toda la verdad hoy revelada será confirmada.

Para los cristianos de la época medieval, era un tema de discusión la perpetua virginidad de María y su santidad personal. Progresivamente llegó a imponerse la idea de una virginidad "antes y después del parto". Con el paso de los siglos por presión de los devotos y el temor de la Iglesia Católica Romana al saber que la verdad iba a salir a relucir, tarde o temprano, asumieron el dogma de la Inmaculada Concepción y el dogma de la Asunción o glorificación de *María,* donde la iglesia plantea que *María* fue asumida en cuerpo y alma al cielo después de su muerte, sin conocer la corrupción del sepulcro. Una forma muy práctica pero mezquina para no revelar los Verdaderos Misterios de la Virgen María, manteniendo así oculto que *Ella* forma parte de la *Santísima Trinidad de Dios.* Ocultando que *María* no fue concebida por ser humano alguno, sino encarnada por obra y gracia del *Espíritu Santo, que es Dios*, su Propio Ser, solo así podría ser la Madre del Cristo, ya que ambos provienen del Propio *Espíritu Santo*, ambos tuvieron una vida santa y ambos al cumplir su misión humana en la tierra ascendieron al firmamento, para morar a la diestra y siniestra del *Espíritu Santo.*

Génesis 3:15 es la profecía de que *María y Jesús* vendrían a la tierra para derrotar a satanás y redimir a toda la humanidad de todo pecado. Esta proclamación hecha por el propio Espíritu Santo a la serpiente inmediatamente después que ésta persuadió a Adán y Eva a cometer el pecado, es la fiel demostración de cuan grande es la misericordia de Dios, que desde el inicio tiene la intención de salvar la humanidad, pero sin imposición, por medio de la salvación por medio de la fe.

Desde la creación el propósito del Espíritu Santo de Dios es que la humanidad logre la salvación por medio de la fe y no por medio de la ley. La gracia tiene preferencia ante la ley, y por ello nos fueron dados *María y Jesús en el Espíritu Santo* como dadores de toda Gracia Divina.

Por medio de la *Santísima Virgen María en el Espíritu Santo*, Jesús reina en el Universo. Los verdaderos misterios de la vida de *María* fueron ocultos por los que reescribieron la Biblia en el siglo IV, hecho este llevado a cabo por los obispos, los escribas y el emperador romano Constantino I. Para lo cual se ingeniaron la idea de llamarla alma mater o Madre oculta y escondida. Y atribuir a su infinita humildad el supuesto anhelo de ella de ocultarse a sí misma y a todas las creaturas, para ser conocida solamente por Dios. Bajo este supuesto ella le pidió a Dios que la ocultara en su concepción, nacimiento, resurrección y asunción. Según planteó San Louis: "Sus propios padres no la conocían y, los ángeles, querubines y serafines se preguntaban con frecuencia unos a otros ¿Quién es ésta? ¿Por qué el Altísimo nos la ocultaba? O, si algo les manifestaba de Ella, era infinitamente más lo que les encubría". Algo que demuestra la gran ignorancia de los más connotados representantes de la Iglesia Cristiana, en el tema de la esencia del Ser Divino, o el interés de éstos en ocultar la verdadera composición del Ser Supremo.

El 12 de abril de 1947, en Tre Fontane, Roma, Nuestra Santísima Madre anunció, "Yo soy la Virgen del Apocalipsis". Gobbi uno de los sacerdotes más connotado del Movimiento Mariano, quien se dice ha recibido más revelaciones de parte de María que cualquier otra persona, asevera que la Virgen María le dijo lo siguiente el 24 de abril de 1980: *"Yo soy la Virgen de la Revelación. En Mí, la obra maestra del Padre se realiza de manera tan perfecta, que Él puede derramar en Mí la Luz de su predilección. El Verbo asume su naturaleza humana en mi seno virginal, y así puede venir a ustedes por medio de mi verdadera función de Madre. El Espíritu Santo me atrae, como imán, hacia lo íntimo de la vida de amor entre el Padre y el Hijo, me transforma interiormente y me asimila tanto a Él que me hace su Esposa. Los llevaré a la plena comprensión de la Sagrada Escritura".*

Aquí podemos ver que *la Virgen María* es la excelente obra maestra de sí misma; quien se ha reservado a sí misma el conocimiento y posesión de Ella misma y Su Creación. *María* es la Madre y Esposa sublime de su Propio Ser que es el Espíritu Santo. Hay de quienes tuvieron a bien humillarla y ocultar su verdadero origen, a sabiendas, y durante tanto tiempo. Aquellos que, para fomentar el poder machista, la consideraron como una simple mujer, una simple sierva del Señor, como si se tratara de una extraña, son mínimas las veces que se le menciona en las Escrituras de la Biblia que fue manipulada por orden del emperador Constantino El Grande y algunos obispos leales a éste. ¡Hay! de aquellos que siempre supieron que ella era la persona más apreciada y amada del Infinito Universo y por machistas lo han ocultado.

La Virgin María es la fuente sellada, en la que sólo puede entrar el Espíritu Santo en las personas del Padre y del Hijo; como Esposo fiel y como Hijo amado. "María es el santuario y tabernáculo de la Santísima Trinidad, donde mora el Espíritu Santo, más magnífica y maravillosamente que en ningún otro lugar del universo, sin exceptuar los querubines, serafines y demás seres del universo, sean estos de carne o de espíritu: a ninguna creatura, por pura que sea, se le permite entrar allí sin privilegio especial", así lo expresó san Luis, el único cristiano que trató de revelar su divinidad, pero no le fue permitido revelarla al mundo como lo hacemos en esta oportunidad, con la plena convicción de que *Ella es Nuestra Señora de la Santísima Trinidad del Espíritu Santo.*

Ella eleva con sus meritos el Trono de la Santísima Trinidad del *Espíritu Santo*, a una altura inaccesible. Su poder y grandeza se extiende hasta sobre el Propio Ser, ya que Ella es su Creadora. Aunque parezca incomprensible, Ella es la propia Energía Divina de la Creación hecha Mujer, Madre y Esposa de su Propio Ser; no existe la Creación sin el Ente Femenino que la Crea, igual que no ha existido el Adán sin primero estar Eva. Pasaron muchos siglos de Eva antes de que llegara el siglo de Adán.

Como parte de la Santísima Trinidad del *Espíritu Santo*, Ella tiene todo el poder, para accionar y hacer milagros, pero Ella siempre entendió que debía dejar que su Hijo cumpliera con la misión asignada por El Espíritu Santo y solo en algunas ocasiones ha hecho ostentación de su poder en la tierra, su poder como parte de la divina trinidad del Ser Supremo, su Propio Ser, su Propio engendro.

Todo el universo está lleno de su gloria y muchos verdaderos cristianos han obligado con su devoción a que Ella haya sido escogida como Patrona de todas las naciones, provincias, diócesis y ciudades alrededor del mundo. Muchas Catedrales han sido consagradas a Dios bajo una de sus múltiples advocaciones. Todas las iglesias católicas tienen un altar en su honor. No hay comarca donde no se dé culto a alguna de sus imágenes milagrosas, donde se cura toda suerte de enfermedades y se obtiene toda clase de bienes. Hoy existen muchas cofradías y congregaciones en su honor. Muchos institutos religiosos han sido colocados bajo su nombre y protección. Miles de congregantes en las asociaciones piadosas y miles de religiosos y religiosas en todas las Órdenes publican sus alabanzas y proclaman su misericordia.

A partir de Hoy, desde el comienzo hasta el fin del Universo, y hasta lo más profundo del centro de la tierra, a diestra y siniestra, todos debemos pregonar para regocijo de todo ser viviente, la Divinidad de la *Virgen María*. Todos los coros angelicales, los hombres y las mujeres, sin importar edad ni condiciones, ni religión, ricos y pobres, y hasta los mismos espíritus contrarios, se ven obligados por la evidencia de la verdad, a proclamar a los cuatros vientos que la Santa Madre es parte de la *Santísima Trinidad del Espíritu Santo; Ella es y por siempre será "Nuestra Señora de la Santísima Trinidad del Espíritu Santo."*

La obra de la *Virgen María* nos enseña a alabar al Ser Supremo por las gracias que el *Espíritu Santo* le otorga y por las bendiciones que Ella derrama sobre el mundo. Podemos encomendar nuestras necesidades a Ella, porque Ella tiene el poder que emana del *Espíritu Santo*, su Propio Ser. Son muchas las personas que han tenido la santa experiencia de estar en contacto con el *Espíritu Santo*, en la presencia de la Divina Trinidad del Espíritu Santo y han manifestado que el Ser Supremo le ha hablado con las tres voces; la de la Madre, la del Padre y la del Hijo desde un solo ente de luz, ya que Ellos tres conforman el *Espíritu Santo*. Estas personas han manifestado que cuando habla la Virgen escuchan una voz femenina de bondad angelical, cuando habla Jesús escuchan una voz varonil de ternura y paciencia, y cuando habla el Padre escuchan una voz que retumba y extrémese.

La *Virgen María* se ha mantenido viniendo a la tierra preparando la segunda venida de Nuestro Señor Jesucristo. A estas visitas en auxilio de seres humanos necesitados, es lo que los cristiano - marianos llamamos las Apariciones de La Virgen. Estas apariciones tienen lugar en diferentes localidades de la tierra y es por esta razón que se le han dado tantos nombres diferentes, dependiendo del lugar donde aparece o del misterio que representa, se le han ido poniendo los nombres, pero en realidad la *Virgen María* es una sola, aunque en algunas ocasiones su rostro adquiere los razgos caracteristicos de la población en donde hace su aparición.

Como se ha revelado aquí, la Santísima *Virgen María* forma parte de la Santísima Trinidad del *Espíritu Santo*. Tres figuraciones diferentes de un mismo Ser Supremo que a su vez son uno mismo, un único Ser. *María*, Madre de Dios hecho hombre forma parte de la divinidad del Ser Supremo, del *Espíritu Santo*. "Antes que el Hijo, vino la Madre y antes que la Madre, el Padre y los tres vinieron por obra y gracia del *Espíritu Santo que es Dios*, del cual son un todo y parte a la vez." "Y cada uno tiene asignado su lugar." Así fue expresado: "Él está allá, pero sigue estando aquí; si despiertas aquí, te despertaras allá".

Para los verdaderos cristianos esta revelación confirma y afirma todo el conjunto de "paradojas marianas" que se han manifestado con el paso del tiempo sobre los Verdaderos Misterios del cristianismo. Podemos analizar como estas paradojas nos confirmar que esta revelación es veraz, ya que la misma hace referencia a las gracias extraordinarias de las que fue depositaria *María* durante su encarnación, y en orden a su divina maternidad. Por ser la madre del Cristo –considerado el Verbo encarnado, Dios mismo–, para concebir el Verbo *María* debía ser el Verbo mismo, igual que el *Espíritu Santo* es Verbo y solo existe un solo Verbo que se expresa a voluntad.

La Virgen *María*, como parte femenina del *Espíritu Santo* es:

*   *la que engendró su Propio Ser,*
*   *la que engendró al Ser que la engendró a ella,*
*   *la que existía antes que toda existencia,*
*   *la que dio el Ser al Ser creador de todo,*
*   *la que encerró en su seno al Inmenso e Infinito Dios,*
*   *aquella que encerró en sus entrañas a quien no cabe en todo el mundo,*
*   *la que sostuvo en sus brazos al que todo lo sustenta,*
*   *la que tuvo obligación de ejercer vigilancia sobre el que todo lo ve,*
*   *la que tuvo a su cuidado al Ser que cuida de todos,*
*   *la que tocó los confines de quien no tiene fin,*
*   *el Verbo hecho Mujer, para ser Madre y Esposa de Dios,*
*   *la parte femenina del Verbo; el cual es Madre, Padre e Hijo unidos en la gracia del Espíritu Santo,*
*   *Nuestra Señora de la Santisima Trindad del Espíritu Santo.*

Muy a pesar de todas las creencias que nos han inculcado durante miles de años, debemos estar claros y no confundir las cosas, cada parte del Ser Supremo tiene su misión. Y la misión de la redención del ser humano le fue encomendada al Espíritu Santo Hijo, encarnado en Jesucristo, pero el principio y el fin de la devoción para la salvación de los verdaderos cristianos es una misión que corresponde a *Jesús* y a *María en el Espíritu Santo* por igual, ya que los tres son en sí un solo ser. *María* es quien crea el enlace entre el Dios- Espíritu y el Dios – Hombre. Jesucristo es el elemento de enlace entre el Espíritu Santo Padre y el Ser Humano, a través de él estamos unidos al Dios Padre. Para llegar al Ser Supremo necesitamos imitar a Jesucristo en el cual permanece toda plenitud y gracia, dada a él, aquí en la tierra, por la *Virgen María y el Espíritu Santo*. A través del Hijo se llega al Padre y a través de Cristo hemos de recibir toda bendición del *Espíritu Santo*. Pero para llegar al *Espíritu Santo*, que es la unión complementaria de la Santísima Trinidad de Dios se debe estar en armonía con las tres Divinas Personas; el Padre, la Madre y el Hijo.

El *Espíritu Santo* es uno y trino a la vez, de forma que, si personalmente te sientes confortable orándole al Padre, obtiene la bondad de las tres Divinas Personas que en verdad es un solo Ser. Pero si te sientes identificado con la Virgen y en armonía con la Madre del Ser que es uno, y si le oras a ella también tus plegarias serán escuchadas igual por los tres, porque ellos son un mismo Espíritu Santo; Y ni se diga del Hijo, siempre que le pides algo a Jesús también se lo estas pidiendo a su Padre y a su Madre. Y siempre que pida con devoción y fe vas a recibir con abundancia toda la gracia que emana del *Espíritu Santo.*

< San Pedro Nolasco fundador de la Orden de Santa María de la Merced, de la redención de los cautivos, una comunidad religiosa que se ha dedicado por siglos a ayudar a los prisioneros y ha tenido mártires y santos, cuenta la historia de un dia estar orando, pidiéndole ayuda a Dios *y, en signo de la misericordia divina, le responde La Virgen María pidiéndole que funde una orden liberadora… Una prueba clara de que La Virgen María, al igual que el Padre y el Hijo, es Dios.*>

Ha habido un gran desenfoque en la humanidad durante todo el transcurso de los tiempos donde se ha perdido el concepto básico de la humanización del Ser Supremo. Hemos pasado por alto que el primer ejemplo que el *Espíritu Santo* nos enseñó fue el de desposar a *María* y luego hacerla madre al engendrar en ella a su Hijo, su propia encarnación, para ante el mundo dar a conocer la esencia del *Espíritu Santo* el cual es uno y tres a la vez. Conformando el primer ejemplo de familia; en el nombre del Padre, de la Madre y del Hijo, en el Espíritu Santo. Ellos quisieron dar ejemplo para que esto llegue a nosotros por convicción y no por imposición. Ni el Padre ni el Hijo han visto con buenos ojos la vejación hecha por el hombre a la mujer en la persona femenina de la Santísima Trinidad del *Espíritu Santo que es Dios.*

La Biblia establece que; "No se ha dado a los hombres sobre la tierra otro nombre (de ser humano) por el cual podamos ser salvados," sino el de Jesús. Pero el Espíritu Santo nos ha dado otro fundamento de salvación, perfección y gloria, en la Virgen María. "Todo edificio que no esté construido sobre rocas firmes, se apoya en arena movediza y tarde o temprano caerá infaliblemente". Todas estas y otras tantas expresiones han sido fuentes de confusión, pero no nos debemos dejar confundir con todos estos preceptos que aplican solo para los hombres, no para la divinidad de la *Virgen María*. Ya que como hemos visto aquí, Ella está por encima de Todo. Ella es la única que ha engendrado al ser que la creó a Ella, en una acción que carece de lógica humana pero no así en los entes divinos.

Debemos arrodillarnos ante la Santísima *Virgen María,* para humildemente pedirle por su Divina Majestad, que perdone la ignorancia de la gran mayoría de los seres humanos, que han menospreciado la unión que la liga a la *Santísima Trinidad del Espíritu Santo*, que es la misma que une al Padre con el Hijo. Debemos también reconocer que, a través del *Espíritu Santo*, Jesús estás siempre con *María,* igual que *María* está siempre con Jesús; *María* está de tal manera trasformada en Jesús por la gracia del *Espíritu Santo*, que Ella ya no vive ni es nada sin Él, igual que Él no es nada sin Ella, y lo propio sucede con el Espíritu Santo. Bajo este gran Misterio Divino, la Madre (Virgen María), el Padre (Jehová o Yahvé) y el Hijo (Jesús) son un mismo ser integrado, en el *Espíritu Santo*, y que habita con todas las criaturas del macro Universo de todas las dimensiones, y cuya energía proviene de su Propio Ser.

Hoy estoy seguro, mi amadísima *Virgen María*, que cuando todos los seres humanos reconozcan la gloria y el amor que reside en la misteriosa y admirable figura, que conforma la Santísima Trinidad del *Espíritu Santo*; Padre, Madre e Hijo. Todos tendremos hacia Ti sentimientos muy diferentes de los que ahora se tienen. Cuando descubramos que tú está unida al Padre y al Hijo tan firmemente que sería más fácil separar la luz del sol, el calor del fuego, el frio del hielo, porque Ellos te aman más ardientemente y te glorifican con mayor perfección que a todas las demás creaturas del Universo.

No es extraño, Santísima *Madre Celestial,* ver la arrogancia de todos los hombres respecto a ti, los cuales te han ignorado solo por el hecho de ser mujer. Pero no solo son los paganos y los herejes, también los propios cristianos te han desconocido. Estos señores hablan muy raramente de Ti, y otros jamás te han rendido el culto que te merece, supuestamente por miedo a ofender la honra de Dios y de Jesús. Estos cristianos a media, al ver que alguien hablar con devoción hacia Ti, Santísima *Virgen María*, con un lenguaje eficaz y persuasivo, sin pena y sin miedo, de una senda inmaculada y sin imperfección y de un secreto maravilloso que nos revela que tú eres parte de la Santísima Trinidad del *Espíritu Santo,* la parte femenina del Ser Supremo, argumentan miles de falsedades, que según ellos prueban que no se debe hablar tanto de Ti, que únicamente se debe hablar de Jesús o de Jehová de los ejércitos. Otros llegan a decir que tú eres una sierva que solo fuiste utilizada por Jehová para su propósito. Cuan sorprendidos quedaran todos cuando te vean a la cabeza de la Suprema Corte Celestial al mando de las estrellas.

Estoy consciente mi amadísima *Virgen María* que el Rosario, el escapulario y la corona como devociones propiamente dichas no son suficiente para alabarte y adorar tu grandeza. Pero muchos de estos supuestos cristianos piensan que esto es suficiente y muchos otros, incluso, piensan que esto es demasiado o que es un abuso. De hecho, cuando estos caballeros encuentran algún devoto de tu grandeza rezando el Rosario o practicando alguna devoción en tu honor, hacen grandes esfuerzos para tratar de "purificarle" el espíritu y limpiar su corazón, aconsejándole que, en lugar de rezar el Rosario, debieran rezar los siete salmos penitenciales. Cuando la verdad es que un rezo no se opone al otro, y por el contrario ambos se complementan y se fortalecen en el Espíritu Santo. Estos señores piden a las personas solo rezar a Jesús o al Padre. Pero, *¿En verdad, complacerá al Señor, quién por temor a desagradarlo, no honra a su amada Madre; su propio Ser?* Consagrarte a la *Virgen María* en vez de alejarte de Jesús te acerca a Él. Porque el que ama al Hijo debe amar a la Madre, igual que el que ama al Hijo ama al Padre, ya que a fin de cuenta es un mismo ser, un solo Espíritu Divino, el *Espíritu Santo.*

La realidad actual es que la mayoría de los estudiosos, incluso cristianos, mientras más sabios más alejados se encuentran de la devoción a la Santísima Madre y muestran una absoluta indiferencia hacia su Divinidad. Guárdanos de estos sentimientos y de este tipo de apatía hacia tu Divina Majestad, Madre Divina. Danos sabiduría y ayúdanos a participar de los sentimientos de gratitud y amor que tú tienes, para con nosotros, tus hijos e hijas, a fin de que podamos amarte y glorificarte, y que ese amor hacia ti nos haga más perfectos y merecedores de tu reino celestial.

Aunque nadie más lo admita concédeme, Santísima *Virgen María,* la honra y la gracia de poder amarte y adorarte por las gracias que tu concedes al *Espíritu Santo.* Concédeme la gracia de alabarte dignamente, a pesar de todos tus detractores, porque no alcanzará misericordia divina aquel que ofende a la Madre bendita. En cambio, el que alabe la Santísima Madre ya tendrá el pase para llegar al Hijo y al Padre, en el seno del Espíritu Santo. Porque aquí está dicho, para alcanzar la misericordia de Jesús, es necesaria una verdadera devoción hacia su Santísima Madre y más aún si esta se difunde con devoción y fe a través de toda la tierra como lo es el difundir este libro por todos los confines de la tierra.

Nada hay entre los cristianos que nos haga pertenecer más plenamente a Jesucristo que la veneración y adoración a su Santísima Madre, aceptada voluntariamente. El hombre y la mujer que profesen su amor a la *Virgen María* nunca estarán fuera de la gracia del *Espíritu Santo.* Los cristianos son llamados repetidas veces en la Biblia servidores de Cristo, y yo les digo que el que sirve a Cristo sirve al Ser Supremo, con lo cual también sirve a María y al Espíritu Santo al mismo tiempo. Está demostrado que el (la) que ama a la *Virgen María* recoge los frutos de sus buenas obras y nunca estará desposeído (a) de la protección del *Espíritu Santo.*

Como hay divinidad en *Jesucristo*, hay divinidad en la *Virgen María*. Siendo Ella la compañera inseparable de su vida, gloria y poder en el cielo y en la tierra, le otorgó respecto y Majestad con todos los derechos y privilegios que a Ella le corresponden por naturaleza. Todos los Dones que provienen del *Espíritu Santo* por obra y gracia, proviene de *María* por naturaleza.

Conforme todos estos planteamientos, podemos convertirnos en servidores del amor a la Divinidad de la *Virgen María*, a fin de serlo más perfectamente de Jesucristo. La Virgen Santísima es el medio del cual debemos servirnos para ir a Él. Pues *María* no es como las demás creaturas, que, si nos apegamos a ellas, pueden separarnos de Dios en lugar de acercarnos a Él. La inclinación más fuerte hacia la que aplastó la serpiente, es la de unirnos a Jesucristo, su Hijo y su Propio Ser; y el mayor deseo de Jesús es que vayamos a Él por medio de su Divina Madre.

Porque no sin razón nos ha dado el *Espíritu Santo* mediadores ante sí mismo, de forma que nos podamos identificar más con el propio Ser Supremo a través de una de sus personificaciones, ya que él conoce nuestra indignidad e incapacidad, se apiadó de nosotros y para darnos acceso a su misericordia nos proveyó de dos poderosos mediadores ante su grandeza; la *Virgen María y Jesucristo*. Porque está tan corrompida nuestra alma que si nos apoyamos sólo en nuestros propios esfuerzos no podremos llegar hasta el Ser Supremo y mucho menos podremos unirnos a Él y que nos escuche. Por tanto, reconocemos en *Jesucristo* y la *Virgen María* los únicos mediadores que nos pueden acercar directamente a su Divina Santidad.

Jesucristo es nuestro mediador de Redención y la *Virgen María* nuestra mediadora de aflicción; Y ambos lo son ante el *Espíritu Santo*. Por Ellos debemos orar juntos toda la humanidad. Por Ellos tenemos acceso ante la Majestad Divina y, sólo apoyados en Ellos, revestidos de sus méritos, debemos presentarnos ante el *Espíritu Santo*, con la humildad y el respeto que se merecen al tener la más alta investidura del Universo, por encima de todo ser, sacerdote, ministro, papa, gobernante, presidente, rey, logia, secta, religión, creencia, pensamiento y ciencia.

Jesucristo es el principal mediador ante el Padre, pero la *Virgen María* es mediadora ante el Mediador mismo, ante el Padre y ante Sí misma. Por Ella vino *Jesucristo* a nosotros y por Ella debemos nosotros ir a Él. Esta relación es como el triangulo equilátero; estando en uno de los vértices puedes llegar a cualquiera de los otros dos que te quedan a la misma distancia, que son exactamente iguales y que solo tienen diferentes nombres para poder diferenciarlos cuando debe llamarlos por separado, porque en realidad son un solo elemento que se llama triangulo equilátero. Si temes ir directamente al *Espíritu Santo*, a causa de su infinita grandeza y de tu pequeñez o pecados, implora con filial confianza la ayuda e intercesión de la dulce y tierna *Virgen María*, la Madre de la Creación. Ella es tierna y bondadosa, es la pura naturaleza, no hay nada austero ni terrible en todo su Ser.

La *Virgen María* es tan bondadosa que nunca ha rechazado a ninguno de los que imploran su intercesión, por más pecadores que hayan sido, pues jamás se ha oído decir que alguien haya sido rechazado al haber acudido confiado y perseverantemente a ella. Ella es como el sol que con la brillantez de sus rayos alumbra todo el Universo y al mismo tiempo, hermosa y apacible como la luna que toma esos rayos y los acomoda para que nuestras vistas puedan apreciar la belleza de la tenue luz, sin sufrir ningún daño. Ella es tan piadosa que tus peticiones jamás serán desoídas, bástale con que le presente alguna súplica, para que Ella la acepte y reciba y se deje vencer amorosamente por las súplicas de sus amadísimos (as) hijos (as).

Para armonizar con *Nuestro Dios Creador* tenemos tres posibles vías: la primera, es el *Espíritu Santo Padre: Yahweh*; La segunda es el *Espíritu Santo Madre:* la Virgen *María*; La tercera es el *Espíritu Santo Hijo: Jesucristo.* Para llegar a Jesucristo hay que ir a *María* nuestra Mediadora de intercesión. Para llegar hasta el Padre hay que ir al Hijo, que es nuestro Mediador de Redención, aunque también se puede llegar al Padre directamente a través de *María*, su amadísima Esposa y su Propio Yo. Y cada uno de los tres nos puede llevar al *Espíritu Santo*; Padre, Madre e Hijo, si logras evolucionar hasta llegar a la dimensión en donde habita la Santísima Trinidad del *Espíritu Santo.*

Es prácticamente imposible, bajo la evolución normal del ser humano, dada su pequeñez y fragilidad, conservar las gracias dadas por el *Espíritu Santo*, a cada hombre y mujer al nacer, ya que, aunque todos estamos formados por partículas divinas, dichas partículas no pueden evolucionar a un ritmo acelerado mientras estemos limitados por nuestra poca fe, y por el mínimo conocimiento de la corrupción de la materia del cuerpo humano que aun la ciencia no puede revelar. Solo cuando nuestra mente y espíritu lleguen a sobrepasar las altas dimensiones podremos lograr armonizar con el *Espíritu Santo*. Los seres humanos solo tenemos tres vías para lograr esto; Jesucristo, *María* y el proceso evolutivo del ser humano a través de la propia *consciencia cósmica.*

Llevamos en la sangre y en todo el cuerpo las partículas divinas del Ser Creador, algo más valioso que el cielo y la tierra, juntos. Pero nuestro cuerpo es corruptible, nuestra alma es débil e inconstante por cualquier cosa se turba y abate, dejando nuestro espíritu a la deriva. Nos creamos falsos demonios, para justificar nuestra debilidad y flaqueza. Seres que supuestamente nos rodean para devorarnos y arrebatarnos en un momento, por un solo pecado, todas las gracias y méritos logrados en muchos años. Su malicia y su astucia deben hacernos temer infinitamente esta desgracia. Pero la verdad es que todo, lo bueno y lo malo, está en nuestras partículas divinas, es decir, dentro de nuestro propio ser, de forma tal que las partículas divinas al mismo tiempo pueden ser partículas malignas. Y éstas van a depender de qué tipo de energía alimenta nuestros cuerpos. Acudes a *María* para que te dé la fuerza y la sabiduría que te haga capaz de conservar los atributos de la creación, nadie mejor que Ella como Madre y creadora conoce la esencia de nuestro ser. *Si alimentas tu alma, tu mente y tu cuerpo con cosas positivas, todo en ti será positivo, en cambio si los alimentas con cosas negativas, todo en ti será negativo.*

Nada mejor que la devoción admirable a la *Virgen María*, para confiar nuestra esencia de vida, ya que Ella nos la guardará como si fuera suya propia. Es difícil perseverar en gracia, a causa de la espantosa corrupción del mundo, en todos los tiempos y eras. Corrupción tal, que se hace prácticamente imposible que algún hombre o mujer pueda vivir sin mancha y sin miedo; miedo por haber fallado o miedo por temor a fallar. Ya que sería un milagro el que una persona se conserve pura en medio de este torbellino de corrupción mundial en todos los niveles sociales, sin ser arrastrada por el mal, del vicio, la infidelidad, la avaricia, la envidia, la inmoralidad, etc. Solo con una verdadera devoción a la *Virgen María*, contra quien nada pudo hacer la serpiente, y con un avance del ser humano en la *Consciencia Cósmica*, se podría conseguir este milagro a favor de toda la humanidad.

<*Soberana Virgen María, Madre de Jesús, Dios Vivo, pues le has parido: Rogad por todos los pecadores para que nos perdone. Líbranos del enemigo que nos combate y concedenos la gloria eterna. Amén.* >

<*Virgen Santísima, rogad por mi, siempre serás alabada y bendita. Rogad por este pecador, a tu amado Hijo, preciosa hermosura de los Angeles, de los Profetas y de los Patriarcas; corona de los Mártires, de los Apóstoles y de los Confesores; gloria de los Serafines, de los Querubines y de las Vírgenes, libradme de aquella espantosa figura cuando mi alma saliere de mi cuerpo. ¡Oh, Santísima fuente de piedad y hermosura de Jesucristo, alegría de la gloria, consolación del clero, remedio en los trabajos! Con Vos, Virgen prudentísima, se alegran los Angeles. Encomendad mi alma y la de todos los fieles cristianos; rogad por nosotros a vuestro bendito hijo, y conducidnos al paraíso eterno, en donde vives y reinas por los siglos de los siglos; y allí te alabaremos eternamente, Amén.* >

La *Virgen María* se ha mantenido viniendo a la tierra, preparando al ser humano para la venida del *Espíritu Santo* con toda su Corte Celestial. A estas visitas en auxilio de pueblos y de seres humanos necesitados, es lo que llamamos "las apariciones de La Virgen". Estas apariciones tienen lugar en diferentes localidades de la tierra y es por esta razón que se le han dado tantos nombres diferentes, ya que dependiendo del lugar donde aparece se le ha ido poniendo diferentes nombres, pero en realidad la *Virgen María* es una sola; Nuestra Señora de la Santísima Trinidad del Espíritu Santo.

Podemos agrupar la mayoría de las advocaciones marianas en diversas categorías:

1) Relativas a los misterios o pasajes de la vida de la Virgen, como la Anunciación, la Asunción, la Presentación, la Inmaculada Concepción, la Divina Providencia, etc.

2) Relativas a verdades teológicas abstractas, como la Esperanza, la Caridad, la Consolación, etc.

3) Relativas a los estados físicos o psicológicos de la Virgen, como los Dolores, la Soledad, etc.

4) Relativas a su condición de mediadora y protectora de la humanidad, como Auxiliadora, las Mercedes, los Remedios, La Sanación, etc.

5) Relativas a frutos, flores, aves... utilizados como símbolos de sus cualidades, como el Pino, la Granada, la Paloma, etc.

6) Relativas a accidentes geográficos, generalmente coincidentes con los parajes donde se encuentran sus santuarios, como el Carmen, el Mar, Fátima, Lourdes, etc.

7) Relativa a su principal Mision en la tierra, la Virgen de Coatlaxopeuh término (náhuatl/azteca) que significa "La que aplastó la serpiente" y se pronuncia en la lengua nativa "quatlasupe" promunciación que los españoles entendían como "Guadalupe" por su gran parecido.

Las advocaciones marianas se suelen nombrar con las fórmulas "Santa María de", "Virgen de" o "Nuestra Señora de". Pero también, las advocaciones suelen dar lugar en muchos casos a nombres propios femeninos, compuestos del nombre María y su advocación: María del Carmen, María de los Dolores, María de Lourdes, etc.

Aunque el nombre sea diferente en cuanto al atributo relativo a la Virgen María siempre se refiere únicamente a ella, así se haga mención de varios nombres en un mismo momento, la instancia es la misma, *la Virgen María; Nuestra Señora de la Santísima Trinidad del Espíritu Santo.*

Entre las diferentes advocaciones de la *Virgen María* tenemos: María Auxiliadora, Nuestra Señora de la Asunción, Nuestra Señora de Hollywood, La Virgen de Regla, Nuestra Señora de la Altagracia, la Virgen de la Caridad del Cobre, Nuestra Señora de Guadalupe, la Virgen de las Mercedes, la Virgen del Carmen, la Virgen de la Inmaculada Concepción, la Virgen de la Divina Providencia, Nuestra Señora de Coromoto, Nuestra Señora de los Ángeles, la Virgen de Fátima, Inmaculado Corazón de María, la Virgen de Covadonga, la Virgen de Montserrat, la Virgen de la Medalla Milagrosa, Nuestra Señora del Rosario, la Virgen de Lourdes, la Virgen de China, Nuestra Señora de Paris, Nuestra Señora de Syracuse, la Virgen de Roma, Nuestra Señora de La Salette, la Virgen de Pontmain, la Virgen de Banneux, la Virgen de pellevoisin, Nuestra Señora de Beauraing, Nuestra Señora de Knock, la Virgen de la Rosa Mistica, Nuestra Señora Chiquinquirá, Nuestra Señora del Perpetuo Socorro, la Virgen del Pilar, la Virgen de la Candelaria, Nuestra Señora de Loreto, Nuestra Señora La Dolorosa del Colegio, Nuestra Señora Aparecida, Nuestra Señora de Luján, Nuestra Señora de la Paz, Nuestra Señora de Suyapa, la Virgen de las Lágrimas, Nuestra Señora de los Treinta y Tres, Nuestra Señora del Carmen del Maipú, la Virgen de Akita, Nuestra Señora de los Milagros de Caacupé, Nuestra Señora de la Presentación del Quinche, Santa María de la Antigua, Nuestra Señora de los Dolores, Nuestra Señora de la Evangelización, Nuestra Señora de "El Viejo", Nuestra Señora de Schoenstatt, la Virgen de Czestochowa, Nuestra Señora de Copacabana, Nuestra Señora de la Franquira, Nuestra Señora de las Nieves, Nuestra Señora de los Desamparados, Nuestra Señora de la Rogativa, Nuestra Señora de la Arrixaca, Nuestra Señora de Rosell, Nuestra Señora del Azahar, Nuestra Señora de la Peña, Santa María Madre de la Eucaristía, Santa María Desatanudos, entre otras.

4.1.- Nuestra Señora de la Altagracia; advocación de la Virgen María.

Nuestra Señora de la Altagracia o Virgen de la Altagracia: es la Santa Madre protectora espiritual de la República Dominicana. Su fiesta patronal es celebrada el 21 de enero en dicho país donde muchos fieles devotos de la Virgen María van desde toda parte del territorio nacional dominicano hasta su templo en la Basílica de Higüey a rendirle culto. Esta devoción se inició en el país durante el primer período colonial, cuando los primeros viajes de los españoles, aunque también fue paseada por otras regiones del mundo.

Los hermanos Alonso y Antonio Trejo fueron quienes llevaron la imagen de la Virgen de la Altagracia al país dominicano; éstos provenían de la localidad de Siruela donde la virgen se le apareció a un agricultor sobre un árbol, y de ahí su nombre de "la Alta Gracia" bajada del cielo. Es también venerada en Garrovillas de Alconétar, otra localidad española, donde la leyenda cuenta que la santísima virgen se le apareció a una niña sobre un gran peñasco. Los Hermanos Trejo fueron los primeros en fundar un trapiche para producir azúcar, que tiempo después daría paso a los famosos ingenios azucareros de la República Dominicana. Los Trejos se mudaron en la villa de Higüey, y de inmediato regalaron la imagen de la Virgen de la Altagracia, para que toda la comunidad la venerara.

La imagen de la Virgen de la Altagracia representa la escena del Nacimiento de Jesús en el Pesebre de Belén, donde se destaca la maternidad de la Virgen. En el cuadro se encuentra la Estrella de Belén, la cual tiene ocho puntas y simboliza el cielo y tiene dos rayos extendiéndose hacia el pesebre, en el cual el Espíritu Santo está señalando las dos divinidades humanizadas, en su hijo Jesús y en su madre María. Por encima de la Virgen hay doce estrellas y en su alrededor hay un resplandor, cual si estuviera revestida de sol. La Virgen también lleva una corona en su cabeza que simboliza que Ella es la Reina del Universo, y un velo sobre la cabeza que simboliza la pureza de la mujer. Delante de la Madre se encuentra el Niño Jesús, dormido sobre pajas y detrás, bien retirado de Ella, está José, vestido con una capa roja y una vela en su mano izquierda. En la imagen también se puede apreciar la figura de María en actitud de adoración, con sus manos unidas en forma de arco. Sobre su pecho se distingue una especie de triángulo blanco, expresión de la divina trinidad representada en ese momento, el cual sube desde el pesebre, donde descansa el niño, hasta casi los hombros de María. El rostro de María se muestra sereno, con un perfil bajo, pero sin reflejar tristeza, sino más bien alegría y paz, en una actitud de meditación. Su cabeza está cubierta con un velo azul oscuro que le llega hasta los hombros y su manto está salpicado de dieciséis pequeñas estrellas, ocho de cada lado. Detrás hay una columna, como señal de que en ese momento aquel pesebre se había convertido en un templo sagrado, porque allí estaban presente dos de las tres divinas personas. La imagen de la Virgen de la Altagracia es un ícono. No hay un elemento, un color ni una relación que no tenga su significado. También es uno de los pocos cuadros alrededor del mundo que está estampado en oro puro.

La Virgen de la Altagracia es venerada en México, en la comunidad de Zapopan, Jalisco, en donde es Patrona, allí se encuentra una capilla dedicada a Nuestra Señora de la Altagracia. El pueblo de la Altagracia, de la Provincia de Córdoba, Argentina, debe el origen de su nombre a la Virgen de la Altagracia. En España, la Virgen de la Altagracia es Patrona de Garrovillas de Alconétar, Cáceres, Siruela, y Badajoz. En Panamá la Virgen de la Altagracia es Patrona de la comunidad de Jobo Dulce, Los Santos, Panamá. En Venezuela es Patrona de Curiepe, Miranda y Quibor, Lara.

4.2.- Nuestra Señora de Guadalupe; advocación de la Virgen María.

El Santuario de Nuestra Señora de Guadalupe es único entre los grandes centros de devoción mariana, porque en él se ha conservado y se venera la hermosísima imagen de la Virgen María, Madre de Dios, en la tilma del humilde indio, Juan Diego, la cual fue pintada con tinta y pinceles que no son del mundo conocido por el ser humano, al menos hasta ahora.

Cuenta la tradición que la Virgen María se le apareció al indio Juan Diego cuando éste iba rumbo al Convento de Tlaltelolco para oír misa. Al amanecer llegó al pie del Tepeyac, y de repente oyó una melodía que provenía de los árboles. Sorprendido se paró, y alzó su vista hacia el cerro y vio que estaba iluminado con una luz como de rayos de sol. Dejó de sonar la música y en seguida oyó una dulce voz procedente de lo alto de la colina, que le decía: "Juanito; querido Juan Dieguito". Por lo cual él subió presurosamente y al llegar a la cumbre vio a la Virgen María, en medio de un arco iris, vestida del esplendor celestial. Su hermosura y mirada bondadosa llenaron su corazón de gozo infinito mientras escuchó las palabras tiernas que ella le dirigió. Ella le dijo que era la

Virgen María, Madre de Dios. Le reveló su deseo de tener un templo allá en el llano donde, como madre piadosa, mostraría todo su amor y misericordia a él y a los suyos y a cuantos aclamaran por su auxilio. La Santa Madre lo mandó a que fuera a la casa del Obispo de México y le dijera que iba de parte de la majestad divina de la Madre de Dios para solicitarle la construcción de un Templo en su honor en el llano indicado por Ella. Cuéntale cuanto has visto, oído y admirado. Y Juan se inclinó ante ella y le dijo: "Señora mía, voy a cumplir tu mandato; me despido de ti, yo, tu humilde siervo."

Juan fue a la casa del Obispo Zumárraga y le dijo todo lo que la Madre de Dios le había dicho. Pero el Obispo dudó de sus palabras, y le dijo que no tenía tiempo para escucharle y le pidió que regresara otro día. Juan regresó a la cumbre de la colina y encontró a la Virgen que ya le estaba esperando. Y con lágrimas de tristeza le contó de su fracaso. Ella le pidió que volviera a casa del Obispo el próximo día. Juan volvió y esta vez corrió con mejor suerte, esta vez el Obispo le escuchó, pero le exigió que le trajera una señal. Juan volvió a la colina, le dijo a María la petición del Obispo y ella le aseguró que le daría la señal que él pedía. Pero Juan se vio imposibilitado de cumplir con este encargo ya que un tío suyo, también llamado Juan, había enfermado gravemente. Por lo cual Juan Diego se apresuró a buscarle un sacerdote en la ciudad, para lo cual tomó una vía diferente para evitar verse con la *Virgen María*. Pero para su sorpresa Ella bajó y salió a su encuentro. Juan se disculpó con Ella por no haber podido cumplir su misión el día anterior. Después de oír las palabras de Juan Diego, ella le respondió: "Oye y ten entendido, hijo mío el más pequeño, que es nada lo que te asusta y aflige. No se turbe tu corazón, no tema esa ni ninguna otra enfermedad o angustia. ¿Acaso no estoy aquí yo, que soy tu madre? ¿No estás bajo mi sombra? ¿No soy tu salud? ¿Qué más te falta? No te aflija la enfermedad de tu tío, que no morirá ahora de ella; está seguro de que ya sanó." Juan se sintió contento al oír estas palabras. Le pidió que le despachara a ver al Obispo para llevarle alguna prueba a fin de que le creyera. Y Ella le dijo: "Sube, hijo mío el más pequeño, a la cumbre donde me viste, encontrará diferentes flores, córtalas y tráemelas." El así lo hizo y las llevó ante la Virgen. Ella tomó las flores en sus manos, las arregló en la tilma y dijo: "Hijo mío el más pequeño, aquí tienes la señal que debes llevar al Señor Obispo. Le dirás en mi nombre que vea en ella mi voluntad y que él tiene que cumplirla. Tú eres mi enviado y eres digno de confianza. Rigurosamente te ordeno que sólo delante del Obispo despliegues tu tilma." Cuando Juan Diego estuvo ante el Obispo, y le contó los detalles de la cuarta aparición de la Santísima Virgen, abrió su tilma para mostrarle las flores, las cuales cayeron al suelo. En ese instante, ante la inmensa sorpresa del Obispo y sus compañeros, apareció la imagen de la Santísima *Virgen María* maravillosamente pintada con los más hermosos colores sobre la burda tela de su manto.

El mismo día, la Santísima *Virgen María* se presentó en la choza de Juan Bernardino, tío de Juan Diego, para curarle de su mortal enfermedad. Su corazón se llenó de gozo cuando Ella le dio el feliz mensaje de que su retrato milagrosamente aparecido en la tilma de Juan Diego, sería el instrumento que aplastaría la idolatría de sus hermanos hacia la serpiente, por medio de la enseñanza que la divina imagen encerraba. Te-coa-tla-xope en la lengua Azteca quiere decir "aplastará la serpiente de piedra." Los españoles oyeron la palabra de los labios de Juan Bernardino. Ellos entendieron que dijo "de Guadalupe". Sorprendidos se preguntaron el por qué de este nombre español, pero los hijos predilectos de América, conocían bien el sentido de la frase en su lengua nativa. Así fue como la imagen y el santuario, adquirieron el nombre de Guadalupe, título que ha llevado hasta ahora. Y así se cumplió lo anunciado por los profetas: *"Y Dios mandará una mujer cuya descendencia aplastará la serpiente y liberará los hijos de Dios".*

Cuenta la Sagrada Escritura que en los tiempos de la antigüedad un gran cometa recorría el espacio sideral. Este cometa tenía la apariencia de una serpiente de fuego. Por lo cual los indios de México le dieron el nombre de Quetzalcoatl que significa serpiente con plumas, y por temor hicieron ídolos de piedra, en forma de serpiente emplumada, los cuales comenzaron a adorar y a ofrecerles sacrificios humanos. Pero después de ver la sagrada imagen de la *Virgen María,* los indios abandonaron sus falsos dioses y abrazaron la fe cristiano - mariana. Unos nueve millones de indígenas se convirtieron al cristianismo en los primeros siete años después de la aparición de la imagen de *Nuestra Señora de la Santísima Trinidad del Espíritu Santo.*

La tilma de Juan Diego en donde la imagen de la Santísima *Virgen María* apareció, está hecha de fibra de maguey, la cual tiene una duración ordinaria máxima de veinte años aproximadamente. Con un tamaño de 195 centímetros de largo por 105 de ancho con una sutura en medio que va de arriba a abajo. Impresa directamente sobre la tela, se encuentra la

Divina imagen de Nuestra Señora de Guadalupe. El cuerpo de ella mide 140 centímetros de alto. Esta imagen de la Santísima Virgen es el único retrato auténtico que se tiene de ella. Su conservación en estado fresco y hermoso por más de cuatro siglos, es considerada milagrosa. La imagen se venera en la Basílica de Nuestra Señora de Guadalupe en la Ciudad de México, donde ocupa el sitio de honor en el altar mayor. Espertos en imagenes digitales y fotografía aseguran que en los ojos de la Virgen de Guadalupe se encuentran grabadas 13 imagenes de personas las cuales aún no han podido ser decifradas.

4.3.- Nuestra Señora de la Caridad del Cobre; advocación de la Virgen María.

La adoración a la Virgen María en la Isla de Cuba inicio con la derrota de Alonso de Ojeda y los primeros conquistadores de Cuba cuando pretendían imponerse a los indios. Estos los enfrentaron obligando a los españoles a huir a través de montes y ciénagas para salvar sus vidas. Llegando al pueblo indio de Cueibá en la zona de Jobabo, en muy mal estado por lo cual tuvieron compasión de ellos y les auxiliaron. Por agradecimiento Alonso de Ojeda construyó una pequeña ermita con ramas de árboles. Y allí colocó una Imagen de la *Virgen María* que era su preciada pertenencia. Cumpliendo así la promesa que había hecho de darle la Imagen a quien le ayudara a salir con vida de aquella situación. También enseñó a los indios a rezar el "Ave María" lo cual se propagó tan rápido entre los indios que más tarde Cuba se llegó a conocer como la isla del "Ave María." Sin conocimientos sobre el cristianismo, los indios de aquel lugar adoraron y rezaron a la Imagen de la Virgen María y mantuvieron la ermita con esmero cuando Ojeda y sus hombres se marcharon.

Cuando comenzó la explotación del cobre en las montañas de la región oriental de la isla de Cuba. Próximo a las minas, los españoles establecieron el hato de Barajagua que contaba con mucho ganado. Por eso era necesaria la sal que prevenía la corrupción de la carne. Una mañana que tres personas salieron a buscar sal en la bahía de Nipe, y mientras iban por la sal ocurrió la aparición de la estatua de la Virgen María. Estos tres hombres eran llamados Juan de Hoyos, Rodrigo de Hoyos y Juan Moreno, conocidos como "los tres Juanes". Así lo contó uno de ellos años más tardes: "...habiendo ranchado en cayo Francés que está en medio de la bahía de Nipe para con buen tiempo ir a las salinas..., estando una mañana el mar calmado salimos de dicho cayo Francés antes de salir el sol, los dichos Juan y Rodrigo de Hoyos y este declarante, embarcados en una canoa para dichas salinas, y apartados de dicho cayo Francés vimos una cosa blanca sobre la espuma del agua, que no distinguimos lo que podía ser, y acercándonos más nos pareció pájaro y ramas secas. Dijeron dichos indios "parece una niña," y en estos discursos, llegados, reconocieron y vieron la imagen de Nuestra Señora de la Santísima Trinidad con el Niño Jesús en los brazos sobre una tablita pequeña, y en dicha tablita unas letras grandes las cuales leyó dicho Rodrigo de Hoyos, y decían: "Yo soy la Virgen de la Caridad," y siendo sus vestiduras de ropaje, se admiraron que no estaban mojadas. Y en esto, llenos de alegría, cogieron sólo tres tercios de sal y se vinieron para el Hato de Barajagua..."

El administrador del término Real de Minas de Cobre, Don Francisco Sánchez de Moya, ordenó levantar una ermita para colocar la imagen y estableció a Rodrigo de Hoyos como capellán. Una noche Rodrigo fue a visitar a la Virgen y notó que no estaba allí. Se organizó una búsqueda sin éxito. A la mañana siguiente, y para la sorpresa de todos, la Virgen estaba de nuevo en su altar, sin que se pudiera explicar, ya que la puerta de la ermita había permanecido cerrada toda la noche. Este hecho se repitió dos o tres veces más hasta que los habitantes de Barajagua pensaron que la Virgen quería cambiar de lugar. Por lo que se trasladó en procesión, con gran pena para ellos, al Templo Parroquial del Cobre. La Virgen María fue recibida con repique de campanas y gran alegría en su nueva casa, donde la situaron sobre el altar mayor. Así llegó a conocerse como la Virgen de la Caridad del Cobre.

Pero en el Cobre se volvió a repetir la desaparición de la Virgen. Pensaron entonces que ella quería estar sobre las montañas de la Sierra Maestra. Esto se confirmó cuando una niña llamada Apolonia subió hasta el cerro de las minas de cobre donde trabajaba su madre. La niña iba persiguiendo mariposas y recogiendo flores cuando, sobre la cima de una de las montañas vio a la Virgen de la Caridad. La noticia de la pequeña Apolonia causó gran revuelo. Unos creían, otros no, pero la niña se mantuvo firme en su testimonio. Por lo cual llevaron a la Virgen a dicho lugar. Desde la aparición de la estatua, la devoción a la Virgen de la Caridad se propagó con una rapidez asombrosa por toda la isla de

Cuba. Con el transcurso de los años se construyó un recinto mayor, este nuevo recinto acoge al creciente número de peregrinos que anualmente visitan el santuario de la Santísima Virgen de la Caridad del Cobre, para las festividades del 8 de septiembre. La Virgen de la Caridad fue coronada por el papa Juan Pablo II como Reina y Patrona de Cuba el sábado 24 de enero de 1998, durante la Santa Misa que celebró en su visita apostólica a Santiago de Cuba.

La primera celebración de la Fiesta de la Virgen de la Caridad del Cobre en el exilio se llevó a cabo el 8 de septiembre de 1961, el mismo día que llegó la imagen de la santísima Virgen a la ciudad de Miami. Esta era la imagen que se había adorado por mucho tiempo en la Parroquia de Guanabo de la Habana. Dicha celebración se llevó a cabo con profunda emoción, presidida por el Arzobispo de Miami, y a partir de la fecha se hizo una tradición que continúa hasta el día de hoy. Pero la imagen de la Virgen no sólo estuvo presente en estas celebraciones, sino que comenzó un recorrido de los campamentos para los niños cubanos exilados que se encontraban sin sus padres. Los cubanos se organizaron para construir una Ermita a la Virgen de la Caridad en el exilio. La primera piedra de la capilla provisional se puso el 20 de mayo de 1967. El 21 de mayo de 1968 el Arzobispo Carrol de Miami, ordena la fundación de la Cofradía de la Virgen de la Caridad para reunir a los devotos para honrar a la Virgen María y con ella evangelizar. Miami cuenta con ciudadanos de todos los países hispanos. Desde los años 80, además de los 126 municipios cubanos, peregrinan también a la ermita de la Virgen de la Caridad del Cobre de forma organizada, todos los países hermanos de la hispanidad durante el mes de octubre.

Los devotos de la Virgen han logrado propagar no solo la devoción a la Virgen de la Caridad, sino hacer de la Ermita un centro de evangelización de irradiación mundial. El instrumento principal de la *Virgen María* para la obra de la Ermita fue desde el principio Monseñor Agustín Román, con la ayuda de las Hermanas de la Caridad que ministran en la Ermita y la Archicofradía. La imagen de la Virgen de la Caridad refleja que el Espíritu Santo está por encima de todo y de todos. En su mano derecha sostiene la Cruz, camino único de salvación, que debe ser abrazado por todos sus hijos. Con la mano izquierda sostiene a su Hijo, el Niño Dios. Así nos enseña la importancia de, imitarla a ella que fue fiel, acompañando a Jesús desde el comienzo de su vida hasta la Cruz. La *Virgen María* es nuestra Madre y Creadora. Ella en tiempo de tormenta, vino para salvar a "los tres Juanes". Igual la Virgen María viene hoy para salvarnos de las tormentas que azotan en nuestras vidas. Así como Ella acompañó a los Apóstoles cuando se reunieron llenos de miedo en Pentecostés. La *Virgen María* nos adentra en su corazón maternal, santuario del Espíritu Santo donde nos forja en otro Cristo, al irradiarnos con su divinidad. La parte femenina del Ser Supremo quiso hacerse mujer de carne y hueso para concebir en su vientre al hombre que se convertiría a su vez en Dios, dando ejemplo al ser humano de que el camino de luz y verdad conduce al Espíritu Santo. Ella es la madre de todos los que guardan la Palabra y de todos los que no la guardan también. La Virgen María nos enseña la importancia de la Maternidad, la dignidad de la mujer que asumió tan gran misión. Por ende, el respeto que merece. La *Virgen María* es la madre de todas las familias, la Madre del Ser, la Madre del Verbo, la Madre de sí misma. Al recurrir a ella, la familia se consolida en la auténtica caridad que ella representa.

La Virgen de la Caridad del Cobre nos enseña que la verdadera patria de cada ser humano es el Universo sin importar la lengua. La patria de la tierra es amada y edificada según nuestras ideas y limitaciones humanas. A medida que en un país sus hijos hacen la voluntad del Espíritu Santo, ese país se enaltece. Pero la gloria debe ser de todo ser humano en cualquier lugar que se encuentre, Dios mando a habitar toda la tierra y donde quiera que vayamos nos acompaña la esencia divina. Y aunque en cada ciudad o nación la Virgen lleve un nombre distinto en verdad existe una sola la Divina Virgen María. María nos enseña que la caridad es paciente, es servicial; la caridad no es envidiosa, no es jactanciosa, no se engríe; es decorosa; no busca su interés; no se irrita; no toma en cuenta el mal; no se alegra de la injusticia; se alegra con la verdad; Todo lo excusa; Todo lo cree; Todo lo espera; Todo lo soporta; La caridad no acaba nunca.

4.4.- Nuestra Señora de Coromoto; advocación de la Virgen María.

Santa María de Coromoto en Guanare de los Cospes o Virgen de Coromoto es la patrona de Venezuela y, desde el 19 de noviembre de 2011 Patrona Principal de la Iglesia arquidiocesana de Caracas luego que la Santa Sede aprobó su designación. Es una advocación mariana, venerada tanto en la ciudad de Guanare, donde apareció hace 368 años, como en toda Venezuela.

Cuando se fundó el pueblo de Guanare en 1591, los indígenas que habitaban en la región, los Cospes, huyeron hacia la selva en el norte de la localidad. Esto dificultaba la evangelización que la Iglesia Católica Romana había emprendido. La aparición de la Virgen ocurrió en esta selva a la que habían huido los nativos, el 8 de septiembre de 1652, donde la *Virgen María* se le apareció al Cacique de los Cospes, el nativo Coromoto, y a su mujer, diciéndole en su propia lengua: *"Vayan a casa de los blancos y pídanles que les eche el agua en la cabeza para poder ir al cielo,"* con esta frase la Virgen le pide a él y a su tribu que se bautizaran. Según la tradición oral, el cacique le relató lo sucedido a su encomendero, don Juan Sánchez, éste le pidió que en ocho días estuviese listo con la tribu para recibir la catequesis y el bautismo. Varios indígenas cospes se convirtieron y se bautizaron, pero no el cacique, debido a que no se sentía a gusto, pues ya él no era el jefe. El nativo Coromoto huyó, la Virgen se le apareció otra vez, y Coromoto, enceguecido por la ira, alza su brazo para agarrarla y desaparece, la aparición se materializó en una estampilla hecha de fibra de árbol que luego se buscó y encontró la reliquia que se venera hoy día en el Santuario Nacional Nuestra Señora de Coromoto.

Cuenta el relato que Coromoto es mordido por una serpiente venenosa y vuelve a Guanare, herido y a punto de morir, comenzó a pedir el bautismo, se lo administró un barinés, y al bautizarse, se convirtió en apóstol y rogó al grupo de indios cospes rebeldes que estaba bajo su mando, que se bautizaran. Después, Coromoto, ahora con el nombre cristiano de Ángel Custodio, murió en buena vejez.

En 1950 el Papa Pío XII la declaró Patrona de Venezuela, el Papa Juan Pablo II la coronó en su visita al Santuario mariano en Guanare y el Papa Benedicto XVI elevó en 2006 al Santuario Nacional de Nuestra Señora de Coromoto a la categoría de Basílica Menor.

En la isla de Tenerife (Isla Canaria, España) se encuentran varias réplicas de la imagen de la patrona de Venezuela, entre ellas:

- En San Cristóbal de la Laguna nos encontramos un barrio que debe su nombre a esta imagen mariana, El Coromoto y donde se encuentra una réplica de la imagen en una diminuta capilla, la ermita de Nuestra Señora del Coromoto, el barrio celebra la festividad de la imagen en los primeros fines de semana del mes de septiembre.

- En el municipio de Candelaria se encuentra una réplica de la Virgen de Coromoto en la Iglesia de Santa Ana, cerca de la Basílica y Real Santuario mariano de la Virgen de la Candelaria (Patrona de Canarias).

- En el municipio de La Guancha se encuentra una imagen de la Virgen de Coromoto en una pequeña ermita en el barrio de la Guancha de abajo, cuya fiesta se celebra el último domingo del mes de mayo.

- En la Iglesia de San Miguel Arcángel en la Ciudad de Villahermosa, Tabasco, México, hay una réplica de la Imagen de Nuestra Señora de Coromoto traída por la Asociación Civil "Unión de Venezolanos en Tabasco" (UVETAB A.C.).

También la podemos encontrar en el centro del pueblo de Bolibar (Bolibar oficialmente y según la ortografía vasca actual) Vizcaya, País Vasco - España. Está la Iglesia de Santo Tomás en cuyo pórtico guarda desde 1959 la capilla con puerta de vidrio dedicada a la Virgen de Coromoto Patrona de Venezuela.

En Madrid en la iglesia San Antonio de Padua (Calle Bravo Murillo, 150), en la capilla primera se encuentra el altar de Nuestra Señora de Coromoto. Encima del Altar se lee: "Nuestra Señora de Coromoto, Patrona de Venezuela". El fondo del retablo es una pintura del cielo con unos ángeles rodeando la imagen de la Virgen de Coromoto. La pintura es obra de Francisco Boira Castells y pertenece al año 1955.

4.5.- Nuestra Señora de la Inmaculada Concepción; advocación de la Virgen María.

El dogma de la Inmaculada Concepción, también conocido como Purísima Concepción, es una creencia del catolicismo que sostiene que María, madre de Jesús, a diferencia de todos los demás seres humanos, no fue alcanzada por el pecado original, sino que, desde el primer instante de su concepción, estuvo libre de todo pecado. No debe confundirse esta doctrina con la de la maternidad virginal de María, que sostiene que

Jesús fue concebido sin intervención de varón y que María permaneció virgen antes, durante y después del embarazo.

Al desarrollar la doctrina de la Inmaculada Concepción, la Iglesia Católica contempla la posición especial de María por ser madre de Cristo, y sostiene que Dios preservó a María libre de todo pecado y, aún más, libre de toda mancha o efecto del pecado original, que había de transmitirse a todos los hombres por ser descendientes de Adán y Eva, en atención a que iba a ser la madre de Jesús, que es también Dios. La doctrina reafirma con la expresión "llena eres de gracia" (*Gratia Plena*) contenida en el saludo del arcángel Gabriel (Luca 1,28), y recogida en la oración del Ave María, este aspecto de ser libre de pecado por la gracia de Dios.

La definición del dogma, contenida en la bula *Ineffabilis Deus*, de 8 de diciembre de 1854, dice lo siguiente:

> ...Para honra de la Santísima Trinidad, para la alegría de la Iglesia católica, con la autoridad de nuestro Señor Jesucristo, con la de los Santos Apóstoles Pedro y Pablo y con la nuestra: Definimos, afirmamos y pronunciamos que la doctrina que sostiene que la Santísima Virgen María fue preservada inmune de toda mancha de culpa original desde el primer instante de su concepción, por singular privilegio y gracia de Dios Omnipotente, en atención a los méritos de Cristo-Jesús, Salvador del género humano, ha sido revelada por Dios y por tanto debe ser firme y constantemente creída por todos los fieles. Por lo cual, si alguno tuviere la temeridad, lo cual Dios no permita, de dudar en su corazón lo que por Nos ha sido definido, sepa y entienda que su propio juicio lo condena, que su fe ha naufragado y que ha caído de la unidad de la Iglesia y que si además osaren manifestar de palabra o por escrito o de otra cualquiera manera externa lo que sintieren en su corazón, por lo mismo quedan sujetos a las penas establecidas por el derecho.

Pío IX, contemplando el mar agitado de Gaeta, escuchó y meditó las palabras del cardenal Luigi Lambruschini: "Beatísimo Padre, Usted no podrá curar el mundo sino con la proclamación del dogma de la Inmaculada Concepción. Sólo esta definición dogmática podrá restablecer el sentido de las verdades cristianas y retraer las inteligencias de las sendas del naturalismo en las que se pierden".

El historiador Francesco Guglieta, experto en la vida de Pío IX, señala que el tema del naturalismo, que despreciaba toda verdad sobrenatural, podría considerarse como la cuestión de fondo que impulsó al Papa a la proclamación del dogma: *La afirmación de la Concepción Inmaculada de la Virgen ponía sólidas bases para afirmar y consolidar la certeza de la primacía de la Gracia y de la obra de la Providencia en la vida de los hombres.* Guglieta señala que Pío IX, pese a su entusiasmo, acogió la idea de realizar una consulta con el episcopado mundial, que expresó su parecer positivo, y llevó finalmente a la proclamación del dogma.

La doctrina de la Inmaculada Concepción no es aceptada por los miembros de las iglesias protestantes. Los protestantes rechazan la doctrina ya que no consideran que el desarrollo dogmático de la teología sea un referente de autoridad y que la mariología en general, incluida la doctrina de la Inmaculada Concepción, no se enseña en la Biblia.

Los protestantes argumentan que, si Jesús necesitó de un vientre sin pecado para nacer sin pecado, también Dios tuvo que haber intervenido en la concepción de la madre de María, en su abuela, y así sucesivamente a lo largo del tiempo. La respuesta del catolicismo es que sólo María tenía que mantenerse libre de pecado pues ella iba a concebir directamente a Cristo, mientras que sus ancestros no. Es decir, que Cristo sí necesitó de un vientre sin pecado, pero María no.

Otro argumento sostenido por los protestantes proviene de los evangelios de Marcos 10:18 y Lucas 18:9. Cuando Jesús es nombrado como *Buen pastor* (Marcos 10:17), replica "Nadie es bueno - excepto Dios". Señalan que con esta frase Cristo enseña que nadie está sin pecado, dejando margen para la conclusión de que él es Dios encarnado. Los católicos señalan que la Biblia entera, y no una frase o sentencia aislada manifiesta la verdadera doctrina de Jesucristo. Aunque la Biblia no dice nada acerca del hecho extraordinario de que María naciera sin pecado.

Otro argumento en contra de la creencia en la Inmaculada Concepción aparece en la primera epístola de San Juan 1: 8 "Si decimos que no tenemos pecado, nos engañamos a nosotros mismos y la verdad no está en nosotros".

Sin embargo, el iniciador del movimiento protestante, Martín Lutero, dijo:

Es dulce y piadoso creer que la infusión del alma de María se efectuó sin pecado original, de modo que en la mismísima infusión de su alma ella fue también purificada del pecado original y adornada con los dones de Dios, recibiendo un alma pura infundida por Dios; de modo que, desde el primer momento que ella comenzó a vivir fue libre de todo pecado.

Sermón: "Sobre el día de la Concepción de la Madre de Dios", 1527.

No obstante, la ley registrada en Levítico 12:1-8 menciona que la mujer que daba luz a un varón tenía que ser inmunda siete días. María cumplió esta ley, según san Lucas 2:22-24.

Eso no indica que María haya pecado. Desde este punto de vista Jesús recibe el bautismo de Juan predicado para el perdón de los pecados, no siendo el mismo Jesús pecador. "Déjame hacer por el momento, porque es necesario que así cumplamos lo ordenado por Dios".

En el XI Concilio de Toledo el rey visigodo Wamba ya era titulado "Defensor de la Purísima Concepción de María", abriendo una línea de fieles devotos entre los reyes hispanos. Monarcas como Fernando III el Santo, Jaime I el Conquistador, el emperador Carlos V o su hijo Felipe II fueron fieles devotos de la Inmaculada y portaron su estandarte en sus campañas militares.

El rey Carlos III, muy afecto a esta advocación mariana, creó una orden en su nombre, la Orden de Carlos III, y la declaró patrona de sus estados.

Desde el siglo XIV existen en España referencias de cofradías creadas en honor a la Inmaculada. La más antigua, en Gerona, data de 1330. En el siglo XVI se revitalizará este fervor con un ingente número de cofradías constituidas bajo la advocación de la Pura y Limpia Concepción de María, hermandades consagradas a las labores caritativas y la asistencia social. Los franciscanos fueron muy fieles a la creencia en la Inmaculada, y contribuyeron a su arraigo y extensión por todo el mundo.

La fiesta de la Inmaculada fue fiesta de guardar en todos los reinos de su Majestad Católica, es decir, en todo el Imperio español, desde 1644; se declaró fiesta de guardar en toda la Iglesia desde 1708 por orden del papa Clemente XI.

España celebra a la Inmaculada como patrona y protectora desde 1644, siendo el 8 de diciembre fiesta de carácter nacional. Durante la celebración de dicha festividad, los sacerdotes españoles tienen el privilegio de vestir casulla azul. Este privilegio fue otorgado por la Santa Sede en 1864, como agradecimiento a la defensa del dogma de la Inmaculada Concepción que hizo España.

- La patrona de la Infantería Española es la Inmaculada Concepción. Este patronazgo tiene su origen en el llamado Milagro de Empel durante las guerras en Flandes.

- El voto a la Inmaculada Concepción se hizo por primera vez en España en el pueblo de Villalpando (Zamora), el 1 de noviembre de 1466, en la iglesia de San Nicolás, seguido por la entonces Villa de Alcázar de San Juan, renovando el voto cada año. Lo hicieron 13 pueblos (Villalpando, Quintanilla del Monte, Cotanes del Monte, Villamayor de Campos, Tapioles, Cañizo, Villar de Fallaves, Villardiga, Prado, Quintanilla del Olmo, San Martín de Valderaudey, Villanueva del Campo, Cerecinos de Campos). Dos manuscritos, uno en pergamino y otro en papel, los dos de 1527, conservan los textos del Voto y de las dos primeras refrendaciones. Éste fue impreso por primera vez en 1668 por F. López de Arrieta, presbítero villalpandino, en León. Las 6 refrendaciones o renovaciones del Voto (1498, 1527, 1904, 1940, 1954 y 1967) se han hecho en la plaza mayor de Villalpando como actos solemnes notariales. Los 5 "notarios de la Purísima" han sido Diego Fernández de Villalpando (1466), Alonso Pérez de Encalada (1498, 1527), Manuel Salas Fernández (1904), Eloy Gómez Silió (1940) y Luis Delgado González (1954 y 1967).

- Puente Genil (Córdoba) fue el primer pueblo de Andalucía en hacer fiesta en honor a la Purísima Concepción. El 26 de octubre de 1617 el Cabildo acuerda hacer una fiesta solemne en defensa inmaculista, pero de manera concreta hizo Voto oficial el 8 de mayo de 1650. En ese año, lo mismo que ocurriera en otras localidades de Andalucía en esta centuria, la población de la antigua Puente de Don Gonzalo sufrió las consecuencias de una epidemia de cólera que asoló la Villa causando numerosas muertes en el vecindario. Aquellos vecinos, angustiados por tal azote y asidos a una gran fe decidieron encomendarse con súplicas y oraciones a la protección de Nuestra Señora la Santísima Madre de Dios, para que por su divina intervención los librara de la contagiosa enfermedad, siendo por ello por lo que prometieron guardar, cumplir y ejecutar siempre el Voto con el que la aclamaron por Patrona y que fidelísimamente viene cumpliéndose anualmente hasta la actualidad. A través del cual se promete festejar el día de su onomástica, el 8 de diciembre, con la renovación del Voto y la celebración de la solemne procesión de la Imagen hasta su santuario. Es la única población que de manera ininterrumpida ha renovado dicho Voto, y ni las guerras ni modismos han conseguido extinguirlo. Fue una iniciativa oficial del Ayuntamiento, una propuesta institucional y no particular como ocurría en otras ciudades, pues cofradías hacían su voto de defensa y, o bien se han extinguido o bien se han renovado esporádicamente y de manera individual. Su iconografía es un tanto peculiar dado que tiene en sus manos al Niño Jesús.

- El templo más importante de la ciudad de Santa Cruz de Tenerife (Canarias), está dedicado a la Inmaculada (Iglesia Matriz de la Concepción). También en la isla de Tenerife la Inmaculada Concepción de la ciudad de San Cristóbal de la Laguna, es la Alcaldesa de la ciudad de La Laguna y Patrona de la Cruz Roja Española de la ciudad de La Laguna.

- Los Colegios Oficiales de Farmacéuticos y las Facultades de Farmacia, también la tienen como patrona.

- El primer templo dedicado a la Inmaculada Concepción en España fue el Monasterio de San Jerónimo en Granada.

- Patrona del pueblo de Torrejoncillo (Cáceres), que cada 30 de noviembre prepara su trono en el retablo de la iglesia; el día 7, a las 10 de la noche sale La Encamisá (declarada Fiesta de interés turístico nacional), que consiste en un jinete portando el estandarte de la Inmaculada Concepción, seguido de dos centenares de jinetes encamisados con sábanas blancas, todos ellos vitoreados por la multitud.

- Patrona de las Nuevas poblaciones que fundó el rey Carlos III, la Carlota, Fuente Palmera.

- En la ciudad de La Línea de la Concepción (Cádiz) lleva el nombre de Concepción en honor de su patrona, a su vez la ciudad posee el Santuario de la Inmaculada Concepción edificada en el siglo XIX. El día de la patrona se procesiona la imagen por las calles de la ciudad.

- También recibe especial veneración en la localidad murciana de Yecla, de donde es patrona y en cuyo honor se celebran importantes fiestas declaradas de Interés turístico nacional.
- Patrona del municipio de Fortuna (Murcia), y titular de su iglesia parroquial.
- Patrona del municipio de Segart (Valencia), y titular de su iglesia parroquial.
- Patrona del municipio de Torremejía (Provincia de Badajoz) y titular de su iglesia parroquial
- Patrona de la pedanía de La Punta (Valencia), y titular de su iglesia parroquial.
- Ostenta el patronazgo y titularidad de la parroquia en la pedanía murciana de Palmar.
- Patrona del municipio almeriense perteneciente a la comarca de La Alpujarra, Alhama de Almería (Almería).
- En el municipio grancanario de Agaete, es la patrona de la villa.
- Es patrona del municipio de Villanueva del Ariscal (Sevilla), cuya bandera reproduce la concepcionista.
- Es patrona del municipio de Arenales de San Gregorio (Ciudad Real). El día 8 de diciembre se celebra la solemne misa y las tradicionales hogueras en honor a la patrona. A pesar de ser este día la solemnidad propiamente dicha, se celebra con mayor importancia el "Día de la Virgen" que suele recaer el sábado más próximo al 9 de mayo, con motivo de la Feria y Fiestas en honor de San Gregorio Nacianceno y la Inmaculada Concepción, ambos patrones de la localidad.
- Es patrona de Nava del Rey (provincia de Valladolid) desde el año 1745, celebrándose desde entonces un novenario en su honor. Con este motivo, la Virgen desciende procesionalmente el 30 de noviembre desde su ermita hasta la parroquia de los Santos Juanes, donde se celebra la novena. Después de los actos litúrgicos, el 8 de diciembre la imagen retorna a su ermita aclamada por los fieles. Ambas procesiones se conocen como la fiesta de *Los Pegotes, nombre que reciben las antorchas con las que se ilumina el recorrido. Entre otras particularidades, las procesiones se celebran por la noche con el recorrido iluminado por hogueras; además la Virgen va dentro de un coche de caballos tirado por mulas. La fiesta está declarada de Interés turístico regional.*

- Horcajo de Santiago, (Cuenca) celebra sus fiestas del *Vitor* en honor a la Inmaculada Concepción, durante los días 7 y 8 de diciembre; declaradas de Interés turístico regional.
- Es patrona de la pedanía ilicitana de Torrellano, en la cual se celebran en su honor las fiestas más importantes en las que tiene lugar una solemne procesión de la imagen de la patrona por todas las calles de la pedanía.
- Es la patrona de la diócesis de Huelva.
- Es la patrona de Torrevieja (Alicante).
- Es la patrona de la diócesis de Asidonia-Jerez.
- Argentina. El 8 de diciembre es feriado nacional.
- Brasil. El 8 de diciembre es feriado en varias ciudades brasileñas, como Angra dos Reis, Dourados, Itapura, Bragança Paulista, Jacareí y Mogi Guacu (patrona de la ciudad), Recife, Salvador, João Pessoa, Campina Grande, Nuevo Mundo, Belo Horizonte, Contagem, Conceição dos Ouros, Divinópolis, Porto Franco, Campos dos Goytacazes, Port Colborne, y así sucesivamente.
- Chile. El 8 de diciembre es feriado nacional, y en la víspera de ese día cada año miles de peregrinos se trasladan mayoritariamente a pie o en bicicleta al Santuario de Lo Vásquez, ubicado en la Ruta 68 (en la que se interrumpe el tránsito de vehículos motorizados), a 85 km de Santiago y 34 km de Valparaíso.
- Colombia. Se trata de un festivo nacional en cuya víspera o madrugada los católicos, niños y adultos, se reúnen en familia o entre amigos para encender velas y faroles en las aceras de las calles en honor de la Virgen María, fiesta conocida también como el día de las Velitas, la cual tradicionalmente da inicio a la época navideña.
- Sicilia. Fiesta nacional, siendo la Virgen de la Inmaculada Concepción protectora de su ejército.
- Estados Unidos de América. En 1792, el obispo de Baltimore, John Carroll, consagró a la recién nacida nación de los Estados Unidos a la protección de la Inmaculada Concepción. En 1847, el papa Pío IX formalizó dicho patronazgo.
- Guatemala. La procesión de la Inmaculada Concepción recorre las calles desde el día 7. En época antigua las calles eran iluminadas con fogatas para el paso de la procesión que hacía su recorrido durante la noche. Posteriormente a la quema de las

fogatas se le llamó la *Quema del Diablo*, tradición para purificar lo material previo a la fiesta de la Inmaculada Concepción y da inicio a las festividades populares de Navidad en el país.

- México. La Catedral metropolitana de la ciudad de México está consagrada a la Inmaculada Concepción de María. La localidad de Celaya, Guanajuato, desde su fundación se amparó a esta advocación siendo traída desde Salamanca una imagen que es considerada aún en la actualidad como la más bella de la provincia franciscana de San Pedro y San Pablo. En el estado de Tamaulipas La Catedral de Tampico, está dedicada a la Inmaculada Concepción. En el estado de Veracruz, la ciudad de Cosamaloapan en la Cuenca del Papaloapan, tiene como santa patrona a la imagen de la "Nuestra Señora de Cosamaloapan", perteneciente a la advocación de la Inmaculada Concepción, figura tallada en madera que según la tradición llegó al pueblo flotando en las aguas del río en el año 1546. En la ciudad de Chignahuapan en el estado de Puebla se erige la Basílica de la Inmaculada Concepción, donde se tiene en el altar una imagen de 14 metros de altura tallada en madera, la cual está registrada como la más grande del mundo (2018). En el municipio de Mazatán (Chiapas), se celebra a la virgen bajo el nombre de Virgen Margarita Concepción, del 29 de noviembre al 8 de diciembre de cada año. Actualmente es Reina de la Diócesis de Tapachula.

- Nicaragua. A partir de finales del siglo XVIII comenzó en la ciudad de León la fiesta de "La gritería" la noche del 7 de diciembre de cada año, víspera de su festividad. El pueblo cristiano volcado en las calles de la ciudad visita los altares preparados en las salas y porches de las casas y al grito de júbilo "¿Quién causa tanta alegría? ¡La Concepción de María!" se reparten dulces típicos. Esta fiesta nacional se hace desde entonces hasta hoy.

- Panamá. El 19 de diciembre de 1988 con la Bula "Ad Perpetuam Rei Memoriam" del papa Juan Pablo II, se crea la diócesis de Colón-Kuna Yala, Panamá en la costa del Caribe. Además, es la patrona de la diócesis de Coclé y venerada en la Basílica Menor Santiago Apóstol de Natá de los Caballeros. Es día feriado nacional y oficialmente Día de la Madre.

- Paraguay. El 8 de diciembre es feriado nacional. La Inmaculada Concepción es venerada bajo la advocación de "Virgen de Caacupé". Ese día y en los previos, miles de personas peregrinan a la ciudad de Caacupé, situada entre las serranías de la Cordillera de los Altos, a unos 54 km al este de la capital paraguaya.
- Perú. El 8 de diciembre es feriado nacional. A su vez en varias regiones incluso Ancash y Huayao, se celebra este día, cantando y bailando la tradicional danza Carrera de Cintas, en la cual los ancashinos celebran a la Virgen.
- Portugal. *Nossa Senhora da Conceição* es patrona de Portugal, siendo festivo ese día.

La Inmaculada Concepción; simbolismo de Luz y Fuego.

- El fuego, desde el inicio de los tiempos, ha despertado en los hombres un sentimiento muy especial: salir de la oscuridad para entrar a la luz, a la verdad y a la vida eterna.
- La tradición de asociarle a la Inmaculada Concepción el encendido de las velitas tiene su propia historia (aunque la historia del fuego se remonte a tiempos antiquísimos, no se tratará aquí más que lo concerniente a su utilización en general en el cristianismo y en particular en la veneración de la Inmaculada Concepción).
- Las primeras menciones al uso de velas o cirios se hallan entre los etruscos, (s. xv a.c., civilización que influyó en los romanos), quienes al parecer las fabricaban de cera, sebo o pez, con mecha de fibras vegetales como el papiro o el junco. Fue costumbre posterior en la Roma pagana alumbrar los santuarios en sus ceremonias, con velas de cera, como ocurría en las llamadas fiestas de Saturno o saturnalias.
- Sin embargo, en la primera centuria de vida del cristianismo nada sugiere en torno al uso de las velas, excepto el uso que hubo de dársele a éstas en el tiempo de la persecución. Mientras los cristianos se refugiaron en sitios oscuros y subterráneos, la necesidad de encender cirios para celebrar los santos misterios se convirtió en una obligatoriedad: "Los cristianos celebraban al principio sus misterios en casas retiradas y en cuevas durante

la noche; y de esto provino que les llamaran lucifugaces..."
(Voltaire 1981:184).

- Terminada la persecución, podríamos decir que pudo haberse iniciado tímida y lentamente a consolidar esta tradición en los siglos posteriores, que luego fue evolucionando. A partir del siglo XII empiezan a aparecer las velas colocadas en los altares de ciertas iglesias, hasta que la costumbre enraizó y se propagó definitivamente en los siglos XV y XVI, que es precisamente la época en que América es invadida y colonizada.

- Los hombres prehispánicos tenían sus propias creencias y prácticas religiosas, pero bastó mucho menos que un siglo para que las costumbres y la cultura de aquellos aborígenes se hubiera trastornado ostensiblemente. España se hallaba en plena fiebre de conquistas, y atravesaba además una época de gran convulsión religiosa, aquella provocada por Lutero en 1519, la cual había desencadenado ese letal movimiento de la contrarreforma, de modo que ésta emigró también con los españoles y marcó con huellas profundas la experiencia religiosa andina.

- Acciones tales como instaurar Tribunales de Santa Inquisición para indios, iniciar un "movimiento de extirpación de idolatrías", expropiación de las tierras de los indios por el derecho que así les concedía una bula papal, y otras vejaciones (Bonilla, comp. 1992), indudablemente terminarían por cercenar las costumbres y creencias de los nativos, a la par que estos se irían adaptando a los hábitos de los colonizadores en un largo camino de mestizaje. Y es en un panorama como éste que empezará en América la costumbre de celebrar el día de la "Inmaculada Concepción", y lo que otrora se hiciera con identidad americana, vino a convertirse en un sincretismo religioso por lo que las fiestas del hombre prehispánico se reemplazaron por las tradicionales españolas. Caso concreto fue la antigua fiesta del Inti raymi (fiesta del sol) que los incas celebraban por la misma época de la solemnidad del Corpus Christi.

- Ahora bien, las fiestas ayudaron sobre todo al nativo para que aprendiera a integrarse en el nuevo estilo de vida, y el elemento lúdico que sobresalía en toda fiesta era la luz, así que las luminarias fueron como la parte visible del júbilo en los villorrios, que en medio de la noche y de la algazara adquiría otras connotaciones. Entre las clases de fiestas que se celebraban, estaban las "repentinas" que consistían en una representación del poder español (una carroza llevaba el retrato del rey entre aclamaciones y vivas). Las "solemnes" correspondían al calendario católico y en esas estaban incluidas todas las fiestas patronales, Semana Santa y Corpus; además, las "patrióticas".

- Algunos registros históricos testimonian lo anterior con formidable detalle. Uno de ellos cuenta cómo fue la llegada del virrey al pueblo limeño, en el año 1556: "...se regocijen cuanto sea posible, y así mandaron que se pregone luego en las plazas y calles de esta ciudad, que la primera noche todos los vecinos y moradores de esta ciudad pongan a primera noche luminarias en lo alto de sus casas y hagan fuegos a sus puertas..." (Libros... Lima, tomo 10, p.128 citado en López 1992:66).

- Y una de las más significativas es la celebrada en Puerto Rico en 1747 y que se refiere a la exaltación al trono de Fernando VI: "Todos demostraron, su alegría con muchas luminarias, que pusieron en ventanas, balcones y calles. La real Fortaleza (morada del gobernador) estaba adornada con cuarenta hachas y más de doscientas velas, tan simétricamente en balcones, corredores y azoteas, que todos querían ver su hermosura, obligados de su extraordinario y abundante adorno, y en la misma conformidad se adornó todos los días que duraron las fiestas, haciéndolo lo mismo el vecindario..." (Boletín...Puerto Rico, Relación Verídica..., p.165 citado en López 1992:67).

- Estas evidencias del uso temprano de las velas en tiempo de la colonia, sugieren que su utilización tenía más un sentido desde lo folklórico y festivo que desde lo religioso y simbólico. De este modo arribamos entonces al momento en que se introduce en Colombia, la celebración de la solemnidad de la Inmaculada Concepción: "La fiesta que hoy inicia el período navideño, la Inmaculada Concepción el 8 de diciembre, se impuso en la América Española por cédula real en 1760, aunque dicha cédula llegó al Cauca en marzo de 1762" (Miñana 1997:23)

- Y es Popayán la ciudad que se lleva el honor de acoger, en primer lugar, esta orden que vino por conducto del papa Clemente, quien decretó: "...que la Inmaculada Concepción fuera tenida, reconocida y reverenciada como principal y universal patrona de las Españas (...) se estableció la costumbre de iluminar la ciudad la noche del 7 de diciembre, en lo que obraba orden infaltable del teniente gobernador o del alcalde" (Arboleda 1956:310).

4.6.- Nuestra Señora de la Divina Providencia; advocación de la Virgen María.

Nuestra Señora de la Divina Providencia es una advocación mariana de la Iglesia Católica que se originó en Italia en el siglo XIII. Actualmente posee una gran veneración en Puerto Rico, de hecho, es la Patrona de Puerto Rico. Su imagen se encuentra en una capilla en la Catedral Metropolitana de San Juan en la capital puertorriqueña.

Al ser nombrado obispo de Puerto Rico el catalán Gil Esteve y Tomás, trajo consigo a Puerto Rico esta devoción que conociera en sus años de seminarista. En las manos de la Divina Providencia tuvo que poner toda su diócesis este prelado, pues encontró a la catedral prácticamente en ruinas y la economía de la diócesis en peores condiciones. La confianza del obispo y su trabajo dieron fruto rápidamente y antes de los cinco años ya había podido reconstruir el templo catedralicio, en el que se estableció el culto y la devoción a la Virgen de la Providencia.

La imagen original venerada por los Siervos de María y otras órdenes religiosas italianas, es un óleo en el que aparece la Virgen con el Divino Niño dormido plácidamente en sus brazos. El título "de la Divina Providencia", se debe a San Felipe Benicio, quinto superior de los Siervos de María, quien al invocar la protección de la Virgen un día en que sus frailes no tenían alimentos, encontró a la puerta del convento dos cestas repletas de alimentos sin que se pudiese conocer su procedencia.

La imagen mandada a hacer por Don Gil Esteve fue tallada en Barcelona (España) según el gusto de la época. Es una imagen sentada, "de ropaje", (es decir, hecha para ser vestida), y estuvo expuesta al culto en la catedral durante 67 años, hasta que en 1920 fue sustituida por otra talla, toda de madera, que es la imagen de Nuestra Señora de la Divina Providencia más familiar y conocida por las comunidades puertorriqueñas.

María se inclina sobre el Niño, que en total actitud de confianza duerme plácidamente en su regazo. Las manos de la Virgen se unen en oración mientras sostiene suavemente la mano izquierda del Divino Infante.

El Papa Pablo VI declaró a Nuestra Señora de la Divina Providencia, como patrona principal de la isla de Puerto Rico mediante un decreto firmado el 19 de noviembre de 1969. En ese documento se decretó también que la solemnidad de la Virgen debía trasladarse del dos de enero, aniversario de su llegada a la isla, al 19 de noviembre, día en que fue descubierta la isla de Borinquén. Se quiso unir así los dos grandes afectos de los puertorriqueños; el amor por su preciosa isla y el amor por la Madre de Dios.

La talla más antigua, que data del 1853, fue la elegida para ser coronada solemnemente durante la reunión del Consejo Episcopal Latino Americano celebrada en San Juan de Puerto Rico el 5 de noviembre de 1976. La víspera del acontecimiento esta imagen fue vilmente quemada en la Parroquia de Santa Teresita de Santurce. La imagen quemada fue enviada a España para ser restaurada. Actualmente espera la construcción del proyectado gran santuario nacional para ser allí colocada.

4.7.- Nuestra Señora del Perpetuo Socorro; advocación de la Virgen María.

La Virgen del Perpetuo Socorro es una advocación mariana. La imagen original es un icono procedente de Creta y venerado en Roma en la iglesia de los Agustinos, a finales del siglo XV, y desde 1866 en la iglesia romana de San Alfonso. La datación del icono es difícil de precisar. Unos los sitúan entre siglos X y XI, y otros a comienzos del siglo XV. Su festividad se celebra el 27 de junio.

El icono original está en el altar mayor de la iglesia de San Alfonso, muy cerca de la Basílica de Santa María la Mayor en Roma. El icono de la Virgen, pintado sobre madera, de 21 por 17 pulgadas, muestra a María con el Niño Jesús. El Niño observa a dos ángeles que le muestran los instrumentos de su futura Pasión mientras agarra fuertemente con las dos manos la de su Madre, quien lo sostiene en sus brazos. El cuadro recuerda la maternidad divina de la Virgen y su cuidado por Jesús desde su concepción hasta su muerte.

Según una tablilla colocada antiguamente al lado del icono con los orígenes de la imagen, la cuna de este cuadro fue la isla de Creta, en el mar Egeo. Un mercader sustrajo el icono de una iglesia, lo escondió entre su equipaje y se embarcó rumbo a otras tierras. Durante la travesía sobrevino una gran tempestad y los pasajeros se encomendaron a Dios y a la Virgen. La leyenda cuenta que el mar recuperó su calma y el pasaje arribó a puerto seguro.

Poco después el mercader llegó a Roma con el cuadro y, tras algunas resistencias de la familia, el icono pasa a ocupar un lugar preferente en la iglesia de San Mateo, regentada por los agustinos. Era el año 1499, en tiempos del papa Alejandro VI. La iglesia de San Mateo era un templo menor entre las grandes basílicas de San Juan de Letrán y Santa María la Mayor. Allí permaneció la imagen del Perpetuo Socorro durante trescientos años. Los escritores de la época narraron ampliamente los milagros atribuidos a la imagen. El siglo XVII parece ser el más intenso en la devoción y culto a la Virgen del Perpetuo Socorro.

En febrero de 1798, con la invasión de Napoleón, sus tropas se apoderan de Italia y destruyen en Roma más de treinta iglesias, entre ellas la de san Mateo. Los religiosos agustinos salvan el cuadro milagroso y se lo llevan consigo. El icono entra en fase de olvido por más de 88 años.

En 1855 los Redentoristas compran unos terrenos al lado de la Via Merulana, muy cerca de Santa María la Mayor. Se llamaba Villa Caserta y en su interior algún día estuvo edificada la iglesia de san Mateo. A través del padre Miguel Marchi se descubre el paradero del icono milagroso. Los hijos de San Alfonso María de Ligorio, el gran cantor de las Glorias de María, solicitan al papa la concesión del Perpetuo Socorro. Es el 11 de diciembre de 1865, y el 19 de enero de 1866 la imagen de Nuestra Señora del Perpetuo Socorro regresa a la iglesia de San Alfonso, en el mismo emplazamiento donde había estado tres siglos.

Restaurada, ocupa el centro del ábside de la iglesia de San Alfonso y su devoción e influencia se extiende a los cinco continentes. Centenares de miles de iconos de Perpetuo Socorro se esparcen por las iglesias, casas y carreteras del mundo. Pío IX dijo, en la audiencia al Superior General de los Redentoristas el 11 de diciembre de 1865: "Dadla a conocer a todo el mundo". Juan Pablo II, en su autobiografía "Don y misterio", al referirse a los orígenes de su vocación sacerdotal, afirma: "No puedo olvidar la trayectoria mariana. La veneración a la Madre de Dios en su forma tradicional me viene de la familia y de la parroquia de Wadowice. Recuerdo, en la iglesia parroquial, una capilla lateral dedicada a la Madre del Perpetuo Socorro a la cual, por la mañana, antes del comienzo de las clases, acudían los estudiantes del instituto. También, al acabar las clases, en las horas de la tarde, iban muchos estudiantes para rezar a la Virgen".

La Virgen del Perpetuo Socorro es patrona de numerosos lugares e instituciones. En España está muy vinculada a los corredores de seguros. Es la patrona de Haití. Existen veinte institutos religiosos acogidos a la Madre del Perpetuo Socorro. Igualmente, diversas instituciones sanitarias, numerosas editoriales, libros, revistas, emisoras de radio mantienen y propagan su devoción.

Teniendo esta advocación mariana como patrona de su congregación, los padres Redentoristas la llevaron a sus misiones en Haití. Allí se le edificó un santuario en Béle-Aire, cerca de Puerto Príncipe, la capital de Haití.

En 1883 una terrible epidemia de viruela azotaba el país. Los devotos acudieron a la Virgen y le hicieron una novena. La epidemia cesó milagrosamente y se decidió nombrarla patrona del país.

En 1993 se celebró con gran regocijo el centenario del milagro y del nombramiento de la Virgen como patrona de Haití. El papa Juan Pablo II visitó Haití para esta celebración y puso al país bajo el amparo de la Virgen del Perpetuo Socorro.

4.8.- Nuestra Señora del Pilar; advocación de la Virgen María.

Nuestra Señora del Pilar o la Virgen del Pilar, es una advocación mariana católica. El 27 de mayo de 1642 el municipio de Zaragoza proclama patrona de la ciudad a la Virgen del Pilar, patronazgo que en las Cortes aragonesas de 1678 se extiende a todo el Reino de Aragón. Acumula diversos patronazgos sobre el Cuerpo de la Guardia Civil (1913), Cuerpo de Correos (1916), Cuerpo de Secretarios, Interventores y Depositarios de Administración Local (1928), Sociedad Mariológica (1940) y Consejo Superior de Misiones (1948). También es patrona de la Hispanidad (no de España, aunque ese día se celebre la Fiesta Nacional). Es venerada en la Catedral-Basílica de Zaragoza (España) a la que da nombre.

La leyenda sobre sus orígenes se remonta al año 40, cuando, de acuerdo con la tradición cristiana, el 2 de enero la Virgen María se apareció a Santiago el Mayor en Caesaraugusta. María llegó a Zaragoza "en carne mortal" —antes de su Asunción— y como testimonio de su visita habría dejado una columna de jaspe conocida popularmente como "el Pilar". Se cuenta que Santiago y los siete primeros convertidos de la ciudad edificaron una primitiva capilla de adobe en la vera del Ebro. Este testimonio es recogido por un manuscrito de 1297 de los Moralia, sive Expositio in Job, de Gregorio Magno, que se custodia en el Archivo del Pilar. La devoción mariana comenzó en los albores del siglo XIII cuando comienzan las primeras peregrinaciones a Santa María la Mayor.

Sobre la iglesia mozárabe preexistente, se erige el templo románico del Pilar poco después de la conquista de Zaragoza por Alfonso I el Batallador (1118) que fue culminado en el siglo XIII. En esta época se documenta en el templo una capilla primitiva para alojar el Pilar, según transmite Diego de Espés en 1240. Para 1293 el templo se encontraba en tan mal estado que el obispo Hugo de Mataplana promovió la restauración del templo y su conversión en la colegiata gótico-mudéjar de Santa María la Mayor con recursos de una bula de Bonifacio VIII que por vez primera menciona la advocación "del Pilar". Actualmente el único vestigio conservado del templo románico del Pilar es el tímpano de la iglesia, que ha sido colocado en la fachada sur de la basílica barroca.

La talla de la Virgen en madera dorada mide treinta y ocho centímetros de altura y descansa sobre una columna de jaspe, resguardada esta por un forro de bronce y plata y cubierta por un manto hasta los pies de la imagen, a excepción de los días dos, doce y veinte de cada mes en que aparece la columna visible en toda su superficie. En la fachada posterior de la capilla se abre el humilladero, donde los fieles pueden venerar a la Santa Columna a través de un óculo abierto al jaspe.

Se trata de una escultura de estilo Gótico tardío franco-borgoñón de hacia 1435 atribuida a Juan de la Huerta, imaginero de Daroca. En cuanto a su iconografía, se observa a María coronada y con túnica y manto, que recoge con su mano derecha, contemplando a Jesús niño que agarra el manto de su madre con la mano derecha y un pájaro con la izquierda. El rostro de la Virgen posee ternura y el niño puede haber sido objeto de una restauración poco cuidadosa.

Probablemente fue una imagen donada por Dalmacio de Mur con el mecenazgo de la reina Blanca de Navarra, mujer de Juan II de Aragón, a raíz de la curación de una enfermedad que aquejó a la reina por entonces.

La imagen representa a la Virgen coronada y ataviada con un vestido gótico abotonado. Se trata de una vestidura ceñida por un cinturón con hebilla que llega hasta los pies y permite discretamente observar el derecho más que el izquierdo. Una gran pieza de paño cubre la cabeza y muestra un peinado ondulado. La mano derecha sostiene un pliegue de la ropa, que cubre todo su abdomen y la mayor parte de sus extremidades inferiores. El Niño Jesús se encuentra en la mano izquierda y mira desde atrás. Aparece desnudo e irradia inocencia. Su figura gira hacia la izquierda y su cabeza apunta al cinturón de la Virgen. La escultura de fábrica gótica se restauró en 1990 por el Instituto del Patrimonio Histórico Español, a iniciativa del Cabildo Metropolitano de Zaragoza.

La Santa Columna está hecha de jaspe, tiene 1.70 metros de altura, un diámetro de 24 centímetros y un forro de bronce y plata. La tradición pilarista afirma que jamás ha variado su ubicación desde la visita de María a Santiago.

El 24 de marzo de 1596 se recibió en el santuario del Pilar el obsequio de Felipe II, que consistía en dos ángeles de plata —obra de Diego Arnal— que sirven de guardia a la Virgen. Son los únicos elementos de la colegiata gótica-mudéjar de Santa María la Mayor que se conservan en la actual basílica barroca.

El templo se articula en tres naves, de igual altura, cubiertas con bóvedas de cañón, en las que se intercalan cúpulas y bóvedas de plato, que descansan sobre robustos pilares. El exterior es de ladrillo caravista, siguiendo la tradición de construcción en ladrillo aragonesa, y el interior revocado en estuco. La nave central se halla dividida por la presencia del altar mayor bajo la cúpula central. El altar está presidido por el gran retablo mayor de la Asunción, perteneciente a la colegiata gótico-mudéjar de Santa María la Mayor de Zaragoza, realizado por Damián Forment en el siglo XVI.

Bajo las otras dos cúpulas elípticas de la nave central, se dispuso la Santa Capilla de la Virgen del Pilar, y el coro y órgano, que también procedían de la colegiata predecesora. Actualmente el coro y órgano, se encuentran desplazados, al siguiente tramo, para dotar de mayor espacio los tramos del altar mayor.

La comunidad cristiana de Caesaraugusta es una de las más antiguas de España, junto a las de Mérita, León y Astorga. Hacia 254 se documenta su existencia en el epistolario de San Cipriano. También consta que el obispo Valerio estuvo en el Concilio de Elvira a inicios del siglo IV y que el Pilar muy probablemente fue sede del concilio antiprisciliancista de 380.

En el siglo IV destaca el canon VIII del concilio de Antioquía —celebrado en la segunda mitad del siglo IV—, que establece la colocación de las imágenes religiosas sobre columnas o pilares. De lo cual deducen estudiosos como Mariano Nougués Secall y Manuel Aramburu que el hecho pudo haber estado inspirado por el conocimiento de la aparición de María a Santiago, aunque dicha tradición era muy popular en el paganismo. De acuerdo con Francisco García Palacios, en este siglo el obispo Atanasio de Zaragoza, discípulo de Santiago, ya utilizaba los símbolos del cristianismo primitivo como el agnus dei.

Hacia 1608 se descubrió en una pared contigua a la Santa Capilla medieval la tumba de un diácono de nombre Lorenzo, que aparentemente habría fallecido en julio de 196. Siguiendo la teoría de Aramburu —aunque Juan Francisco Andrés de Uztarroz puso en duda que el epígrafe de la tumba hubiese sido escrito en las postrimerías del siglo II— la capilla pilarista funcionaba activamente en 196 y contaba ya con varios diáconos ordenados. Del siglo II datarían también las comunicaciones subterráneas de la iglesia del Pilar con varios sitios de la ciudad cesaraugustana. En 1718, al desmontar la primitiva plaza del Pilar, se descubrieron comunicaciones entre una casa particular y el templo. Se cree que fueron construidas cerca del 130 después de Cristo, cuando los judíos comenzaron a utilizar las catacumbas para practicar su religión perseguida por el emperador Adriano, táctica que poco tiempo después adaptarían las primitivas comunidades cristianas.

Para estudiar el siglo III existe mayor diversidad de documentos que aportan información a la historia del Pilar. Se tiene constancia de que el obispo Valero de Zaragoza edificó un salón anejo al templo conocido como la "sala valeriana". También se discute la existencia de la capilla del Pilar durante las persecuciones de Diocleciano, aunque numerosas fuentes indican que testigos visitaron el templo durante aquellos años, como Caledonio, obispo de Braga.

En noviembre de 380 se convocó a un concilio nacional en la ciudad de Zaragoza, presidido por el obispo Valerio II de Zaragoza. El acta del concilio es firmada por doce obispos. Se infiere que esta catedral tenía representadas, en pintura o en bajorrelieve, veinticuatro escenas del Antiguo Testamento y el mismo número para el Nuevo Testamento. En el arco fronterizo figuraba el Pantocrátor y los veinticuatro ancianos.

Aparentemente, el poeta tardorromano Aurelio Prudencio redactó una oda a los mártires de Zaragoza entre 380 y 395. De acuerdo con algunas interpretaciones, en una de las estrofas de su composición alude al templo del Pilar como "templo" y "casa llena de ángeles". Sin embargo, Juan de Arruego, Antonio de Nebrija y Lupercio Leonardo de Argensola, cada quien por su cuenta, desecharon esta teoría al afirmar que Aurelio Prudencio se refería a toda la ciudad de Zaragoza y no al Pilar en particular. Cualquiera que haya sido el caso, es seguro que para el siglo IV la capilla del Pilar había sido ampliada y contaba con espacio suficiente para albergar a los dieciochos mártires que, según la tradición, murieron durante las persecuciones en los albores del siglo IV.

El mismo Prudencio fue comisionado para escribir glosas sencillas a algunas escenas del templo, pero al colocar la explicación al Santo Pilar redactó algo insólito: "la Columna (atado) a la cual fue flagelado el Señor". Gracias a este testimonio autores como Lupercio Leonardo de Argensola, Diego Murillo, Manuel Aramburu y José Félix de Amada especularon que la Santa Columna podía ser la que sirvió para atar a Cristo en la flagelación o que incluso era una porción de ella. Al respecto escribió Lupercio:

Dicen que el Pilar que vemos en la santa Capilla fue traído por los ángeles. Siendo así como la tradición asegura, debemos de dar alguna causa digna de que tales ministros lo trajesen y de que la Virgen se pusiese sobre él; pues ¿qué causa más verosímil que haber sido aquel en que Nuestro Señor Jesucristo fue azotado? Yo así lo oí predicar siendo niño al padre Gobierno. (Daniel Lasagabáster Arratíbel, Historia de la Santa Capilla de Nuestra Señora del Pilar, Zaragoza (Reyes de Aragón, 5): D. Lasagabáster, 1999, pág. 201. ISBN 84-605-8648-0.)

Otro testimonio sobre la veneración a la Virgen en los tiempos del bajo imperio es uno de los bajorrelieves del sarcófago de Santa Engracia, donde se representa el descenso de los cielos de la Virgen para entrevistarse con Santiago. Se conoce desde el siglo IV.

Con la llegada de los visigodos a Hispania se suscitaron numerosos conflictos religiosos entre las dos principales doctrinas de la época: el arrianismo y el catolicismo romano. Gracias a los Concilios de Toledo, a la conversión del rey Recaredo y a mártires como San Hermenegildo, paulatinamente el reino visigodo experimentó una transición unificadora hacia el catolicismo.

Se ha puesto en duda la supervivencia de la capilla del Pilar en el siglo V, debido a las severas invasiones sufridas por Hispania en la época.

Existen testimonios que afirman que en 542 la estola de San Vicente, resguardada en el Pilar, fue llevada en procesión hasta París, donde Chideberto la requirió en agradecimiento por haber levantado el cerco de la ciudad. Asimismo, se relata que en esta centuria fue muy común la denominación de "basílica de San Vicente" para el templo del Pilar.

En el siglo VI se atestigua también el uso de la misa propia de la Virgen del Pilar, que había utilizado desde 368 el misal mozárabe. También se conoce un documento fechado en 645 por Chindasvinto — una donación— donde se menciona el templo del Pilar como fundado por el apóstol Santiago. Por último, en este siglo ocupó la cátedra zaragozana el obispo San Braulio, documentado como obispo entre 626 y 651 y cuya tumba se encontró en el Pilar en 1290. Se encuentra sepultado cerca del altar mayor.

Durante las últimas décadas de la dominación visigótica, la sede episcopal de Zaragoza y el templo del Pilar alcanzaron su mayor esplendor. Braulio de Zaragoza es la figura señera de estos años, aunque, de acuerdo con Daniel Lasagabáster, existe cierta extrañeza porque Braulio jamás comentó en sus textos la existencia del edículo y la tradición pilarista.

Duchesne esgrimió este argumento contra la predicación de Santiago. Z. García Villada lo aplica a la Visita de la Virgen a Zaragoza. Lo considera importante ya que calla el hecho de la aparición Idacio, Orosio, Juan de Viclara, S. Isidoro de Sevilla, S. Ildefonso de Toledo, S. Braulio y Prudencio, que parece debían registrarlo. Y añade: "Causa extrañeza el que Braulio no aprovechara cualquier ocasión para escribir algo sobre un acontecimiento tan glorioso como el de la Virgen del Pilar". Aquí está precisamente el error de García Villada. En el siglo VII el objeto de la tradición pilarista se centraba en un edículo insignificante de 4 x 2 m, situado en descampado donde se echaban desperdicios, lugar inhóspito fuera de las murallas. ¡Qué tenía que decir Orosio sobre este edículo! Daniel Lasagabáster Arratíbel, Historia de la Santa Capilla de Nuestra Señora del Pilar, Zaragoza (Reyes de Aragón, 5): D. Lasagabáster, 1999, pág. 189. ISBN 84-605-8648-0.

En 716 los musulmanes capturaron Zaragoza y la nombraron Saraqusta. Asimismo, aunque importaron su religión y construyeron la mezquita mayor de Saraqusta al Baida, "Zaragoza la Blanca", una de las más antiguas de Al-Ándalus, la religión cristiana fue permitida y el Pilar se convirtió en uno de sus baluartes. Durante aquella época, según las crónicas, se formó incluso la Cofradía de la Bienaventurada Virgen María del Pilar. Arruego señala que en el siglo VIII, cuando inicia la islamización en Zaragoza, la catedralidad pasó al templo del Pilar.

En el siglo IX se hace mención de los obispos Sénior, quien trasladó al Pilar el cadáver de San Vicente, y Eleca, participante de numerosos concilios y personaje relevante en el cristianismo español de dicha centuria.

Es aquí cuando Aimoino escribe su Historia del traslado de San Vicente, donde describe la iglesia mozárabe del Pilar en el mismo emplazamiento del templo barroco. En torno a ella se congregaba la comunidad cristiana de Zaragoza.

Hacia 985 el barcelonés Moción, hijo de Froya, hace una donación a la iglesia mozárabe de Santa María la Mayor y a las Santas Masas de Zaragoza. En su testamento heredaba cien sueldos "ad Santa María". El pergamino se conserva en el archivo de la Archidiócesis de Barcelona. Este testimonio permite afirmar que el templo pilarista existía desde la época visigótica, pues, a pesar de la tolerancia religiosa islámica, no se permitía construir nuevas iglesias.

Las capitulaciones firmadas el 18 de diciembre de 1118, luego de la conquista de Zaragoza, otorgaban a los musulmanes ciertas concesiones entre las que se incluía el plazo de un año para abandonar la ciudad e instalarse extramuros, y practicando su religión. Alfonso el Batallador le otorgó el patronazgo de la capilla del Pilar a Gastón IV de Bearn, adalid de la toma de Zaragoza. De acuerdo con Lasagabáster, el hecho de que los dos encargados del Pilar tras la conquista, Pedro de Librana y Gastón IV, fueran franceses, es una prueba de que la devoción pilarista era ya bastante conocida en Europa.

Pedro de Librana fue nombrado obispo de Zaragoza, y al constatar el lamentable y ruinoso estado del templo de Santa María, extendió la siguiente carta:

"Habéis oído contar (audivistis) con suficiente detalle que, con la ayuda del cielo, alcanzada con vuestras oraciones, y el arrojo de los esforzados combatientes ha sido conquistada la ciudad de Zaragoza por las armas cristianas y que ha sido liberada la iglesia de la bienaventurada Virgen María, después de haber permanecido durante mucho tiempo sujeta ¡oh dolor! al dominio de los infieles sarracenos. De antaño sabéis (novistis) que esta iglesia es prevalente (pollere), antecede a todas por su bienaventurada y antigua nombradía de santidad y dignidad. Sin embargo, debo daros a conocer que ahora, como consecuencia de la triste cautividad anterior, carece de todo lo necesario. Sabed que se halla en estado ruinoso por la falta de reparaciones durante el largo cautiverio y que carece de todo. No se cuenta con medios para restaurar sus destrozados muros y reponer los ornamentos. Los clérigos que día y noche se dedican allí al servicio divino no disponen de vivienda ni de medios de subsistencia. Acudimos, pues, suplicantes a vuestra benevolencia a fin de que, si corporalmente no la podéis visitar, al menos la visitéis con la generosa oblación de vuestras limosnas. (...) A los que se compadezcan de esta iglesia, privada de los recursos más necesarios y, condoliéndose de los gemidos de su pobreza, entreguen un denario, o lo que puedan, para su restauración, nosotros, confiados en la divina clemencia, en la autoridad del papa Gelasio, del arzobispo de Toledo y de todos los obispos de España, les concedemos indulgencia plenaria. Los demás conseguirán la remisión de sus pecados en conformidad a la cuantía de sus limosnas y al mérito de sus buenas obras. Aquellos que ofrezcan hospitalidad a nuestro arcediano Miorrando y acompañantes, portadores de nuestra carta, consigan de Dios la vida eterna." (Daniel Lasagabáster Arratíbel, Historia de la Santa Capilla de Nuestra Señora del Pilar, Zaragoza (Reyes de Aragón, 5): D. Lasagabáster, 1999. ISBN 84-605-8648-0.)

Así, entre 1119 y 1120 el arcediano Miorrando recorrió varias diócesis de España, Italia y Francia en busca de donativos para restaurar la capilla pilarista. De acuerdo con los testimonios escritos debe haber obtenido una generosa suma que le permitió a Pedro de Librana emprender cuanto antes las tareas que había señalado.

Es en el siglo XII cuando el Pilar recibe numerosos obsequios que atestiguan la existencia de la tradición pilarista durante la dominación islámica. El más destacado es el olifante de Gastón IV de Bearn, donado por su viuda Talesa de Aragón y resguardado en el Museo del Pilar. En 1138 se fundará la primera congregación de agustinos. Seis bulas de los papas Eugenio III, Alejandro III y Celestino III otorgan importancia al Pilar de Zaragoza. De igual modo, el templo fue favorecido por los reyes de Aragón —tanto de la Casa de Aragón como de la Casa de Trastámara— desde Ramón Berenguer IV hasta el rey Fernando II, así como Alfonso VII de León y Sancho II de Navarra. Así, el Pilar se convierte en un prestigiado y reconocido templo de culto mariano.

Ya en el siglo XIII la tradición pilarista se difunde por toda España y poco después se funda la primera cofradía. Es importante señalar que el pueblo aragonés ya conocía a la Santa Capilla como "Santa María del Pilar", aunque el templo en el que se asentaba era llamado "de Santa María la Mayor". Hasta bien entrado el siglo XV se empleará el título de "Santa María la Mayor y del Pilar".

Para 1261 fuertes riadas dañaron severamente la estructura del templo románico de Santa María. En 1291 el recién llegado obispo Hugo de Mataplana decidió emprender la restauración de la iglesia y su conversión al estilo gótico, tan en boga durante aquellos años. En marzo de 1293 ordena al canónigo obrero idear una solución para mejorar el estado del templo pilarista. A este hecho se le considera el fin del templo románico y el inicio de la historia de la colegiata gótico-mudéjar. En 1296 Hugo de Mataplana viajó a la Santa Sede para obtener el apoyo del papa Bonifacio VIII. Aunque Mataplana falleció estando en Roma, el pontífice expidió poco después la bula Mirabilis Deus, para acicatear al pueblo a colaborar en las obras de restauración del Pilar de Zaragoza.

En 1318 un documento de Juan XXII menciona a Santa María la Mayor de Zaragoza como "edificada por Santiago en el año 40" y también afirma que dicho templo es el más antiguo de España. Sin embargo, incurre en un error bastante común: señalar que la colegiata fue edificada en 40 cuando su construcción data de varios siglos después. Pero este dato permite conocer que para los canónigos la Santa Capilla y el templo gótico formaban parte de un solo conjunto.

De acuerdo con fuentes de la época, la reina Blanca de Navarra, esposa de Juan II el Grande, experimentó una curación milagrosa atribuida a la Virgen del Pilar y en agradecimiento marchó al santuario en julio de 1434.

Entre 1434 y 1435 se originó en la sacristía del claustro un incendio que arrasó con varias joyas y con el retablo de alabastro del templo. Es aceptada casi unánimemente la teoría de que el camarín de la Virgen y el Santo Pilar resultaron indemnes del siniestro. No existen indicios de que el fuego haya alcanzado a la colegiata gótica. La imagen que hoy se venera de la Virgen del Pilar, elaborada en estilo gótico tardío por un imaginero de Daroca, muy probablemente fue una donación de la reina Blanca y del arzobispo Dalmau de Mur. En este siglo continuaron las concesiones al Pilar, otorgadas por Juan II y su hijo Fernando II.

Los fieles y la nobleza de Aragón colaboraron en las obras para restaurar los daños del incendio. Las paredes fueron cubiertas con bajorrelieves que representaban la aparición de la Virgen a Santiago. También se emprendió la construcción de un nuevo retablo, "de alabastro, de los más claros y transparentes que he visto, donde hay algunas figuras de bulto muy bien labradas, puestas dentro de sus nichos y el samblaje y lo demás del retablo hecho con gran primor. Acompañan a todo esto otras molduras y figuras pequeñas de alabastro, que están en lo restante de la pared a una parte y a otra".

El arzobispo Alonso de Aragón, hijo de Fernando el Católico, fue el responsable de transformar la iglesia en estilo gótico y a él se debe el magnífico retablo tallado por Damián Forment (1512-1518). En el siglo XVI la Casa de Austria entró a gobernar en España y continuó la tradición de la dinastía aragonesa de otorgar privilegios y protecciones al santuario del Pilar. En 1530 la decisión de Clemente VII de exceder la jurisdicción episcopal del Pilar generó un conflicto interno en los arzobispados locales. La Seo interpuso un pleito por la catedralidad que fue resuelto hasta 1676, cuando Clemente X fusionó los cabildos de la Seo y del Pilar, con lo que dio origen al Cabildo Metropolitano de Zaragoza.

Ya entrado el siglo XVI la iglesia gótica experimenta su transformación al estilo mudéjar. En esta centuria ocurren hechos de trascendencia para el templo, como la construcción de una bóveda estrellada de crucería flamígera llena de florones relucientes de oro (1504-1515), a semejanza de las que adornaban el Palacio de la Aljafería.

El 29 de marzo de 1640 ocurrió el suceso conocido como Milagro de Calanda, pues el cojo Miguel Pellicer afirmó que por intercesión de la Virgen del Pilar le fue restituida la pierna derecha, que había perdido en un accidente. El hecho obtuvo gran relevancia en todo el reino, y el 27 de abril de 1641 se dictaminó como milagro. Ya el 27 de mayo de 1642, el municipio de Zaragoza proclama patrona de la ciudad a la Virgen del Pilar.

La devoción a la Virgen del Pilar se había extendido por toda España, y en 1678 el virrey Pedro Antonio de Aragón llamó a Cortes en nombre del rey Carlos II, a fin de declarar a la Virgen como patrona de Aragón.

El 1904 fue el año declarado por Pío X como "jubilar mariano". Durante este período varias damas de España comenzaron a invitar al pueblo a recaudar fondos para coronar solemnemente a la Virgen. El 28 de septiembre, gracias a la intervención de la condesa de Guiomar, Pío X otorgó su apoyo a la causa.

La corona fue construida en los talleres Ansorena de Madrid gracias al patrocinio de un grupo encabezado por la reina María Cristina de Habsburgo-Lorena. El 28 de abril de 1905 el arzobispo zaragozano Juan de Soldevilla llevó las coronas a Roma para ser bendecidas por el Papa.

El 20 de mayo fue el día en que se coronó a la Virgen del Pilar. Prelados de toda España y representantes diplomáticos acudieron a la ceremonia, donde también estuvo presente un número hasta entonces inusitado de peregrinos. A las doce en punto del día el obispo coronó al Niño y después a la figura de la Virgen, en medio de una atmósfera de emoción generalizada. Días después comenzaron las peregrinaciones, realizadas por grupos, ya que no era posible obtener alojamiento en la ciudad para todos los peregrinos. En memoria de la coronación canónica, cada día 20 del mes la Virgen no lleva manto.

La Virgen del Pilar fue la sexta imagen mariana de España en recibir la Coronación Canónica después de las imágenes de la Virgen de Montserrat (1881), la Virgen de la Merced de Barcelona (1889), la Virgen de la Candelaria de Tenerife (1889), la Virgen de los Reyes de Sevilla (1904) y la Virgen de la Misericordia de Reus (1904).

La madrugada del 3 de agosto de 1936, durante la Guerra Civil Española, el trimotor republicano Fokker lanzó tres bombas, de 50 kilogramos cada una, sobre las torres de la Basílica del Pilar. Una de ellas quedó clavada en la Basílica del Pilar, otra atravesó el techo y la última logró penetrar la bóveda del coreto de la Virgen y causar serios daños en el marco dorado de La adoración del nombre de Dios, de Goya. Ninguna de ellas logró estallar ni causar daños de consideración, hecho que fue atribuido a un milagro de la Virgen. Las bombas fueron desactivadas y hoy en día se exhiben en pilastras cercanas a la Santa Capilla.

Un Congreso Mariológico y Mariano Internacional se llevo a cabo en la Basílica en octubre de 1979. A pesar de que el papa Juan Pablo II no asistió, para dicha celebración se mandó remodelar las cúpulas y los tejados del templo.

Se atribuyen a la intercesión de la Virgen del Pilar diversos milagros, entre los que destacan la asombrosa curación de doña Blanca de Navarra, a la que se creía muerta, y las de invidentes como el niño Manuel Tomás Serrano y el organista Domingo de Saludes o el llamado "Milagro de Calanda", por el que al mendigo Miguel Pellicer, nacido en Calanda, se le restituyó la pierna que le fue amputada en octubre de 1637. Este suceso extraordinario ocurrió el 29 de marzo de 1640 y fue proclamado como milagro el 27 de abril de 1641 por el arzobispo Pedro Apaolaza Ramírez, tras un proceso en el que intervinieron tres jueces civiles y fueron interrogados veinticinco testigos. Ese mismo año, el rey Felipe IV mandó ir a palacio a Miguel Pellicer y arrodillándose ante él le besó la pierna. Este hecho prodigioso determinó que en 1642 la Virgen del Pilar se convirtiera en co-patrona de Zaragoza junto a San Valero. Más mundanos resultan otros hechos que se le atribuyen, como liberaciones de presos, superación de pruebas o éxitos económicos y deportivos.

Entre las campañas militares que los católicos consideran obra de su intercesión se cuenta la toma de Zaragoza de manos musulmanas en 1118, la resistencia ante el ejército francés durante la Guerra de Independencia Española y la protección del templo en la guerra Civil Española. De esta última se narra el bombardeo sufrido por el templo el 3 de agosto de 1936, cuando fueron arrojadas sobre la Basílica de El Pilar cuatro bombas que no estallaron. Las cargas que cayeron en el templo se exponen a los lados del Camarín de la Virgen e integran la larga lista de hechos milagrosos atribuidos a la Virgen María del Pilar.

4.9.- Nuestra Señora de Chiquinquirá; advocación de la Virgen María.

Nuestra Señora del Rosario de Chiquinquirá es una de las advocaciones con que se venera a la Virgen María en el catolicismo. Es la patrona y reina de Colombia, del Estado Zulia en Venezuela y de la ciudad de Caraz, en el departamento de Ancash en Perú.

En Colombia la imagen descansa en la Basílica de Nuestra Señora del Rosario de Chiquinquirá, a donde acuden miles de peregrinos no solo el día de su fiesta patronal el 9 de julio sino todos los domingos, cuando se celebran las misas y procesiones. El 3 de julio de 1986 el Papa Juan Pablo II visitó el santuario y oró por la paz de Colombia a los pies de la Virgen María. El 9 de julio de 1999 el lienzo visitó por última vez la ciudad de Bogotá para presidir la oración por la paz. Se le conoce por el nombre de la ciudad de Chiquinquirá, donde tuvo lugar la primera de sus manifestaciones milagrosas, y donde reposa el lienzo orginal.

Una imagen de la Virgen de Chiquinquira de Venezuela descansa en la Basílica de Maracaibo. En esa ciudad, cada año, el 18 de noviembre, se celebra la tradicional "Feria de la Chinita" y se realizan misas y procesiones en honor a la Virgen.

La historia se remonta al siglo XVI cuando los frailes y dominicos realizaban expediciones de evangelización en la región del centro del país. Un caballero proveniente de España, Antonio de Santana, en 1560 obtiene la encomienda de la región para levantar una casa dotada con diferentes dependencias, apropiada para la administración de los colonos, los indígenas y esclavos; además debía construir una capilla para oficios religiosos en Suta. Posteriormente de España llega un fraile colaborador en las misiones, fray Andrés Jadraque que ve la necesidad de dotar la capilla con un lienzo o cuadro de la Virgen del Rosario, advocación promulgada por la Orden Dominicana a la cual pertenecía el religioso. De esa manera acuden a un pintor también español Alonso de Narváez que vivía en la ciudad de Tunja, Boyacá, cercana a la región, para pedirle que pintara a la Virgen del Rosario. Todos acuerdan poner al lado de la Virgen a sus santos de devoción, San Antonio de Padua y San Andrés por ser el primer patrono del encomendero que solicitaba la imagen y el segundo, del fraile que la había mandado a hacer. Para el año de 1562 la pintura hecha de algodón indígena que media 125 cm de ancho por 111 de alto ya estaba en la capilla y allí permaneció por más de una década hasta aproximadamente el año 1574. Por entonces, la capilla, que tenía techo de paja se deteriora por consecuencia de la humedad, al punto que la imagen quedó prácticamente borrada. La imagen estaba en tan mal estado que fue llevada dentro de la misma región a la población de

Chiquinquirá, allí fue abandonada en una habitación que muy raras veces fue usada como capilla u oratorio. Se dice que incluso el lienzo sirvió para secar granos al sol.

La crónica histórica (elaborada al año siguiente de los acontecimientos) señalan que en el año 1586 María Ramos, una mujer del lugar, sabiendo que el lienzo había guardado la imagen de la Virgen María, decide reparar el viejo oratorio y el lienzo maltratado, otorgándole el mejor lugar de la capilla. Diariamente oraba y pedía a la Virgen del Rosario que se manifestara, hasta que el 26 de diciembre de 1586 cuando María salía del oratorio, una mujer indígena llamada Isabel junto a su pequeño hijo al pasar por el lugar le gritaron a María: "mire, mire Señora...", al dirigir su mirada a la pintura ésta brillaba con resplandores y la imagen, que estaba irreconocible, se había restaurado con sus colores y brillo originales; los agujeros y rasguños de la tela desaparecieron. Desde entonces empezó la devoción a la advocación conocida como "Nuestra Señora del Rosario de Chiquinquirá".

El santuario fue confiado a la orden de los Dominicos, quienes construyeron un convento a su lado, guardando la imagen hasta tiempos presentes. Tras un fuerte terremoto, ocurrido en 1785, los frailes deciden construir una nueva basílica en otro lugar de la población y trasladar allí la imagen de la Virgen. Esto generó protestas por parte de los vecinos de Chiquinquirá. Pese a todo, la nueva iglesia se edificó y la imagen fue trasladada en torno a 1823.

La devoción de la gente por esta imagen se evidencia en múltiples acontecimientos, que van desde las tradicionales "romerías" o grandes peregrinaciones hechas al lugar, pasando por la música popular, hasta hechos históricos protagonizados por personajes como virreyes, obispos y políticos, comenzando con el mismo Simón Bolívar, quien no sólo recibió para su Campaña Libertadora los tesoros y joyas del cuadro, sino que él mismo fue en varias ocasiones a orar por el éxito de su empresa. Finalmente, el gobierno de la República de Colombia decidió en 1919, consagrar el país a la Virgen de Chiquinquirá como su Reina y Patrona. El 9 de julio de 1919 el presidente Marco Fidel Suárez coronó a la Virgen de Chiquinquirá como Reina de Colombia en una ceremonia realizada en la Plaza de Bolívar de Bogotá en presencia del Nuncio Apostólico y varios obispos.

En algunas ocasiones la imagen ha sido trasladada con gran pompa, a la ciudad de Bogotá (unos 120 km al sur) con el fin de pedir a Dios por el fin de guerras, catástrofes o epidemias. El último traslado de este tipo ocurrió en 1999.

Cuenta la historia que una humilde anciana lavandera habitante de un barrio humilde de Nueva Zamora de Maracaibo denominado El Saladillo, en la provincia de Venezuela cumplía su faena en las orillas de la laguna de Coquivacoa cuando una tablita llegó a sus manos, sin ninguna particularidad que la hiciere especial, pero al parecer la misma fue recogida por la lavandera dándole la utilidad de tapa para la tinaja de agua. Al tiempo a la anciana le pareció reconocer en la tablita una imagen muy borrosa de carácter religioso y quizá por reverencia la colocó en una de sus paredes. El martes 18 de noviembre de 1709 se encontraba absorta en sus que haceres, por lo que no prestó atención a una serie de golpes que se escuchaban en la pared donde colgaba la imagen. Los golpes se escucharon de nuevo, pero ella no se movió. Sin embargo, a la tercera vez, se dirigió extrañada al lugar de donde venían los golpes y sorprendida vio cómo en la tablita se apreciaba claramente la imagen de la Virgen de Chiquinquirá y salia de ella una luz brillante. La sorpresa de tal fenómeno la llevó a la calle donde comenzó a gritar: "Milagro, milagro" y con esto se dio inicio a la gran devoción de los zulianos hacia la Madre de Jesucristo. La imagen se presume fue lanzada como despojo en aguas del mar, de un saqueo de algún pirata en el por aquel entonces Virreinato de la Nueva Granada (hoy Colombia) y se desconoce cuánto tiempo pudo estar flotando en las aguas del mar hasta llegar a la Laguna de Coquivacoa (hoy Lago de Maracaibo). La mirada de la Virgen en la imagen viene dada hacia la izquierda, como dando a presumir que sigue su camino a la entonces Provincia de Venezuela, haciéndose desde entonces la "indocumentada" más querida de este país, presagiando quizá también el gran éxodo de colombianos que han llegado a Venezuela. Y Luego del portento similar al ocurrido en el vecino Virreinato se quiso trasladar la Imagen a la Catedral de Nueva Zamora de Maracaibo y de hecho se logró hacer hasta cierto tramo de las adyacencias al templo, pero llegada a un lugar determinado la imagen empezó a ponerse pesada en extremo, hasta el punto que hubo que bajarla y dejarla en tierra, sin que luego de esto pudiera ser levantada de nuevo. En vista de las circunstancias a alguno de los pobladores se le ocurrió que quizá la providencia deseaba que la imagen no estuviera en el templo mayor, junto a los mantuanos (los adinerados de la época) sino en la ermita en construcción para ese momento de San Juan de Dios (más acorde con los más desposeídos) hacia el oeste de la ciudad. La sugerencia fue tomada en cuenta y sorprendentemente la imagen recobró su peso original y llegó con honores a la mencionada ermita, hoy convertida en Basílica Menor dedicada a Nuestra Señora del Rosario de Chiquinquirá y San Juan de Dios, en la cual se venera desde entonces.

Ciclo festivo: enmarcado en la celebración de la Feria, a la par del cronograma formal y religioso de actividades se desarrollan otros eventos populares y de masas de acuerdo a las creencias de los fieles. Todos los 18 de noviembre Maracaibo y el Estado Zulia en general, han venido celebrando la fiesta de la Chinita, como cariñosamente se le denomina en el país, fecha que se ha convertido a partir de ese entonces, en ocasión de fiestas para los fieles del pueblo zuliano y sus alrededores. Con el alumbrado de la avenida Bella Vista, al son de la gaita (música originada en la época colonial y que hoy en día está dedicada en gran medida a la celebración de las fiestas de la Virgen y protestas del pueblo zuliano), fuegos artificiales que alumbran el cielo marabino, chimbangueles (música de tambores) que retumban, bandas orquestales hay un marco de fiesta, acompañando a la Virgen en su recorrido por las calles donde se dice ocurrió el milagro de la renovación, tal como también sucedió en Chiquinquirá, Colombia.

La devoción a la Virgen del Rosario de Chiquinquirá es muy grande en la ciudad de Maracaibo y a la misma se le atribuyen multiplicidad de favores, algunos de los más sorprendentes se han exaltado en hermosos vitrales en la misma Basílica.

La Virgen del Rosario de Chiquinquirá es la formal patrona de la Ciudad de Maracaibo, el estado Zulia y de la Guardia Nacional de la República Bolivariana de Venezuela, fue coronada canónicamente con las ofrendas de oro junto a piedras preciosas y semipreciosas tales como rubíes, zafiros y esmeraldas que su pueblo le ha obsequiado desde la colonia. Dicha corona está sostenida por cuatro ángeles de plata. En la época hispánica la tabla fue cubierta en sus bordes con un repujado de oro, ciertos adornos sobre la imagen como coronas para la Virgen y el niño, la aureola, etc., los cuales han sido retirados en su mayoría a excepción de la corona. Cuenta la imagen con un cetro de oro, zafiros y esmeraldas; la imagen también cuenta con una corona elaborada con piedras denominadas "tumas" obsequio de la etnia guajira.

La imagen de Nuestra Señora del Rosario de Chiquinquirá se ha trasladado en varias oportunidades a múltiples sitios; una de las más recordadas fue cuando visitó la capital de la República y de manera más frecuente ha sido paseada por las diferentes parroquias del estado Zulia, trasladándose en lanchas por el lago y los ríos, en vehículos terrestres y hasta en helicóptero. Hoy estas visitas continúan, pero haciendo uso de una réplica por resguardo de la imagen original.

Las celebraciones en honor a la Virgen del Rosario de Chiquinquirá, dejaron de ser las modestas fiestas patronales del pasado para adquirir características internacionales de festejo de gran complejidad donde confluyen eventos religiosos y populares, todos reunidos bajo el nombre da la Feria Internacional de la Chinita.

En ella se realizan las famosas corridas de toros, bailes en sitios públicos y privados de la ciudad, amaneceres gaiteros, juegos de béisbol, la gran gala de la belleza, (concurso de belleza que permite elegir a la soberana que será la reina de la feria por todo el año, el desfile de carrozas y comparsas, además muchas otras actividades.

El 18 de noviembre es un día importante el que todos los marabinos (naturales de Maracaibo) le hacen un homenaje a la Virgen de Chiquinquirá. Ese día es conocido y celebrado como (La Feria De La Chinita) y se celebra con mucho entusiasmo, alegría, fe y fidelidad por todos los habitantes de la ciudad. A la par se desarrolla el juego de béisbol Copa la Chinita, actividad deportiva muy frecuentada por la fanaticada zuliana, que se reúne (luego de una larga noche de parranda) a darle ánimo y apoyo al equipo pelotero de las Águilas del Zulia. A la semana siguiente se realiza la procesión de la Aurora y en ella se pasea la imagen desde la basílica a las 3:00 de la madrugada, para que junto a su pueblo reciba el día en la calle. Finalmente, el domingo siguiente se restituye la imagen a su camerino.

En España: Desde el año 2004 en Madrid (España) veneran a la Virgen de Chiquinquirá y se celebra la feria de la Chinita igual que en Maracaibo (Venezuela) celebrando así el día de la patrona en España, la celebración se hace en el 17, 18 y 19 de noviembre, dando así inicio a la celebración cada año de la feria a la patrona de España, Colombia y Venezuela y en diciembre se hace también actividades de la feria en España el día especial de la patrona es el mismo día que se celebra en Maracaibo con una misa y después una serenata gaitera con el grupo entre palos y alegrías y también el grupo gaitero madridcaibo es gaita.

4.10.- Nuestra Señora de los Ángeles; advocación de la Virgen María.

Nuestra Señora de los Ángeles es una advocación de la Virgen María en la Iglesia Católica Romana. Este culto es originario de España, en Getafe, cerca de Madrid, y fue traído a América por los conquistadores españoles.

La Virgen de los Ángeles fue declarada Patrona de Costa Rica y protectora de las Américas por el Papa Juan Pablo II.

La celebración de Nuestra Señora de los Ángeles se realiza en la ciudad de Cartago, Costa Rica, desde finales del siglo XIX se realiza una romería hasta el santuario cada 2 de agosto, en la Basílica de los Ángeles.

También hay templos a la misma advocación en Italia, España, México, Estados Unidos y Argentina.

En 2005 esta imagen fue llevada al Vaticano, en Roma. El Papa Benedicto XVI la bendijo, y la colocaron en la Basílica Santa María de la Luz, a la que peregrinan muchos inmigrantes.

En el Período Colonial, Cartago era la principal ciudad para españoles en Costa Rica y su capital provincial. A su alrededor había varios pueblos para indígenas nativos. En 1635, los mulatos vivían dispersos al este de la ciudad, pues las leyes españolas prohibían que los mulatos libres, o pardos, pasaran de la Cruz de Caravaca.

La historia dice que el 2 de agosto de 1635, una joven mulata llamada Juana Pereira, iba a lavar ropa como de costumbre, y se encontró una pequeña estatua, de una muñeca con un bebe en brazos, similar a la Virgen María, en medio del bosque, sobre una roca, cerca de un manantial, en el lugar llamado "La Puebla de los Pardos". Ella decidió llevársela para su casa, donde la guardo en un cajón envuelta en un paño de tela. Al día siguiente, Juana volvió al sitio del primer hallazgo, se encontró una muñeca de piedra igual a la encontrada el día anterior, hizo lo mismo, se la llevo para su casa, para guardarla junto a la otra, pero cuando llego a buscarla se dio cuenta que no estaba, así volvió a guardar la imagen encontrada nuevamente, lo mismo sucedió al tercer día, pero esta vez se la llevo al sacerdote de la localidad, Alonso de Sandoval, quien la guardó en una caja, y se olvidó de ella. Al día siguiente abrió la caja y, para su sorpresa, no estaba. Juana Pereira volvió al lugar de las apariciones y encontró ahí la imagen, así que se la llevó al sacerdote y este la guardó dentro del sagrario. Al día siguiente abrió el sagrario y no la encontró, por lo que declaró que aquello era un mensaje de la Virgen María, ella deseaba estar en el bosque, sobre la roca, por lo que construyeron un pequeño templo en su honor, donde actualmente se encuentra la Basílica de los Ángeles, y a su alrededor se empezaron a agrupar los pardos.

La pequeña imagen de 20 centímetros fue bautizada con el nombre de Virgen de los Ángeles, porque el 2 de agosto los franciscanos celebran la fiesta de Nuestra Señora de los Ángeles (Getafe). Por esta razón, se tiene la certeza de que el hallazgo ocurrió ese día, pero no así la fecha exacta. Se estima que fue antes de 1639 aunque algunos dan por un hecho que fue en 1635.

La joven que tuvo el honor de encontrar la imagen de Nuestra Señora de los Ángeles parece que se perdió en la Historia de Costa Rica. Se sabe que existió pues los escritos de la época y de la Iglesia lo comprueban, sin embargo, no se le dio seguimiento después del hallazgo de "la Negrita".

El segundo Arzobispo de San José, Monseñor Víctor Sanabria Martínez, intentó recuperar datos sobre esa mulata. En sus investigaciones detectó que la mayoría de mujeres de esa zona se llamaban Juana y llevaban por apellido Pereira. Al no dar con la identidad de esta muchacha la llamó "Juana Pereira" como un homenaje a todas las mulatas que conocieron a la verdadera joven que dio con la imagen de Nuestra Señora de los Ángeles. En ellas se pretendió extender ese honor a toda la cultura indígena y afrodescendente de Costa Rica.

Según otras fuentes, en esa época era muy popular la imaginería religiosa en el Valle Central de Costa Rica. Hay mucha documentación sobre maestros, oficiales y aprendices que se especializaban en hacer imágenes en madera o piedra, para venderlas en el mercado local. La administración del gobernador español Gregorio de Sandoval Anaya y González de Alcalá, el obispo español Fernando Núñez y el párroco de Cartago, Alonso de Sandoval, en los años del hallazgo, se caracterizó por establecer varias iglesias en "Pueblos de Indios" en los alrededores de Cartago, y la ermita de la "Puebla de Pardos" fue obra suya.

La estatuilla fue realizada con la técnica del cincelado en jade (técnica indígena heredada a través del mestizaje), piedra volcánica en la base, y grafito para colorearla.

La composición de la Negrita, se ha dicho, que consiste en tres diferentes piedras: el grafito, jade y roca volcánica. Los arqueólogos se muestran muy interesados en esa composición debido a que resulta muy difícil, casi imposible, unir las tres piedras; sin embargo, coinciden al señalar que la imagen de la Virgen tiene características de todas ellas.

Se tienen investigaciones que en esa época no había grafito en Costa Rica, sólo en Europa, mientras que en el Viejo Continente no se contaba con las otras dos rocas. Con base en esa realidad, se podría concluir que la imagen tiene características de los dos continentes. Es de 20 cm de alto, le llaman la Negrita pese a que su verdadero color es un gris-verduzco. Los rasgos de la Virgen son de mestiza, específicamente mulata. Ella ve hacia el frente, mientras que su Hijo la ve directamente a los ojos, y con su manita le toca el corazón.

Algunos coinciden que esa narración describe a la Virgen María asunta al cielo en cuerpo y alma. Es por ese motivo que la Familia del Valle, los joyeros personales de la Virgen, le construyeron un trono muy especial. Es todo en oro con piedras preciosas, la mayoría donadas por fieles agradecidos por un favor. En total, la estructura mide un metro de alto. Es fácilmente observable que la imagen de la virgen de Los Ángeles, cumple con la descripción del Apocalipsis, en el versículo 12:1: "Apareció en el cielo una gran señal, una mujer vestida de oro con doce estrellas sobre su cabeza y la luna bajo sus pies". En el punto más alto del resplandor sobresale el pectoral (cruz que usan los obispos sobre su pecho) que donó el arzobispo de San José, Monseñor Otón Castro. En la base de la estructura se colocó el escudo de Costa Rica que fue un regalo del entonces mandatario, Daniel Oduber. Al emblema nacional se le agregaron algunos anillos que donó Monseñor Rodríguez para recordar a su madre en la Imagen de la Negrita.

La Iglesia se fue levantando con el aporte de los pobladores, muchos de los cuales tenían fincas de cacao. Para 1777 se inicia la elaboración del altar actual, razón por la cual se encuentran las tallas con estilizadas hojas rodeando una talla de mazorca de cacao grande y debajo de esta una incipiente o en crecimiento. A los dos lados están tallados unos canastos de frutos que son una alegoría a la abundancia de favores, milagros y alimento para sus feligreses. La cúpula es, en realidad, una enorme corona en la que se ve el anagrama de la Virgen María y cuyo remate final lo es la imagen de San Miguel Arcángel, quien vence al demonio.

Actualmente se encuentra en ese lugar la Basílica de Los Ángeles, sitio de devoción y peregrinación para el pueblo católico costarricense y centroamericano. Entre el 25 de julio y 2 de agosto de cada año, la plaza de la Basílica, recibe aproximadamente 2,500,000 personas (cifra no oficial, ya que datos de la UCR han mostrado que los romeros alcanzan números máximos de 800,000), nacionales y extranjeros, para mostrar su devoción a la Virgen, que en su mayoría llegan caminando desde sitios rurales como Guanacaste y San Vito, o de la misma ciudad de San José, a esta tradición se la llama ROMERÍA e inician desde el 25 de julio. Al lado de la Basílica se encuentra un manantial de agua bendita, los fieles que llegan a la Basílica recogen el agua en botellas con la forma de la virgen, y algunos se lavan partes de su cuerpo o todo el cuerpo para pedir un favor o ser sanados. En la Basílica se encuentra la sala de exvotos, lugar donde los fieles dejan una medallita con la forma de la parte del cuerpo que le sanó la Virgen o un recuerdo del milagro. Son muchos los favores que ha hecho la Virgen y por eso los costarricenses la quieren como su reina y madre.

4.11.- Nuestra Señora de las Mercedes; advocación de la Virgen María.

La Santísima Virgen María se le apareció a San Pedro Nolasco, en 1218, recomendándole que fundara una comunidad religiosa que se dedicara a auxiliar a los cautivos que eran llevados a sitios lejanos. De esta manera nace esta advocación mariana en España para luego difundirse por el resto del mundo.

San Pedro Nolasco, inspirado por la Santísima Virgen María, fundó una orden dedicada a la merced o misericordia. Su misión era la misericordia para con los cristianos cautivos en manos de los musulmanes. Muchos de los miembros de la orden canjeaban sus vidas por la de presos y esclavos. Fue apoyado por el rey Jaime el Conquistador y aconsejado por San Raimundo de Peñafort.

San Pedro Nolasco y sus frailes muy devotos de la Virgen María, la tomaron como patrona y guía. Su espiritualidad es fundamentada en Jesús el liberador de la humanidad y en la Santísima Virgen, la Madre liberadora. Los mercedarios querían ser caballeros de la Virgen María al servicio de su obra redentora. Por eso la honran como Madre de la Merced o Virgen Redentora.

En 1272, tras la muerte del fundador, los frailes toman oficialmente el nombre de La Orden de Santa María de la Merced, de la redención de los cautivos, pero son más conocidos como mercedarios. El Padre Antonio Quexal en 1406, siendo general de la Merced, dice: "María es fundamento y cabeza de nuestra orden".

Esta comunidad religiosa se ha dedicado por siglos a ayudar a los prisioneros y ha tenido mártires y santos. Sus religiosos rescataron muchísimos cautivos que estaban presos en manos de los feroces sarracenos.

El Padre Gaver, en 1400, relata como La Virgen llama a San Pedro Nolasco y le revela su deseo de ser liberadora a través de una orden dedicada a la liberación.

Nolasco le pide ayuda a Dios y, en signo de la misericordia divina, le responde La Virgen María diciéndole que funde una orden liberadora.

Desde el año 1259 los padres Mercedarios empiezan a difundir la devoción a Nuestra Señora de la Merced (o de las Mercedes) la cual se extiende por el mundo.

Los mercedarios llegan al continente americano y pronto la devoción a la Virgen de la Merced se propaga ampliamente. En República Dominicana, Perú, Argentina y muchos otros países, la Virgen de la Merced es muy conocida y amada.

En los últimos siglos de la Edad Media, los árabes tenían en su poder al sur y el levante español y sus vidas en vilo. Los turcos y sarracenos habían infestado el Mediterráneo, y atacaban a los barcos que desembarcaban en las costas llevándose cautivos; a muchos.

Un alma caritativa, suscitada por Dios, a favor de los cautivos, fue San Pedro Nolasco, de Barcelona, llamado el Cónsul de la Libertad. Se preguntaba cómo poner remedio a tan triste situación y le rogaba insistentemente a Dios.

Pronto empezó a actuar en la compra y rescate de cautivos, vendiendo cuanto tenía. La noche del 1 de agosto de 1218, Nolasco estando en oración, se le apareció la Virgen María, le animó en sus intentos y le transmitió el mandato de fundar la Orden Religiosa de la Merced para redención de cautivos. Pocos días después, Nolasco cumplía el mandato. Los mercedarios se comprometían con un cuarto voto: liberar a otros más debiles en la fe quedando como rehenes, si fuera necesario.

De este modo, a través de los miembros de la Nueva Orden, la Virgen María, Madre y Corredentora, Medianera de todas las gracias, aliviaría a sus hijos cautivos y a todos los que suplicaban a ella, gimiendo y llorando en este valle de lágrimas. A todos daría la merced de su favor.

La Virgen María tendrá desde ahora la advocación de la Merced, o más bello todavía en plural: Nuestra Señora de las Mercedes, indicando así la abundancia incontable de sus gracias.

Nuestra Señora de las Mercedes concedería a sus hijos la merced de la liberación. Alfonso X el Sabio decía que "sacar a los hombres de cautivo es cosa que place mucho a Dios, porque es obra de la Merced".

Bajo la protección de Nuestra Señora de la Merced, los frailes mercedarios realizaron una labor ingente. Como ingentes fueron los sufrimientos de San Pedro Nolasco, San Ramón Nonato y San Pedro Armengol. Y no faltaron mártires como San Serapio, San Pedro Pascual y otros muchos.

El culto a Nuestra Señora de la Merced se extendió muy pronto por Cataluña y por toda España, por Francia y por Italia, a partir del siglo XIII. El año 1265 aparecieron las primeras monjas mercedarias. Los mercedarios estuvieron entre los primeros misioneros de América. En la Española o República Dominicana, por ejemplo, misionó Fray Gabriel Téllez (Tirso de Molina).

Barcelona se gloría de haber sido escogida por Nuestra Señora de la Merced como lugar de su aparición y la tiene por celestial patrona. "Princesa de Barcelona, protegiu nostra ciutat."

En el museo de Valencia hay un cuadro de Vicente López en el que varias figuras vuelven su rostro hacia la Virgen de la Merced, como implorándole, mientras la Virgen abre sus brazos y extiende su manto, cubriéndolos a todos con amor, reflejando así su título de Santa María de la Merced.

La ciudad argentina de Tucumán, fue fundada por don Diego de Villarroel en 1565, pero el día de Nuestra Señora de las Mercedes de 1685 fue trasladada al sitio actual.

El Cabildo en 1687 nombró a Nuestra Señora de las Mercedes como Patrona y Abogada de la ciudad, por los muchos favores que la Virgen dispensó a los tucumanos.

La victoria argentina en la batalla de Tucumán del 24 de septiembre de 1812, es acreditada a Nuestra Señora de las Mercedes. En ella se decidió la suerte de las Provincias Unidas del Río de la Plata. Los españoles eran unos tres mil y los argentinos apenas mil ochocientos. Belgrano, el general argentino, puso su confianza en Dios y en Nuestra Señora de las Mercedes, a quien eligió por Patrona de su Ejército.

En la mañana del 24 de septiembre de 1812, día del combate, el general Belgrano estuvo orando largo rato ante el altar de la Virgen.

El ejército argentino obtuvo la victoria. En el parte que transmitió al Gobierno, Belgrano hizo resaltar que la victoria se obtuvo el día de Nuestra Señora de las Mercedes, bajo cuya protección se habían puesto las tropas.

El parte dice textualmente: "La patria puede gloriarse de la completa victoria que han tenido sus armas el día 24 del corriente, día de Nuestra Señora de las Mercedes bajo cuya protección nos pusimos ".

El general Belgrano puso en manos de la imagen de la Virgen su bastón de mando. La entrega se efectuó durante una solemne procesión con todo el ejército, que terminó en el Campo de las Carreras, donde se había librado la batalla.

Belgrano se dirigió hacia las andas en que era conducida la imagen de Nuestra Señora de las Mercedes, y le entregó el bastón que llevaba, poniéndolo en las manos de la Virgen y proclamándola como Generala del Ejército.

Al tener conocimiento de estos actos de devoción las religiosas de Buenos Aires, remitieron a Belgrano cuatro mil escapularios de Nuestra Señora de la Merced para que los distribuyera a las tropas. El batallón de Tucuman se congregó antes de partir rumbo a Salta, frente al atrio del templo de Merced, donde se les entregaron los escapularios, tanto los jefes como oficiales y tropas los colocaron sobre sus uniformes.

El 20 de febrero de 1813 los argentinos que buscaban su independencia se enfrentaron nuevamente con los españoles en Salta. Antes de entrar en combate, Belgrano recordó a sus tropas el poder y valimiento de María Santísima y les exhortó a poner en Ella su confianza. Formuló también el voto de ofrendarle los trofeos de la victoria si por su intercesión la obtenía.

Con la ayuda de la Madre de Dios vencieron nuevamente a los españoles, y de las cinco banderas que cayeron en poder de Belgrano, una la destinó a Nuestra Señora de las Mercedes de Tucumán, dos a la Virgen de Luján y dos a la Catedral de Buenos Aires.

A partir del año 1812, el culto a Nuestra Señora de las Mercedes adquiere una gran solemnidad y popularidad. En 1813, el Cabildo de Tucumán pide al gobierno eclesiástico la declaración del vice patronato de Nuestra Señora de las Mercedes "que se venera en la Iglesia de su religión" y ordena de su parte que los poderes públicos celebren anualmente su fiesta el 24 de septiembre. La Autoridad Eclesiástica, por Decreto especial, declara el 24 de septiembre de 1813 festivo en homenaje a Nuestra Señora de las Mercedes.

Después del 31 de agosto de 1843, es declarada oficialmente Vice Patrona, jurando su día por festivo y disponiendo se celebre cada año una Misa solemne con asistencia del Magistrado y que por la tarde se saque la imagen de la Santísima Virgen en procesión, como prueba de gratitud por los beneficios dispensados.

Al cumplirse el centenario de la batalla y victoria de Tucumán, la imagen de Nuestra Señora de las Mercedes fue coronada solemnemente, en nombre del Papa San Pio X, en 1912.

El 22 de junio de 1943, el Presidente de la República, General Pedro P. Ramírez, por decreto aprobado el día anterior con sus ministros, dispuso por el artículo 1ro.:

"Quedan reconocidas con el grado de Generala del Ejército Argentino: la Santísima Virgen María, bajo la advocación de Nuestra Señora de las Mercedes, y la Santísima Virgen María, bajo la advocación de Nuestra Señora del Carmen".

Los artículos 2,3 y 5 se refieren a la imposición de la banda y faja que corresponde a los generales de la nación. El gobierno argentino proclama así, solemnemente, ante el mundo, su religiosidad.

En 1945, el Gobierno Nacional designó a Nuestra Señora de las Mercedes Patrona Principal de la Aeronáutica Militar.

En Santa Fe la imagen se venera en el templo del Milagro, Paraná se venera en la catedral, en Córdoba en la Iglesia de los Padres Mercedarios, y así en muchos otros lugares.

En la República Dominicana una de las imágenes de gran devoción, y la más antigua es la de Nuestra Señora de las Mercedes.

En marzo de 1495 Cristóbal Colón, acompañado de unos cuantos españoles, tuvo que enfrentar a un crecido número de indios acaudillados por un cacique. Levantaron una trinchera y junto a ella colocaron una gran cruz de madera.

Los indios lograron desalojar a los españoles, quienes de inmediato se replegaron a un cerro. Mientras tanto los indios prendieron fuego a la cruz y con hachas intentaban destruirla, sin poder lograrlo. Ante la agresividad de los indios, Colón y la mayoría de la tropa decidieron retirarse del lugar. Sin embargo, el mercedario Fray Juan Infante, confesor de Colón, que llevaba consigo una imagen de Nuestra Señora de las Mercedes, exhortó a los españoles a seguir combatiendo y les prometió la victoria en nombre de la Virgen.

Al día siguiente las fuerzas de Colón obtuvieron una increíble victoria frente a los indios. Cuenta la historia que en medio del combate se apareció la Virgen de las Mercedes y los indios, a pesar de que estaban ganando la batalla, salieron huyendo y se dispersaron por los montes. Luego de este suceso se construyó un santuario a Nuestra Señora de las Mercedes en la misma cumbre del cerro donde Colón y sus hombres libraron la batalla contra los indios rebeldes.

En el Perú la devoción a Nuestra Señora de las Mercedes se remonta a los tiempos de la fundación de Lima. Consta que los Padres Mercedarios, que llegaron al Perú junto con los conquistadores, habían edificado ya su primitiva iglesia conventual hacia 1535, templo que sirvió como la primera parroquia de Lima hasta la construcción de la Iglesia Mayor en 1540.

Los Mercedarios no sólo evangelizaron a la región, sino que fueron gestores del desarrollo de la ciudad al edificar los hermosos templos que hoy se conservan como valioso patrimonio histórico, cultural y religioso.

Junto con estos frailes llegó su celestial patrona, la Virgen de la Merced, advocación mariana del siglo XIII.

Esta Orden de la Merced, aprobada en 1235 como orden militar por el Papa Gregorio IX, logró liberar a miles de cristianos prisioneros, convirtiéndose posteriormente en una dedicada a las misiones, la enseñanza y a las labores en el campo social. Los frailes mercedarios tomaron su hábito de las vestiduras que llevaba la Virgen en la aparición al fundador de la orden.

La imagen de la Virgen de la Merced viste totalmente de blanco; sobre su larga túnica lleva un escapulario en el que está impreso, a la altura del pecho, el escudo de la orden. Un manto blanco cubre sus hombros y su larga cabellera aparece velada por una fina mantilla de encajes. En unas imágenes se la representa de pie y en otras sentadas; unas veces se muestra con el Niño en los brazos y otras los tiene extendidos mostrando un cetro real en la mano derecha y en la otra unas cadenas abiertas, símbolo de liberación. Esta es la apariencia de la hermosa imagen que se venera en la Basílica de la Merced, en la capital limeña, que fue entronizada a comienzos del siglo XVII y que ha sido considerada como patrona de la capital.

Fue proclamada en 1730 "Patrona de los Campos del Perú"; "Patrona de las Armas de la República" en 1823; y al cumplirse el primer centenario de la independencia de la nación, la imagen fue solemnemente coronada y recibió el título de "Gran Mariscala del Perú" el día 24 de septiembre de 1921, solemnidad de Nuestra Señora de la Merced, desde entonces, declarado fiesta nacional, ocasión en que cada año el ejército le rinde honores a su alta jerarquía militar de "Mariscala". La imagen porta numerosas condecoraciones otorgadas por la república de Perú y sus gobernantes e instituciones nacionales. En 1970 el cabildo de Lima le otorgó las "Llaves de la ciudad" y en 1971 el presidente de la República le impuso la Gran Cruz Peruana al Mérito Naval, gestos que demuestran el cariño y la devoción del Perú a esta advocación considerada por muchos como su Patrona Nacional.

4.12.- María Auxiliadora; advocación de la Virgen María.

Los cristianos de la antigüedad en Éfeso, Constantinopla, Jerusalén, Atenas, Grecia, Turquía, Egipto, Antioquía y Alejandría llamaban a la Santísima Virgen María con el nombre de Auxiliadora, en griego "Boetéia", que significa "La que trae auxilios desde el cielo". Los dos títulos que más se leen en los antiguos monumentos de Oriente son: Teotocos y Boetéia, es decir, Madre de Dios y Auxiliadora. El gran orador Proclo dijo, a mediado del siglo V: "La Madre de Dios es nuestra Auxiliadora porque nos trae auxilios de lo alto". Sabas de Cesarea, un siglo más tarde, llamó a la Virgen "Auxiliadora de los que sufren" y narra el hecho de un enfermo gravísimo que llevado junto a una imagen de la Virgen María recuperó la salud y que aquella imagen de la "Auxiliadora de los enfermos" se volvió sumamente popular entre la gente de su época. El gran poeta Greco Romano Melone, en ese mismo siglo, llama a la Virgen María "Auxiliadora de los que rezan y ayuda de los que somos débiles" y pide que recemos para que Ella sea también "Auxiliadora de los que gobiernan" y así cumplamos lo que dijo Cristo: "Demos al gobernante lo que es del gobernante" y con lo que dijo Jeremías: "Oremos por la nación en donde estemos viviendo, porque su bien será nuestro bien". Las naciones de Asia menor celebran la fiesta de María Auxiliadora el 1º de octubre. En Europa y América se celebre el 24 de mayo. Sofronio, Arzobispo de Jerusalén dijo: "María es Auxiliadora de los que están en la tierra y la alegría de los que están en el cielo". Juan Damasceno, famoso predicador cristiano, es el primero en propagar la famosa frase: "María Auxiliadora ruega por nosotros". Y repite: "La Virgen es auxiliadora para conseguir la salvación. Auxiliadora para evitar los peligros, Auxiliadora en la hora de la muerte". Germán, Arzobispo de Constantinopla, dijo: "Oh María Tú eres Poderosa Auxiliadora de los pobres, valiente Auxiliadora contra los enemigos de la fe. Auxiliadora del pueblo humilde que necesita de tu ayuda".

La Basílica de María Auxiliadora fue consagrada el 9 de junio de 1868, en la ciudad de Turín, Italia. Su construcción estuvo a cargo San Juan Bosco, un campesino de origen humilde que quedó huérfano a los tres años. Que para estudiar tuvo que pedir limosnas. La Santísima Virgen María se le apareció en sueños y le mandó a que adquiriera "conocimiento y paciencia", ya que el Espíritu Santo de Dios lo había destinado para educar a muchos niños pobres. Ya siendo hombre, nuevamente se le apareció la Virgen María y le pidió que le construyera un templo y que la invocara con el nombre de Auxiliadora. Empezó la obra del templo con tres monedas de veinte centavos. Pero fueron tantos los milagros que María Auxiliadora empezó a hacer en favor de sus devotos, que en sólo cuatro años estuvo terminada la gran Basílica. El santo solía repetir: "Cada ladrillo de este templo corresponde a un milagro de la Santísima Virgen". Desde aquel santuario empezó a propagarse por el mundo la devoción a la Madre de Dios bajo el título de Auxiliadora, y son tantos los favores que la Virgen María concede a quienes la invocan con el título de Auxiliadora, que ésta devoción ha llegado a ser una de las más populares en todo el mundo. San Juan Bosco decía: "Propagad la devoción a María Auxiliadora y veréis lo que son milagros" y recomendaba repetir muchas veces esta pequeña oración: "María Auxiliadora, rogad por nosotros". (Historia de la Devoción a María Auxiliadora. Aciprensa.com)

4.13.- Nuestra Señora de Lourdes; advocación de la Virgen María.

La advocación católica de Nuestra Señora de Lourdes hace referencia a las dieciocho apariciones de la Virgen María que Bernadette Soubirous (1844-1879) afirmó haber presenciado en la gruta de Massabielle, a orillas del río Gave, en las afueras de la población de Lourdes, Francia, en las estribaciones de los Pirineos, en 1858.

Ya en vida de Bernadette, multitud de católicos creyeron en las apariciones de la Virgen María como vehículo de la gracia del Espíritu Santo de Dios, su propio Ser, y el papa Pío IX autorizó al obispo local para que permitiera la veneración de la Virgen María en Lourdes en 1862, unos diecisiete años antes de la muerte de Bernadette.

Bernadette Soubirous fue proclamada santa por el papa Pío XI en 8 de diciembre de 1933. Desde entonces, la advocación de la Virgen María como Nuestra Señora de Lourdes ha sido motivo de gran veneración, y su santuario es uno de los más visitados del mundo.

Los cristianos de la Iglesia católica invocan a Nuestra Señora de Lourdes como patrona de los enfermos.

Bernadette Soubirous, una adolescente pobre y analfabeta de catorce años, aseguró haber visto en 18 ocasiones a la Virgen María en una gruta del paraje de Massabielle, al occidente del poblado de Lourdes entre el 11 de febrero y el 16 de julio de 1858.

En la tercera aparición, la niña habló con la Señora en gascón, dialecto occitano que se usa en la zona, la cual se dirigió a ella usando el "usted" (*voi*) de cortesía y pidiéndole: "¿Me haría usted el favor de venir aquí durante quince días?" (*Boulet aoue era gracia de bié aci penden quinze dias?*) Bernadette le prometió que lo haría. A su vez, la Señora le anunció que no le prometía hacerla feliz en este mundo, sino en el otro.

En sucesivas apariciones, el mensaje fue tomando cuerpo:

- Invitación a la Penitencia y a la oración por los pecadores (21 de febrero).
- Invitación a vivir una pobreza más evangélica.
- Solicitud de que se hicieran procesiones a la gruta y le fuera erigida allí una capilla (2 de marzo).

El 25 de febrero, según testificó Bernadette, la Virgen le dijo que fuera a tomar agua de la fuente y que comiera de las plantas que crecían libremente allí. Ella interpretó que debía ir a tomar agua del cercano río Gave y hacia allá se dirigió. Pero la Señora le enseñó con el dedo que escarbara en el suelo. Al excavar en el fango e intentar beber, Bernadette ensució su rostro, y sus gestos y apariencia fueron motivo de escepticismo por parte de muchas de las mas de 350 personas presentes, ya que el manantial no se manifestó de inmediato. Sin embargo, poco después surgió una fuente de agua que, hasta el día de hoy, es meta de peregrinaciones por parte de muchos católicos y que ha sido testigo de numerosos milagros. El manantial que brotó aquel 25 de febrero de 1858 produce cien mil litros de agua por día, de forma continua desde aquella fecha hasta nuestros días.

Ante la reiterada petición de Bernardette de que revelara su nombre, el 25 de marzo de 1858 (en su decimosexta aparición) la Señora le dijo: *"Que soy la Immaculada Councepciou"* ("Yo soy la Inmaculada Concepción"). El dogma católico de la Inmaculada Concepción de la Virgen María había sido solemnemente proclamado el 8 de diciembre de 1854, tres años antes. La expresión resultaba ajena al vocabulario de Bernadette y, en principio, fue motivo de desconcierto, tanto en el propio Padre Peyramale -párroco de Lourdes- como en otras autoridades eclesiásticas y civiles. Sin embargo, Bernadette Soubirous mantuvo una consistente actitud de calma durante todos los incisivos interrogatorios que se le hicieron, sin cambiar su historia ni su actitud, ni pretender tener un conocimiento más allá de lo dicho respecto de las visiones descritas.

El último interrogatorio ante la comisión eclesiástica, presidida por el obispo de Tarbes, Laurence, fue el 1 de diciembre de 1860. El anciano obispo terminó emocionado, al repetir Bernardita el gesto y las palabras que la Virgen hiciera el 25 de marzo de 1858: "Yo soy la Inmaculada Concepción".

El 18 de enero de 1862, el anciano obispo de Tarbes publicó la carta pastoral con la cual declaró que "la Inmaculada Madre de Dios se ha aparecido verdaderamente a Bernardita". En ese mismo año, el papa Pío IX autorizó al obispo local para que permitiera la veneración de la Virgen María en Lourdes. Desde entonces los diversos pontífices han apoyado de varias formas la devoción y la peregrinación al santuario. El papa Pío X extendió la celebración de la memoria a toda la Iglesia. El papa Pío XI ratificó definitivamente la celebración de Nuestra Señora de Lourdes al beatificar a Bernadette Soubirous el 6 de junio de 1925, y canonizarla en la Solemnidad de la Inmaculada Concepción del Año Santo de la Redención, el 8 de diciembre de 1933. En 1937, el mismo Pío XI nombró a Eugenio Pacelli como Delegado Papal para visitar y venerar personalmente a la Virgen María en Lourdes. El 8 de septiembre de 1953, en conmemoración del centenario del dogma de la Inmaculada

Concepción, el papa Pío XII, decretó en su Carta Encíclica Fulgens Corona la celebración de un Año Mariano (el primero en la historia de la Iglesia católica) en todo el mundo, mientras describía los sucesos de Lourdes con las siguientes palabras:

"Y parece como si la Virgen Santísima hubiera querido confirmar de una manera prodigiosa el dictamen que el Vicario de su divino Hijo en la tierra, con el aplauso de toda la Iglesia, había pronunciado. Pues no habían pasado aún cuatro años cuando cerca de un pueblo de Francia, en las estribaciones de los Pirineos, la Santísima Virgen, vestida de blanco, cubierta con cándido manto y ceñida su cintura de faja azul, se apareció con aspecto juvenil y afable en la cueva de Massabielle a una niña inocente y sencilla, a la que, como insistiera en saber el nombre de quien se le había dignado aparecer, ella, con una suave sonrisa y alzando los ojos al cielo, respondió: "Yo soy la Inmaculada Concepción». Bien entendieron esto, como era natural, los fieles, que en muchedumbres casi innumerables, acudiendo de todas las partes en piadosas peregrinaciones a la gruta de Lourdes, reavivaron su fe, estimularon su piedad y se esforzaron por ajustar su vida a los preceptos de Cristo". (Pío XII, Carta encíclica Fulgens Corona, N° 3-4)

Las apariciones fueron revelaciones privadas y no públicas, por lo cual la Iglesia católica no las considera artículos de fe -no incorporaron material nuevo como objeto de fe de la Iglesia católica, ni se requiere de sus fieles que crean en ellas-. En la fe de la Iglesia católica, Dios elige a quién curar y por qué medios, pues "vuestros pensamientos no son los míos, ni vuestros caminos son mis caminos, dice el Señor" (Isaías 55, 8). En el decir de Blaise Pascal, "Dios tiene sus razones que nuestra razón no conoce".

Por otra parte, las autoridades de la Iglesia católica han expresado explícitamente su devoción a Nuestra Señora de Lourdes de distintas formas. El 25 de marzo de 1958, centenario de aquella aparición en la que la "Señora" se presentó con las palabras "Yo soy la Inmaculada Concepción", el cardenal Angelo G. Roncalli, luego papa y beato Juan XXIII, consagró la gran Basílica subterránea de San Pío X. En la clausura del centenario de las apariciones de Lourdes, lo expresó así: "La Iglesia, por la voz de sus papas, no cesa de recomendar a los católicos que presten atención al mensaje de Lourdes".

El calendario litúrgico católico celebra la "Festividad de Nuestra Señora de Lourdes" el día de la primera aparición, es decir, el 11 de febrero. En 1992, el papa Juan Pablo II instituyó la celebración de la "Jornada Mundial del Enfermo" a realizarse el 11 de febrero de cada año, en memoria litúrgica de Nuestra Señora de Lourdes.

En 1983 y 2004, Juan Pablo II en persona visitó Lourdes, al igual que lo haría su sucesor Benedicto XVI el 15 de septiembre de 2008, en conmemoración del 150 aniversario de las apariciones de 1858.

Hoy, el Santuario de Nuestra Señora de Lourdes es uno de los sitios principales de peregrinaje católico en el mundo. Con una población de aproximadamente 15,000 habitantes, Lourdes recibe actualmente la visita de unos 6,000,000 de peregrinos por año.

La imagen de la Virgen de Lourdes que los fieles católicos veneran sigue en general la descripción que Bernadette hiciera de Nuestra Señora:

- Joven.
- Vestida de blanco con una cinta de color azul a la cintura.
- Con las manos juntas en actitud orante.
- Con un rosario colgándole del brazo.
- Con una rosa dorada en cada pie.

La Iglesia Católica siempre consideró a la Virgen María como una figura íntimamente próxima a todo sufrimiento humano, desde aquel momento descrito por el Evangelio según San Juan:

> *"Junto a la cruz de Jesús, estaban su madre y la hermana de su madre, María, mujer de Cleofás y María Magdalena. Jesús, viendo a su madre y junto a ella al discípulo a quien amaba, dice a su madre: "Mujer, ahí tienes a tu hijo." Luego dice al discípulo: "Ahí tienes a tu madre". Y desde aquella hora el discípulo la acogió en su casa".* Juan 19, 25-27

A partir de los hechos testimoniados por Bernadette Soubirous, la Iglesia Católica consideró a la Virgen María, en su advocación de Nuestra Señora de Lourdes, la patrona de los enfermos.

Es importante señalar que tanto las apariciones de Lourdes como la existencia de hechos "no explicables científicamente por las leyes naturales" no constituyen artículos de fe —estos últimos incluidos en el credo—.

"Le Bureau des Constatations Médicales" y de "Le Comité Médical International" de Lourdes, que rigen el análisis científico de las curaciones producidas en Lourdes, lo hacen de forma sumamente estricta. De los aproximadamente 7,000 expedientes de curación registrados desde las apariciones, sólo 67 casos han sido reconocidos por la Iglesia como milagros en un siglo y medio. "La Iglesia siempre ha sido muy cuidadosa acerca de las curaciones", dijo el facultativo francés Patrick Theillier, director de la oficina médica. "Prefiere no reconocer un milagro verdadero a proclamar uno donde no existe". En efecto, tal es el grado de rigor manifestado en este tema que la curación de Marie Bailly, aquejada de peritonitis tuberculosa en último estadio (el famoso "Dossier 54" de los Archivos de "Le Bureau des Constatations Médicales" de Lourdes), y testimoniada por el mismísimo -y por entonces escéptico- Dr. Alexis Carrel (Premio Nobel de Fisiología o Medicina en 1912), no se encuentra incluida entre los casos considerados "milagrosos" por la Iglesia católica, simplemente por una constatación insuficiente del estado psíquico de la paciente previo a su curación.

La persona más joven que se considera recibió esa gracia fue un niño de 2 años: Justin Bouhort, de Lourdes (Francia), que padecía hipotrepsia crónica post infecciosa con retardo del desarrollo motor. El más reciente reconocimiento de un milagro por parte de la Iglesia Católica sobrevino en el año 2005. Asimismo, se reconoció que 6 milagros tuvieron lugar por intercesión de Nuestra Señora de Lourdes sin que los enfermos viajaran a Lourdes. La mayoría de los milagros se produjeron por contacto con el agua de Lourdes (49 milagros de los 67). Para que una curación se considere "milagrosa" se deben cumplimentar una serie de requisitos, entre los que se cuentan:

- Que la dolencia sea incurable, desde un punto de vista científico.
- Que se haya puesto de manifiesto la total ineficacia de los medicamentos o protocolos empleados en su tratamiento.
- Que la curación haya sobrevenido de forma súbita y no gradual.
- Que la curación haya sido absoluta, con efectos duraderos, y no solamente una remisión.
- Que la curación no sea el resultado de una interpretación derivada del estado psíquico de la persona.
- Algunos de 67 casos de curación considerados "milagrosos" por la Iglesia católica son los siguientes:

- Jeanne Fretel, de Rennes (Francia). Visitó Lourdes el 10 de mayo de 1948, a los 31 años. Tenía peritonitis tuberculosa, con enflaquecimiento extremo y fiebre. Fue llevada a Lourdes en estado comatoso. Le fue dado un fragmento minúsculo de Eucaristía y despertó. Se informó que fue "inmediata y permanentemente curada" esa noche mientras yacía en su silla de ruedas al lado del manantial. Ella todavía no se había bañado en el manantial, ni bebido de su agua. Su curación fue reconocida oficialmente el 11 de noviembre de 1950.

- Hermano Léo Schwager, de Fribourg (Suiza). Visitó Lourdes el 30 de abril de 1952, a la edad de 28 años. Sufría esclerosis múltiple desde los 5 años. Su curación fue reconocida oficialmente el 18 de diciembre de 1960.

- Alicia Couteault, de Bouille-Loretz (Francia). Visitó Lourdes el 15 de mayo de 1952, a la edad de 34 años. Sufría esclerosis múltiple desde hacía tres años. Su curación fue reconocida oficialmente el 16 de julio de 1956.

- Marie Bigot, de La Richardais (Francia). Visitó Lourdes en dos oportunidades, el 8 de octubre de 1953 y 10 de octubre de 1954, a la edad de 31 y 32 años respectivamente. Padecía de aracnoiditis a nivel de la fosa posterior (causal de su ceguera, sordera y hemiplegia). Su curación fue reconocida oficialmente en Rennes, el 15 de agosto de 1956.

- Ginette Nouvel, de Carmaux (Francia). Visitó Lourdes el 21 de septiembre de 1954 a la edad de 26 años. Padecía el Síndrome de Budd-Chiari (trombosis de las ramas principales de las venas suprahepáticas). Su curación fue reconocida el 31 de mayo de 1963 en la diócesis de Albi.

- Elisa Aloi, luego Elisa Varcalli, de Patti (Italia). Visitó Lourdes el 5 de junio de 1958, a la edad de 27 años. Padecía tuberculosis osteoarticular y fístulas en diversos sitios del miembro inferior derecho. Su curación fue reconocida el 26 de mayo de 1965 en la diócesis de Messina (Italia).

- Juliette Tamburini, de Marsella (Francia). Visitó Lourdes el 17 de julio de 1959, a la edad de 22 años. Padecía osteoperiostitis femoral con fístulas y epistaxis. Su curación fue reconocida el 11 de mayo de 1965 en la diócesis de Marsella.

- Vittorio Micheli, de Scurelle (Italia). Visitó Lourdes el 1 de junio de 1963, a la edad de 23 años. Padecía de sarcoma (cáncer) de pelvis. Su tumor canceroso era tan grande y terrible que desencajó su muslo izquierdo, dejando su pierna izquierda paralizada. Después de ser bañado en las aguas del manantial, se liberó del dolor y pudo caminar. La disminución del tamaño del tumor se produjo de inmediato, aunque la verificación final se realizó en febrero de 1964, fecha en la que no sólo el tumor había desaparecido por completo, sino que además se había recalcificado la unión con la cadera, habiendo retornado Vittorio a su vida normal. La curación fue reconocida el 26 de mayo de 1976 en la diócesis de Trento.

- Serge Perrin, de Lion d'Angers (Francia). Visitó Lourdes el 1 de mayo de 1970 a la edad de 41 años. Sufría de hemiplejía recurrente del lado derecho, con lesiones oculares, por trombosis bilateral de la arteria carótida. Los síntomas, que incluían dolor de cabeza, deterioro del habla y de la visión, y parálisis parcial del lado derecho, comenzaron sin advertencia previa en febrero de 1964. Durante los siguientes seis años vivió confinado a una silla de ruedas, casi ciego. En 1969 viajó a Lourdes, retornando en el mismo estado alarmante. Durante su peregrinaje a Lourdes en 1970, sintió un calor repentino de pies a cabeza, retornando su visión y su capacidad de caminar sin ayuda alguna. Regresó de Lourdes con la confirmación médica de hallarse curado. Su curación fue reconocida oficialmente el 17 de junio de 1978 en la diócesis de Angers.

- Delizia Cirolli, luego Delizia Costa, de Paternò (Sicilia, Italia). Visitó Lourdes el 24 de diciembre de 1976 a la edad de 12 años. Padecía del Sarcoma de Ewing en la rodilla derecha. Los doctores sugirieron la amputación pues el avance de la enfermedad podría resultar fatal, pero sus padres se rehusaron. La madre llevó a la niña a Lourdes. A su retorno a Italia, el tumor evidenció una rápida regresión hasta desaparecer toda evidencia del mismo. El tumor dejó su tibia angulada, requiriéndose una operación correctiva (osteotomía). La niña recomenzó a caminar, comer, y vivir normalmente. Su curación fue reconocida el 28 de junio de 1989 en la diócesis de Catania (Italia). Ella se hizo enfermera.

- Jean-Pierre Bély, de La Couronne (Francia). Visitó Lourdes el 9 de octubre de 1987, a la edad de 51 años. Padecía esclerosis múltiple desde 1972 y su estado se deterioró año tras año. Cuando partió en peregrinación a Lourdes, el 5 de octubre de 1987, había sido reconocido por el sistema sanitario francés con un grado de invalidez total. En Lourdes, después de recibir la unción de los enfermos en la explanada del Santuario, experimentó una profunda paz interior. Repentinamente, recobró la sensibilidad táctil y pudo moverse nuevamente. En el acto, él no se atrevió a ponerse de pie. En la noche siguiente, una voz interior le repitió: «Levántate y anda», lo cual hizo. Como a él mismo le gustaba destacar: "el Señor ha curado primero mi corazón, y luego mi cuerpo". El médico que le atendió, Dr. Patrick Fontanaud, agnóstico, reconoció abiertamente que resulta científicamente inexplicable lo que sucedió. Después de 12 años de investigaciones médicas, su curación fue oficialmente reconocida el 9 de febrero de 1999 en la diócesis de Angoulême. Una comisión canónica declaró que esa curación fue "un signo eficaz de Cristo Salvador, que se consumó por la intercesión de Nuestra Señora de Lourdes". Aquí se puede ver que la Virgen y Cristo son un mismo ente divino, los cuales obran dentro del Espíritu Santo.
- Anna Santaniello de Salerno (Italia). Nacida, en 1911, sufría una cardiopatía severa derivada de fiebre reumática aguda, conocida en el ambiente científico como enfermedad de Bouillaud. Como consecuencia de su enfermedad, tenía dificultades para hablar, estaba incapacitada para caminar, y presentaba ataques de asma severos, cianosis en el rostro y los labios, y edemas en los miembros inferiores. El 16 de agosto de 1952, a la edad de 41 años, peregrinó a Lourdes con la organización italiana UNITALSI (Unión Nacional Italiana de Transporte de Enfermos a Lourdes y al Santuario Internacional). Ella hizo el viaje a Lourdes en tren en una camilla. Durante su estancia encontró asilo en Notre-Dame, precursor de la actual Casa de Nuestra Señora, en el Santuario, siendo objeto de vigilancia constante. El 19 de agosto de 1952 fue conducida e introducida a la piscina de Lourdes en camilla, saliendo del agua por sus propios medios. Esa misma tarde, participó de la procesión

mariana de las antorchas. El Comité Médico Internacional de Lourdes calificó la curación de la mujer de "extraordinaria" en 1961. El 21 de septiembre de 2005, la curación milagrosa de Anna Santaniello fue reconocida oficialmente por monseñor Gerardo Pierro, arzobispo de la diócesis de Salerno (Italia), cuando ella contaba con 94 años de edad. Anna Santaniello confió más tarde que, estando enferma, no oró para sí misma en la gruta de Lourdes, sino por un joven de veinte años, Nicolino, que había perdido el uso de sus piernas después de un accidente. Permaneció soltera y, en el ejercicio de la profesión de enfermera pediátrica, trató desde su regreso a Italia a cientos de niños desfavorecidos.

Para los creyentes católicos, científicos o no, la atención no se centra en lo sorprendente o extraordinario de los hechos ocurridos, sino en el Espíritu Santo de Dios, de cuya autoridad emana el poder para realizarlos. Al igual que Jesús en los evangelios, "cuya discreción reduce al mínimo el riesgo de una posible interpretación mágica", los creyentes son llamados a vivir estos sucesos de forma sencilla, desconfiando de las grandes palabras.

Una curación extraordinaria es un desafío, pero ciertamente sería desafortunado plantearlo como un "desafío a la ciencia". Es más bien un desafío para el espíritu humano. En Lourdes, la Iglesia católica considera que, por intercesión de la Virgen María, se han producido muchos más cambios de vida que curaciones del cuerpo. Aunque no se trató de una conversión abrupta, sino gradual, la de Alexis Carrel es quizá la más conocida, por tratarse de un científico laureado con el Premio Nobel de Fisiología o Medicina en 1912. (Nuestra Señora de Lourdes, wikipedia.com)

No corresponde tratar de dilucidar el misterio que encierra toda conversión, pero sí se puede hacer una aproximación al converso, describir su trayectoria antes y después de su encuentro con el misterio, estudiar el contexto y subrayar lo que tiene de significativo para nuestros días.

El Dr. Alexis Carrel provenía de una familia católica devota y fue educado por los jesuitas. Sin embargo, al momento de ingresar a la Universidad, ya no practicaba su religión. Él era un estudiante de medicina de segundo año cuando el presidente francés, Marie Francois

Sadi Carnot, fue asesinado por un anarquista en Lyon en 1894. El cuchillo del anarquista había cortado una arteria de primer orden, por lo que el presidente murió luego de dos días de agonía. En esos tiempos, la sutura de un vaso sanguíneo grande todavía era un tema sin solución segura. El joven estudiante de medicina Carrel decidió resolver el problema. Julius H. Comroe, profesor emérito del Cardiovascular Research Institute (University of California at San Francisco) escribió: "Carrel ganó el Premio Nobel en Fisiología y Medicina en 1912, y no lo ganó por alguna investigación oscura y esotérica, sino "en reconocimiento a su trabajo en sutura vascular y en trasplantes de vasos sanguíneos y órganos." Entre 1901 y 1910, Alexis Carrel, utilizando animales de experimento, efectuó todas las acciones y desarrolló todas las técnicas conocidas hoy en cirugía vascular (...)."

Seis años más tarde de sus inicios, ya médico y asistente en el Departamento de Anatomía, Carrel leyó su trabajo científico publicado en la Sociedad de Medicina de Lyon el 12 de mayo de 1902. Ese trabajo científico hizo historia y lo catapultaría a la fama una década después, como Carrel intuía que lo haría. Dos semanas más tarde se encontró en el tren que llevó a Marie Bailly a Lourdes. Lo que pasó desde ese momento durante los siguientes cinco días fue escrito por Carrel después, aunque el manuscrito fue publicado en 1948 bajo el título "*Le voyage de Lourdes, suivi de fragments de journal et de méditations*", cuatro años después de su muerte ocurrida en noviembre de 1944. En 1950, fue publicado en una traducción al inglés como "*The Voyage to Lourdes*".

Un colega de Alexis Carrel y ex-compañero de clases le pidió que tomara su lugar como médico a cargo de un tren que trasladaba gente enferma a Lourdes. Carrel estaba interesado en Lourdes, pero no para evaluar la "autenticidad" de los milagros. En esos momentos, el no creía en milagros. Él estaba interesado en justipreciar de forma personal la velocidad con que se producía la curación de diferentes enfermedades o lesiones informadas en Lourdes. Dotado de un fino sentido de observación, sus amigos decían de él que tenía "el ojo en la espalda..."

De entre los enfermos, el Dr. Alexis Carrel fijó su atención en una joven enferma agonizante, Marie Bailly (a quien él llamó con el seudónimo de "Marie Ferrand" en sus escritos -publicados de forma póstuma bajo el título de "Un viaje a Lourdes"-). Marie Bailly estaba afectada por peritonitis tuberculosa en último estadio, una enfermedad ciertamente mortal en esa época.

La historia de Marie Bailly es bien conocida en el ámbito médico. Toda su familia había muerto de tuberculosis. Ella había tenido úlceras tuberculosas, lesiones de los pulmones, y luego, una peritonitis, diagnosticada tanto por un médico general como por un cirujano reconocido de Burdeos, Bromilloux. Su estado era muy grave y podía morir en cualquier momento. El médico había expresado que de la única forma que ella podría curarse era con un milagro.

Retirando los cobertores, el cuerpo de Marie estaba expuesto de nuevo. El abdomen estaba hinchado como antes, pero algo más pronunciado en el lado izquierdo... "Temo que se me muera entre las manos...", habría declarado Carrel. Cuando el tren arribó a Lourdes, la joven Marie Bailly estaba semiconsciente, pero al llegar ella al Hospital de Lourdes propiamente dicho, ella estaba consciente. Carrel tenía una visión tan pesimista de la condición de la joven que prometió "convertirse en monje" si ella llegaba con vida a la Gruta, situada apenas a 400 metros del hospital. Por insistencia de Marie Bailly, una jarra llena de agua del manantial de Lourdes fue vertida tres veces sobre el abdomen, ciertamente muy hinchado, de la joven. Media hora más tarde, el pulso de la joven comenzó a disminuir y el vientre hasta entonces hinchado se acható. Durante ese tiempo, Marie Bailly permaneció totalmente consciente. Carrel quedó perplejo: el científico que regía su interior se negó a aceptar la posibilidad de un milagro, pero su mente tampoco lograba obtener una conclusión empírica y pragmática.

La curación repentina de Marie Bailly se dio a conocer ampliamente en Lyon, junto con el hecho de que Carrel estuvo presente durante su curación. Un periódico publicó un artículo, implicando que Carrel se negaba a creer en el milagro. En consecuencia, el Dr. Carrel se vio compelido a publicar una respuesta que no agradó a nadie. Él criticó a los creyentes por tomar con demasiada facilidad algo inusual como si se tratara de milagro. Y, por otra parte, reprochó a quienes se negaban a mirar los hechos cada vez que parecía ser un milagro (implicando en gran medida a los miembros de la comunidad médica).

Medio año después el Dr. Carrel tuvo que abandonar la Facultad de Medicina. Primero fue a París, de allí a Montreal, de allí a la Universidad de Chicago, y desde allí, a través de una conferencia en la Universidad Johns Hopkins, el Instituto Rockefeller. El caso de Marie Bailly se convirtió en una gran noticia en Francia recién a partir de 1913, después que Alexis Carrel, con el halo del Premio Nobel de Fisiología/Medicina de 1912, volvió de visita a Francia.

Los detalles más precisos sobre los hechos de importancia que constituyen la columna vertebral del "caso Bailly" se pueden obtener del "Dossier 54", en los archivos de "Le Bureau des Constatations Médicales", organismo que, junto con "Le Comité Médical International", rige el análisis científico de las curaciones producidas en Lourdes. El "Dossier 54" también se encuentra en la introducción redactada por Stanley L. Jaki (ganador del Premio Templeton 1987) en ocasión de una re-edición del libro de Carrel "Un viaje a Lourdes".

Marie Bailly nació en 1878. Tanto su padre, un óptico, como su madre murieron de tuberculosis. De sus cinco hermanos, sólo uno no sufrió esa enfermedad. Ella tenía veinte años cuando se evidenciaron por primera vez los síntomas de la tuberculosis pulmonar. Un año más tarde, se le diagnosticó meningitis tuberculosa, de la que se recuperó repentinamente cuando utilizó agua de Lourdes. Dos años más tarde, en 1901, sufrió peritonitis tuberculosa. Poco después, ella ya no podía retener los alimentos. En marzo de 1902, los médicos en Lyon se negaron a operarla por miedo a que ella muriera en la mesa de operaciones.

El 25 de mayo de 1902, le rogó a sus amigos que la metieran "de contrabando" en un tren que llevaba enfermos a Lourdes. Ella tenía que ser objeto de tránsito ilícito ya que, por regla general, estaba prohibido llevar a gente moribunda en esos trenes. El tren partió de Lyon al mediodía. A las 2 de la mañana siguiente, ella se estaba muriendo. Se llamó a Alexis Carrel. Él le suministró morfina a la luz de una lámpara de kerosene y permaneció con ella. Tres horas más tarde, él diagnosticó ese caso como peritonitis tuberculosa y dijo a media voz que no iba a llegar a Lourdes con vida. El diagnóstico inmediato en ese tiempo dependía en gran medida de un procedimiento de palpación.

En Lourdes, Marie Bailly fue examinada por varios médicos. El 27 de mayo, ella insistió en ser llevada a la Gruta, aunque los médicos (entre ellos Carrel) tenían miedo de que muriera en el camino. El "Expediente 54" ("Dossier 54") del Archivo de la Oficina Médica contiene las declaraciones inmediatas realizadas por tres médicos, incluyendo el propio Carrel, y el testimonio de Marie Bailly, que escribió en noviembre y entregó a Carrel, quien lo remitió debidamente a la Oficina Médica de Lourdes. Los aspectos más destacados del testimonio de la propia Marie Bailly son los siguientes:

Al llegar a los baños contiguos a la gruta, no se le permitió la inmersión. Pidió que un poco de agua de los baños se derramara sobre su abdomen. Esto le causó un dolor punzante en todo el cuerpo. Aun así, ella pidió se repitiera. La segunda vez, ella sintió mucho menos dolor. Cuando el agua se vertió sobre su abdomen por tercera vez, le daba una sensación muy agradable. Mientras tanto Carrel estaba detrás de ella, con un bloc de notas en sus manos. Marcó el momento, el pulso, la expresión facial y otros datos clínicos, como testigo ocular. El abdomen, enormemente hinchado y muy duro, comenzó a aplanarse y, en un plazo de 30 minutos, había desaparecido la hinchazón por completo. No se observó ningún tipo de descarga corporal.

Ella fue llevada primero a la Basílica y, a continuación, a la Oficina Médica, donde fue examinada de nuevo por varios médicos, entre ellos Carrel. Por la noche, ella se sentó en su cama y cenó sin vomitar. A la mañana siguiente, se levantó por sí misma y ya estaba vestida cuando Carrel la volvió a ver.

Carrel no podía dejar de registrar que ella estaba curada. "¿Qué vas a hacer con tu vida ahora?", le preguntó Carrel. "Me uniré a las Hermanas de la Caridad para pasar mi vida cuidando a los enfermos", fue la respuesta de Marie Bailly. Al día siguiente, Marie Bailly se subió al tren por su cuenta y, después de un viaje de 24 horas en duros bancos, llegó renovada a Lyon. Allí tomó el tranvía y se fue a la casa familiar, donde tendría que "probar" que ella era realmente Marie Bailly, la misma que sólo cinco días antes había salido de Lyon en un estado crítico.

Carrel continuó tomando un gran interés en ella. Le pidió a un psiquiatra que la pusiera a prueba cada dos semanas, lo que se realizó durante cuatro meses. Ella fue examinada regularmente en busca de trazas de la tuberculosis. A fines de noviembre, ella fue declarada en buen estado de salud, tanto física como mental. En diciembre, ella entró en el noviciado en París. Sin tener una recaída, ella vivió la vida ardua de una Hermana de la Caridad hasta 1937.

Carrel tenía ante sí un problema. Si alguien conocía los hechos del caso era él, quien humanamente sabía lo que pasó con Marie Bailly. Sin embargo, no se atrevía a creer que algo más que simplemente las fuerzas naturales habían intervenido en la recuperación repentina de

Marie Bailly. Continuó regresando a Lourdes para poder ver otras curaciones repentinas. Él esperaba percibir de esta forma alguna fuerza puramente natural que produjera las llamadas curaciones "milagrosas" y que lo hiciera a través del poder de la oración, al cual él consideraba una fuerza psíquica puramente natural. La prueba de ello está en su famoso libro "*L'homme, cet inconnu*" ("La Incógnita del Hombre - El Hombre, Ese Desconocido"), que apareció publicado por primera vez en francés en 1934, luego en inglés y, posteriormente, en treinta idiomas. Allí se hace referencia, precisamente en este sentido, a varios de los milagros de Lourdes.

Para entonces, habían pasado treinta y dos años desde que Carrel había estado detrás de la camilla de Marie Bailly. En todos esos años, se había entrevistado con sacerdotes una y otra vez. Se reunió con teólogos, o mejor dicho, algunos teólogos lo buscaron a él, con la esperanza de que Carrel les diera una confirmación "científica" de los milagros. Nada de esto parecía haberlo acercado a la fe de su infancia. Entonces, Marie Bailly murió en 1937 a la edad de 58 años.

Al año siguiente, Carrel se topó con un sacerdote, Rector del Seminario Mayor en Rennes, con quien desarrolló rápidamente una relación. El Rector le sugirió ver a un monje trapense, Alexis Presse. El Padre Alexis había pasado una década restaurando y reabriendo abadías en ruinas en toda Francia. En 1939 comenzó a trabajar en una abadía en ruinas en Bouquen, a sólo una hora en automóvil de la residencia de verano de Carrel en Bretaña. Cuando se dirigía con su esposa, Carrel permaneció refunfuñando y dijo: "El encuentro con los sacerdotes le hace a uno más daño que bien". Al llegar a las ruinas vino un monje, el Padre Alexis, miró a Carrel, quien comenzó a sentir "algo extraño corriendo a través de él". Cuatro años más tarde, en noviembre de 1944, Carrel se moría en París. El mensaje fue enviado al Padre Alexis en Bretaña. El monje abordó un tren militar que transportaba bananas de América a las tropas que seguían combatiendo a los alemanes más allá de París. Llegó justo a tiempo. Carrel pidió los sacramentos antes de morir, el 5 de noviembre de 1944. Eduardo de la Hera hizo una descripción de los conversos que quizá se corresponda con la de Alexis Carrel, un converso de "Nuestra Señora de Lourdes":

> *"Los conversos son esas personas que, después de haber vivido al margen de toda fe religiosa, un día inolvidable dieron un viraje*

tan intenso a la trayectoria de su vida que cambiaron de rumbo.
Y comenzaron, si se me permite la expresión, a "tomarse en serio
a Dios". Dios trastocó sus vidas. En cierto sentido, se las complicó.
Alguien pudo ver en ellos a seres sugestionados, alucinados o
alienados. Pero no, ellos no se salieron de este mundo: el suyo y el
de todos, el único que tenemos. (...) Tampoco se transformaron
en fanáticos de lo religioso. Supieron, simplemente, mostrarse
coherentes con su verdad y respetuosos con la verdad de los otros."
Eduardo de la Hera

Esta es la esencia de lo que realmente le sucedió en Lourdes a aquel hombre laureado con el premio Nobel. La totalidad del famoso "Dossier 54" brinda sólo la mitad de la respuesta a la pregunta: ¿Qué ocurrió realmente? La otra mitad no se trata tanto de medicina, sino que se enmarca en el plano de la fe católica.

Por cierto, esta curación no fue reconocida como "milagrosa" por la Iglesia. El caso de Marie Bailly, fue discutido en varias ocasiones en distintos niveles por la Oficina Médica de Lourdes y, finalmente, en París, en su nivel más alto, por el Comité Internacional. Era el año 1964. Se tomó la decisión en contra de la naturaleza milagrosa de la cura. ¿La razón?

Debido a que los primeros médicos que la atendieron no habían considerado la posibilidad de un embarazo psicológico (pseudociesis) –para lo cual se requeriría de más informes psicológicos y psiquiátricos previos a la curación–, el Comité Internacional decidió fallar en contra de la recomendación de considerar a la curación de Marie Bailly para su aprobación eclesiástica como "milagro". Se podría suponer que se trataba de una suposición descabellada. ¿Podrían tantos médicos diagnosticar incorrectamente semejante caso? ¿Podrían todos los médicos equivocarse al momento de palpar la pesada mucosidad del abdomen? Esto, debido a que la peritonitis de Marie Bailly no producía una mucosidad líquida, sino pesada. La palpación puede fácilmente establecer la presencia de esa mucosidad densa y pesada, especialmente cuando se presenta en grandes cantidades. Más aún, ¿a dónde había ido a parar toda esa pesada mucosidad en sólo 30 minutos? Por último, Marie Bailly había superado todas las pruebas psicológicas posteriores a su curación con gran éxito. Ella resultó ser una persona equilibrada, con sentido común y difícilmente impresionable.

Sin embargo, el fallo fue en contra, a fin de excluir la más mínima posibilidad de error en la certificación de ese hecho como "milagroso". Eso, aunque quien firmara en representación de la ciencia médica que se trataba de un hecho inexplicable fuera un Premio Nobel de Fisiología o Medicina.

En cierto sentido, las contribuciones del Dr. Alexis Carrel en el campo de la medicina no perduraron en el reconocimiento que se les debería, ni siquiera por parte de sus colegas científicos. En el artículo antes mencionado, Julius H. Comroe señaló: "En 1974, antes de iniciar una charla a un grupo de científicos cardiovasculares en su reunión anual, le entregué a cada uno una tarjeta que tenía en la parte superior esta requisitoria: «Sin consultar a nadie, por favor escriba a continuación del nombre de cada persona (mencionada), aquélla que considera fue su mayor contribución a la ciencia biomédica». Seguían cuatro nombres, uno de los cuales era Alexis Carrel. Cuando las respuestas fueron tabuladas, encontré que sólo 7 de los 111 que retornaron sus tarjetas conocían sus grandes contribuciones a la cirugía vascular, 33 sólo conocían sus últimos trabajos sobre cultivos de órganos, y 71 escribieron después del nombre de Carrel: NOADE -nunca oí acerca de él-."11 Sin embargo, el renacimiento espiritual de Alexis Carrel llegó a ser uno de los ejemplos más reconocidos de conversiones en Lourdes.

En su libro póstumo "Viaje a Lourdes", el protagonista lleva el seudónimo de Dr. "Lerrac", que es su apellido al revés, Carrel. Allí, Alexis Carrel escribió:

"Y él se fue a la gruta, a contemplar atentamente la imagen de la Virgen María, las muletas que, como exvotos, llenaban las paredes iluminadas por el resplandor de los cirios, cuya incesante humareda había ennegrecido la roca... Lerrac tomó asiento en una silla al lado de un campesino anciano y permaneció inmóvil largo rato con la cabeza entre las manos, mecido por los cánticos nocturnos, mientras del fondo de su alma brotaba esta plegaria: "Virgen Santa, socorro de los desgraciados que te imploran humildemente, sálvame. Creo en ti, has querido responder a mi duda con un gran milagro. No lo comprendo y dudo todavía. Pero mi gran deseo y el objeto supremo de todas mis aspiraciones es ahora creer, creer apasionada y ciegamente

sin discutir ni criticar nunca más. Tu nombre es más bello que el sol de la mañana. Acoge al inquieto pecador, que con el corazón turbado y la frente surcada por las arrugas se agita, corriendo tras las quimeras. Bajo los profundos y duros consejos de mi orgullo intelectual yace, desgraciadamente ahogado todavía, un sueño, el más seductor de todos los sueños: el de creer en ti y amarte como te aman los monjes de alma pura..." Eran las tres de la madrugada y a Lerrac le pareció que la serenidad que presidía todas las cosas había descendido también a su alma, inundándola de calma y dulzura. Las preocupaciones de la vida cotidiana, las hipótesis, las teorías y las inquietudes intelectuales habían desaparecido de su mente. Tuvo la impresión de que, bajo la mano de la Virgen, había alcanzado la certidumbre y hasta creyó sentir su admirable y pacificadora dulzura de una manera tan profunda que, sin la menor inquietud, alejó la amenaza de un retorno a la duda." Alexis Carrel

Quizá el número total de curaciones declaradas como milagros sólo sea un dato anecdótico, puesto que la importancia de "Nuestra Señora de Lourdes" viene dada por el renacimiento espiritual de aquellos que a ella acuden.

"Nuestras indagaciones no llegarán nunca a dilucidar el misterio de un renacer espiritual y de los caminos de la gracia. Con todo, puede pretenderse ver cómo se encuadra en su época, cómo la moldea y es moldeado por ella." Romano Guardini

El 24 de septiembre de 2008, el Arzobispo de Canterbury y primado de la Comunión Anglicana Rowan Williams peregrinó al mismísimo Santuario de Nuestra Señora de Lourdes para honrar a la Inmaculada Concepción, predicando ante 20,000 personas en la Eucaristía Internacional. En su homilía destacó:

"María se nos presenta aquí como la primera misionera, "el primer mensajero del Evangelio", como la llamó el obispo de Lourdes, Perrier: el primer ser humano que llevó la buena nueva de Jesucristo a otra persona; cosa que hace simplemente

308 JUAN DE LA CRUZ

llevando a Cristo dentro de sí. Ella nos recuerda que la misión comienza no con la entrega de un mensaje hecho de palabras sino en el camino hacia otra persona con Jesús en el corazón.

Ella atestigua la primordial importancia de, sencillamente, llevar a Jesús, incluso antes de que existan las palabras o las acciones para mostrarle y explicarle. (...) Cuando María se le apareció a Bernadette, la primera vez lo hizo como una figura anónima, una hermosa mujer, una «cosa» misteriosa, no identificada aún como la Madre Inmaculada del Señor. Y Bernadette –inculta, carente de instrucción doctrinal– saltó de gozo, reconociendo que allí había vida, que allí estaba la cura.

Recordad sus narraciones en las que habla de sus movimientos agraciados y ligeros a las órdenes de la Señora; como si ella, al igual que Juan en el vientre de Isabel, comenzara a bailar siguiendo la música del Verbo Encarnado que lleva su Madre.

Sólo poco a poco encontrará Bernadette las palabras para que el mundo sepa; sólo poco a poco, podríamos decir, descubre cómo escuchar a la Señora y referir lo que tiene que decirnos. (...) Los vecinos, los maestros y el clero de la parroquia de Bernadette sabían lo que pensaban que necesitaban saber sobre la Madre de Dios, pero tuvieron que quedar sorprendidos por esta adolescente incapaz de expresarse, inerme e insignificante que había saltado de gozo reconociendo haber encontrado a María como madre, hermana, portadora de su Señor y Redentor. (...) Hoy aquí, con Isabel y Bernadette, decimos con agradecido estupor: "¿Qué he hecho para merecerme que la madre de mi Señor haya venido hasta mí?" Y reconocemos que el deseo de nuestro corazón ha sido satisfecho y lo más profundo de nuestro ser ha sido llevado a una nueva vida." Rowan Williams, Arzobispo de Canterbury y primado de la Comunión Anglicana

Este hecho fue considerado como muy significativo en orden a la unidad de los cristianos y fue seguido por la visita histórica del Papa Benedicto XVI al primado anglicano el 17 de septiembre de 2010, en ocasión del 50 aniversario del primer encuentro de un Papa y un Arzobispo de Canterbury en los tiempos modernos, el de Juan XXIII y el arzobispo Geoffrey Fisher, en diciembre de 1960. A ello a su vez siguió el recibimiento de Benedicto XVI a Rowan Williams en el Vaticano el 18 de noviembre de 2010, poco después de que cinco obispos anglicanos anunciaran su pase a la Iglesia católica, aprovechando el nuevo ordinariato creado a tal fin por la Santa Sede. En tal ocasión, el Papa Benedicto XVI y Rowan Williams oraron juntos. En el sentir de la Iglesia, Nuestra Señora de Lourdes constituye un camino de superación de las divisiones entre los cristianos, en orden al cumplimiento del mandato de Jesús: "Que todos sean uno". Juan 17:21.

4.14.- Nuestra Señora del Rosario; advocación de la Virgen María.

Nuestra Señora del Rosario o Virgen del Rosario es una advocación mariana venerada en la Iglesia Católica, por lo que celebra el 7 de octubre la fiesta de la *Bienaventurada Virgen María del Santísimo Rosario.*

Cuenta la leyenda que la Virgen María se apareció en 1208 a Santo Domingo de Guzmán en una capilla del monasterio de Prouilhe, Francia, con un rosario en las manos, le enseñó a rezarlo y le dijo que lo predicara entre los hombres; además, le ofreció diferentes promesas referentes al rosario. El santo se lo enseñó a los soldados liderados por su amigo Simón IV de Montfort antes de la Batalla de Muret, cuya victoria se atribuyó a la Virgen. Por ello, Montfort erigió la primera capilla dedicada a esta advocación.

Un creciente número de hombres se unió a la obra apostólica de Santo Domingo y, con la aprobación del Santo Padre, Domingo formó la Orden de Predicadores (más conocidos como Dominicos). Con gran celo predicaban, enseñaban y los frutos de conversión crecían. A medida que la orden crecía, se extendieron a diferentes países como misioneros para la gloria de Dios y de la Virgen María.

El rosario se mantuvo como la oración predilecta durante casi dos siglos. Cuando la devoción empezó a disminuir, la Virgen María se apareció a Alano de la Rupe y le dijo que reviviera dicha devoción. La Virgen María le dijo también que se necesitarían volúmenes inmensos para registrar todos los milagros logrados por medio del rosario y reiteró las promesas dadas a Santo Domingo referentes al rosario.

Las Promesas de Nuestra Señora, Reina del Rosario, tomadas de los escritos del Beato Alano:

1. Quien rece constantemente mi Rosario, recibirá cualquier gracia que me pida.
2. Prometo mi especialísima protección y grandes beneficios a los que devotamente recen mi Rosario.
3. El Rosario es el escudo contra el infierno, destruye el vicio, libra de los pecados y abate las herejías.
4. El Rosario hace germinar las virtudes para que las almas consigan la misericordia divina. Sustituye en el corazón de los hombres el amor del mundo con el amor de Dios y los eleva a desear las cosas celestiales y eternas.
5. El alma que se me encomiende por el Rosario no perecerá.
6. El que con devoción rece mi Rosario, considerando sus sagrados misterios, no se verá oprimido por la desgracia, ni morirá de muerte desgraciada, se convertirá si es pecador, perseverará en gracia si es justo y, en todo caso será admitido a la vida eterna.
7. Los verdaderos devotos de mi Rosario no morirán sin los Sacramentos.
8. Todos los que rezan mi Rosario tendrán en vida y en muerte la luz y la plenitud de la gracia y serán partícipes de los méritos bienaventurados.
9. Libraré bien pronto del Purgatorio a las almas devotas a mi Rosario.
10. Los hijos de mi Rosario gozarán en el cielo de una gloria singular.
11. Todo cuanto me pidan por medio del Rosario se alcanzará prontamente.
12. Socorreré en sus necesidades a los que propaguen mi Rosario.
13. He solicitado a mi Hijo la gracia de que todos los cofrades y devotos tengan en vida y en muerte como hermanos a todos los bienaventurados de la corte celestial.
14. Los que rezan Rosario son todos hijos míos muy amados y hermanos de mi Unigénito Jesús.
15. La devoción al Santo rosario es una señal manifiesta de predestinación de gloria.

En estas promesas hechas por la Virgen María, no hay que ser muy errudito para ver que estamos frente a la demostración de que Ella es el Propio Ser Supremo. Aquí en nungun momento Ella dice voy a anteceder ante Dios por el que rece el Rosario, Ella asume en primera potencia "Yo Socorreré", "Yo Libraré", etc., de forma que estamos ante la presencia de una de las divinidades del Ser Supremo, del Espiritu Santo de Dios; estamos frente a la persona femenina de la Santisima Trinidad de Dios; Nuestra Señora de la Santísima Trinidad de Dios.

En el siglo XV la devoción por el Santo Rosario había decaído, por lo que nuevamente la imagen de Nuestra Señora de la Santísima Trinidad de Dios se apareció al beato Alano de la Rupe, le pidió que la reviviera, que recogiera en un libro todos los milagros llevados a cabo por el rosario y le recordó las promesas que siglos atrás dio a Santo Domingo.

En el siglo XVI, San Pío V instauró su fecha el 7 de octubre, aniversario de la victoria en la Batalla de Lepanto, donde las fuerzas cristianas derrotaron a los turcos que invadían Europa (atribuida a la Virgen), denominándola Nuestra Señora de las Victorias; además, agregó a la letanía de la Virgen el título de Auxilio de los Cristianos. Su sucesor, Gregorio XIII, cambió el nombre de su festividad al de Nuestra Señora del Rosario. A causa de la victoria en la batalla de Temesvár en 1716, atribuida por Clemente XI a la imagen, el papa ordenó que su fiesta se celebrase por la Iglesia universal. León XIII, cuya devoción por esta advocación hizo que fuera apodado "el Papa del Rosario", escribió unas encíclicas referentes al rosario, consagró el mes de octubre al rosario e incluyó el título de Reina del Santísimo Rosario en la letanía de la Virgen.

Como anécdotas, tanto la Virgen de Lourdes en su aparición de 1858 como la de Fátima en 1917 pidieron a sus aparecidos que rezasen el rosario. Gran parte de los papas del siglo XX fueron muy devotos de esta advocación, y Juan Pablo II manifestó en 1978 que el rosario era su oración preferida.

Es patrona de multitud de ciudades y localidades repartidas por todo el mundo, así como de las batallas cristianas:

Europa y con ella toda la cristiandad estaba en grave peligro de extinción. Los Musulmanes se proponían hacer desaparecer, a punta de espada, el cristianismo. Ya habían tomado Tierra Santa, Constantinopla, Grecia, Albania, África del Norte y España. En esas extensas regiones el cristianismo era perseguido, y muchos mártires derramaron su sangre, muchas diócesis desaparecieron completamente. Después de 700 años de lucha por la reconquista, España y Portugal pudieron librarse del dominio musulmán. Esa lucha comenzó a los pies de la Virgen de

Covadonga y culminó con la conquista de Granada, cuando los reyes católicos, Fernando e Isabel, pudieron definitivamente expulsar a los moros de la península en el 1492. Esta victoria tuvo una importancia incalculable ya que en ese mismo año ocurrió el descubrimiento de América y la fe cristiana comenzó a propagarse en el nuevo continente.

En la época del Papa Pío V (1566 - 1572), los musulmanes controlaban el Mar Mediterráneo y preparaban la invasión de la Europa cristiana. Los reyes católicos de Europa estaban divididos y parecían no darse cuenta del peligro inminente. El Papa pidió ayuda, pero se le hizo poco caso. El 17 de septiembre de 1569 pidió que se rezase el Santo Rosario. Por fin en 1571 se estableció una liga para la defensa de Europa. El 7 de octubre de 1571 se encontraron las flotas cristianas y musulmanas en el Golfo de Corinto, cerca de la ciudad griega de Lepanto. La flota cristiana, compuesta de soldados de los Estados Papales, de Venecia, Génova y España y comandada por Don Juan de Austria, entró en batalla contra un enemigo muy superior en tamaño. Se jugaba el todo por el todo. Antes del ataque, las tropas cristianas rezaron el santo rosario con devoción. La batalla de Lepanto duró hasta altas horas de la tarde, pero, al final los cristianos resultaron victoriosos.

En Roma, el Papa se hallaba recitando el rosario en tanto se había logrado la decisiva y milagrosa victoria para los cristianos. El poder de los turcos en el mar se había disuelto para siempre. El Papa salió de su capilla y, guiado por una inspiración, anunció con mucha calma que la Santísima Virgen María había otorgado la victoria. Semanas más tarde llegó el mensaje de la victoria de parte de Don Juan, quién desde un principio, le atribuyó el triunfo de su flota a la poderosa intercesión de Nuestra Señora del Rosario. Agradecido con Nuestra Madre, el Papa Pío V instituyó la fiesta de Nuestra Señora de las Victorias y agregó a las Letanía de la Santísima Virgen el título de "Auxilio de los Cristianos". Más adelante, el Papa Gregorio III cambió la fiesta a la de Nuestra Señora del Rosario.

Los turcos seguían siendo poderosos en tierra y, en el siglo siguiente, invadieron a Europa desde el Este y, después de tomar enormes territorios, sitiaron a Viena, capital de Austria. Una vez más, las tropas enemigas eran muy superiores. Si conquistaban la ciudad toda Europa se hacía muy vulnerable. El emperador puso su esperanza en Nuestra Señora del Rosario. Hubo gran lucha y derramamiento de sangre y la ciudad parecía perdida. El alivio llegó el día de la fiesta del Santo

Nombre de María, 12 de septiembre, de 1683, cuando el rey de Polonia, conduciendo un ejército de rescate, derrotó a los turcos.

El Príncipe Eugenio de Saboya derrotó en Temesvar (en la Rumania moderna) a un ejército turco dos veces más grande que el suyo, el 5 de agosto de 1716, que en aquel entonces era la fiesta de Nuestra Señora de las Nieves. El Papa Clemente XI atribuyó esta victoria a la devoción manifestada a Nuestra Señora del Rosario. En acción de gracias, mandó que la fiesta del Santo Rosario fuera celebrada por la Iglesia universal.

Un gran apóstol del rosario en familia es el Padre Patrick Peyton, quién llevó a cabo los primeros planes para que se hiciera una cruzada a nivel mundial del rosario en familia en el Holy Cross College, Washington D.C., en enero de 1942. Hizo esta cruzada en acción de gracias a María Santísima por la restauración de su salud. De una forma maravillosa la cruzada se propagó por todo el mundo con el lema: "La familia que reza unida, permanece unida".

A lo largo de los siglos los Papas han fomentado la pía devoción del rezo del rosario y le han otorgado indulgencias.

Dijo Nuestro Señor: "Donde dos o tres estén reunidos en mi nombre, allí estoy yo en medio de ellos" (Mateo 18:20). El rosario en familia es algo maravilloso. Es un modo práctico de fortalecer la unidad de la vida familiar. Es una oración al alcance de todos. Los Papas, especialmente los más recientes, han hecho gran énfasis sobre la importancia del rosario en familia.

El Papa dominico, San Pío V (1566 - 1572) dio el encargo a su congregación de propagar el santo rosario. Muchos Papas han sido grandes devotos del rosario y lo han propagado con profunda convicción y confianza.

Su Santidad León XIII escribió doce encíclicas referentes al rosario. Insistió en el rezo del rosario en familia, consagró el mes de octubre al rosario e insertó el título de "Reina del Santísimo Rosario" en la Letanía de la Virgen. Por todo esto mereció el título de "El Papa del Rosario"

Su Santidad Juan Pablo II nos insistió en el rezo del Santo Rosario. Recen en familia, en grupos. Recen en privado. Inviten a todos a rezar. No tengan miedo de compartir la fe. Nada más importante. El mundo está en crisis. Nuestras fuerzas humanas no son suficientes. La victoria vendrá una vez más por la Virgen María.

A la Virgen María le encanta el rosario. Es la oración de los sencillos y de los grandes. Es tan simple, que está al alcance de todos; se puede rezar en cualquier parte y a cualquier hora. El rosario honra a Dios y a la Santísima Virgen de un modo especial. La Virgen llevaba un rosario en la mano cuando se le apareció a Bernardita en Lourdes. Cuando se les apareció a los tres pastorcitos en Fátima, también tenía un rosario. Fue en Fátima donde ella misma se identificó con el título de "La Señora del Rosario".

4.15.- Nuestra Señora de Fátima; advocación de la Virgen María.

La Virgen María se le apareció en seis ocasiones en 1917 a tres niños; Lucía de 10 años, Francisco de 9 años, y Jacinta de 7 años. En los momentos que estos estaban llevando las ovejas a las colinas que pertenecían al padre de Lucía conocidas como Ensenada de Irene en Fátima, Portugal. Fue ahí donde la Santísima Virgen María, bajo el nombre de Nuestra Señora del Rosario se les apareció en seis ocasiones en 1917, con la excepción de una séptima vez en 1920 en la cual sólo se le apareció a Lucía. En este periodo, el mundo atravesaba, simultáneamente, por los estragos catastróficos de tres eventos que cambiarian el rumbo de la humanidad: 1) La pandemia de la gripe española que en 40 meses mató aproximadamente 100 millones de personas en todo el mundo, incluyendo a Francisco y a Jacinta, 2) La Primera Guerra Mundial en la que murieron más de 50 millones de habitantes, y 3) La revolución Rusa que cambiaría el sistema económico, político y social de muchos países de la tierra, en el cual se sumergió casi la mitad de los habitantes del planeta.

El relato histórico anterior lo hacemos para ubicar al lector en el contexto bajo el cual la Virgen de Fátima intercede por el ser humano para paliar los males morales y sociales, a través de sus mensajes hace cien años.

Cuando Nuestra Señora de Fátima se apareció a los niños vestía con un manto extraordinariamente blanco, con un borde de oro que caía hasta sus pies. En sus manos llevaba el Rosario que parecían estrellas relucientes, con un crucifijo que era la gema más radiante por sobre todas las demás. Le dijo a Lucia que Ella venía del cielo que no temieran. La presencia de la Virgen María le producía felicidad y un gozo confiado.

En la primera aparición la Divina Madre les dijo a los niños que regresaran a este mismo sitio todos los días trece de cada mes durante seis meses a la misma hora para Ella revelarle sus deseos. Luego volvería una séptima vez. Lucía cuenta que mientras la Virgen María pronunciaba estas palabras, abría sus manos, y fueron cubiertos por una luz celestial que provenía directamente de sus manos y esta luz que penetró sus almas y corazones les hacía comprender que de alguna forma provenía del propio Espíritu Santo de Dios. La luz los hacía sentirse abrazados por Ella. Luego por un impulso de Gracia Divina cayeron de rodillas repitiendo desde lo más profundo de sus corazones: **"Oh Santísima Trinidad, te adoramos. Mi Dios, mi Dios, te amo en el Santísimo Sacramento."**

< Este es otro hecho, palpable, que demuestra y confirma la revelación que hacemos en este libro sobre la divinidad de la Virgen María. Ella es el Propio Ser Supremo, la personificación femenina de la Santísima Trinidad del Espíritu Santo de Dios. >

Los niños permanecieron de rodillas en el torrente de esta fuente de luz maravillosa, hasta que *Nuestra Señora de la Santísima Trinidad* habló de nuevo. Ella le habló sobre la guerra en Europa, de la cual estos niños no tenían ninguna noción. La Santísima Virgen María le pidió que rezaran el Rosario todos los días, para traer la paz al mundo con el final de la guerra. Después de haberle dicho esto, la Divina Madre se comenzó a elevar lentamente hacia el este, hasta desaparecer en el firmamento. La luz que la rodeaba se confundía entre las estrellas, como si el cielo la absolviera.

Lucía había pedido a los otros niños que mantuvieran todo en secreto, sabiendo las dificultades que ellos experimentarían si estos eventos se supieran. Sin embargo, Jacinta no pudo contener su entusiasmo, y prontamente olvidó su promesa y le reveló todo a su madre, quien la escuchó pacientemente pero no le creyó, pensando que era una invención de la niña. Entre toda la familia solo su padre estuvo inclinado a aceptar la historia como verdad. El creyó en la honestidad de su hija, y como tenía alguna apreciación de las obras de Dios, se convirtió en el primer creyente de las apariciones de la *Virgen María en Fátima*.

La madre de Lucía, cuando finalmente le contaron lo que había ocurrido, creyó que su propia hija era la instigadora de un fraude, o más aún de una blasfemia. Lucía recordó rápidamente lo que la Virgen María le había dicho sobre el hecho de que ellos sufrirían mucho. María Rosa, la madre de Lucía, no pudo hacer que ésta se retractara, aún bajo amenazas. Finalmente la llevó donde el sacerdote de la parroquia, para sin éxito, tratar de que ella se retractara. El 13 de Junio, cuando los niños estaban con la Virgen, les revelaron que Ella tenía pocos creyentes, y muchos en contra en las comunidades de Aljustrel y de Fátima. En esta oportunidad cuando ellos llegaron vieron que había una pequeña multitud esperándolos y por lo cual ellos rezaron el Rosario junto con la multitud que estaba presente. Al llegar la Virgen ellos vieron el reflejo de la luz que se le acercaba y luego a Nuestra Señora del Rosario a orilla del roble. La Divina Virgen le dijo: quiero que vengan aquí el próximo mes. Quiero que continúen diciendo el Rosario todos los días. Después de cada misterio, mis hijos, quiero que recen de la siguiente manera; "Oh mi buen Jesús, perdona nuestros pecados, líbranos del fuego del infierno. Lleva a todas las almas al cielo, especialmente a las más necesitadas de tu Divina Misericordia." Quiero que aprenda a leer y escribir, y luego les diré que más quiero de ustedes. También quiero que sepan que pronto me llevaré a Jacinta y a Francisco al cielo, pero tú Lucia te quedarás un tiempo más aquí, ya que Jesús desea que tú me hagas conocer y amar en la tierra. El también desea que tú establezca devoción en el mundo entero a mi Inmaculado Corazón. Pero tú no estarás sola, hija mía, no te sientas triste porque yo estaré contigo siempre y mi Inmaculado Corazón será tu consuelo y el camino que te llevará hasta Dios."

Habiendo la Divina *Virgen María* dicho estas últimas palabras, abrió sus manos, y les transmitió como la primera vez, el reflejo de esa luz intensa que le hizo sentir que estaban sumergidos dentro del mismo Dios. Jacinta y Francisco parecían estar en la parte de la luz que se elevaba hacia los Cielos, mientras que Lucía estaba en la parte que se derramaba sobre la tierra. En frente de la palma de la mano derecha de Nuestra Señora del Rosario estaba un corazón rodeado de espinas que parecían clavársele. Esto le hizo pensar que éste era el Inmaculado Corazón de la *Virgen María* ofrecido por los pecados de la humanidad, deseando ansiosamente curación. Esta segunda aparición terminó como en la primera ocasión, con Nuestra Señora elevándose hacia el este y desapareciendo en la inmensidad del cielo.

La aparición de la *Virgen María* del 13 de Julio se convirtió en la más controversial del mensaje de Fátima, proveyendo un secreto en tres partes que los niños guardaron celosamente. En las primeras dos partes, la visión del infierno y la profecía del futuro rol de Rusia y cómo prevenirlo, no fueron reveladas hasta que Lucía las escribió en su tercer diario, en obediencia al obispo, en 1941. La tercera parte, comúnmente conocido como el Tercer Secreto, fue más tarde comunicado al obispo, quien lo envió sin leer al Papa Pío XII. En esta aparición la Santa Virgen dijo a los niños; "quiero que vengan aquí el día trece del próximo mes. Quiero que continúen rezando el Rosario todos los días en honor a Nuestra Señora del Rosario, para obtener la paz del mundo y el final de la guerra, *porque sólo Ella puede obtenerlo*. Deben venir aquí todos los meses, y en octubre yo les diré quién soy y lo que quiero de ustedes. Después haré un milagro para que todos crean… Y curaré algunas personas de las que ustedes me pidan, pero otras no las curaré."

< *Fíjese aquí, está bien claro, cuando la Virgen María le dice a los niños: "… continúen rezando el Rosario todos los días en honor a Nuestra Señora del Rosario… porque solo Ella puede obtener la paz del mundo y el final de la guerra." Vuelvo y hago hincapiés: "Solo Ella puede lograrlo", es decir, nadie más puede. Está claro que en este momento la Virgen María está revelando su poder y autoridad por sobre todas las cosas, algo que solo siendo en Propio Ser Supremo, el Propio Espíritu Santo de Dios, podría hacer. Luego les dice: "…y en octubre yo les diré quién soy y lo que quiero de ustedes. Después haré un milagro para que todos crean…" "… curaré algunas personas de las que ustedes me pidan, pero otras no las curaré."* >

< *Es decir, aquí vemos que en ningún momento la Virgen dice que intercederá antes Dios o antes Jesús para que cure a algunas personas. Ella aquí establece Su Propia Autoridad, afirmando categórica; "haré un milagro para que todos crean…" "…CURARÉ algunas personas, pero a otras no las curaré", es decir, Ella curará, no que pedirá que otra entidad cure.* >

La *Virgen María* continúa diciéndole a los niños; "**…También quiero que ustedes hagan sacrificios por los pecadores, y digan seguido, especialmente cuando hagan un sacrificio: Oh Jesús, esto es por amor a Ti, por la conversión de los pecadores, y en reparación por las ofensas cometidas contra el Inmaculado Corazón de María.**"

< *Aquí claramente la Virgen María está reclamando por las ofensas cometidas por los hombres en contra de su Divina Majestad al no haberla reconocido como parte del Espíritu Santo de Dios.* >

… Y continúa narrando Lucia: "mientras Nuestra Señora de Fátima decía estas palabras abrió sus manos una vez más, como lo había hecho en los dos meses anteriores. Los rayos de luz parecían penetrar la tierra, y vieron como si fuera un mar de fuego. Sumergidos en este fuego estaban demonios y almas en formas humanas, como tizones transparentes en llamas, todos negros o color bronce quemado, flotando en el fuego, ahora levantadas en el aire por las llamas que salían de ellos mismos juntos a grandes nubes de humo, se caían por todos lados como chispas entre enormes fuegos, sin peso o equilibrio, entre chillidos y gemidos de dolor y desesperación, que nos horrorizaron y nos hicieron temblar de miedo. Los demonios podían distinguirse por su similitud aterradora y repugnante a miedosos animales desconocidos, negros y transparentes como carbones en llamas. Horrorizados y como pidiendo auxilio, miramos hacia Nuestra Señora, quien nos dijo, tan amable y tristemente: "Ustedes han visto el infierno, donde van las almas de los pobres pecadores. Es para salvarlos que Dios quiere establecer en el mundo una devoción a mi Inmaculado Corazón. Si ustedes hacen lo que yo les diga, muchas almas se salvarán, y habrá paz. Esta guerra cesará, pero si los hombres no dejan de ofender a Dios, otra guerra más terrible comenzará muy pronto. Cuando ustedes vean una noche que es iluminada por una luz extraña y desconocida sabrán que esta es la señal que Dios les dará que indicará que está a punto de castigar al mundo con la guerra y el hambre."

La Divina Virgen María de Fátima vino al mundo en estas fechas y en este lugar para pedir que Rusia fuera consagrada a su Inmaculado Corazón, y pedir que los primeros sábados de cada mes se hicieran comuniones en nombre de la santísima Madre para el perdón de todos los pecados del mundo. Si estos deseos se cumplen, Rusia se convertirá y habrá paz, si no, Rusia repartirá sus errores alrededor del mundo, trayendo nuevas guerras y persecuciones a la Iglesia, los justos serán martirizados y el Santo Padre tendrá que sufrir mucho, ciertas naciones serán aniquiladas. Pero al final el Inmaculado Corazón de María triunfará. El Santo Padre consagrará a Rusia a la Virgen María, y esta será convertida y el mundo disfrutará de un período de paz. En Portugal la fe siempre será preservada. Luego, al igual que todas las veces anteriores, Nuestra Señora del Rosario comenzó a ascender hacia el este, hasta que finalmente desapareció en la inmensa oscuridad del firmamento.

La posesión del Secreto probó ser una gran prueba para los tres pequeños niños de 10, 9 y 7 años. Sus familias, sus vecinos, devotos y creyentes de las apariciones, y el clero, trataron sin éxito que fuera revelado. Finalmente, en cuanto el día de la aparición se acercaba hasta el gobierno civil, que era secular y venenosamente anti clerical, alarmado por el número de personas que estaban interesándose en los eventos de

Fátima, atentaron con arrebatárselos y de alguna manera demostrar que todo era un fraude. Con el pretexto de proveerles su propio automóvil, para que los niños pudieran trasladarse seguramente en medio de la multitud que rodeaba sus hogares, el administrador civil o alcalde del distrito en el que estaba ubicado el pueblo de Fátima, llegó a Aljustrel en la mañana del 13 de agosto. En un intento para desconocer la verdad, sin éxito, el 11 de agosto, Arturo Santos, un influyente funcionario, planeó una trampa para que los niños quedaran bajo su custodia para forzarlos a revelar todo. Este se ofreció para llevar a los tres niños y a sus padres a ver al párroco, pero al llegar a la casa parroquial él abandonó a los padres llevándose solo a los niños hasta la cedes del distrito en Vila Nova de Ourem. Aquí él intentó persuadirlos, los amenazó de muerte y los encerró en una celda con diferentes criminales para hacerlos retractarse de su historia, sin ningún resultado. A pesar de sus edades, su fe en la Virgen María y su coraje fueron imperturbables.

En Cova al mediodía del día 13 de agosto, los signos externos característicos de la aparición de la Virgen María se hicieron visibles para la multitud, la mayor multitud hasta el momento. Después que estos signos terminaron la multitud se dispersó, sin saber del juicio de los niños, el cual duró dos días. Así en la fiesta de la Asunción el 15 de agosto, el Administrador condujo a los niños de nuevo al pueblo de Fátima y los dejó frente a la rectoría. Aquí fueron vistos por la gente que salía de Misa tratando de averiguar con el padre de Lucía dónde habían estado los niños. Este fue el único esfuerzo serio por parte de las autoridades por intervenir con Nuestra Señora de Fátima.

Esta situación hizo que los planes de la Virgen se retrasaran un poco. El domingo 19 Lucía, su hermano Juan y Francisco estaban pastoreando sus ovejas en un lugar llamado Valinhos. Era alrededor de las 4 de la tarde, presintiendo que la Virgen estaba a punto de aparecer, Lucía le ofreció unos cuantos centavos a Juan para que fuera a buscar a Jacinta. Mientras ella y Francisco esperaban vieron la luz típica. Tan pronto como Jacinta llegó se apareció la Virgen María. Y les dijo; "vengan otra vez a Cova da Iria el trece del mes que viene, y continúen rezando el Rosario todos los días. El último día yo haré un milagro para que todos crean. Con las ofrendas que las gentes están dejando aquí quiero que hagan dos andas -para cargar estatuas- para la fiesta de Nuestra Señora del Rosario. Quiero que Lucía y Jacinta lleven una de ellas con dos niñas más. Ustedes dos se vestirán de blanco. Y también quiero que Francisco, con tres niños, cargue la otra. Los niños también han de vestir de blanco. Lo que quede de las ofrendas ayudará para la construcción de la capilla que ha de ser construida aquí.

A pesar de las burlas causadas por la prensa secular y atea, miles de personas se reunieron en Cova para la aparición del mes de septiembre. Ahora mientras se rezaba el Rosario la multitud pudo ver a los niños ponerse de pie mirando hacia el este y ver como sus rostros cambiaron asombrosamente. Las demás personas no podían ver a la Virgen, pero esta vez personas que estaban cerca de Lucía la escucharon preguntar: ¿Qué quieres de mí? Pero no alcanzaron a oír la respuesta de la Virgen; "continúen diciendo el Rosario, mis hijos. Díganlo todos los días para que cese la guerra. En octubre vendrá Nuestro Señor, así como Nuestra Señora del Perpetuo Socorro y Nuestra Señora del Monte Carmelo. San José se aparecerá con el Niño Jesús para bendecir al mundo. A Dios le agradan sus sacrificios, pero no quiere que se pongan los cordones de noche para ir a dormir. Sólo pónganselos durante el día.

A Lucía le preocupaba que mucha gente creyera que ella era una impostora y un fraude, por lo cual pedían que fuera colgada o quemada. Por lo cual la Virgen María le prometió que en octubre haría un milagro para que le creyeran.

Durante la noche del 12 al 13 de octubre había llovido toda la noche, empapando el suelo y a los miles de peregrinos que viajaban a Fátima de todas partes para ver la aparición de Nuestra Señora. A pie, por carro y carrozas venían, entrando a la zona de Cova por el camino de Fátima, hasta llegar al sitio de las apariciones en donde se construyó la capillita y la estatua de Nuestra Señora del Rosario de Fátima. En cuanto a los niños, lograron llegar a Cova entre las adulaciones y el escepticismo que las gentes les manifestaba. Cuando llegaron encontraron críticos que cuestionaban su veracidad y la puntualidad de la aparición, quien había prometido llegar al medio día. Ya habían pasado las doce según la hora oficial del país. Sin embargo, cuando el sol había llegado a su apogeo Nuestra Señora se apareció como había dicho. **Y les dijo; "quiero que se construya una capilla aquí en mi honor. Quiero que continúen diciendo el Rosario todos los días. La guerra pronto terminará, y los soldados regresarán a sus hogares."** En esta ocasión la Virgen María le dijo; **"Yo soy la Señora del Rosario". En cuanto a tus peticiones debo decirte que algunas serán concedidas, y otras las debo negar. Las personas deben rehacer sus vidas y pedir perdón**

por sus pecados. No deben de ofender más a Nuestro Señor, ya lo han ofendido demasiado.

Mientras Nuestra Señora del Rosario se eleva hacia el este Ella tornó las palmas de sus manos hacia el cielo oscuro. Aunque la lluvia había cedido, nubes oscuras continuaban al oscurecer el sol, que de repente se escapa entre ellos y se ve como un suave disco de plata. En este momento dos distintas apariciones pudieron ser vistas, el fenómeno del sol presenciado por unos 70,000 espectadores y aquella que fue vista sólo por los niños. Después que la Virgen se desapareció en la inmensa distancia del firmamento, se vio la figura de San José y el Niño Jesús haciendo la señal de la cruz con sus manos. Luego cuando esta aparición terminó vieron a Nuestro Señor Jesucristo y a la Virgen María con el aspecto de la Dolorosa. Nuestro Señor Jesucristo parecía bendecir al mundo al igual que lo hizo San José. Cuando esta aparición desapareció, nuevamente se vio a Nuestra Señora, esta vez con el aspecto de Nuestra Señora del Carmen.

Según continúa narrando Lucía en su diario; "A la una en punto de la tarde, mediodía solar, la lluvia cesó, el cielo de color gris nacarado iluminaba la vasta región árida con una extraña luz. El sol tenía como un velo de gasa transparente que hacía fácil el mirarlo fijamente. El tono grisáceo madre perla que se tornó en una lámina de plata que se rompió cuando las nubes se abrían y el sol de plata envuelto en el mismo velo de luz gris, se vio girar y moverse en el círculo de las nubes abiertas. De todas las bocas se escuchó un gemido y las personas cayeron de rodillas sobre el suelo fangoso".

…. Y continúa diciendo Lucía, "la luz se tornó en un azul precioso, como si atravesara el vitral de una catedral y esparció sus rayos sobre las personas que estaban de rodillas con los brazos extendidos. El azul desapareció lentamente y luego la luz pareció traspasar un cristal amarillo. La luz amarilla tiñó los pañuelos blancos, las faldas oscuras de las mujeres. Lo mismo sucedió en los árboles, las piedras y en la sierra. La gente lloraba y oraba con la cabeza descubierta ante la presencia del milagro que habían esperado. Los segundos parecían como horas, así de intensos eran".

Según la hermana Lucía, esa tarde en Fátima, todos podían mirar con facilidad el sol, que por alguna razón no les cegaba. El Sol parecía titilar primero en un sentido y luego en otro. Sus rayos se esparcían en muchas direcciones y pintaban todas las cosas en diferentes colores, los árboles, la gente el aire y la tierra. Pero lo más extraordinario era que el sol no lastimaba sus ojos. Todo estaba tranquilo y en silencio y todos miraban hacia arriba, hacia el sol, el cual de pronto comenzó a moverse y a danzar en el cielo, hasta que parecía desprenderse de su lugar y caer sobre los presentes. Era algo extraordinariamente asombroso. El sol transformó todo de diferentes colores – amarillo, azul y blanco, entonces se sacudió y tembló, parecía una rueda de fuego que caía sobre la gente. Empezaron a gritar "¡nos va a matar a todos!", otros clamaron a Nuestro Señor para que los salvara. Cuando al fin el sol dejó de saltar y de moverse todos respiraron aliviados. Aun estaban vivos, y el milagro predicho por los niños fue visto por todos.

Era para entonces cerca de las 2 de la tarde. EL sol unos momentos antes había aparecido entre unas nubes, las cuales lo ocultaban y brillaba clara e intensamente, atrayendo todas las miradas. Se veía como un disco con un aro claramente marcado, luminoso y resplandeciente, pero que no hacía daño a los ojos de los presentes. La luz era de un color naranja claro y resplandeciente que tenía algo del brillo de una perla. No se parecía en nada a la luna en una noche clara porque al uno verlo y sentirlo parecía un cuerpo vivo. No era una esfera como la luna ni tenía el mismo color o matiz. Perecía como una rueda de cristal hecha de la madre de todas las perlas. No se podía confundir con el sol visto a través de la neblina ya que no había neblina en ese momento, porque no era opaca, difusa ni cubierta con un velo. Esa tarde, en Fátima daba luz y calor y aparentaba un claro cofre con un arco bien definido.

Esta fue la última aparición en Fátima para Jacinta y Francisco. Pero no para Lucía a la cual Nuestra Señora del Rosario se la apareció una séptima vez en 1920, como lo había prometido la Virgen María el mes de mayo. Esta vez Lucía estaba en oración, antes de dejar Fátima para ir a un internado de niñas. Nuestra Señora del Rosario vino para pedirle que se dedicara enteramente a Dios.

Gracias a las revelaciones de Nuestra Señora de la Santísima Trinidad, San Juan Pablo II hizo intentos reales por reconocer la divinidad de la Virgen Marías, como reina de la corte de las estrellas celestiales. También fue el único papa que trató de reencausar la Iglesia Católica Romana por el sendero del verdadero cristianismo, en su vano esfuerzo reconoció el poder de la parte femenina del Espíritu Santo de Dios y el papel de María Magdalena como Apóstola de los Apóstoles. En el día de la Juventud colocó a "La María del Nuevo Advenimiento" como especial y divinamente asociada con el Día Mundial de la Juventud, el cual Juan Pablo II promovió durante varios años. Esta fue adorada durante toda la noche en la vigilia de oración de los peregrinos que se reunieron con el papa más cristiano de la era de la Iglesia Católica Romana. En esta oportunidad, en sus pláticas, Juan Pablo II por momentos se dirigió personalmente a la Virgen María en el cielo. El papa comenzó su discurso diciendo: "Con mi corazón lleno de alabanza para la Reina del Cielo, el signo de la esperanza y la fuente de consuelo en nuestro peregrinaje de fe a la Jerusalén celestial, les saludo a todos ustedes que están presentes en esta solemne liturgia. En esta liturgia les presento a ustedes, a María, como la mujer vestida del sol, ¡oh mujer vestida del sol, la juventud del mundo te saluda con tanto amor! En María la victoria final de la vida sobre la muerte ya es una realidad."

<*Es evidente, aquí, que el papa Juan Pablo II hace esfuerzo por resaltar algo que la Iglesia Católica Romana ha ocultado durante toda la historia de la humanidad de la era cristiana, la Verdadera Majestad y Divinidad de María en el cielo y la tierra.* >

Durante su vida, el Papa Juan Pablo II manifestó haber rezado todos los días a la Virgen María, a la cual él le atribuyó haber salvado su vida. "En cierto momento del 13 de mayo de 1981, durante una audiencia papal al aire libre en la Plaza de San Pedro, en presencia de 75,000 personas y ante la vista de unos 11 millones de televidentes, el Papa Juan Pablo II divisó a una niña que llevaba un pequeño retrato de Nuestra Señora de Fátima. Justamente al inclinarse para hacerle una ligera caricia a la niña, el asesino Mehmet Ali Agca, descargó dos tiros precisamente en dirección de donde momentos antes le había apuntado a la cabeza del papa. El asesino falló los tiros a la cabeza del papa porque este se inclinó en ese preciso momento a reverenciar la imagen de la Virgen María. A la par que dos peregrinos caían al suelo levemente herido, se oyeron dos disparos más, y esta vez la sangre de Juan Pablo II manchaba su blanca sotana papal, pero sus heridas no fueron mortales. El 13 de mayo de 1991 y otra vez en la misma fecha de 1994, Juan Pablo II fue a Fátima y dio gracias a Nuestra Señora de Fátima por haberle salvado la vida en el atentado de asesinato de 1981. El Papa Juan Pablo II fue el hombre más convencido, después de San Luis, de la divinidad de la Virgen María. Y ningún hombre de la actualidad ha sido más devoto de la parte femenina de Dios. Juan Pablo II dedicó a sí mismo y su pontificado a Nuestra Señora la Virgen María, llevó la M de María en su escudo de armas; su lema personal, bordado en latín en el interior de sus capas, es "totus tuus sum María" que significa "María, soy todo tuyo".

Juan Pablo II estuvo plenamente convencido, como lo están miles de personas más, de que fue María la que puso fin al comunismo en toda Europa. Su fe está firmemente basada en las insignes profecías que María pronunciara en Fátima en 1917. De acuerdo a la Hermana Lucía, que formaba parte del grupo de niños y niñas que afirmó haberla visto. La Virgen predijo el surgimiento del totalitarismo soviético mucho antes de que esto se hiciera realidad. En una visión subsiguiente, ella le indicó al papa y a sus obispos que dedicaran a Rusia a su Inmaculado Corazón para de esa manera poner fin al comunismo. Los esfuerzos del papado por llevar a cabo dicha encomienda fracasaron en los años 1942, 1952, y 1982. Fue Juan Pablo II quien finalmente cumplió la orden en 1984, un año después subió al poder Mijail Gorbachov quien inició la caída del imperio soviético. El mundo reconocerá a su debido tiempo que la derrota del comunismo fue resultado de la intercesión del divino poder de Nuestra Señora de la Santísima Trinidad de Dios.

Las iglesias del mundo se están uniendo sobre puntos comunes de fe, gracias a la intervención bondadosa de la Virgen María. Ella a pesar de saber que los portadores de la fe, no portan una verdadera fe porque en el pasado todo fue distorsionado, se afianza a su bondad infinita con la esperanza en el hombre y la mujer del comienzo de los tiempos. El comienzo de la era cristiano-mariana del Espíritu Santo de Dios que a de marca su inicio en el presente milenio. En donde lo que parecía acercarte a Dios, te alejará y lo que parecía alejarte de Dios, te acercará. Debemos reconocer que fue Luis Grignon de Montfort el gran peregrino que por primera vez dedicó su vida y su ministerio a adorar a la Virgen María. Cuando él era seminarista se ganó un viaje especial a un Santuario de la Virgen María que era concedido a los más sobresalientes de sus clases. Y al llegar al santuario permaneció ocho horas seguidas, inmóvil, rezando de rodillas. Esto demuestra a la misma vez la paciencia y la devoción de Luis, quien fue el primer cristiano en reconocer la divinidad de María. El llegó a conocer a María más que cualquier otro mortal. Para él sus dos mejores amigos eran Jesús y María. Su primera Misa quiso celebrarla en un altar de la Virgen María, y durante muchos años la Catedral de Nuestra Señora de París fue su templo preferido y su refugio.

Al investigar sobre las revelaciones de este libro pude encontrar gran similitud en algunos análisis de los autores de "El Trueno De La Justicia" en cuanto a la visión de que María se refiere a sí misma como la que "aplastaría la serpiente", en el fin de los tiempos, puesto que ella es la "mujer" de Génesis 3:15. Examinando con detenimiento este pasaje bíblico vemos que esta interpretación es correcta. En Génesis 3:15 dice: "Y pondré enemistad entre ti y la mujer, y entre tu simiente y la simiente suya; ésta te herirá en la cabeza, y tú le herirás en el calcañar". Este versículo es una profecía y a la vez una promesa de que algún día vendría una mujer, y "esta te herirá en la cabeza, y tú la herirás en el calcañar". Como se puede interpretar claramente dice que la mujer herirás a la serpiente, de todo modo vencería al enemigo asestándole un golpe fatal en la cabeza al final de los tiempos. Esta profecía fue complementada en Apocalipsis 12 y cumplida con las apariciones de la Virgen de Fátima: "Una gran señal apareció en el cielo: una Mujer, vestida de sol, con la luna bajo sus pies y una corona de doce estrellas sobre su cabeza". Si se analizan los relatos de los niños y las niñas que interactuaron en estas apariciones podemos identificar a Nuestra Señora de Fátima como la representación bíblica de la Mujer vestida del sol.

Pero hay otro punto neurálgico en el cual coinciden algunas revelaciones del antiguo testamento, del nuevo testamento, y de algunos videntes de diferentes épocas, y que fue una orden dada por Nuestra Señora de Fátima a la jerarquía eclesiástica a través de Lucia, en "el tercer secreto" de la Virgen de Fátima dado a los niños, el cual ningún Papa se ha atrevido a cumplir desde 1960. Este punto es el establecimiento, o mas bien la transferencia, de la sede central de la iglesia al santuario de la Virgen de Fátima en Portugal. Esta petición fue especificada, claramente, por Santa Lucia, y por lo cual ella pidió que la carta que contenía "el tercer secreto" fuera abierta solo después de 1960. Nuestra Señora de Fátima pide incluso que la piedra angular que cubre la tumba de Pedro, el primer Santo Padre, sea trasladada al Santuario de la Virgen de Fátima. Este año 2020, se cumplen 100 años de la petición del Espíritu Santo de Dios a través de la Virgen, pero también se cumplen 60 años de que esta petición debio ser ejecutada. Han pasado cinco Papas, y seis con el actual, que han postergado la ejecución de transferir la dirección de la iglesia cristiana hacia la basilica de la Virgen María en Fátima.

4.16.- Nuestra Señora del Carmen; advocación de la Virgen María.

La más antigua devoción a la Virgen María, con más de veinte siglos. El nombre del Carmen viene del Monte Carmelo o "viña de Dios" que está en Tierra Santa. Según el Libro de los Reyes, allí vivió el Profeta Elías con un grupo de jóvenes, dedicados a la oración. Corría el año 300 antes de Cristo, y una gran sequía asolaba la región; el Profeta subió a la montaña para pedir lluvia y divisó una nube de luminosa blancura de la cual brotaba el agua en abundancia; comprendió que la visión era un símbolo de la llegada del Salvador esperado, que nacería de una doncella inmaculada para traer una lluvia de bendiciones. Desde entonces, aquella pequeña comunidad se dedicó a rezar por la que sería Madre del Redentor, comenzando así la devoción a Nuestra Señora del Carmen (o Carmelo).

Muchos acontecimientos han sucedido a través del tiempo en dicha localidad, pero las oraciones continuaron elevándose desde el Carmelo: es que los hombres y las instituciones pasan, pero las obras del Espíritu Santo de Dios permanecen porque participan un poco de su eternidad. Así encarnó la parte femenina del Espíritu Santo de Dios en la Virgen María y llega a ser la Madre del Salvador: según la tradición visitó a los monjes y los estimuló a continuar sus oraciones. Luego vino la pasión y muerte, seguidas de la resurrección y marcha al Cielo de Jesús, y más tarde de su Madre. Luego vendrían las invasiones musulmanas, pero las oraciones del Carmelo no se interrumpen, sino que los monjes deciden trasladarse a Europa. Allí los encontramos en el Siglo XIII: su Superior, San Simón Stock estaba en oración, preocupado por nuevas persecuciones, cuando se le aparece la mismísima Madre de Dios para decirle: "amadísimo hijo, recibe el Escapulario de mi orden para que quien muriese llevándolo piadosamente, no padezca el fuego eterno". El Papa Gregorio XIII declaró verdadera esta aparición después de serios estudios, y basándose en los favores que recibían los que usaban el Escapulario. También fue reconocida esta aparición por el Papa Juan XXII, que recibió una nueva aparición de la Virgen María, en la que prometía sacar del purgatorio el primer sábado después de su muerte a sus devotos.

Esta devoción se difundió por toda Europa y contó con Santos de la talla de San Juan De la Cruz y Santa Teresa; no es extraño que llegara a América y acompañara el despertar a la fe de nuestros indígenas que la veneraron desde mediados del siglo XVI. Ya en el siglo XVIII se encuentra en Mendoza, Argentina, la imagen que hoy es venerada allí, pues don Pedro de Núñez "caballero de gran fortuna y devoción, donó la imagen y todo lo necesario para el culto de la Virgen del Carmen". Primero estuvo en el templo de los Padres Jesuitas estando fundada la Cofradía. En 1776, a raíz de la expulsión de la Orden, la imagen fue trasladada a San Francisco, desde donde presidiría una de las más bellas jornadas de la historia. Llega el año 1814, momento en el que San Martín hizo de los pacíficos habitantes de Cuyo, heroicos soldados forjadores de libertad, pero ellos necesitaron una Madre que los ampare y de sentido a tanto sacrificio. Es conocida la profunda devoción que el Libertador profesó a la Virgen María y que lo hizo nombrarla Generala de su Ejército, superando los respetos humanos de una época en la que el liberalismo había impuesto la idea de que "la religión es asunto privado". Tanta importancia dio al tema, que lo decidió con su Estado Mayor, según dice Espejo en su obra El Paso de los Andes: "la devoción a la Virgen del Carmen estaba muy arraigada en Cuyo y casi todos los soldados llevaban su escapulario, por eso fue ella la que tuvo preferencia" dice, y más adelante describe la brillante ceremonia (5 de enero de 1817) durante la cual San Martín le entrega su bastón de mando, la nombra Generala, y hace bendecir también la Bandera de los Andes, "saludada por dianas y la banda con cajas y clarines, mientras rompía una salva de veintiún cañonazos, ante el ejército de gran gala y todo el pueblo de Mendoza". Más tarde, después de sus triunfos, entregará definitivamente su bastón, esta vez en el silencio que acompaña a todo lo grande y dejando aquella conocida carta: "la protección que ha prestado al Ejército de los Andes su Patrona y Generala la Virgen del Carmen son demasiado visibles..." Ambas reliquias, el bastón y la carta, se conservan hoy en el Camarín de la Virgen María, como mudos testigos de la parte que Ella tuvo en la grandeza de alma del Libertador. Siendo Generala del Ejército Argentino, junto a la banda, acompaña a la imagen nuestra bandera, así como también las banderas de Perú y Chile, al ser esta advocación Patrona de los 2 países vecinos.

Por inquietud de Fray Leonardo Maldonado, el Papa Pío X, decretó: "que la Sagrada Imagen de la Virgen María bajo el título del Carmen que se venera en la Iglesia de San Francisco en Mendoza, sea con voto solemne coronada con corona de oro". Apoyó su resolución en la "Suficiente constancia que existe de la popular veneración de la imagen, de su fama y celebridad como también de las gracias admirables y celestiales, dones concedidos copiosamente por ella". La corona, ofrenda de sus devotos, le fue impuesta en memorable ceremonia el 8 de septiembre de 1911 y es un recuerdo de tal solemnidad que se decretó tal día como Fiesta Patronal de la Provincia y en ese día, desde 1950 es también honrada muy especialmente la Santísima Virgen del Carmen de Cuyo, en las escuelas de Mendoza, como Patrona de la Escuela Primaria, instituida en tal carácter por decisión superior; y de la educación en sus tres niveles por decreto del 30-08-80. En 1982 fue declarada Patrona de la 8º Brigada de Montaña. (La Virgen del Carmen, usuarios.advance.com)

En las palabras de Benedicto XVI, (15, VII, 06): "El Carmelo, alto promontorio que se yergue en la costa oriental del Mar Mediterráneo, a la altura de Galilea, tiene en sus faldas numerosas grutas naturales, predilectas de los eremitas. El más célebre de estos hombres de Dios fue el gran profeta Elías, quien en el siglo IX antes de Cristo defendió valientemente de la contaminación de los cultos idolátricos la pureza de la fe en el Dios único y verdadero. Inspirándose en la figura de Elías, surgió la Orden contemplativa de los "Carmelitas", familia religiosa que cuenta entre sus miembros con grandes santos, como Juan de la Cruz, Teresa de Ávila, Teresa del Niño Jesús y Teresa Benedicta de la Cruz (en el siglo, Edith Stein). Los Carmelitas han difundido en el pueblo cristiano la devoción a la Santísima Virgen del Monte Carmelo, señalándola como modelo de oración, de contemplación y de dedicación a Dios. María, en efecto, antes y de modo insuperable, creyó y experimentó que Jesús, Verbo encarnado, es el culmen, la cumbre del encuentro del hombre con Dios. Acogiendo plenamente la Palabra, "llegó felizmente a la santa montaña" (Oración de la colecta de la Memoria), y vive para siempre, en alma y cuerpo, con el Señor. A la Reina del Monte Carmelo deseo hoy confiar todas las comunidades de vida contemplativa esparcidas por el mundo, de manera especial las de la Orden Carmelitana, entre las que recuerdo el monasterio de Quart, no muy lejano de aquí (Valle de Aosta). Que María ayude a cada cristiano a encontrar a Dios en el silencio de la oración.

El Escapulario era usado como símbolo de unión con una orden religiosa y su espiritualidad desde antes del siglo X, aun viviendo la vida corriente en medio del mundo. Consistían en una franja de tela igual al hábito de los religiosos, que se introducía por la cabeza cayendo hacia adelante y detrás de los hombros, de ahí su nombre que viene del Latín "scapulae" que significa "hombros". Originalmente era un vestido superpuesto que cae de los hombros y lo llevaban los monjes durante su trabajo. Con el tiempo redujeron su tamaño hasta el actual y se le dio el sentido de ser la cruz de cada día que, como discípulos de Cristo llevamos sobre nuestros hombros. Para los Carmelitas particularmente, pasó a expresar la dedicación especial a la Virgen Santísima y el deseo de imitar su vida de entrega a Cristo y a los demás. Pero lo más importante es que no se trata de un amuleto o de algo con poderes mágicos. Es un signo sacramental que hace presente el amor de la Virgen hacia quienes son buenos hijos de Dios, viven en su amistad, o sea gracia y cumplen su ley. Hoy se sustituye para el uso diario por la medalla correspondiente, ambos reciben las mismas indulgencias y pueden ser usados por quienes no pertenecen a la Cofradía.

El Escapulario es un signo externo, sacramental, que presupone una vida de gracia. La preparación conveniente, consiste en: 1- Ser muy devotos de la Santísima Virgen María, en especial bajo la advocación del Carmen de Cuyo. 2 - Participar en todas las ceremonias que se realizan en su honor. 3 - Saber que es un compromiso de por vida, una Alianza entre Nuestra Señora y el que lo recibe. 4 - Tener una conducta de acuerdo a las normas y leyes de la Iglesia. 5 - Unas de las condiciones primordiales impuestas por la Santísima Virgen del Carmen, es el uso permanente de este escapulario, o la medalla que lo reemplazó. Ésta debe ser con la imagen de la Virgen y el Sagrado Corazón en el reverso. 6 - Todas las personas que conforman la Hermandad del Carmelo, prometen rezar el Santo Rosario diariamente o al menos 3 Avemarías en honor a su Patrona.

El escapulario de la Santísima Virgen María se impone todo los 1° miércoles de mes, el 16 de julio y durante la novena, a las personas que lo deseen recibir. La promesa de la Virgen del Carmen a San Simón Stock fue que quien muriese con el escapulario no padecerá del fuego eterno. En otra aparición al Papa Juan XXII, prometió sacar del purgatorio a las almas que muriesen piadosamente, con el escapulario, en el sábado siguiente a su muerte.

"La devoción del escapulario del Carmen ha hecho descender sobre el mundo una copiosa lluvia de gracias espirituales y temporales" (Pío XII, 6-VIII-1950).

El escapulario carmelita es un sacramental, es decir un objeto religioso que la Iglesia ha aprobado como signo que nos ayuda a vivir santamente y a aumentar nuestra devoción. Los sacramentales deben mover nuestros corazones a renunciar a todo pecado, incluso al venial.

El escapulario, al ser un sacramental, no nos comunica gracias como hacen los sacramentos, sino que nos disponen al amor a Dios y a la verdadera contrición del pecado si los recibimos con devoción.

Los seres humanos nos comunicamos por símbolos. Así como tenemos banderas, escudos y también uniformes que nos identifican. Las comunidades religiosas llevan su hábito como signo de su consagración a Dios.

Los laicos no pueden llevar hábito, pero los que desean asociarse a los religiosos en su búsqueda de la santidad pueden usar el escapulario. La Virgen dio a los Carmelitas el escapulario como un hábito miniatura que todos los devotos pueden llevar para significar su consagración a ella. Consiste en un cordón que se lleva al cuello con dos piezas pequeñas de tela color café, una sobre el pecho y la otra sobre la espalda. Se usa bajo la ropa, junto con el rosario y la medalla milagrosa, el escapulario es uno de los más importantes sacramentales marianos.

San Alfonso Ligorio, doctor de la Iglesia, manifiesta: "Así como los hombres se enorgullecen de que otros usen su uniforme, así Nuestra Señora Madre María está satisfecha cuando sus servidores usan su escapulario como prueba de que se han dedicado a su servicio, y son miembros de la familia de la Madre de Dios."

En el año 1246 nombraron a San Simón Stock general de la Orden Carmelita. Este comprendió que, sin una intervención de la Virgen María, a la orden le quedaba poco tiempo. Simón recurrió a María poniendo la orden bajo su amparo, ya que ellos le pertenecían. En su oración la llamó "La flor del Carmelo" y la "Estrella del Mar" y le suplicó la protección para toda la comunidad. En respuesta a esta ferviente oración, el 16 de julio de 1251 se le apareció la Virgen a San Simón Stock y le dio el escapulario para la orden con la siguiente promesa:

> "Este debe ser un signo y privilegio para ti y para todos los Carmelitas: quien muera usando el escapulario no sufrirá el fuego eterno".

Aunque el escapulario fue dado a los Carmelitas, muchos laicos con el tiempo fueron sintiendo el llamado de vivir una vida más comprometida con la espiritualidad carmelita y así se comenzó la cofradía del escapulario, donde se agregaban muchos laicos por medio de la devoción a la Virgen María y al uso del escapulario. La Iglesia ha extendido el privilegio del escapulario a los laicos.

La Santísima Virgen María se apareció al Papa Juan XXII en el siglo XIV y le prometió para quienes cumplieran los requisitos de esta devoción que "como Madre de Misericordia con mis ruegos, oraciones, méritos y protección especial, les ayudaré para que, libres cuanto antes de sus penas, (...) sean trasladadas sus almas a la bienaventuranza".

Desde entonces, muchos papas, santos y teólogos católicos han explicado que, según esta promesa, quien tenga la devoción al escapulario y lo use, recibirá de María Santísima a la hora de la muerte, la gracia de la perseverancia en el estado de gracia (sin pecado mortal) o la gracia de la contrición (arrepentimiento). Por parte del devoto, el escapulario es una señal de su compromiso a vivir la vida cristiana siguiendo el ejemplo perfecto de la Virgen Santísima.

El escapulario tiene 3 significados:

1- El amor y la protección maternal de María: El signo es una tela o manto pequeño. Vemos como María cuando nace Jesús lo envuelve en un manto. La Madre siempre trata de cobijar a sus hijos. Envolver en su manto es una señal muy maternal de protección y cuidado. Señal de que nos envuelve en su amor maternal. Nos hace suyos. Nos cubre de la ignominia de nuestra desnudes espiritual.

2- Pertenencia a María: Llevamos una marca que nos distingue como sus hijos escogidos. El escapulario se convierte en el símbolo de nuestra consagración a María. Consagración significa pertenecer a María, es decir reconocer su misión maternal sobre nosotros y entregarnos a ella para dejarnos guiar, enseñar, moldear por Ella y en su corazón. Así podremos ser usados por Ella para la extensión del Reino de su Hijo.

3- El suave yugo de Cristo: "Carguen sobre ustedes mi yugo y aprendan de mí, porque soy paciente y humilde de corazón, y así encontrarán alivio. Porque mi yugo es suave y mi carga liviana". (Mateo 11:29-30)

En 1950 Papa Pío XII escribió acerca del escapulario: "que sea tu signo de consagración al Inmaculado Corazón de María, lo cual estamos particularmente necesitando en estos tiempos tan peligrosos". En estas palabras del Papa vemos una vez más devoción a la Virgen del Carmen es devoción a la Inmaculada. Quien lleve el escapulario debe estar consciente de su consagración a Dios y a la Virgen y ser consecuente en sus pensamientos, palabras y obras.

<El escapulario simboliza ese yugo que Jesús nos invita a cargar pero que María nos ayuda a llevar. Quién lleva el escapulario debe identificarse como católico sin temor a los rechazos y dificultades que ese yugo le traiga.>

El escapulario es un signo de nuestra identidad cristiano - mariana, vinculados de íntimamente a la Virgen María con el propósito de vivir plenamente según nuestro bautismo. Representa nuestra decisión de seguir a Jesús por María en el espíritu de los religiosos, pero adaptado a la propia vocación. Esto requiere que seamos humildes, castos y obedientes por amor a Dios.

Al usar el escapulario constantemente hacemos silenciosa petición de asistencia continua a la Santísima Madre. La Virgen María nos enseña e intercede para que recibamos las gracias para vivir como ella, abiertos de corazón al Señor, escuchando Su Palabra, orando, descubriendo a Dios en la vida diaria, y cercano a las necesidades de nuestros hermanos. El escapulario además es un recuerdo de que nuestra meta es el cielo y todo lo de este mundo está pasando.

En momentos de tentación, tomamos el escapulario en nuestras manos e invocamos la asistencia de la Madre, resueltos a ser fieles al Señor. Ella nos dirige hacia el Sagrado Corazón de su Hijo Divino y el demonio es forzado a retroceder vencido.

Imposición del Escapulario:

- La imposición se hace preferentemente en comunidad.
- Es necesario que en la celebración quede bien expresado el sentido espiritual de las gracias unidas al Escapulario de la Virgen del Carmen y los compromisos asumidos con este signo de devoción a la Santísima Virgen.
- El primer escapulario debe ser bendecido por un sacerdote e impuesto por él mientras dice la oración:

"Recibe este escapulario bendito y pide a la Virgen Santísima que, por sus méritos, lo lleves sin ninguna mancha de pecado y que te proteja de todo mal y te lleve a la vida eterna".

Una vez bendecido el primer escapulario, el devoto no necesita pedir la bendición para escapularios posteriores.

Los escapularios gastados, si han sido bendecidos no se deben echar a la basura. Se pueden quemar o enterrar como signo de respeto.

Por su parte, la medalla-escapulario tiene en una cara la imagen del Sagrado Corazón de Jesús y la imagen de la Bienaventurada Virgen María en su reverso. En 1910, el Papa Pío X declaró que, una persona válidamente investida en su escapulario de tela podía llevar la medalla-escapulario en su lugar, provisto que tuviera razones legítimas para sustituir su escapulario de tela por la medalla- escapulario. Esta concesión fue hecha a petición de los misioneros en los países del trópico, donde los escapularios de tela se deterioran pronto. Ahora bien, el Papa Pío X y su sucesor, el Papa Benedicto XV, expresaron su profundo deseo de que las personas continuaran llevando el escapulario de tela cuando fuera posible, y que no sustituyeran el escapulario de tela por la medalla escapulario sin que medie primero razón suficiente. La vanidad o el miedo a profesar su fe en público no pueden ser razones que satisfagan a Nuestra Señora. Estas personas corren el riesgo de no recibir la promesa del escapulario del Carmen. ("Otorga mucha importancia a tu escapulario" del Apostolado Mundial de Fátima, Washington, NJ 07882-0976 USA).

Los Papas y Santos han alertado muchas veces acerca de no abusar de la promesa de nuestra madre como si nos pudiéramos salvar llevando el escapulario sin conversión. El Papa Pío XI nos advierte: "aunque es cierto que la Virgen María ama de manera especial a quienes son devotos de ella, aquellos que desean tenerla como auxilio a la hora de la muerte, deben en vida ganarse dicho privilegio con una vida de rechazo al pecado y viviendo para darle honor"

Vivir en pecado y usar el escapulario como ancla de salvación es cometer pecado de presunción ya que la fe y la fidelidad a los mandamientos es necesaria para todos los que buscan el amor y la protección de Nuestra Señora.

San Claude de la Colombiere advierte: "Tu preguntas: ¿y si yo quisiera morir con mis pecados?, yo te respondo, entonces morirás en pecado, pero no morirás con tu escapulario"

El Privilegio Sabatino es una promesa de la Virgen que consiste en la liberación del purgatorio, el primer sábado (día que la Iglesia ha dedicado a la Virgen), después de la muerte por medio de una intercesión especial de la Virgen. Se originó en una bula o edicto que fue proclamado por el Papa Juan XXII en marzo 3, 1322 como resultado de una aparición que tuvo de la Virgen en la que prometió para aquellos que cumplieran los requisitos de esta devoción que "como Madre de Misericordia, con mis ruegos, oraciones, méritos y protección especial, les ayudaré para que, libres cuanto antes de sus penas, sean trasladadas sus almas a la bienaventuranza".

Condiciones para que aplique este privilegio

1) Usar el escapulario con fidelidad.
2) Observar castidad de acuerdo al estado de vida.
3) Rezo del oficio de la Virgen (oraciones y lecturas en honor a la Virgen) o rezar diariamente 5 décadas del rosario.

El Papa Pablo V confirmó en una proclamación oficial que se podía enseñar acerca del privilegio sabatino a todos los creyentes.

Es evidente que la Virgen María quiere revelarnos de manera especial el escapulario. Reporta Lucia (vidente de la Virgen de Fátima, luego convertida en la Hermana María del Inmaculado Corazón), que en la última aparición (octubre, 1917, día del milagro del sol), la Virgen María vino vestida con el hábito carmelita y con el escapulario en la mano y recordó que sus verdaderos hijos lo llevaran con reverencia. También pidió que los que se consagraran a ella lo usaran como signo de dicha consagración.

El Papa Pío XII habló frecuentemente del Escapulario. En 1951, aniversario 700 de la aparición de Nuestra Señora a San Simón Stock, el Papa ante una numerosa audiencia en Roma exhortó a que se usara el Escapulario como "Signo de Consagración al Inmaculado Corazón de María" (tal como pidió la Virgen en Fátima). El Escapulario también representa el dulce yugo de Jesús que María nos ayuda a sobrellevar. Y finalmente, el Papa continuó, El Escapulario nos marca como hijos escogidos de María y se convierte para nosotros (como lo llaman los alemanes) en un "Vestido de Gracia".

El mismo día que San Simón Stock recibió de María el Escapulario y la promesa, el fue llamado a asistir a un moribundo que estaba desesperado. Cuando llegó puso el Escapulario sobre el hombre, pidiéndole a la Virgen María que mantuviera la promesa que le acababa de hacer. Inmediatamente el hombre se arrepintió, se confesó y murió en gracia de Dios".

El Beato Papa Gregorio X fue enterrado con su escapulario solo 25 años después de la Visión del Escapulario. 600 años más tarde cuando abrieron su tumba, su escapulario estaba intacto.

San Alfonso Ligorio y San Juan Bosco tenían una especial devoción a la Virgen del Carmen y usaban el Escapulario. Cuando murió San Alfonso Ligorio le enterraron con sus vestiduras sacerdotales y con su Escapulario. Muchos años después cuando abrieron su tumba encontraron que su cuerpo y todas las vestimentas estaban hechas polvo, sin embargo, su Escapulario estaba intacto. El Escapulario de San Alfonso está en exhibición en su Monasterio en Roma.

San Alfonso Ligorio nos dice: "Herejes modernos se burlan del uso del Escapulario. Lo desacreditan como una insignificancia vana y absurda."

San Pedro Claver, se hizo esclavo de los esclavos por amor. Cada mes llegaba a Cartagena, Colombia un barco con esclavos. San Pedro se esforzaba por la salvación de cada uno. Organizaba catequistas, los preparaba para el bautismo y los investía con el Escapulario. Algunos clérigos acusaron al santo de celo indiscreto. Sin embargo, él continuó su obra hasta tener más de 300,000 conversos.

San Claudio de Colombiere (director espiritual de Santa Margarita María) manifestó: "Yo quería saber si María en realidad se había interesado en mí, y en el Escapulario Ella me ha dado la seguridad más palpable. Sólo necesito abrir mis ojos, Ella ha otorgado su protección a este Escapulario: "Quien muera vestido en él no sufrirá el fuego eterno". Y agregó; "Debido a que todas las formas de amar a la Santísima Virgen y las diversas maneras de expresar ese amor no pueden ser igualmente agradables a ella y por consiguiente no nos ayudan en el mismo grado para alcanzar el cielo, lo digo sin vacilar ni un momento, ¡El Escapulario Carmelita es su predilecto!", y continúa diciendo; "Ninguna devoción ha sido confirmada con mayor número de milagros auténticos que el Escapulario Carmelita".

"Un sacerdote de Chicago fue llamado para ir a asistir a un moribundo que había estado lejos de su fe y de los sacramentos por muchos años. El moribundo no quiso recibirlo, ni hablar con él. Pero el sacerdote insistió y le enseñó el Escapulario que llevaba. Le preguntó si le permitiría ponérselo. El hombre aceptó con tal que el sacerdote lo dejara en paz. Una hora más tarde el moribundo mandó a llamar al sacerdote pues deseaba confesarse y morir en gracia y amistad con Dios"

El demonio odia el Escapulario. Un día al Venerable Francisco Yepes se le cayó el Escapulario. Mientras se lo ponía, el demonio aulló: "¡Quítate el hábito que nos arrebata tantas almas!".

Un misionero Carmelita de Tierra Santa fue llamado a suministrar la unción de los enfermos en el año 1944. Notó que mientras caminaba, sus pies se hundían cada vez más en el fango hasta que, tratando de encontrar tierra firme, se deslizó en un pozo de fango en el que se hundía hacia la muerte. Pensó en la Virgen y besó su hábito el cual era Escapulario. Miró entonces hacía la Montaña del Carmelo gritando: "¡Santa Madre del Carmelo! ¡Ayúdame! ¡Sálvame!". Un momento más tarde se encontró en terreno sólido. Atestiguó más tarde: "Sé que fui salvado por la Santísima Virgen por medio de su Escapulario Carmelita. Mis zapatos desaparecieron en el lodo y yo estaba cubierto de él, pero caminé las dos millas que faltaban, alabando a María".

En el verano de 1845 el barco inglés, "Rey del Océano" se hallaba en medio de un feroz huracán. Las olas lo azotaban sin piedad y el fin parecía cercano. Un ministro protestante llamado Fisher en compañía de su esposa e hijos y otros pasajeros fueron a la cubierta para suplicar misericordia y perdón. Entre la tripulación se encontraba el irlandés John McAuliffe. Al mirar la gravedad de la situación, el joven abrió su camisa, se quitó el Escapulario y, haciendo con él la Señal de la Cruz sobre las furiosas olas, lo lanzó al océano. En ese preciso momento el viento se calmó. Solamente una ola más llegó a la cubierta, trayendo con ella el Escapulario que quedó depositado a los pies del muchacho.

Durante lo acontecido el ministro había estado observando cuidadosamente las acciones de McAuliffe y fue testigo del milagro. Al interrogar al joven se informaron acerca de la Santísima Virgen y su Escapulario. El Señor Fisher y su familia resolvieron ingresar en la Iglesia Católica lo más pronto posible y así disfrutar la gran protección del Escapulario de Nuestra Señora de la Santísima Trinidad de Dios.

En mayo de 1957, un sacerdote Carmelita en Alemania publicó una historia extraordinaria de cómo el Escapulario había librado un hogar del fuego. Una hilera completa de casas se había incendiado en Westboden, Alemania. Los piadosos residentes de una casa de dos familias, al ver el fuego, inmediatamente colgaron un Escapulario a la puerta de la entrada principal. Centellas volaron sobre ella y alrededor de ella, pero la casa permaneció intacta. En 5 horas, 22 hogares habían sido reducidos a cenizas. La única construcción que permaneció intacta, en medio de la destrucción, fue aquella que tenía el Escapulario adherido a su puerta. Los cientos de personas que vinieron a ver el lugar que el Escapulario había salvado son testigos oculares del poder del Escapulario y de la intercesión de Nuestra Señora de la Santísima Trinidad del Espíritu Santo.

En octubre de 1952, un oficial de la Fuerza Aérea en Texas escribió lo siguiente: "Seis meses después de comenzar a usar el Escapulario, experimenté un notable cambio en mi vida. Casi inmediatamente comencé a asistir a Misa todos los días. Durante la cuaresma viví fervorosamente como nunca lo había hecho. Fui iniciado en la práctica de la meditación y me encontré realizando débiles intentos en al camino de la perfección. He estado tratando de vivir con Dios y doy el crédito al Escapulario de María".

Recordemos que el escapulario es un signo poderoso del amor y protección maternal de María y de su llamada a una vida de santidad y sin pecado. Usar el escapulario es una respuesta de amor a la Madre que vino a darnos un regalo de su misericordia. Debemos usarlo como recordatorio que le pertenecemos a ella, que deseamos imitarla y vivir en gracia bajo su manto protector. Se puede ganar indulgencia plenaria:

- el día en que se recibe el escapulario
- el 16 de mayo, en la Festividad de San Simón Stock.
- el 16 de julio, en la Solemnidad de la Santísima Virgen del Carmen,
- el 20 de julio, en la Festividad del Profeta San Elías.
- el 1 de octubre, en la Festividad de Santa Teresita del Niño Jesús.
- el 15 de octubre, en la Festividad de Santa Teresa de Jesús.
- el 14 de noviembre, en la Festividad de todos los Santos de la Orden.
- el 14 de diciembre, en la Festividad de San Juan De La Cruz.

5.0.- La Virgen María en el Espíritu Santo en éste nuevo milenio

El Padre Nicolás Schwizer sostiene que hoy en día, más que nunca, nuestro camino como cristianos cuesta mucho. Infidelidad, duda, desorientación e inseguridad, aun en medio de la propia Iglesia, dificultan nuestra vida cristiana. Según Él, precisamos más claridad y seguridad, buscamos una luz para poder orientarnos en la oscuridad de nuestro tiempo. Esta luz para nosotros es la *Virgen María*. Ella es el modelo vital y la enseñanza intuitiva para la vida de todos los seres humanos y muy especialmente para la vida de los creyentes en la Santísima Trinidad del Espíritu Santo.

La *Virgen María* es nuestro modelo vital, es la luz que nos guía a través de la tiniebla que arropa el mundo hoy dia. Ella es la única vacuna que puede salvar a la humanidad de esta terrible pandemia que afecta al mundo. El Padre Nicolás Schwizer la destaca como reverso de Eva, como nueva Eva. Sabemos que Eva es compañera y ayudante de Adán en el pecado original, en la ruina del género humano. También *María* no es mero instrumento pasivo, sino compañera y ayudante del Espíritu Santo y Jesucristo para la salvación del mundo. La desobediencia y la incredulidad de Eva son compensadas por la obediencia y la fe de *María*. Eva trajo la muerte, *María* trae la vida. Así la Virgen inmaculada, la nueva Eva se nos revela como el Ser Supremo. En este mundo del mal, el Espíritu Santo conserva la idea original de pureza y santidad del paraíso en la persona de la *Virgen María*. Concebida por el Propio Espíritu Santo, su Propio Ser, sin pecado, para junto al Padre y el Hijo consustancialse en el seno de la Santísima Trinidad de Dios.

La Santísima *Virgen María* representa la perfección de la obra del *Espíritu Santo de Dios* y es en Ella en donde se conjuga la esencia de la redención de Cristo en toda su plenitud. La Biblia no expresa en su contenido la verdadera grandeza de la divina personalidad de *María* como la parte femenina de la Santísima Trinidad del *Espíritu Santo de Dios*. Ella, aunque encarnó en una figura humana siempre ha sido parte del Ser Supremo al igual que su Hijo, Jesucristo y el Propio *Espíritu Santo de Dios*.

Por eso, el ángel Gabriel declaró que Ella está "llena de gracia". Aunque en verdad, toda su persona está a plenitud llena de todos los dones del *Espíritu Santo de Dios*, ya que toda perfección y redención proviene de Su Propio Ser. Desde su encarnación Ella vino con la armonía perfecta entre su cuerpo, alma y espíritu santo. Cuando miramos la imagen de la *Virgen María* se despiertan en nosotros grandes sentimientos de deseos y esperanzas.

El *Espíritu Santo de Dios* nos eligió antes de la creación del mundo, para tener la oportunidad de ser parte de Él. Todos los seres humanos fuimos creados a imagen y semejante del *Espíritu Santo de Dios* y todos (as) tenemos la oportunidad de convertirnos en hombres y mujeres nuevos (as). El *Espíritu Santo de Dios* nos infundió a través del bautismo la vida divina de *María* y de Cristo y todos debemos aspirar a mantener este don durante toda nuestra vida.

A través del bautismo en el *Espíritu Santo de Dios* todos somos llamados, a convertirnos en seres humanos nuevos, a imagen de Cristo y de la *Virgen María*. Todos debemos imitar a la *María* y a *Jesús*, y procurar cumplir la misión de "Hágase en mí tu voluntad" para lograr alcanzar la sintonía con el *Espíritu Santo de Dios*. Y así ver nacer y crecer en nosotros el hombre nuevo, que tanto admiramos en *Jesús* y la mujer nueva que admiramos en *María*.

La Santísima *Virgen María* es modelo de renovación y esperanza, pero también, Madre y Educadora de hombres y mujeres nuevos (as). Su seno, en el que Dios se formó, es el mejor molde para forjar seres humanos a imagen del *Espíritu Santo de Dios*. Los padres de la Iglesia la llamaron no sólo creatura del paraíso, sino también la puerta del paraíso. Puerta al paraíso porque nos atrae y educa hacia ese ideal, y nos introduce en el paraíso. (Padre Nicolás Schwizer, catholic.net)

5.1.- La Virgen María; un camino seguro para la salvación.

No debemos dejarnos confundir, no hay ningún riesgo en el culto mariano: Muchos argumentan erróneamente que *María* aparte de Cristo, que le hace "competencia", y que se coloca como "pantalla" entre Dios y nosotros. En el origen de ese temor suelen encontrarse experiencias negativas, provocadas por prácticas desviadas del culto Mariana, o enfoques falsos sobre la persona de *María*. Pero tales temores no corresponden a la realidad querida por el *Espíritu Santo* y así es proclamada por la *Iglesia Cristiano Mariana del Espíritu Santo* en su vida y en su doctrina.

La Santísima Trinidad del *Espíritu Santo* es el verdadero centro de nuestra fe, es la razón verdadera de nuestra confianza, es el último fin de nuestro amor. Jesucristo y la *Virgen María* son los medios dispuestos por el *Espíritu Santo* para ayudar al ser humano a lograr una sintonía armoniosa con Él. En el Dios trino, *Jesús y María,* ambos forman parte de los misterios centrales de la fe cristiano - mariana, *Jesús* representa la parte masculina del Ser y *María* la parte femenina, y ambos fueron formados en un único "Ente Divino" llamado *Espíritu Santo.*

"Haced lo que él os diga" son las últimas palabras de la *Virgen María* conservadas en el Evangelio mutilado de la Biblia. Y más que a los sirvientes de la boda, son palabras dirigidas a los hombres y las mujeres de todos los tiempos. Es lamentable que muchas otras palabras expresadas por Ella en momentos trascendentales del nacimiento de nuestra era, no fueran recogidas en estos importantes relatos para conocer más profundamente todo el anhelo, la vivencia y la misión de *María* en su ministerio. Hoy en día, se hace difícil reconocer que *María* es el verdadero centro de la fe cristiana. Ella por su papel protagónico en la historia general de la salvación y en la creación es por obligación el centro de enfoque de los hombres y las mujeres de los nuevos tiempos.

Juan Pablo II dijo: "*María* estuvo de verdad unida a *Jesús*. No se han conservado en el Evangelio muchas palabras suyas; pero las que han quedado nos llevan de nuevo a su Hijo y a su palabra. En Caná de Galilea se dirigió a los sirvientes con estas palabras: "Hagan lo que él os diga.""

En la actualidad la *Virgen María* sigue repitiendo esas mismas palabras "Hagan lo que él os diga" que viene a ser igual que "hagan lo que Yo os diga" o "hagan lo que el Espíritu Santo diga."

La *Virgen María* es para nosotros el camino normal hacia la salvación a través de la Santísima Trinidad. Ya que, si el camino por el cual *Jesús* llegó al ser humano es *María*, entonces, precisamente *María* es el camino por el que nosotros podremos llegar a Cristo. Cuando le damos a *María* un lugar privilegiado en nuestros corazones, y nos confiamos a su educación, entonces estamos en el camino hacia su Hijo, que es su propio ser. Entonces Ella nos conduce hacia Cristo en el *Espíritu Santo de Dios*. Es consciente de esta verdad que el Papa Pío X dijo: "*María* no sólo es el camino normal hacia Cristo sino también el camino más fácil, más corto y más seguro hacia Cristo", y continúa diciendo sobre Ella: "La Divina *Virgen María* nos regala un conocimiento vital de Cristo."

La devoción a La *Virgen María* es uno de los grandes dones que el *Espíritu Santo* le ha dado al pueblo: lo demuestra el gran entusiasmo con el cual se ha recibido la imagen de la Virgen en todos los lugares. Y cuanto más amamos a la Virgen, más amamos a Cristo Jesús. Ya que Ellos son en sí, un solo Ser en el Espíritu Santo.

La divinidad de *María*, representa la divinidad femenina y maternal de la Santísima Trinidad del *Espíritu Santo*. Ella nos regala familiaridad con el mundo sobrenatural y hace de la fe cristiano mariana una similitud entre la vida en la Iglesia y en el hogar, de hombres y mujeres formando familias como madres, padres, hijos, hijas, hermanos y hermanas. El poder de *María* explica la fuerza y el arraigo de la devoción mariana en el pueblo a pesar de que las intensiones de los hombres del cristianismo han sido tenerla relegada a un simple papel de sierva, a pesar de ser Ella la verdadera Reina del Universo.

Estudiando un poco sobre los principales Santos de todos los tiempos podemos darnos cuenta que cada uno de ellos y cada una de ellas, prueban con su vida la verdad y la importancia de *María* en el camino del cristianismo. Han sido casi sin excepción hombres y mujeres con una gran *devoción mariana*. Muchos de ellos hasta se han consagrado a la Virgen y Ella, sin falta, los ha conducido a la Santísima Trinidad del *Espíritu Santo*. Esto demuestra que todo el amor que le regalamos a la Divina *Virgen María*, Ella lo lleva hacia las entrañas en donde nace el Altísimo. Es así como nuestro amor encuentra, por medio de *María*, el camino más fácil, más corto, más seguro y más fecundo hacia *el Espíritu Santo*.

La vida de la *Virgen María*, por su propio origen, está complementada en la composición del *Espíritu Santo* con la vida de Nuestro Señor Jesucristo. La *Virgen María* es divina, santa y llena de toda la Gracia de su Espíritu Creador. Ella es el principio de su propio infinito, Ella representa el primer momento de la existencia del Ser. Ella es llamada sagrario, tabernáculo, santuario del Espíritu Santo. *María* cohabita en el *Espíritu Santo* de un modo del todo singular y superior. El Espíritu de santidad actúa en la *Virgen María* y a través de Ella.

El Espíritu Santo siempre ha actuado junto con la Virgen. A través de la unión de Ellos nació Jesucristo, "el Hijo de Dios". El *Espíritu Santo* y *María* son el Padre y la Madre de *Jesucristo,* y los tres forman en Sí un solo Ser Divino. La Parte Femenina del *Espíritu Santo* encarnó en la figura humana de la Santísima *Virgen María* de manera totalmente voluntaria y libre, para entregarse al *Espíritu Santo,* y a través de esta relación dar ejemplo de unión y sacrificio familiar como la Primera Familia del Universo.

El *Espíritu Santo* quiso dar ejemplo de esposa, de madre y de hermana a través de su encarnación en la *Virgen María*, y dar ejemplo de padre, de hijo y de hermano en la persona de *Jesucristo.* Cada uno de Ellos tenía que recorrer su propio camino para la creación de la fe. Y cuando llegó la gran Hora del sacrificio, sobre el monte Calvario, fueron controlados en Ella los deseos y necesidades naturales de madre. En ese momento, todo quedó sujeto a la voluntad del *Espíritu Santo*. Cuán difícil fue para Ella soportar en su presencia la crucifixión de su Hijo y aunque ambos tenían el poder para cambiar la situación fue también su propia y voluntaria decisión que todos estos hechos sucedieran de la manera en que sucedieron. Ambos estaban seguros de que todo debía consumarse de esa manera para Ellos poder adentrarse de un modo más perfecto dando ejemplo de vida y sacrificio a la humanidad.

A pesar de su divinidad, *María* ha sido ejemplo de bondad humana. A pesar de que los seres humanos no le habíamos sabido reconocer su verdadera posición en la creación, Ella no se ha molestado con nosotros y se ha mantenido dando amparo a los necesitados del mundo.

En el principio del cristianismo *María* dio muestras de ser instrumento principal de la fe al convertirse en el Espíritu de Pentecostés. En dicha ocasión, *María* condujo a los apóstoles y discípulos a la sala del Cenáculo, les transmitió su anhelo profundo de que Ellos cumplieran con la voluntad del *Espíritu Santo* y les dio las fuerzas del Altísimo para que obraran sobre toda la Iglesia de tal manera.

En Pentecostés se colmó en *María* la luz del *Espíritu Santo*. Allí quedó completamente compenetrada y transformada en Él. Ya en su vida tuvo un cuerpo humano espiritualizado, es decir, el Espíritu transformado en un cuerpo de carne y hueso, el cual no podía ser destruido ya que no era corruptible. Después de Pentecostés quedó preparada para la ascensión en cuerpo y alma hacia su origen; el *Espíritu Santo*, en el seno de la Santísima Trinidad de Dios. Ella y su hijo, *Jesús,* nos dieron ejemplo de cómo nosotros también podemos insertarnos en el *Espíritu Santo.*

El mejor de los regalos del *Espíritu Santo* a la humanidad, después de su creación es la encarnación de *María* para engendrar a su hijo *Jesús. Jesús* moribundo sobre la cruz, a pesar de quedar desposeído de todo, poseía aún el Tesoro más preciado del universo, Su Divina Madre. La cual nos entregó para que en su partida Ella siguiera protegiéndonos. Juan 19, 25-27 nos narra este episodio de *Jesús* en sus últimos minutos sobre la cruz, y la fortaleza de su madre parada frente a Él sin flaqueza a pesar del dolor que desgarraba su alma, desprovista de toda divinidad. En dicha narración se hace notar que las tres mujeres más amadas por *Jesús* estaban presente en el momento del reparto de las vestiduras y del sorteo de la túnica del Salvador. Juan deja bien explicito aquí que esa túnica era obra de *María,* la madre de Jesús, y que es precisamente ese sorteo lo que hace brotar los recuerdos en la cabeza del moribundo y lo que le impulsa a fijar su atención en el grupo de discípulas que hacían guardia al pie de la cruz. Ya que el grupo de curiosos se habían alejados a sus diferentes quehaceres. Quedando únicamente los soldados de guardia y el pequeño grupo de mujeres fieles, ya que todos los demás Apóstoles varones, por miedo, no estaban en ese importante momento junto al Mesías crucificado.

El grupo de mujeres fieles estaba encabezado por *María,* la madre del Hijo de Dios, quien yacía moribundo colgado en la cruz. Pero Ella no estaba sola, había a su lado otras dos mujeres: Martha la hermana de su Madre y María Magdalena una fiel seguidora. Tal como lo narra Juan el evangelista, estaban allí junto a la cruz: "*María,* su madre; Martha, la hermana de su madre, la esposa de Cleofás; y María Magdalena". Las tres mujeres se acercaron a la cruz, para tratar de percibir el último aliento de *Jesús,* ya que ninguna ley les impedía a los parientes acercarse a los condenados. Los soldados custodiaban las cruces para impedir cualquier posible forma de manifestación de las multitudes seguidoras de *Jesús;* pero no apartaban a los curiosos que se acercaban a ver en pequeños grupos. Realmente poco podían los guardias temer de aquellas tres mujeres indefensas. Los mismos soldados debían de tener compasión de aquel condenado a quien tantas gente seguía y a la hora de la verdad, solo tres fieles mujeres le quedaron.

Sabemos que estas tres mujeres estaban paradas junto a la cruz y que se mantuvieron firmes hasta el último suspiro de *Jesús. María* tuvo algún momento de desmayo dentro de su condición humana, ya que Ella había sido despojado en esos momentos, y por voluntad propia, de su divinidad, para poder sufrir, "en carne propia", a la par que su hijo, aquellos terribles momentos de la crucifixión. Pero la divina Madre siempre tuvo el soporte de María Magdalena, quien a partir de aquel día se convirtió en su hija por petición del propio *Jesús* que entre sus últimas palabras les dijo a ambas: "Madre, he ahí a tu hija; Hija, he ahí a tu madre". Este hecho trascendental, los manipuladores de la palabra de Dios, al escribir la Biblia se lo atribuyeron a Juan, aunque el propio evangelista describe claramente que el discípulo que más amaba *Jesús* era María Magdalena.

La *Virgen María* es mucho más que una simple devoción, más que una bandera, más que una santa patrona, Ella es el verdadero origen de la vida, el origen del Creador. Debemos reconocer la divinidad de *María*, y colocarla en su justa dimensión conjuntamente con el Espíritu Santo y su Hijo Jesús. *María* es la genuina representación de la síntesis entre fe y vida, entre lo divino y lo humano. Modificando un poco las palabras del Padre José Kentenich diríamos: Quien quiere ser constructor y colaborador para el mundo actual, ha de vincularse a *María*. Han de vincularse a Ella todos los humanos, sin importar pueblos, razas, ni culturas, para que Ella los conduzca hacia la Santísima Trinidad del *Espíritu Santo*.

María nos enseña, con su ser y su actuar, que toda perfección y redención viene del *Espíritu Santo*, en la que Ella y Jesucristo se condensa en total plenitud. En *María* el *Espíritu Santo* puede documentar la perfección de su obra. *María*, como persona humana, es quien más plenamente realiza el ideal del ser humano como cristianos en este tercer milenio. Con Ella podemos encontrar el paraíso perdido, de deseos y esperanzas, y lograr la perfecta armonía entre el cuerpo, el alma y el espíritu.

Todos los cristianos somos convertidos en seres humanos nuevos, el día de nuestro bautismo. En ese momento, el *Espíritu Santo* nos infunde en el alma las vidas divinas de Cristo y *María*. Lo que para la santa Madre y su Hijo es un don, para nosotros es una lucha de toda la vida. Por lo cual, todos (as) nosotros (as) somos llamados (as), a convertirnos en hombres y mujeres nuevos (as), en armonía con la imagen de Cristo y de *María*. Todos nosotros somos invitados a imitar a *Jesús* y a la *Virgen María* en el *Espíritu Santo*, y a abrirnos a su voluntad, haciendo nuestra vida según sus deseos. El Verbo se hizo carne en *María y Jesús*, y hoy se sigue haciendo carne en los hombres y las mujeres devotos de *María y Jesús en el Espíritu Santo*.

María es plenitud de amor. Su vida y sus actos de hoy día comprueba que eso es cierto. Porque lo que más caracteriza su vida, es que Ella vive en plena comunión de amor no sólo con el *Espíritu Santo*, sino también con los seres humanos. Así aparece la *Virgen María* desde las primeras escenas del Evangelio hasta nuestros días con sus apariciones gloriosas y generosas. Ella vive ligada por hondos lazos de amor a los seres humanos de todos los tiempos.

El *Espíritu Santo* está siempre en *María y María* está siempre el *Espíritu Santo*. Desde el mismo instante en que ella fue encarnada, la creó a plenitud con todos sus propios dones. Por eso *María* es también llamada "la Inmaculada", la sin pecado. Para pecar se necesita no cumplir con el mandato de amar a Dios y al prójimo, lo cual Ella cumple plenamente ya que Ella es en sí el propio Dios en su parte femenina.

La salvación a través de Jesucristo, igual como sucede a través de *María,* comienza con la liberación del pecado y el retorno a una vida plena de amor. Lo cual se logra a través de la apertura del corazón hacia el Ser Divino y a todos nuestros congéneres, mientras que al mismo tiempo echamos fuera el egoísmo y el orgullo. Pidámosle a la *Virgen María* que nos ayude a liberarnos de todo lo que en el corazón se opone al amor. Pidámosle fuerzas para vencer en nosotros mismos el orgullo y el egoísmo, que nos separan cada vez más a uno de los otros. Pidámosle que abra nuestros corazones al amor hacia Dios y los demás seres humanos. El que abre su corazón al amor, por vivir en comunión con la Santísima Trinidad del Espíritu Santo y con sus congéneres, está ya salvado, y liberado de los mezquinos sentimientos que autodestruyen el ser humano.

La *Virgen María* nos enseña que el amor nos ayuda a ser solidarios y compasivos. Ella comparte dentro del *Espíritu Santo* con el *Padre* y *el Hijo,* su grandeza divina y su misión. Su amor y su compasión se han convertido en comunión de vida y obra, y en comunión en la alegría y en la aflicción.

Nuestra Señora de la Santísima Trinidad posee un carisma, un don especial para unir los corazones y abrirlos al amor, para hacernos hermanos y hermanas. Ella quiere hacernos comprender que toda la felicidad del Evangelio de su Hijo se resume en estas simples palabras: vivir en comunión con el Espíritu Santo de Dios y con nuestros semejantes. *La Virgen* quiere que los seres humanos vivamos en un ambiente de unidad y de amor. Nos pide crearlo, cultivarlo y perfeccionarlo permanentemente en nuestros hogares, nuestros lugares de trabajo, nuestros vecindarios y nuestros grupos, asi como también a través de las redes sociales y el internet. Ella nos invita, a la vez, a construir todos juntos; gobernantes y gobernados, ricos y pobres, empleadores y empleados, sacerdotes y laicos, una sociedad más justa, más humana, más solidaria que manifieste su ayuda real a los que sufren, a los que dependen de nosotros y a los que se acercan a nosotros.

Todas estas situaciones son la realidad del mundo moderno en el cual nos ha tocado vivir y el cual debemos dejar como herencia a nuestros hijos y nuestras hijas. Por lo cual es preciso, hoy más que nunca, dar vida, dar luz, dar esperanza, dando a conocer la grandeza del Espíritu Santo, en sus tres divinas personas; Padre, Madre e Hijo. El único que puede redimir todos los pecados del mundo, devolvernos el valor y la dignidad, y darnos vida en abundancia por toda la eternidad. En estos precisos momentos del tercer milenio debemos vivir un nuevo adviento, una nueva espera de la manifestación de la *Santísima Trinidad del Espíritu Santo* en un mundo que tanto necesita re-encontrar su origen, lo cual solo podremos lograr poniéndonos en sintonía con *el Espíritu Santo* a través de una de sus personificaciones humanas: Yahvé, *Jesús o la Virgen María*.

Para que *Jesús* viniera al mundo se necesitaron dos elementos: la encarnación de la parte femenina del Espíritu Santo, en *María*, y la Obra y Gracia del Propio Espíritu Santo en el divino vientre de *María*. De esta forma quedó establecido que todo advenimiento de Cristo para el mundo, requiere de la acción conjunta de la Santísima Trinidad del Espíritu Santo, en las Divinas Personas del Espíritu Santo (el Padre), la Virgen María (la Madre) y el propio Jesús (el Hijo).

Necesitamos establecer la verdadera composición de la Santísima Trinidad del Espíritu Santo para pedir por una nueva efusión del Espíritu Santo en un nuevo pentecostés en el que todos los fieles reconozcamos la real personalidad de la *Virgen María* en el *Espíritu Santo*. Juntos todos unidos sin sectarismo preparar un nuevo Advenimiento, una nueva era de fe y esperanza.

La unión del Espíritu Santo Padre y del Espíritu Santo Madre, encarnada en *María*, dio como resultado el engendro del Espíritu Santo

Hijo, el cual es llamado Jesús. Pero lo maravilloso de esta misión es que no se limita a aquel preciso momento sino, que es una misión que se manifiesta eternamente en las almas, para promover que, por la unión divina de ambos, Cristo nazca en cada corazón que se abra a él día tras día. Todas las gracias llegan a nosotros desde el *Espíritu Santo Padre* a través de los meritos de Dios Madre y Dios Hijo. Se distribuyen a través de la obra de *María*, no solo como un reflejo de su santidad, sino también como parte central de la Suprema Divinidad que Ella ostenta. Como esposa del Espíritu Santo Padre y debido a su relación intima y estrecha con El, *María* colabora libre y conscientemente en el trabajo y la obra de santificación del *Espíritu Santo*, su Propio Ser.

Está comprobado que *María* no es el simple instrumento humano del *Espíritu Santo*, es el reflejo de su propia obra en el proceso de santificación de las almas. Ella lleva a todas las almas las gracias ganadas por su propio Ser, en Cristo, el cordero de Dios sacrificado en la Cruz. Vemos como la presencia de *María,* irremediablemente atrae el derramamiento del Espíritu Santo en la Iglesia, ya que en Sí es su propio Ser. *María* es la Parte femenina del Ser Supremo en el *Espíritu Santo*. *María* siempre se ha mantenido entre nosotros, pero Hoy más que nunca *María* ha estado visitando el mundo, de una manera jamás antes vista, posiblemente en espera de que nosotros hagamos conciencia de su divinidad antes de Ella traer un nuevo pentecostés sobre la Iglesia y el mundo. *María* está actuando en el *Espíritu Santo* para traer un nuevo advenimiento de Cristo a la Iglesia y al mundo, como una continuación del pasaje de la visitación y el de Pentecostés.

Nosotros hemos visto en la Iglesia en los últimos 50 años una gran manifestación del Espíritu Santo de Dios que parece ser un signo de los tiempos que nos revela las primicias de avanzar a un nuevo pentecostés en donde todos los seres humanos tendremos un total y pleno conocimiento sobre "Jesús y la *Virgen María* en el *Espíritu Santo.*" Como podemos apreciar en las palabras del Papa Pablo VI: "Que necesidad, primera y última, advertimos para esta nuestra Iglesia bendita y querida? Que necesita realmente? Lo debemos decir, temblorosos y en oración, porque es su misterio, es su vida: es el Espíritu Santo, animador y santificador de la Iglesia, su aliento divino, el viento de sus velas, su principio unificador, su fuente interior de luz y de energía, su apoyo y su consolador, su manantial de carisma y de cantos, su paz y su gozo, su prenda y preludio de vida bienaventurada y eterna. La Iglesia tiene necesidad de un perenne Pentecostés: necesita fuego en el corazón, palabra en los labios, profecía en la mirada. La Iglesia necesita ser templo del Espíritu Santo, es decir, de total limpieza y de vida interior. La Iglesia y el mundo necesitan más que nunca que el prodigio de Pentecostés se prolongue en la historia". (Pablo VI, 1972)

La Iglesia necesita un nuevo pentecostés y para lograrlo debemos unirnos en oración para ponernos en contacto con *Jesús y la Virgen María en el Espíritu Santo*, y dejarnos guiar, formar y moldear por su ser. "El reconocimiento de la divinidad de *María*, renueva maravillosamente nuestra era de fe haciendo surgir un nuevo Pentecostés, y concede que la nueva Iglesia cristiano mariana del Espíritu Santo, se mantenga orando perseverantemente e insistentemente como un solo corazón y una sola mente, juntos con *Jesús y la Virgen María en el Espíritu Santo que es Dios,* promoviendo así el reinado divino de la verdadera Santísima Trinidad, un reino de justicia, de amor y de paz".

A través de estas oraciones el *Espíritu Santo* nos está revelando el papel relevante de *María*, y al igual que la primera venida del Mesías fue a través de la encarnación de *María* y del poder del Espíritu Santo, este nuevo advenimiento o resurgir del cuerpo místico, se está desarrollando a través de la *Virgen María en el Espíritu Santo*. Está demostrado que *María* juega un papel indispensable en esta preparación de la Iglesia cristiano mariana para que juntos clámenos al *Espíritu Santo*, "Ven, Señor", "Ven y Reina, haciendo tu voluntad en el corazón de todo hombre y toda mujer".

El *Espíritu Santo* se ha manifestado en estos tiempos para revelarnos la verdadera divinidad de María, ya que en el pasado la mezquindad de los hombres la mantuvo oculta de este mundo en un punto más bajo que la más insignificante mujer. Pero hoy el Espíritu Santo quiere hacernos ver que Él Propio Dios es obra maestra de sus propias manos y por eso Él quiere ser alabado y glorificado a través de nuestra contemplación de las maravillas que hoy en día está haciendo la *Virgen María* en la humanidad.

María es el camino por donde vino Nuestro Señor Jesucristo a nosotros la primera vez, y sigue siendo el camino por donde nosotros podemos llegar a Él. Ella es el medio más seguro y el camino directo para encontrar a Jesucristo y hallarle perfectamente. De forma tal que, si la salvación del mundo comenzó por medio de la encarnación de *María*, es por medio de Ella que debemos alcanzar la plenitud del *Espíritu Santo* en su Hijo. Ella resplandece en estos momentos, más que nunca, en misericordia, poder y gracia.

Tal y como planteará el papa san Juan Pablo II: "Es precisamente porque el Espíritu Santo quiere revelar y manifestar poderosamente a *María* en estos tiempos de gran dificultad para la Iglesia, que la estrategia específica para la victoria de la Iglesia sobre el Príncipe de la Oscuridad es La consagración al *Inmaculado Corazón de María*. La victoria si llega, llegara por medio de *María...Cristo vencerá por medio de Ella*, porque Él quiere que las victorias de la Iglesia en el mundo contemporáneo y en el mundo futuro estén unidas a Ella." (Juan Pablo II; Cruzando el umbral de la Esperanza).

De igual manera pudimos ver en los relatos sobre la Virgen de Fátima que Ella le dijo a la niña Lucia: **"Al final mi Inmaculado Corazón triunfara"**. Por lo cual debemos estar confiados y con la fe bien en alto, en que este triunfo del Inmaculado Corazón de María y el triunfo del Espíritu Santo de Dios en este nuevo pentecostés son un mismo triunfo; el triunfo de *"Jesús y la Virgen María en el Espíritu Santo."*

Este gran triunfo conjunto de Jesús y la *Virgen María* en el Espíritu Santo, en la Iglesia y el mundo, traerá consigo un nuevo advenimiento de Cristo, en una era en la cual, como dijo el papa san Juan Pablo II, la humanidad parece haber perdido su conciencia y su corazón. Es en estos precisos momentos en los cuales más necesitamos del corazón inmaculado de *María y de Jesús*, hoy que el hombre cada vez más endurece su corazón, estrechando la barrera entre el bien y el mal, siendo incapaz de entregar un amor verdadero, a no ser a la avaricia y a lo mundano.

El *Espíritu Santo* se hizo mujer fecunda, en *María*. Con Ella, en Ella y de Ella produjo a su obra maestra, que es Él mismo, hecho hombre, en *Jesús*. Por ello, cuanto más compenetrados estemos con *María*, más poderoso y fecundo será el Espíritu Santo al depositar sus dones sobre cada uno de nosotros para reproducir la gran obra de Jesucristo.

El *Espíritu Santo* no solo quiere que la divinidad de *María* se conozca, sino que lo ha hecho una condición para establecer su nuevo reinado, con una nueva presencia espiritual de *Jesús* y la *Virgen María*, en un nuevo pentecostés. De forma tal, que su Iglesia, sus gentes y las naciones sean consagradas al Inmaculado corazón de *María*, para que siendo Ella reina de nuestros corazones, nos lleve por el camino seguro y nos prepare para el Reinado del Corazón Inmaculado de Jesús.

Ahora bien, la gracia del *Espíritu Santo*, es y será por siempre Cristo; él es el único revelador y portador ante el hombre del amor del Creador. Y esto nos lleva a descubrir el verdadero misterio que se asignó *María*. Ella, desde el primer instante de su encarnación, es de Cristo. Es decir, desde el primer momento de su existencia, Ella participa de forma anticipada de la acción redentora y santificadora que llevaría a cabo el Hijo eterno de Ella y del Espíritu Santo, el mismo que, mediante la Encarnación, se convirtió en su propio hijo. *María* es la Madre del mismo Ser que la engendró a Ella. San Juan Pablo II expresó acertadamente este misterio al decir: "María recibe la vida de aquél al que ella misma dio la vida". (*Redemptoris Mater*, 10).

La maternidad divina de *María* fue un hecho absolutamente único e irrepetible: el *Espíritu Santo de Dios* se hizo hombre en las entrañas de la *Virgen María, su Propio Ser*. Con la relación entre el *Espíritu Santo Padre* y el *Espíritu Santo Madre*, representado en *María*, se engendró el hijo de Dios. La acción del Espíritu Santo en *María*, su propio Ser, fue el primer Pentecostés, y es aquí cuando el Espíritu Santo irrumpió sobre todos los creyentes, igual como lo hace hoy día *María*, en sus diferentes advocaciones alrededor del mundo.

5.2.- Bibliografía:

- Amada, José Félix de. Compendio de los milagros de Nuestra Señora del Pilar, Zaragoza, 1680.
- Antonov, Vladimir. "La Enseñanza Original de Jesús Cristo". Traducción del ruso al español por Oscar Orchard, Alfredo Salazar, y Anton Teplyy. 2007
- Ariza, Alberto E. O.P., Hagiografía de Nuestra Señora de Chiquinquirá. Bogotá, Editorial Iqueima, 1950.
- Braaten y Jensen, editores, Christian Dogmatics, Philadelphia, PA: Fortress Press, 1984, tomo 1, pp. 90 – 400.
- Cardinal Francis George and Barbara Reid. Abiding Word, Vol. I, p. 57
- De La Cruz, Juan. Los Verdaderos Misterios del Cristianismo. Editora Palibrio, 2012.
- Díez Macho, Alejandro & Piñero, Antonio. *Apócrifos del antiguo testamento*. Madrid: Ediciones Cristiandad.

- Díez Macho, Alejandro (1984). *Tomo I.* Introducción General. ISBN 978-84-7057-361-3.
- Díez Macho, Alejandro (1984). Tomo IV. Ciclo de Henoc. ISBN 978-84-7057-353-8.
- Díez Macho, Alejandro (1987). Tomo V. Testamentos o discursos de Dios. ISBN 978-84-7057-421-4.
- Eerdmans, B. Eerdman's Handbook to the History of Christianity, Grand Rapids, MI: Eerdmans Publishing Co., 1977, p. 164.
- E. H. Klotsche, The History of Christian Doctrine, Grand Rapids, MI: Baker Book House, 1979, p. 69.
- García Bazán, Francisco. (2003) *La Gnosis eterna. Antología de textos gnósticos griegos, latinos y coptos.* Madrid: Editorial Trotta. ISBN 978-84-8164-585-9.
- Gil Zúñiga, José Daniel. "El culto a la Virgen de Los Ángeles (1824-1935): una aproximación a la mentalidad religiosa en Costa Rica". Tesis de Licenciatura, Universidad Nacional, 1982, Costa Rica.
- Gonzalez, J.L. A History of Christian Thought, Nashville, TN: Abingdon Press, 1970, vol. 1, p. 247- 325.
- Grandes Temas Bíblicos; Libros CLIE -Galvani, 113 -08224 Terrassa (Barcelona)
- Jonas, Hans (2003). La religión gnóstica. El mensaje del Dios Extraño y los comienzos del cristianismo. 2da. ed. Editorial Siruela, Madrid. ISBN 978-84-7844-492-2.
- Juan Pablo II; Cruzando el umbral de la Esperanza.
- Juan Pablo II; *Redemptoris Mater.*
- Maxwell, Mervyn (1989). Dios Revela el Futuro. Pacific Press, t. 2, pp. 321, 328, 346, 347
- Montfort, San Luis María Grignion. Tratado de la Verdadera Devoción a la Santísima Virgen, Parte 1-3
- Neve, J.L. A History of Christian Thought, The United Lutheran Publication House, 1943, vol. 1, p. 119.
- Payá, Miguel Andrés; María, Esposa del Espíritu. www.franciscanos.org
- Pieper, Francis D.D., Christian Dogmatics, St. Louis, MO: Concordia Publishing House, 1951, Vol. 1, p. 350-385.

- Piñero, Antonio (2009). *Tomo VI. Escritos apocalípticos.* ISBN 978-84-7057-542-6.
- Piñero, Antonio. (2009) Textos Gnósticos de Nag Hammadi. 2da. Edición. Editorial Trotta: Madrid. Volumen II. Traducción, introducción y notas de Antonio Piñero, José Montserrat Torrents, Francisco García Bazán, Fernando Bermejo y Ramón Trevijano. ISBN 978-84-8164-885-0.
- Richard A. Lauersdorf. Winter Haven, Florida. 20 de abril de 1999
- Richardson, Padre. The Office of the Holy Spirit. pp. 121-213
- Rodríguez, Antonio. La Religión judía. Editorial Cristiana. pp. 347-351.
- Santos Otero, Aurelio de (2009). Los evangelios apócrifos. 1ra. Ed. Edición. Madrid: B. A. C. ISBN 978-84-220-1409-6.
- White, Elena. (1909). El Camino a Cristo. Pacific Press. pp. 33, 34, 47, 48
- W.W. Westphal. Convención de la CELC, abril de 1999, Winter Haven, Florida.
- The Catholic Encyclopedia.
- Our Orthodox Christian Faith)

www.aciprensa.com/Historia de la Devoción a María Auxiliadora.
www.adoremosalquevive.com "No tengan miedo les he dado mi espíritu". Adela Galindo.
www.arquimercedes-lujan.com.ar/wp.../Boletin-N°-5.pdf
www.bienaventurada.com/Mariologia01.pdf
www.celam.org/.../Documento_Conclusivo_Santo_Domingo
www.corazones.org; María, Esposa del Espíritu Santo. Adela Galindo.
www.corazones.org; El Espíritu Santo y la Virgen María en el Nuevo Milenio. Adela Galindo.
www.es.catholic.net/María La Llena de Amor
www.google.com P. Javier Rodríguez Orozco, PENTECOSTES JUVENIL.
www.obispadodecadizyceuta.org/ María Madre de Dios y Madre Nuestra.
www.op.org.ar/ La Virgen María en la actual.
www.pijamasurf.com/ Asherah la Esposa de Dios fue editada de la Biblia.

www.regnummariae.org/la_bienaventurada.htm
www.unican.es/NR/.../MariaenlafedelaIglesia.pdf
www.usuarios.advance.com/la-virgen-del-Carmen.
www.wikipedia.com/La Virgen de la Altagracia
www.wikipedia.com/Nuestra Señora del Rosario
www.wikipedia.com/La Virgen de Fátima.
www.wikipedia.com/La Virgen de la Caridad del Cobre.
www.wikipedia.com/La Virgen de Guadalupe.
www.wikipedia.com /La Virgen de Coromoto
www.wikipedia.com/La Virgen de las Mercedes
www.wikipedia.com/Nuestra Señora de Lourdes
www.wikipedia.com/La Virgen del Carmen
www.wikipedia.com/Nuestra Señora de Los Ángeles
www.wikipedia.com/La Virgen del Rosario de Chiquinquirá.
www.wikipedia.com/La Virgen del Pilar
www.wikipedia.com/Nuestra Señora del Perpetuo Socorro
www.wikipedia.com/Nuestra Señora de la Divina Providencia
www.wikipedia.com/Nuestra Señora de la Inmaculada Concepción

Printed in the United States
By Bookmasters